ARCHIVES AND
SPECIAL COLLECTIONS AS
SITES OF CONTESTATION

ARCHIVES AND SPECIAL COLLECTIONS AS SITES OF CONTESTATION

Mary Kandiuk, Editor

LIBRARY JUICE PRESS
SACRAMENTO, CA

Published in 2020 by Library Juice Press

Library Juice Press
PO Box 188784
Sacramento, CA 95822

http://libraryjuicepress.com/

This book is printed on acid-free paper.

Library of Congress Cataloging-in-Publication Data

Names: Kandiuk, Mary, 1956- editor.
Title: Archives and special collections as sites of contestation / Mary
   Kandiuk, editor.
Description: Sacramento, CA : Library Juice Press, 2020. | Includes
   bibliographical references and index. | Summary: "Explores the
   reinterpretation and resituating of archives and special collections
   held by libraries, examines the development and stewardship of archives
   and special collections within a social justice framework, and describes
   the use of critical practice by libraries and librarians to shape and
   negotiate the acquisition, cataloguing, promotion and use of archives
   and special collections"-- Provided by publisher.
Identifiers: LCCN 2020011059 | ISBN 9781634000628 (paperback)
Subjects: LCSH: Libraries and society. | Libraries--Social aspects. |
   Archives--Social aspects. | Libraries--Special collections.
Classification: LCC Z716.4 .A73 2020 | DDC 021.2--dc23
LC record available at https://lccn.loc.gov/2020011059

Table of Contents

Introduction

This edited collection provides an opportunity for librarians, archivists, and allied professionals to share their efforts to apply a critical practice perspective to their work with archives and special collections. Librarians and archivists strive to resituate and reinterpret existing hegemonic collections and are committed to democratizing the historical record through the development of collections from a social justice perspective. There is a recognition on their parts that furthering justice requires disrupting archival practices and structures. The strategies librarians and archivists employ are driven by questioning past practices and entrenched power structures, and approaching their work through a new and critical lens.

Common threads run throughout the chapters with many authors raising the same issues and concerns. That archives and libraries are not in fact neutral and that historical, political, social, and economic forces influence what they collect, how they shape what they collect, and how they make available what they collect is a theme that resonates throughout the collection. This in turn has a profound effect on what stories are told and what voices are heard. Colonial practices have dominated recordkeeping, description, and spaces, and a culture of privilege and exclusion has prevailed over community access and engagement. There is strong interest in documenting historical injustices and reaching out to historically marginalized communities, thereby transforming interpretations and creating new narratives. During this period of transition, librarians and archivists re-examine their spaces as well as their work from a critical perspective and look to create archives and special collections

1

that are welcoming and inclusive. The goals are not without political and ethical challenges and the methods and means undertaken in pursuit of them are varied and ambitious. A brief synopsis of the chapters and the topics they address follows.

Lara K. Aase discusses the reconsideration of collections and materials that reflect bias and cultural insensitivity in a Native-American serving, non-tribal liberal arts college in the Southwestern United States. She describes the challenges of balancing the protection of cultural property while facing potential accusations of censorship and the problematic nature of the Library of Congress classification system.

Kimberley Bell and Jillian Sparks describe their experience creating exhibitions and instruction around newsletters from local Kingston, Ontario prisoner communities and their outreach to these communities. They provide guidance to those wishing to identify marginalized voices and bring their narratives to light.

Elizabeth Call and Miranda Mims discuss the shift at their institutions to rethink collection practices and document social justice activities in the Greater Rochester Area. They focus on community engagement and developing community partnerships—in this case, with the homeless.

François Dansereau addresses the question of power dynamics in the archives from the perspective of hegemonic masculinity. He questions the notions of objectivity and neutrality, and examines the practices that have reinforced and reproduced masculine authority in special collections and archives.

Jesse Ryan Erickson examines special collections reading rooms as colonial spaces that contribute to exclusion and reinforce hierarchical and patriarchal power relations. He offers alternative approaches to the spatiality of special collections that recognize and challenge its Eurocentric heritage, as well as alternatives for the development of spaces that encourage transparency and that welcome and reflect marginalized communities.

Daniel German addresses the moral, ethical, and legal issues when dealing with sensitive materials. He examines the pros and cons of access, and he provides approaches for handling materials and navigating pitfalls.

Melanie Hardbattle describes how a digitization project relating to the Komagata Maru incident of 1914, when passengers from the British Punjab were denied entry to Canada, raised awareness of injustices and provided opportunities to build trust with local communities to collect materials and create and shape the historical record.

Elizabeth Hobart describes the ethical challenges facing catalogers and uses cataloging examples to illustrate the powerful role of the cataloger in combating silences and censorship in the catalog while highlighting the limitations of Library of Congress Subject Headings.

Heidi L.M. Jacobs uses the case of a digitization project relating to an all-Black baseball team, the 1934 Chatham Coloured All-Stars, to raise questions regarding librarians' roles in shaping knowledge *vis-à-vis* collecting and providing access. She discusses how digitization projects are informed by many material and ideological assumptions related to power and representation.

Peggy Keeran, Katherine Crowe, and Jennifer Bowers describe their efforts to create social justice experiences in the archives using instruction informed by critical information literacy and archival social justice. The question of the political nature of archives is raised, as is the question of who is included and excluded. They describe the need to deconstruct records and challenge dominant narratives.

Clayton McCarl raises questions of power, ethics, and race relating to a collaborative digital scholarly editing project dealing with community leader, philanthropist, and humanitarian Eartha M.M. White. He discusses the challenges and limitations and strategies for partnering with local communities.

Krista McCracken and Skylee-Storm Hogan describe their work with the Shingwauk Residential Schools Centre and how archives can use technology to disrupt colonial historical narratives and integrate Indigenous knowledge and perspectives within archival description and arrangement. Community engagement allows for the creation of new forms of archival understanding.

Jessica Ruzek, Roger Gillis, and Diana Doublet describe their efforts relating to the contextualization of a digital exhibit dealing with Rudyard

Kipling to enable critical engagement and scholarship. The creation of the Kipling Scrapbooks Digital Exhibit provided an opportunity to further social justice and discourse.

Anne S.K. Turkos and Jason G. Speck highlight the important purpose and validity of archives in the context of contestation and memory relating to memorialization. They describe the role of the archives and the challenges of navigating the call for the renaming of a university football stadium.

Margarita Vargas-Betancourt, Jessica L. English, Melissa Jerome, and Angelibel Soto address the limitations and biases of Anglo-American cataloging and metadata standards. They describe their efforts to provide greater access to Spanish language materials and the creation of a digitization project relating to Cuban Americans to challenge the colonial and hegemonic nature of special collections.

Gregory L. Williams and Maureen Burns describe a multi-institutional digitization initiative relating to Japanese Americans and the use of critical practice to shape an archival project whose materials deal with racism, political and social strife, and controversy. Community outreach initiatives have contributed to the creation of a deeper understanding and democratized record.

Katrina Windon and Lori Birrell discuss the critical approach to archival contracts and raise awareness of ethical issues, including potential inequities, calling for donor education and transparency. They explore the concept of information literacy within the context of informed consent and rights negotiation as part of the archival donation process.

Mary Kandiuk

Acknowledgements

I would like to take this opportunity to thank Rory Litwin, publisher, and Alison Lewis, editor, at Library Juice Press, for their enthusiastic response to this proposal and support for this work. Thank you, Rory Litwin and Library Juice Press, for providing an important publishing venue for critical scholarship in librarianship. I would also like to acknowledge the contributors and thank them for sharing their experience and knowledge and for their commitment to social justice through their work with archives and special collections. Sincere thanks and appreciation to Jill Flohil, a truly exceptional copy editor who kept us all on track. I would like to acknowledge York University and York University Libraries for supporting the scholarly research of librarians. And a special thank you to Nicholas Thompson for his feedback and support.

Mary Kandiuk
February 2020

Chapter 1

CENSORSHIP OR STEWARDSHIP? STRATEGIES FOR MANAGING BIASED PUBLICATIONS AND INDIGENOUS TRADITIONAL KNOWLEDGE IN SPECIAL COLLECTIONS LIBRARIES

Lara K. Aase

INTRODUCTION

Special collections, especially legacy collections that are more than fifty years old and those acquired primarily by donation, often hold materials that prove problematic for librarians and archivists in the twenty-first century. In the United States, the 1960s saw a boom in funding for libraries, archives, and museums, concurrent with more representative inclusion of marginalized cultures in dominant-culture[1] institutions. Notably, with the American Indian Movement and other expressions of protest and advocacy, Native Americans have had increasingly more voice and influence in the US since the 1970s. But material published

---

1. "The terms 'whiteness' and 'dominant culture' … are used inter-changeably and can be defined as invisible, visible, and hyper-visible hierarchically privileged positions of Eurocentric cultural standards and values" with their attendant social and institutional advantages. Anthony Dunbar, "Introducing Critical Race Theory to Archival Discourse: Getting the Conversation Started," *Archival Science* 6, no. 1 (2006): 113. I use the terms "Native" and "Indigenous" (as adjectives) and "Native American" interchangeably when referring to descendants of the original peoples of what is now called North America. I also capitalize all words for races/ethnicities, because *not* capitalizing some names for races/ethnicities, especially "White," suggests that they are the default or assumed race.

or collected before that time is distinctly marked by White bias, because most authors, publishers, librarians, and archivists in this country have historically been White, and "if we are what we keep, then, following human nature, we generally keep what we are, what we are most comfortable with, what we know, what our social and educational backgrounds made us."[2] In recent years, with generally decreased funding, special collections have often come to rely heavily, sometimes exclusively, on donations, resulting in less choice about acquisitions and a limited ability to enhance their holdings to be more inclusive of non-dominant points of view. The result may be a "special" collection that's not so special, including a predominance of White authors, biased perspectives, and dated research materials. On the other hand, truly special collections may contain material that needs so many restrictions that access becomes highly limited, particularly when the material relates to Indigenous peoples.

I am a non-Native, White librarian serving a majority Native American user population at the Delaney Southwest Research Library in the Center of Southwest Studies (CSWS) at Fort Lewis College (FLC) in Durango, Colorado. FLC is a Native American-Serving Nontribal Institution where 47% of the student body is "multicultural" (35% is tribally affiliated, 11% is Hispanic, and many students come from multiple racial and ethnic backgrounds). The CSWS building houses not only our library, archives, and museum, but also the Department of Native American and Indigenous Studies; perhaps for that reason and because of our collection's scope—which includes Native American regional history and culture—more Native than non-Native students visit our library. In my experience, in a library that focuses on underrepresented populations, both bias and cultural sensitivity may hinder the institutional mission to provide excellence in service and quality of materials, to engage with users from a variety of backgrounds and cultures, to

---

2. Terry Cook, "'We Are What We Keep; We Keep What We Are': Archival Appraisal Past, Present and Future," *Journal of the Society of Archivists* 32, no. 2 (2011): 174-75.

collaborate with diverse organizations, and to recognize multiple points of view with fairness.

In a closed-stacks environment, some amount of bias can be hidden (and only visible in the catalog through notoriously slow-to-change subject headings such as "Indians"), but where stacks are open and browsable, bias is on full display right on the shelves. For instance, more than half of our holdings fall in the Library of Congress Classification (LCC) sections E and F, largely between E51 and E99, but LCC is not comprehensive enough to organize Indigenous North American history and culture effectively (or to consider it part of the modern world; E51-99 is still listed as "Pre-Columbian," preceding the "Discovery of America and early explorations"). There is little sense of collocation when books on Diné (Navajo) silversmithing live at both E98.A7 and E99.N3, with thirty-two shelves in between, and when a silversmithing book falls between a book on sheep herding and one on film anthologies. There is no place in the B class for Native American religious thought, but we own several hundred books with subject headings "Indian" AND "religion" OR "mythology," interspersed throughout the E class. Beyond problems with Library of Congress subject headings (LCSH) and classification, cringe-worthy titles such as *In Search of the Wild Indian* or *Sgt. Fred Platten's Ten Years on the Trail of the Redskins* or *Injun Babies* offend even mainstream sensibilities now, but were published within the last 100 years with no sense of irony, shame, or self-awareness.

Other items in our collection contain private cultural knowledge—Traditional Knowledge (TK), or Traditional Cultural Expressions (TCE)—the intellectual property of specific groups. Those items include books containing details about Indigenous religious ceremonies that were never intended to be made public; photos of people who did not give their consent to be photographed; illustrated plates of objects that are meant to be ephemeral; and oral histories that contain songs or stories that should not be heard at certain times of year or by non-tribal members. Ideally, access to that information would be restricted according to the wishes of the people whose knowledge is represented, especially because the information was obtained as a direct result of colonization, genocide, and appropriation.[3]

Moreover, some published materials contain both biased viewpoints and culturally privileged information. We have a large collection of gray literature anthropology and archaeology reports interspersed throughout the E, F, and G classes, most of which objectify Indigenous peoples or perceive them as "prehistoric"; many of those publications, like other early twentieth-century anthropological books and journals about the U.S. Southwest, include photographs of human remains and burial goods. Legal restrictions in the Native American Graves Protection and Repatriation Act (NAGPRA) do not apply to publications, and the Protocols for Native American Archival Materials (PNAAM) pertain primarily to unique archival holdings of TCE (oral histories, handwritten documents) rather than published material. Particularly given the demographics of our main user group, Native American undergraduate students, it is culturally insensitive to leave such material out for unserendipitous discovery, but moving it away from public view risks the accusation of censorship.

I constantly find myself explaining, if not apologizing for, the content and arrangement of our collection, as if I were the parent of a cantankerous child yelling family secrets during a tantrum in a grocery store. I have also had to justify some of my professional decisions to academic colleagues, as if defending my parental discipline choices to disapproving bystanders. In an effort to avoid such tensions, I have looked for ways to be a better caretaker of difficult materials, to provide them with an appropriate home environment through an understanding of their backgrounds, limitations, and needs, and an awareness of the effects they may have on people. In doing so, if I seem parental (or paternalistic, or patronizing), that attitude is one I take toward the books under my care, not toward library users. Because I want to be a

---

3. Kay Mathiesen, "A Defense of Native Americans' Rights over Traditional Cultural Expressions," *American Archivist* 75, no. 2 (2012): 478.

good steward for our collection, I have thought a great deal about the issues involved, teasing apart my own feelings from my understanding of professional ethics and putting them back together, researching other opinions, and experimenting with different solutions.

ISSUES

Archives Versus Libraries

"Special collections" may refer to archival or library collections or both, and may, therefore, include unique original materials as well as published material. Published material may have intrinsic value based on rarity, or book collections may be "special" because they bring together items not collocated elsewhere. Generally, special collections, whether of books or archival material, do not circulate and are not physically browsable, relying on respect des fonds, topical collections, finding aids, and pathfinders to organize materials for users. But at the CSWS library, our stacks are open to public browsing, with LC classes and item location codes as the only organizing principles.

NAGPRA federal law applies primarily to museums, while the PNAAM guidelines apply to archival holdings and only tangentially to libraries. But as Teresa Olwick Grose points out, "Some tribes have chosen to interpret the scope of NAGPRA to include not only artifacts identified as belonging to these categories but also the information attendant to these artifacts as well," extending the spirit of the law to archives, libraries, and other sources and repositories of information. The Hopi Tribe, for instance, "formally presents its interest into all published and unpublished field notes derived from research on the Hopi Tribe. Of specific interest to us are field notes and other records that document esoteric, ritual, and privileged information on religious and ceremonial practices and customs. ... We are also requesting that you place an immediate moratorium on all research activities which require access to Hopi archival material by universities, colleges, independent researchers, and organizations not authorized by the Hopi Tribe and whose purpose do not address current repatriation efforts of the Tribe."[4] By specifying its interest in *published* as well as unpublished records, the Hopi Tribe proclaimed tribal rights not only to the physical artifacts of anthropological field notes (which, if unpublished, are unique items of intrinsic value unlikely to be replicated or duplicated elsewhere), but also to the ideas contained in such records. When those ideas are published, or made public, it may seem futile to try to put the genie back in the bottle, especially now that so much information is available online. The effort not only to possess such information but to keep it away from others may seem quixotic, especially since the copyright clock started ticking again in 2019 and more and more material will be entering the public domain. But the challenges of making that effort do not outweigh the need to do so; as Kay Mathiesen states, "A right is a morally imperative demand, which cannot be put aside simply because it is inconvenient or difficult to respect."[5]

Recent support from professional organizations is bringing the stance of archives and special collections libraries closer together and in line with improved cultural awareness. In August 2018, the Society of American Archivists (SAA) endorsed the PNAAM, commendably acknowledging that "Many of the original criticisms of the Protocols were based in the language of cultural insensitivity and white supremacy" and that "endorsement of these Protocols is long overdue. We regret and apologize that SAA did not take action to endorse the Protocols sooner and engage in more appropriate discussion."[6] In January 2019, the Rare Books and Manuscripts Section of the Association of College & Research Libraries (ACRL), a division of the American Library Association (ALA), included language about inclusivity, respect, and

---

4. Teresa Olwick Grose, "Reading the Bones: Information Content, Value, and Ownership Issues Raised by the Native American Graves Protection and Repatriation Act," *Journal of the American Society for Information Science* 48, no. 7 (1996): 626.

5. Mathiesen, "A Defense of Native Americans' Rights," 481.

6. "SAA Council Endorsement of Protocols for Native American Archival Materials." Society of American Archivists, 2018. https://www2.archivists.org/statements/saa-council-endorsement-of-protocols-for-native-american-archival-materials.

community involvement in its draft Code of Ethics for Special Collections Librarians. The Preamble states,

> As stewards of the cultural record, special collections practitioners also bear an added responsibility to represent historically underrepresented and marginalized voices, recognizing that diversity is complex and intersectional, and that silences, gaps, and poor description in the cultural record related to historical biases have the potential to do great harm. Special collections practitioners should strive to maintain mutually responsible relationships with the individuals and communities that produce the books, manuscripts, and other materials that comprise collections.[7]

Traditional Cultural Expressions, Intellectual Property, and Privacy

In the wake of the enacting of NAGPRA in 1990 and the drafting of the PNAAM in 2006, many authors have written about Indigenous cultural property and group property rights. As Mathiesen points out, the rights specified in the PNAAM are not legally binding, but they are moral rights to be respected in the same way that those in the ALA's *Library Bill of Rights* are "held up as guides for the ethical conduct of library professionals."[8] Cherity M. Bacon states that, although in practice Native American rights fall under U.S. federal intellectual property law, "As sovereign governments, Native American communities should possess the inherent right to maintain and protect their cultural material and intellectual property in accordance with tribal laws and traditions."[9] Jeffrey Mifflin heralds potential legal changes, reminding us that patent, trademark, and copyright law historically have adapted to rather than prescribed social practices.[10] Jennifer O'Neal mainly addresses Native

---

7. "Draft Code of Ethics for Special Collections Librarians: Preamble." Rare Books and Manuscripts Section, Association of College and Research Libraries. Email attachment to RBMS listserv, January 20, 2019.

8. Mathiesen, "A Defense of Native Americans' Rights," 457-58.

9. Cherity M. Bacon, "Native American Concerns About Museums and Archives Policies on Tangible and Intangible Cultural Property," *Archifacts* October-April (2011-2012): 44.

10. Jeffrey Mifflin, "Regarding Indigenous Knowledge in Archives," in *Through the Archival Looking Glass: A Reader on Diversity and Inclusion,* eds. Mary A. Caldera and

peoples' "right to know" as outlined by Vine Deloria Jr. as a framework for establishing and developing tribal archives, repatriating Indigenous information, affirming Native Americans' intellectual property rights, defining best practices for the care of Indigenous collections,[11] and defending peoples' right to have access to their own cultural information. On the flip side, Mathiesen's argument for the group right to informational privacy, similar to recent European ideas about the "right to be forgotten" online, maintains that

> groups need privacy just as individuals do. Groups face threats from invasions of privacy, and members can only enjoy certain benefits when their collective privacy is respected. Privacy protects and enhances the capacity of a group to enjoy collective autonomy, which enhances the lives of its members. And, the important social functions that groups play in creating meaning and a sense of belonging for their members require a measure of group privacy. If avoiding bad consequences, promoting good consequences, protecting autonomy and human dignity, creating and maintaining social relationships, and providing a context of meaning constitute the moral grounds for an individual right to privacy, then they also constitute the moral grounds for a group right to privacy. To the extent that one is committed to protecting individual privacy, one should also be committed to protecting a group right to cultural privacy.[12]

So far, most of what has been written about Indigenous group cultural property has been in the context of museums and archives, where unique artifacts and documents fall under NAGPRA law or the PNAAM guidelines. But implicit, and sometimes explicit,[13] in the arguments protecting tangible cultural property is a defense of Indigenous peoples' rights to their intangible cultural property. Historically, much of that cultural property was obtained, often immorally, during White settler expansion into western North America and during the early

---

Kathryn M. Neal (Chicago, IL: Society of American Archivists, 2014), 78.

11. Jennifer O'Neal, "'The Right to Know': Decolonizing Native American Archives," *Journal of Western Archives* 6, no. 1 (2015): 1-17.

12. Mathiesen, "A Defense of Native Americans' Rights," 476.

13. Mathiesen, "A Defense of Native Americans' Rights"; Bacon, "Native American Concerns."

twentieth century as American Boasian anthropology began to take off. For example, White anthropologists who focused their research on the Zuni people knew it was against the tribe's wishes to sketch or photograph ceremonies, but they did so regardless; one even hid her Bureau of American Ethnography-issued camera up her sleeve to do so.[14] Anthropologists' transcriptions of ceremonial knowledge into text was equally invasive, and equally prevalent.[15] Because Indigenous TK was new to people of European descent, they saw such information as exotic and marketable, and because settlers' concepts of privacy only extended to themselves, they felt no compunction about making other people's information public. Indeed, the early twentieth-century photographer Edward S. Curtis thought of Indigenous North Americans as a "vanishing race," a point of view somewhat understandable given the U.S. government's practice of genocide and forced cultural assimilation.

In the same way that I feel it is morally repugnant to seek out snuff films to watch, even if they are freely available online, I feel it is wrong for me to seek out cultural information obtained illicitly and expressly against people's will, even if that information has been published and printed widely. At the same time, as a librarian and a proponent of civil liberties, I also think it is wrong to censor information. There is no perfect solution to this contradiction, because the right to privacy is in conflict with the right to information. The ACRL draft *Code of Ethics for Special Collections Librarians* recognizes that potential for ambiguity, saying, "When values come into conflict, practitioners must bring their experience and judgment to bear on each case in order to arrive at the best solution. Practitioners also have a responsibility to center ethical practice in decision-making, resisting pressure to sacrifice ethical values for the sake of pragmatism whenever possible."[16]

---

14. Gwyneira Isaac, *Mediating Knowledges: Origins of a Zuni Tribal Museum* (Tucson: University of Arizona Press, 2007), 72-78.

15. "Zunis' perception of the act of duplication ... does not differentiate between different types of inscription—photographic or textual; they see both as transforming powerful knowledge into another form or vessel." Isaac, *Mediating Knowledges*, 80.

16. "Draft Code of Ethics for Special Collections Librarians: Preamble."

Professionally, therefore, I prefer to err on the side of caution and to restrict access for a number of reasons. I do not believe the pursuit of knowledge for its own sake trumps an individual's or a culture's desire for privacy. I came to this decision through reading the words of Zuni religious leader Octavius Seowtewa, who said, "We do not want to risk the death of our culture just to satisfy your curiosity."[17] That statement convinced me that what I had seen previously as an inalienable right to knowledge was neither a right nor a necessity, but merely a personal desire rooted in post-Renaissance European values. As Grose writes, "Western philosophy in general includes the concept that scientific endeavor ultimately benefits all humankind. This idea is often used to rationalize the preemption of power over information and information sources,"[18] often to the detriment of the humans who are the subjects of scientific endeavor—which is why modern academic research needs Institutional Review Board approval. The right to find out information about people stops where it impinges upon their right to privacy.[19] Finally, I think it is incumbent on all people to take other people's wishes into account and to respect them, if there is no vital reason not to. I believe that, after centuries of oppression of Indigenous peoples by folks who look like me, I would rather make the effort to treat Native peoples with respect than to perpetuate the status quo.

Authority, Authorship, Authenticity, and Appropriation

Of course, ideals about respecting cultural wishes must be translated into reality, and figuring out what those wishes are, whose they are, and how

17. Quoted in Miranda Hayes Belarde-Lewis, "From Six Directions: Documenting and Protecting Zuni Knowledge in Multiple Environments" (PhD Dissertation, University of Washington, 2013), 4.

18. Grose, "Reading the Bones," 630.

19. "Universal Declaration of Human Rights," United Nations, 1948. http://www.un .org/en/universal-declaration-human-rights/. The Universal Declaration of Human Rights, Article 12, states that people are entitled to protection of their privacy, whereas Article 19 protects the freedoms of opinion and expression, including the freedom— but not the obligation—to "seek, receive, and impart information."

to follow them can be problematic. As Mifflin asks, "Who, within each Native American nation, would have the authority to make decisions about cultural sensitivity? The most vocal members of a community do not always represent the majority view."[20] His question apparently presumes that a democratic majority's view is the correct one, that Native American nations do not have authoritative bodies to make that sort of decision, and perhaps even that outspoken Indigenous people are not to be trusted. But, on the contrary, in the U.S., there are 183 Tribal Historic Preservation Officers (THPOs; e.g., seven in Arizona, fifteen in New Mexico), each "designated by a federally-recognized Indian tribe to direct a program approved by the National Park Service" to enact a tribal historic preservation plan emphasizing "the importance of the oral tradition...consulting Tribal elders and spiritual leaders with special knowledge of the Tribe's traditions...[and] protecting 'traditional cultural properties'."[21] There are also tribal governments whose representatives speak for their people, like the Hon. Fred S. Vallo Sr., governor of Acoma Pueblo in 2015, who defended Acoma intellectual property rights against unauthorized publication.[22] And often the most outspoken individuals are those with important things to say. Dr. Debbie Reese, who founded the blog *American Indians in Children's Literature* and was selected to give the ALA/Association of Library Service to Children 2019 Arbuthnot Honor Lecture, is highly critical of stereotypes and cultural appropriation. Tribally enrolled at Nambe Owingeh, she has drawn fire for her views, but she has also changed the landscape of children's literature and made it more representative of Native peoples' truths. The members of the Diné Writers' Collective, Saad Bee Hozho, are award-winning

---

20. Mifflin, "Regarding Indigenous Knowledge in Archives," 75.

21. "THPOs." NATHPO: National Association of Tribal Historic Preservation Officers, 2019, http://www.nathpo.org/thpos/what-are-thpos/.

22. Khristaan D. Villela, "Controversy Erupts over Peter Nabokov's Publication of 'The Origin Myth of Acoma Pueblo,'" *Santa Fe New Mexican, Pasatiempo*, January 15, 2016. http://www.santafenewmexican.com/pasatiempo/columns/viajes_pin-torescos/controversy-erupts-over-peter-nabokov-s-publication-of-the-origin/article_1bcbe12b-b5c2-527e-93e9-1759fec994c5.html.

Navajo Nation authors who wrote a joint critique of a self-identifying Ohkay Owingeh author's appropriation of Diné cultural beliefs.[23] They took the bold step of calling out a Native American author for a textual approach more often used by White authors, showing us that accusations of cultural appropriation need not be racially or ethnically directed and that cultural property and privacy rights pertain to the group, not to any one individual. Finding a path through the thickets of authority and appropriateness can be daunting, but "best practices give the research community hope that an increasingly authentic, Native-led narrative is forthcoming, one that equitably balances the goal of access with the need to respect tribal privacy concerns."[24]

SOME SOLUTIONS

New World Views Versus New Worldviews

If you manage a collection of books on Indigenous topics and, like me, are not yourself Indigenous to the land where you live, here are some recommendations I have learned from colleagues, teachers, and my own research and observations. First, find out what group or groups of people lived where you live prior to European settlement. Learn about their history of contact with invading cultures, what languages they spoke historically and what they speak now, and their traditional ways of transmitting, collecting, and accessing information. Start to think of yourself as a guest in a foreign country and, like a good guest, learn how to behave with respect to your hosts on their own terms. In your heart, thank them for allowing you to stay. In real life, especially in conversation, practice humility, maintain a sense of humor about yourself, avoid generalizations, eschew stereotypes, and make no assumptions,

---

23. Saad Bee Hozho/Diné Writers' Collective, "Trail of Lightning is an Appropriation of Diné Cultural Beliefs," *Indian Country Today*, November 5, 2018, https://newsmaven.io/indiancountrytoday/opinion/trail-of-lightning-is-an-appropriation-of-din%C3%A9-cultural-beliefs-4tvSMvEfNE-i7AE10W7nQg/.

24. Naomi Bishop, Jonathan Pringle, and Carissa Tsosie, "Connecting Cline Library with Tribal Communities: A Case Study," *Collection Management* 42, no. 3-4 (2017): 249.

remembering that there are 573 federally recognized tribal nations in the U.S. alone. Don't ask about private information, especially about traditional religious beliefs and ceremonies, and question your own motivations for wanting answers. In your library, whether or not your institution is Native-American serving, if you imagine that all your users are Indigenous, you will be better able to identify problems and improve services for everybody, because you will be thinking inclusively. As O'Neal writes, we should "expand our Western theoretical frameworks and open up to the notion that perhaps these theories are not useful for all collections, especially those with ethnic communities and other minorities with long histories of oppression and injustices. This expansion will ensure that the profession considers and explores a variety of perspectives and ways of knowing that can positively influence the stewardship of these collections."[25]

Standards

Many standards already exist that can guide librarians and archivists to curate Indigenous special collections more effectively. Professional organizations, academic institutions, and individual special collections may endorse these standards officially or use them to inform policy and direct practice.

- *Aboriginal and Torres Strait Islander Protocols for Libraries, Archives and Information Services*. Written in 1995 and updated in 2012, these Protocols provide an outline for cultural awareness and reconciliation as well as community involvement.
- *Protocols for Native American Archival Materials*. Written in 2006 and formally endorsed by the SAA in 2018, the PNAAM emphasize collective knowledge, group ownership of intellectual property, oral as well as written tradition, and the importance of appropriate access to cultural materials.

---

25. O'Neal, "'The Right to Know,'" 15.

- *United Nations Declaration of the Rights of Indigenous Peoples.* Adopted by the United Nations in 2007, this instrument defines the minimum standards for the "survival, dignity and well-being of the indigenous peoples of the world."[26]

Collection Development Policy

A collection development policy is vital for a special collection that includes either Indigenous TK or biased materials. A good collection development policy addresses user needs, outlines collection subject areas and collecting priorities, and provides guidelines for deaccessioning. A better policy will also address planning, public relations, and staffing, and for libraries with Native American content, the best policy will address TK and biased publications as well. Given the history of publishing on topics related to Native American peoples, it is safe to assume that any collection of significant size containing books published before the 1960s or books by non-Native authors on Indigenous topics will include biased materials and information that should be private.

All user populations are different, but keeping in mind that at least some users of every library are Indigenous (and that there is no way to tell by looking) may encourage policy makers to choose inclusive language. Recognizing that historically underrepresented, misrepresented, and marginalized people are stakeholders will strengthen policy development and inspire new ideas for strategic planning and public relations. When addressing staffing in a collection development policy, it is important to note that ethical collection management is the duty of the *role* of librarian or archivist and should not depend on the views of the *individual* who happens to have the job. For that reason, the collection development policy should be the basis of posted job descriptions, and both should include wording about care for TK and TCE in collections.

Because special collections libraries often prioritize local history, a collection development policy is a good place to list overtly the Native

---

26. "United Nations Declaration on the Rights of Indigenous Peoples." United Nations, 2007. https://www.un.org/development/desa/indigenouspeoples/wp-content/uploads/sites/19/2018/11/UNDRIP_E_web.pdf.

nations whose information is part of that local history, as does the *Special Collections Policy for the Montana State Libraries*.[27] Making the effort to verify and use tribes' own names for themselves, rather than using names in colonizing languages only, shows respect for tribal sovereignty. Montana State University Libraries' special collections policy also provides good examples of specific collection levels within the collection scope. Special collections generally do not need to keep items at Levels 1 and 2, but because deaccession guidelines can be part of a collection development policy, it may be helpful to explore criteria for all collection levels here, especially for librarians who experience pushback when attempting to weed materials or turn down donations. Considering an item's quality of content, how long it may retain research or monetary value, its author's credentials, and its tone or manner of presenting ideas, all through the lens of cultural awareness, will help librarians decide what to keep and where to keep it.

Level 1 (do not add/ready to deaccession). Besides duplicates or unremarkable different editions, low-value books in poor condition, and outdated scientific texts without historic value, I also include in this category run-of-the-mill "pan-Indian" publications by non-Native authors. Unless such books are egregious examples of bias, racism, cultural appropriation, or misinformation (see Level 2), they do not add to scholarly knowledge. There is no need to keep a plethora of microaggressions on hand.

Level 2 (low research value). This level includes items that have not been used recently or at all, but that may have historiographic value for future scholars. Their research value is not in the information they contain, which is outdated and biased, but in how they present it, as examples of the cultural context of their publication. If enough exempla can be combined into a collection, the collection may rise to Levels 4 or 5. Examples from the CSWS library include *Indians of Today* (1936), *Colorado Indians! A Kid's Look at Our State's Chiefs, Tribes, Reservations,*

---

27. "Special Collections Development Policy for the Montana State University Libraries." Montana State University Libraries, November 2010. http://www.lib.montana.edu/collections/special_collections_development_policy.pdf.

Powwows, Lore & More from the Past & the Present (1998), and books by fraudulent White authors pretending to have Native identity (e.g., Iron Eyes Cody, Grey Owl, Chief Buffalo Child Long Lance, Forrest Carter, Manitonquat, Jamake Highwater, Nasdijj, and GaWaNi Pony Boy). If left on the shelf at their derived catalog records' call numbers, books like those might be consulted as legitimate resources rather than as historic or cultural artifacts. Collocating such items in collections designated as "historiography," "literary forgery," and the like contextualizes them and makes them worth keeping.

Level 3 (general interest and study). This is the hardest level to weed (and it forms the bulk of the CSWS collection). Determining whether an item belongs in Level 3 or Level 1 can be time-consuming and rarely feels worth the effort in a special collections environment. Periodic collection evaluations, including current market value research (which student workers can be trained to perform), review of use statistics, and an analysis of subject holdings *vis-à-vis* the library's statement of scope, will help librarians make judgment calls. Cultural specificity, or a focus on particular peoples rather than Native Americans generally, is preferable.[28]

One category of books that deserves special attention is anything by non-Native authors that has the word "red" in the title (or other loaded words like "savage," "massacre," and even "wild" and "warrior") in reference to Indigenous peoples. Such books are unavoidable and some are indispensable, but seeing stereotypical or offensive terms in bulk on the shelves or in the Online Public Access Catalog (OPAC) is oppressive, and may be particularly offensive to Native American library users.[29] Because controversial books are more likely to go missing from library collections, they may need to be housed in more secure areas.

---

28. Loriene Roy, "Recovering Native Identity: Developing Readers' Advisory Services for Non-Reservation Native Americans," in *Developing Readers' Advisory Services: Concepts and Commitments*, eds. Kathleen de la Peña McCook and Gary O. Rolstad (New York, NY: Neal-Schuman Publishers, 1993), 74.

29. Lara K. Aase, "There Is No View From Nowhere: User Experience Research at

Level 4 (supports independent research). Items in this category directly serve research patrons, have critical merit, and will maintain their appeal over time. For Native American and Indigenous studies, the best resources are quite recent – the academic discipline was established after 1970 – and they should be held in circulating university libraries as well as in special collections.

Because Level 4 items are research resources, they are also quite likely to contain TK and sensitive material, especially when publications predate NAGPRA. When possible, Level 4 items should be evaluated case-by-case, consulting with THPOs for guidance if necessary. Minimal background research and common sense can answer many questions, however; for instance, despite what the Internet might imply, images of the Hopi Snake Dance, ceremonial Diné sandpaintings, and Zuni Kachina masks are instances of private TK that tribes did not wish to be made public. Similarly, it is understandable that people might not appreciate the publication of photographs of their relatives' corpses and would not have given their permission to publish, had they been asked.

It is up to each special collections library to determine how it wants to house and provide access to published TK. Repatriation is an option; I have heard that some tribes actively purchase out-of-print books in order to keep information private. Doing so raises the market value of available books, which is important for librarians to know, since items that may once have had little value are now scarce or rare and may need more security. In the case of gray literature, such as limited-print anthropological reports, even if NAGPRA does not directly restrict access, other federal laws may, such as the Archaeological Resources Protection Act of 1979 and the National Historic Preservation Act of 1966. In fact, those laws even apply to information contained in journal articles. Even if details about archaeological sites are available online in articles published years ago and recently digitized, that does not guarantee that the information is legally accessible.

Because of the difficulties inherent in dealing with books containing TK, I recommend against circulating such materials or housing them in open stacks, which is not usually an issue in special collections libraries. They should be in closed stacks or vaulted, and available to patrons only by request after checking into a reading room. If it is not feasible or acceptable to restrict access on a need-to-know basis (remembering that in many cases restriction is legally required), informing patrons of the wishes of the source community is simple enough and shows consideration, not only of Indigenous cultural property, but also of patrons' desire to do the right thing. That consideration is especially important when a researcher belongs to the source community and wishes to respect cultural norms. As Karen Underhill writes, "Privileged access to information based on gender, initiate status, age, clan, society, and role can be a form of protection for a community, in contrast to the American democratic traditions of open access to information resources and intellectual freedom."[30]

Level 5 (distinguishing, comprehensive collections). Items in this category are likely to be scarce, rare, or monetarily valuable, the jewels in the crown of a special collections library. They are the books scholars travel to consult, and their value is often increased by belonging to a collection of similar items. At the CSWS library, our collection of historic children's books by Native American authors and illustrators (many of them signed first editions) is such a collection, not because of the market value of the books but because we have so many of them in one place. Formerly, these books were scattered throughout various LC classes or intermixed with other juvenile titles (including books like *Colorado Indians!* mentioned earlier). When they were separated from the rest of the collection, brought together, and arranged chronologically, however, they became a microcosm of Native American identity and accomplishment in the twentieth century.

---

30. Karen Underhill, "Protocols for Native American Archival Materials," *RBM: A Journal of Rare Books, Manuscripts, and Cultural Heritage* 7, no. 2 (2006): 138.

Other Policy Considerations: Deeds of Gift and Memoranda of Agreement

Rather than relying on institutional memory as a guide or a verbal conversation with a donor as an agreement, it is a good idea to write the library's approach to TK and TCE into policy and into the wording of the Deed of Gift form. Northern Arizona University's (NAU) Special Collections and Archives (SCA) "is open about its collaborations with identified representatives from particular communities and how those conversations may result in restrictions placed on items identified as sacred or ceremonial in nature. … [D]onors concerned about such restrictions may choose to donate materials to another institution with more relaxed policies about cultural sensitivity."[31] NAU's SCA make an effort to cultivate a diverse donor pool, with the goal of obtaining diversity in donations. NAU also holds Memoranda of Agreement with tribal representatives. For example, the Hopi Cultural Preservation Office (HCPO) has agreed to provide consultation and assistance with issues of cultural sensitivity and naming conventions, while the SCA forwards digitization and publication requests for Hopi ceremonial materials to the HCPO for approval, shares storage space, and deaccessions and transfers specific ceremonial images to the tribe.[32]

Library Procedures

Collection Management, Cataloging, and Access

The CSWS library was a semi-circulating collection from about 2014 to 2018, with open stacks access to about 80% of its material. In an effort to provide an organizational structure that LCC lacks and to mitigate the effect on users of chance discovery of offensive or private information, I modified some existing systems to improve collocation. The simplest fix for us was to establish topical special collections and change the database location codes of items added to those collections. A database

---

31. Bishop, Pringle, and Tsosie, "Connecting Cline Library," 249-50.
32. Bishop, Pringle, and Tsosie, "Connecting Cline Library," 251.

list of items in any given location can be the basis of a pathfinder, to which our archives and museum may add items. This solution allows us to serve our users' interests in issues such as social justice, Indigenous self-determination, and historical bias without significant deaccessions and without necessarily moving collections out of public view. The only newly established collection now housed in the vault is the Anthropology/Archaeology Collection, because of the preponderance of legally restricted site information, culturally sensitive images of human remains, and unique or scarce publications that the CSWS would not be able to replace. General-interest anthropology and archaeology books remain on the regular shelves and can be browsed by the public, but patrons who wish to see Levels 4 and 5 materials must speak to library staff, who then inform them of federal laws and the content and distinct value of vaulted items. Future special collections with new location codes may include Historiography of Native American and Indigenous Studies, Literary Forgeries, Genealogy, and Indigenous Education (including material on boarding schools, the Bureau of Indian Education, and the history of Fort Lewis College; this will contextualize titles such as *The Red Man, Indians at Work,* and *Blue Coats, Red Skins & Black Gowns: 100 Years of Fort Lewis*).

One advantage of using location codes is the ability to reshelve entire collections in bulk without having to change call numbers. In the case of one new special collection, Children's Books, I also modified LC call numbers in order to add research value. We have about 300 children's books on Indigenous topics by both Native and non-Native authors, and only a handful of children's books on other topics. For the bulk of the collection, the facets I wanted to emphasize, in order, were a juvenile audience (PZ), Indigenous topic (Cutter .I53; other topics use Cutters such as .F for Hispanic American subjects and .QE for paleontology), Native identity of at least one creator (or lack thereof, indicated by IAI for "Indigenous author or illustrator" or NI for "non-Indigenous"), chronology (i.e., year of publication), the name of the author (or Native American illustrator), and that person's tribal affiliation in the language of the tribe. The overall structure and some of those facets follow LC, but the use of "I" as a Cutter letter, using illustrators' instead of authors' names in some cases, and including tribal affiliation, are all departures from LCC. Thus, a recent edition of Pablita Velarde's *Old Father Story Teller* is at call number PZ .I53 IAI 1989 Velarde Tewa, rather than E98.F6 V4 1989 (where retellings of all Native American folktales live, subdivided further only by author's last name), while *Cowboy Sam and the Indians* is at PZ .I53 NI 1954 Chandler (instead of in PZ and collocated with other children's books, subdivided by authors' last names). By prioritizing publication years over authors' names, I sacrificed seeing all of an author's books in one place in favor of delineating the chronological developments in children's books on Indigenous topics, from separate Native and non-Native viewpoints.

Using location codes and modified LC call numbers adds value to previously haphazardly organized materials through collocation and shelf arrangement that facilitate browsing. Such changes can breathe new life into outdated material by creating a collection of use to researchers. Jennifer Bowers, Katherine Crowe, and Peggy Keeran address a similar approach in their discussion of captivity narratives, a subgenre of biased publications "about Indians capturing and holding white men, women, and children. ... Although a few of the memoirs did not show the captors as savages, the majority were propaganda intended to create anxiety about Native peoples."[33] Such a collection will be valuable for historians, literary scholars, and those who study race and ethnicity. If it makes more sense to change call numbers than to create collections, rather than throwing the LC baby out with the bathwater, consider using MARC field 090 for locally assigned LC-type call numbers in the way that serves your collection best, perhaps by moving books on Indigenous religions to the BL2500s and books on Southwest Pueblo silversmithing to NK7112. Archaeology and Anthropology topics could be moved to the GN800 area. Conversely, all pre-Columbian Western Hemisphere topics could stay in E, and information on modern Indigenous peoples

33. Jennifer Bowers, Katherine Crowe, and Peggy Keeran, "'If You Want the History of a White Man, You Go to the Library': Critiquing Our Legacy, Addressing Our Library Collections Gaps," *Collection Management* 42, no. 3-4 (2017): 168.

could fall into its own new class (my vote is I for Indigenous). For any of those alternatives, Cutter numbers can correlate to main LC classes in order to provide more comprehensive collocation through facets. If a collection is large enough, better ways to group Indigenous peoples (instead of using the colonial names for tribes in alphabetical order) are to arrange them geographically or linguistically. Cutter subdivisions can be mapped against Indigenous-centric cataloging systems like Brian Deer's and further modified for the needs of the local user group or the collection.

Finally, catalogers have the power to modify OCLC records, to create high-quality original records and share them with OCLC, and to enhance metadata by "deepen[ing] context for materials with parallel traditional knowledge descriptions, making them available alongside digitized materials ... providing a space for enhanced community description."[34] Catalogers and other interested contributors can also request new LC subject headings. A joint group of library professionals from the American Indian Library Association and the Seminar on the Acquisition of Latin American Library Materials has created a Subject Authority Cooperative Program (SACO) funnel for "Latin American and Indigenous Peoples of the Americas" to contribute suggestions to LCSH.[35] Anyone can join the group or use its resources to improve subject access by suggesting unbiased terminology.[36] Other changes can be undertaken by subject liaisons, who can create pathfinders that bring materials together conceptually, even if they remain separate on the shelves. And archivists can look into database options (like Mukurtu and ArchivesSpace, among others) that have filtering features to restrict access.

Acquisitions

34. Bishop, Pringle, and Tsosie, "Connecting Cline Library," 250.

35. "PCC SACO Funnel Projects." Library of Congress, 2019. https://www.loc.gov/aba/pcc/saco/funnelsaco.html.

36. Violet Fox, "The Cataloging Lab [LAIPA Funnel]," The Cataloging Lab, 2019. http://cataloginglab.org/.

Through self-education and collaboration with local communities, acquisitions librarians can build better quality Native American collections. Learning what cultural information people want shared and how they prefer to preserve it (which may be orally) will help librarians find the best means to deal with TK, perhaps partnering with archivists or public historians to collect and digitize oral histories. Digital librarians can seek out online databases such as *American Indian Newspapers* for curated content produced by and for Native Americans, and serials librarians should consider purchasing subscriptions to the print versions of newspapers as community resources for Native American patrons.[37] When selecting books, librarians must be highly attuned to authors' tones and points of view, keeping in mind that, in addition to appropriating TK, non-Native authors have sometimes falsely claimed tribal affiliation to bolster their credentials. "Plastic shamans" are not the only people guilty of appropriation; well-intentioned non-Native authors who believe they are "speaking for those who can't speak for themselves" profit, nonetheless, from book sales, while also propagating a condescending attitude that assumes Indigenous people are unable to express themselves in print. A more helpful approach is to create quiet spaces for Native voices and then remember not to speak over them. As Bowers, Crowe, and Keeran write, "white archivists and librarians can, when wanted and welcomed, play a role in preserving the history of Native American communities without requiring community members to relinquish autonomy over their history, their ways of knowing, and their own narrative(s)."[38]

Public Service, Reference, and Instruction

---

37. Sarah R. Kostelecky, David A. Hurley, Jolene Manus, and Paulita Aguilar, "Centering Indigenous Knowledge: Three Southwestern Tribal College and University Library Collections," *Collection Management* 42, no. 3-4 (2017): 190; Kevin Brown, "The Role of an Indigenous Nations Library Program and the Advancement of Indigenous Knowledge," *Collection Management* 42, no. 3-4 (2017): 202.

38. Bowers, Crowe, and Keeran, "If You Want the History of a White Man," 165.

To discover if library services are wanted and welcomed, culturally informed user experience research can be eye-opening and can lead to immediate changes that make patrons feel more welcome.[39] Short of undertaking a full research project, reference librarians can adopt Loriene Roy's readers' advisory suggestions for non-reservation Native Americans and adapt them for user groups that include multiple cultures, including Native Americans.[40]

- Advertise your willingness to help, both through outreach efforts and by coming out from behind the reference desk. People who are unaccustomed to special collections environments will appreciate a respectful and gentle introduction to norms such as leaving backpacks and bags at the front desk, showing ID and signing in, and using only pencils. People who are accustomed to a society that views them as "other" may at first misconstrue such standards as discriminatory or condescending behavior, which can lead to awkward interactions. It can help to remember that library professionals are in the position of serving patrons, not the other way around.

- Develop interview skills, keeping in mind that different cultures have different comfort thresholds with the amount and intimacy levels of conversation. Approach patrons rather than waiting for them to come to you. Practice active listening, ask questions, and follow the patron's lead. As Roy points out, "Communication may be based on a new etiquette where eye contact is seen as invasive, close physical proximity intimidating, and silence and long pauses valued."[41]

- Facilitate browsing, if relevant (see section "Collection Management, Cataloging, and Access" above). When creating book

---

39. Bishop, Pringle, and Tsosie, "Connecting Cline Library," 252; Aase, "There Is No View From Nowhere," 139-58.

40. Roy (after Ross), "Recovering Native Identity," 74-76.

41. Roy, "Recovering Native Identity," 75.

displays, feature Indigenous authors and illustrators and avoid displaying biased material unless explicitly pointing out historic racism. Complement book displays with related items from your institution's archives or museum to help contextualize traditional cultural expressions. Remember that holiday displays (particularly for Thanksgiving) may not resonate in the same way with all cultures. Make use of the library website to display digital exhibitions, which can be especially effective at drawing in patrons who live far away.

- Provide lists, finding aids, and pathfinders. Creating topical special collections will make this easy. Remember to include non-print resources like oral histories and musical recordings. Provide online digital access where culturally appropriate, respecting group privacy.
- Let readers share their enthusiasm. When appropriate and not in violation of patrons' privacy, ask about their research. What you learn may help you to help other users in the future. Make the library a gathering place for people to find community space. Provide culturally appropriate programming, including traditional storytellers. The American Indian Library Association's "Talk Story" grant can help facilitate such programs.[42]
- Encourage all library staff to read. Help other staff members to develop ethnic competency along with you.

I would make one additional suggestion for academic librarians:
- Perform inreach as well as outreach. Talk to faculty and students about using oral histories (including print collections of stories, such as *Navajo Stories of the Long Walk Period*) as primary source material. Provide library instruction to teach about historic bias and gaps, the limitations of LC Classification, and the

---

42. "Talk Story: Sharing Stories, Sharing Culture." AILA/APALA, 2019. http://talkstorytogether.org/.

non-neutrality of LC subject headings. Encourage students to read problematic materials critically, respond to what they read, share inaccuracies with you, and suggest improvements.

Human Resources

Last, and perhaps most important, we should all do what we can to increase the representation of Indigenous people in the library profession. The most direct influence we can have as librarians may be in training student workers and interns and discussing these ideas with them. We can also support organizations such as the American Indian Library Association and its Youth Literature Award, the Knowledge River program at the University of Arizona Information School, the Indigenous Information Research Group at the University of Washington iSchool, and the ALA Spectrum Scholarship program. If (following Terry Cook) through archives and libraries we are what we keep and we keep what we are, we must expand *who* we are as a profession.

CONCLUSION

"Those who are not given archival dignity, archival voice, archival legitimacy, will remain suppressed and marginalized."[43] For that reason, our settler-centric approach to special collections management needs rethinking. Because special collections vary in their scope and accessibility, it is difficult to prescribe guidelines that apply to every institution, or even most of them. The approaches I describe as having been implemented at the CSWS library are still nascent and may never be completed. Ceasing circulation, restricting access, creating new locations and collections, and reclassifying materials are administrative as well as collection-management hurdles to jump, and it is difficult to call out collection bias and infringement of cultural privacy without seeming self-censoring. As Mathiesen points out, however, "the fact that problems might arise as we try to implement policies to protect these rights does not provide a

---

43. Cook, "We Are What We Keep," 183.

justification for refusing to do so."[44] Because of their historical value, we must retain our special collections, but we must also find new ways to curate old ideas and traditional Indigenous knowledge.

ACKNOWLEDGMENTS

I would like to thank my 2018-2019 student employees, interns, and contract employees for their help in evaluating the CSWS library collection, bringing biased materials and TK to my attention, and reclassifying topical collections: Tabitha Andersen, Britni Billy, Cassidy Brunson, Tirzah Camacho, Rayna Henry, Summer Shomo, J'Kye Wientjes, and Shawna Yazzie.

I also owe a debt of gratitude to my professional colleagues for all they continue to teach me about cultural awareness and library ethics: Naomi Bishop, Dr. Kay Holmes, Dr. Sandy Littletree, Valerie Nye, Dr. Debbie Reese, and Dr. Loriene Roy.

Bibliography

Aase, Lara K. "There Is No View from Nowhere: User Experience Research at the Center of Southwest Studies Library." *Collection Management* 42, no. 3-4 (2017): 139-58.

"Aboriginal and Torres Strait Islander Protocols for Libraries, Archives and Information Services." Aboriginal and Torres Strait Islander Library, Information and Resource Network. 2012. http://atsilirn. aiatsis.gov.au/protocols.php.

Bacon, Cherity M. "Native American Concerns About Museums and Archives Policies on Tangible and Intangible Cultural Property." *Archifacts* (October-April, 2011-2012): 35-48.

Belarde-Lewis, Miranda Hayes. "From Six Directions: Documenting and Protecting Zuni Knowledge in Multiple Environments." PhD Dissertation, University of Washington, 2013.

Bishop, Naomi, Jonathan Pringle, and Carissa Tsosie. "Connecting Cline

---

44. Mathiesen, "A Defense of Native Americans' Rights," 480.

Library with Tribal Communities: A Case Study." *Collection Management* 42, no. 3-4 (2017): 240-55.

Bolcer, John. "The Protocols for Native American Archival Materials: Considerations and Concerns from the Perspective of a Non-Tribal Archivist." *Easy Access* 24, no. 4 (2009): 3-6.

Bowers, Jennifer, Katherine Crowe, and Peggy Keeran. "'If You Want the History of a White Man, You Go to the Library': Critiquing Our Legacy, Addressing Our Library Collections Gaps." *Collection Management* 42, no. 3-4 (2017): 159-79.

Brown, Kevin. "The Role of an Indigenous Nations Library Program and the Advancement of Indigenous Knowledge." *Collection Management* 42, no. 3-4 (2017): 196-207.

Cook, Terry. "'We Are What We Keep; We Keep What We Are': Archival Appraisal Past, Present and Future." *Journal of the Society of Archivists* 32, no. 2 (2011): 173-89.

"Draft Code of Ethics for Special Collections Librarians." Rare Books and Manuscripts Section, Association of College and Research Libraries. Email attachment to RBMS listserv, January 20, 2019.

Dunbar, Anthony. "Introducing Critical Race Theory to Archival Discourse: Getting the Conversation Started." *Archival Science* 6, no. 1 (2006): 109-29.

Fox, Violet. "The Cataloging Lab [LAIPA Funnel]." The Cataloging Lab. 2019. http://cataloginglab.org/.

Grose, Teresa Olwick. "Reading the Bones: Information Content, Value, and Ownership Issues Raised by the Native American Graves Protection and Repatriation Act." *Journal of the American Society for Information Science* 48, no. 7 (1996): 624-31.

Hurley, David. "Oral Tradition and Tribal College Libraries: Problems and Promise." *Alki* 18, no. 1 (2002): 19, 27.

Isaac, Gwyneira. *Mediating Knowledges: Origins of a Zuni Tribal Museum.* Tucson: University of Arizona Press, 2007.

Joffrion, Elizabeth, and Natalia Fernández. "Collaborations between Tribal and Non-Tribal Organizations: Suggested Best Practices for Sharing Expertise, Knowledge, and Cultural Resources." *American Archivist* 78, no. 1 (2015): 192-237.

Kostelecky, Sarah R., David A. Hurley, Jolene Manus, and Paulita Aguilar. "Centering Indigenous Knowledge: Three Southwestern Tribal College and University Library Collections." *Collection Management* 42, no. 3-4 (2017): 180-95.

Lee, Deborah. "Indigenous Knowledges and the University Library." *Canadian Journal of Native Education* 31, no. 1 (2008): 149-61.

Mathiesen, Kay. "A Defense of Native Americans' Rights over Traditional Cultural Expressions." *American Archivist* 75, no. 2 (2012): 456-81.

Mifflin, Jeffrey. "Regarding Indigenous Knowledge in Archives." In *Through the Archival Looking Glass: A Reader on Diversity and Inclusion*, 61-90. Edited by Mary A. Caldera and Kathryn M. Neal. Chicago, IL: Society of American Archivists, 2014.

O'Neal, Jennifer. "Respect, Recognition, and Reciprocity: The Protocols for Native American Archival Materials." In *Identity Palimpsests: Archiving Ethnicity in the US and Canada*, 125-42. Edited by Dominique Daniel and Amalia Levi. Sacramento, CA: Litwin Press, 2014.

O'Neal, Jennifer. "'The Right to Know': Decolonizing Native American Archives." *Journal of Western Archives* 6, no. 1 (2015): 1-17.

"PCC SACO Funnel Projects." Library of Congress. 2019. https://www.loc.gov/aba/pcc/saco/funnelsaco.html.

"Protocols for Native American Archival Materials." First Archivist Circle. 2006. http://www2.nau.edu/libnap-p/index.html.

Roy, Loriene. "Recovering Native Identity: Developing Readers' Advisory Services for Non-Reservation Native Americans." In *Developing Readers' Advisory Services: Concepts and Commitments*, 73-77. Edited by Kathleen de la Peña McCook and Gary O. Rolstad. New York, NY: Neal-Schuman Publishers, 1993.

Saad Bee Hozho/Diné Writers' Collective. "Trail of Lightning is an Appropriation of Diné Cultural Beliefs." *Indian Country Today*, November 5, 2018. https://newsmaven.io/indiancountrytoday/opinion/trail-of-lightning-is-an-appropriation-of-din%C3%A9-cultural-beliefs-

4tvSMvEfNE-i7AE10W7nQg/.

"SAA Council Endorsement of Protocols for Native American Archival Materials." Society of American Archivists, 2018. https://www2. archivists.org/statements/saa-council-endorsement-of-protocols-for-native-american-archival-materials.

"Special Collections Development Policy for the Montana State University Libraries." Montana State University Libraries, November 2010. http://www.lib.montana.edu/collections/special_collections_development_policy.pdf.

"Talk Story: Sharing Stories, Sharing Culture." AILA/APALA, 2019. http:// talkstorytogether.org/.

"THPOs." NATHPO: National Association of Tribal Historic Preservation Officers, 2019. http://www.nathpo.org/thpos/what-are-thpos/.

Underhill, Karen. "Protocols for Native American Archival Materials." RBM: A Journal of Rare Books, Manuscripts, and Cultural Heritage 7, no. 2 (2006): 134-45.

"United Nations Declaration on the Rights of Indigenous Peoples." United Nations, 2007. https://www.un.org/development/desa/ indigenouspeoples/wp-content/uploads/sites/19/2018/11/ UNDRIP_E_web.pdf.

"Universal Declaration of Human Rights." United Nations, 1948. http:// www.un.org/en/universal-declaration-human-rights/.

Villela, Khristaan D. "Controversy Erupts over Peter Nabokov's Publication of 'The Origin Myth of Acoma Pueblo.'" Santa Fe New Mexican, Pasatiempo, January 15, 2016. http://www.santafenewmexican.com/ pasatiempo/columns/viajes_pintorescos/controversy-erupts-over-peter-nabokov-s-publication-of-the-origin/article_1bcbe12b-b5c2-527e-93e9-1759fec994c5.html.

in Saskatchewan, *Transition* from British Columbia Penitentiary, *Pen-O-Rama* from St. Vincent De Paul Penitentiary in Quebec, *The Beacon* from Dorchester Prison in New Brunswick, and *The Mountain Echo* from Manitoba Penitentiary. These newsletters or "joint magazines" were professional in their production from their stories to the quality of printing. Although these early newsletters were consistent in their content—all containing regular features, lengthy sports columns, humor, a census of the prison population, and a "greetings" column—each newsletter maintained its own unique style and tone.

Produced and edited by inmates, the majority of whom had little or no printing training and limited formal education, these publications provided a more direct representation of prison life to the public.[6] Although the editors of *The Telescope* indicate that the newsletter was written by regular inmates, most of the writing was done by inmate editors. It was difficult for editors to find writers who would follow the policies set by prison administrators. The editors' jobs were not easy. They had to appease the administration and follow the policies or risk punishment, such as having their "good time" reduced, being relieved of their duties as editors, or risk being labeled "uncooperative." In addition, they had to be mindful of the inmate population and walk a fine line between the two—the personal ramifications of upsetting the inmate population could be harsh. Although editors had many hoops to jump through, they were not forced to publish the viewpoints of the prison administration. This was most evident in 1957, when *The Telescope* was not published for an entire year because editors and administrators could not agree on policies for the newsletter.

Well-produced, many with beautiful silkscreen covers, the early KP newsletters were hand-set and printed from linotype. Two different crews—editing and production—were involved in the creation of the publications. Resenting interference, the inmate compositors, press-men, and linotype operators separated themselves from the editors. In the middle of the twentieth century, KP was the only institution in the

---

6. Canada, *Report of the Commissioner of Penitentiaries*, 18.

Kingston area that had an inmate print shop; in addition to printing *The Telescope*, they also printed *The Collin's Bay Diamond*. Around 1962, the newsletters began to change and the high-quality look of the publications, which featured silkscreen and woodcut covers, disappeared and were replaced by mimeographed, and later photocopied, product. By 1968, all of the original Canadian penal press publications had ceased publication.[7]

Opened in 1935, the Prison for Women, commonly known as P4W, the only federal women's penitentiary in Canada, operated in Kingston until 1995 and was decommissioned in 2000.[8] *Tightwire*, the most notable publication from P4W, was first published in 1972 and endured for over two decades.[9] As its name implies, it existed within a dangerous and precarious situation requiring the art of maintaining balance. The editors at *Tightwire* faced the same problems their colleagues at other institutions did, balancing two opposing views with little room for compromise. However, because P4W was the only women's penitentiary, there was little prisoner movement and the newsletter enjoyed continuity of editors and staff that their male counterparts did not. Like the other prison newsletters, *Tightwire* included poetry, art, letters to the editor, humor, sports, and a large Indigenous section. Featured on the covers and throughout the publication, the artwork is exceptional and, like the stories, often intense and deeply personal. Lacking a print shop, *Tightwire's* editions were photocopied and not reminiscent of the quality of *The Telescope*. However, producing the newsletter in this way cut costs considerably and made it much easier for the editors to meet publication deadlines.

From the inception of the Canadian penal press in 1950, beginning with the publication of *The Telescope*, the various newsletters went through many changes. Produced in institutional print shops, woodcuts

---

7. Gaucher, "Canadian Penal Press," 10.

8. After KP opened in 1835, female inmates were incarcerated alongside the men, until P4W became operational in 1934.

9. Prior to having their own newsletter, the women contributed on a regular basis to *The K.P. Telescope* in a column called "Feminine Features."

Figure 3. Inmate in the printing shop at Kingston Penitentiary, c.1953.
Used with permission from Canada's Penitentiary Museum/
Musée Pénitentiaire du Canada.

and attractive silkscreen art graced the covers of the earliest magazines, eventually giving way to black and white photocopies. Originally
endorsed by corrections administration and inmates alike, the support
and enthusiasm eventually fell by the wayside as the hoped-for outcomes
suggested by the Archambault Report of 1938 failed to materialize.
In 2019, *Out of Bounds* (a prison newsletter from William Head Institution, a minimum security prison on Vancouver Island) is the only

outside-directed prison newsletter still produced in Canada.[10] Not without its share of problems, it was banned in 2017 by BC Corrections officials for containing "anti-corrections messaging."[11] The ban has since been rescinded.

Prison Newsletter Exhibit

Focusing on prison newsletters from Kingston area prisons, W.D. Jordan Rare Books and Special Collections mounted an exhibit called Prison Sentences[12] in the winter of 2016 that provided an in-depth look at these newsletters. Examining the content and historical significance of the publications and drawing attention to the high quality of the publications, especially in the 1950s and 60s, the exhibit provided context and highlighted the tension in which the newsletters were produced.

The idea to have an exhibit of this material came about after the Canadian Penitentiary Museum donated a number of newsletters to the Queen's University Archives, which then passed along the items to the W.D. Jordan Rare Books and Special Collections. This addition to the existing collection of prison newsletters increased our holdings to more than ten linear feet of prison newsletters, the majority from KP, Collin's Bay, and P4W. Many of the pre-existing newsletters in the W.D. Jordan Rare Books and Special Collections were donated by John Alexander Edmison (1909-1980) Q.C., a member of the four-man Fauteux Committee (1953-1956) appointed by the Minister of Justice to study probation, parole, and clemency problems.[13] Later, Edmison

---

10. *The Gabber Express*, which is currently published in Matsqui Institution, a medium security institution on the Federal Reserve land that is shared with Fraser Valley Institution and Pacific Institution, located in the community of Abbotsford, British Columbia, is not an outside-directed newsletter.

11. Sunny Dhillon, "BC Corrections Rescinds Ban on Two of Three Prisoner Publications," Globe and Mail March 15, (2017): https://www.theglobeandmail.com/news/british-columbia/bc-corrections-rescinds-ban-on-two-of-three-prisoner-publications/article34317966/.

12. For an audio tour of the exhibit, please see https://library.queensu.ca/about-us/news-events/prison-sentences-penitentiary-literature-kingston.

13. Queen's University Archives holds the John Alexander Edmison fonds, donated by Mrs. J.A. Edmison.

Figure 4. Exhibit poster.

was appointed as a member of the first Parole Board of Canada from 1959 to 1969. Educated at Queen's University and McGill, Edmison was interested in crime prevention, penal reform, and the welfare of ex-prisoners, topics that he wrote and spoke about often. He was a frequent guest editor in the early newsletters and his work in prison reform earned him the reputation of being "a good friend of this magazine."[14]

Totaling six display cases, the exhibit covered the history of the Canadian penal press, social issues within the prisons, how the newsletters were printed, personal narrative books written inside Kingston area prisons, and a sample of writings from famous political prisoners, with one case devoted entirely to *Tightwire*. Issues that mattered to the inmates were highlighted in the "Writer's Block: Social Issues on the Inside" case, featuring stories that captured the attention of prisoners. Headlining the *Joyceville Journal* in March 1965 is a reprinted article, "Capital Punishment—End to Hanging," an issue that found its way into the pages of the newsletters until a moratorium on the death penalty was announced in 1967.[15] "Put Them to Work" is a reprinted article from *The Ottawa Evening Citizen* that strongly supports inmates working for their keep; heartily endorsed by the editors of *The Collin's Bay Diamond*, the article was included in the July 1954 issue. Drug addiction was also a topic of interest and therefore frequently featured in the newsletters. One story from the 1950s, about the deaths of two inmates at P4W, implored the government and the legal system to address the problem. Law reform was also a popular topic, serving to inform the inmates and the public of changes in the legal system.

In addition to material from the W.D. Jordan Rare Books and Special Collections, we borrowed from the Queen's Archives and the Canadian Penitentiary Museum; a goal of the exhibit was to promote this historical material to the community and have the collection used as a resource. In determining how best to recoup the voices of this marginalized group, the curator had to be mindful of the victims' voices. Emphasizing the rehabilitative nature of the newsletters and the attempt at transparency

---

14. *The K.P. Telescope*, vol. 3 no. 1, 1952. 6.

15. It was 1998 before Canada fully abolished capital punishment. The last execution of prisoners occurred in 1962. Paul Gendreau, and Wayne Renke, "Capital Punishment," *The Canadian Encyclopedia*. Historica Canada. Article published February 6, 2006, last modified December 7, 2017. https://www.thecanadianencyclopedia.ca/en/article/capital-punishment.

by prison officials as a result of the Archambault Report, the intent was to highlight the collection as a primary source, not to glorify the writings and lives of the inmates. Interestingly, although perhaps not surprising given that Kingston is known as Canada's "Penitentiary City," the exhibit generated much local interest. Kingston residents pride themselves on living in a prison town, but it was former inmates who displayed the most interest in the exhibit. In particular, a former inmate writer whose books were on display as part of the narratives written in prison visited the library and donated additional books to the collection. Rather than being a painful journey to the past, he described it as an opportunity for reflection. Writing, he said, was a means of escape and an attempt to deal with personal issues.

Out of this former inmate writer's relationship with the collection began another, this time with the coordinator of an online resource called *The Penal Press—A History of Prison from Within*.[16] Run by Professor Melissa Munn from Okanagan College in British Columbia, this website provides open access to these documents. Munn's visit to the exhibit in 2016 led to a discussion about newsletter volumes that *The Penal Press* was missing, and Queen's agreed to scan and supply them. It was also during Munn's visit that she met the former inmate writer, and the two sparked the idea of taking the newsletters back to their prison beginnings.

Student Research: Can the Incarcerated Speak?

In conjunction with the prison newsletter exhibit, Queen's University History professor Steven Maynard built his upper-level "Foucault for Historians" course around the newsletter collection. His students researched the collection for their final seminar papers; consequently, they were not limited to just one special collections class session, but instead became experienced reading room users. Collaborating, we recognized that the newsletters provided students with the opportunity to

---

16. *The Penal Press—A History of Prison from Within*, accessed December 31, 2018, http://penalpress.com/.

conduct hands-on research with primary sources, develop research skills, learn how to handle rare materials, and prepare for future independent work in special collections.

Exploring the theme, "Can the Incarcerated Speak? Prison Newsletters as Power/Knowledge," students were required "to assess the value of the newsletters as sources for writing a Foucauldian-inspired history of the prison." Michel Foucault's famous work, *Discipline and Punish: The Birth of the Prison*, a history of the modern penal system, was first published in 1975; there, he presented his analysis and theories on the history of prisons and the structure of power. Prior to its publication, Foucault helped to establish the Groupe d'Information Sur Les Prisons (The Prisons Information Group, or the GIP) in 1971. On February 8, 1971, he presented the GIP's manifesto to the public:

> We propose to make known what the prison is: who goes there, how and why they go there, what happens there, and what the life of the prisoners is, and that, equally, of the surveillance personnel; what the buildings, the food, and hygiene are like; how the internal regulations, medical control, and the workshops function; how one gets out and what it is to be, in our society, one of those who came out.[17]

Rather than rely on official government reports and statistics, the GIP compiled information through questionnaires and shared it through pamphlets and other print media with the goal of publicizing prisoners' experiences. The questionnaires were more authentic than government reports, because they allowed prisoners to speak for themselves.

Using this Foucauldian context, students were tasked with considering whether the newsletters similarly presented the "authentic" voice of prisoners, and whether they provided an accurate account of marginalized voices more generally. The students grappled with, not only these questions (insofar as the newsletters were vetted by prison administrators), but also with what it means to encounter the newsletters in a

---

17. Salar Mohandesi, "Manifesto of the Groupe d'Information Sur Les Prisons (1971)," *Viewpoint Magazine*, February 16, 2016, https://www.viewpointmag.com/2016/02/16/manifesto-of-the-groupe -dinformation-sur-les-prisons-1971/.

special collections library. They considered how libraries and archives arrange and present collections and what authority and power curators have over collections. In preparation for their archival research, students attended a session in our reading room where they were introduced to handling materials and were presented with the provenance of the collection. Discussing the history of the penal press and how the newsletters were produced enabled us to provide context while leaving the question of authentic voice to be answered by the students. Because students consulted this material throughout the semester, we placed the newsletters on a cart organized by title for ease of access and to keep the items on hold. At the beginning of their projects, students could browse the collection on the cart and then choose one box to consult. The prison newsletter exhibit was concurrently on display and we removed items from the exhibit upon request. Students dropped in during our regular reading room hours and were not required to make appointments. However, students often requested to consult with the exhibit curator and other librarians as they made sense of the collection and formulated their ideas.

The goals of the seminar paper and course are best framed within the context of the ACRL RBMS-SAA's Guidelines for Primary Source Literacy, specifically the learning objectives listed under number four: "Interpret, Analyze, and Evaluate."[18] The first three objectives include:

A. Assess the appropriateness of a primary source for meeting the goals of a specific research or creative project.

B. Critically evaluate the perspective of the creator(s) of a primary source, including tone, subjectivity, and biases, and consider how these relate to the original purpose(s) and audience(s) of the source.

---

18. ACRL RBMS-SAA Joint Task Force (2017), "Guidelines for Primary Source Literacy," approved February 12, 2018, http://www.ala.org/acrl/sites/ala.org.acrl/files/content/standards/Primary%20Source%20Literacy2018.pdf, 5.

C. Situate a primary source in context by applying knowledge about the time and culture in which it was created; the author or creator; its format, genre, publication history; or related materials in a collection.[19]

Students were prompted to devise research strategies to focus their browsing and reading of the collection. They were required to narrow their topics to, for example, a run of newsletters produced at one institution, how prisoners documented and reacted to violent events like the prison riots at KP, or to pick a theme such as women/gender or racialization/incarceration to track across newsletters. Settling on topics, the students engaged in the task of finding appropriate evidence from the primary source. The second and third learning objectives tie back to the question of whether the newsletters accurately convey the prisoners' voices. Students had to consider that the newsletters were not only read by fellow inmates, but circulated to subscribers. However, the content they produced also had to pass through an editorial board of both inmates and prison administrators. These interventions, or mediations of the prisoners' voices, tie back to the course theme: are these prisoners authentically speaking for themselves, and what are the Foucauldian power dynamics at work? The question of power or authority directly relates to the fourth through sixth learning objectives:

D. As part of the analysis of available resources, identify, interrogate, and consider the reasons for silences, gaps, contradictions, or evidence of power relationships in the documentary record and how they impact the research process.

E. Factor physical and material elements into the interpretation of primary sources, including the relationship between container (binding, media, or overall physical attributes) and informational

---

19. ACRL RBMS-SAA Joint Task Force (2017), "Guidelines for Primary Source Literacy," 5.

content, and the relationship of original sources to physical or digital copies of those sources.

F. Demonstrate historical empathy, curiosity about the past, and appreciation for historical sources and historical actors.[20]

The prison newsletters are unique in that they offered a space for a variety of inmates to share their voices in various forms, from essays to poetry to cartoons. As students examined the newsletters, many focused on how prisoners advocated for parole reform or traced one author across time and prisons as inmates were transferred to different institutions. While a number of the newsletters are available online, students were frequently in our reading room and a number of them wrote about the physical interaction with the materials and the quality of production. One of the greatest outcomes of this course and assignment was the continued interest in the newsletters. Students returned the following year to use the collection for different History courses, recognizing that the inmates' writings were valuable and viable sources for their research. One student in particular has chosen to pursue research in the history of insane asylums and prison health care as part of her medical school studies. Their papers and continued research affirm that the prison newsletters do present an authentic view of the prison experience.

Outside of the History department, English graduate students have critically engaged with the Indigenous inmate writings throughout the collection, focusing on P4W's *Tightwire*. In his course, "Incarcerating Indigenous Peoples: Cultural and Political Perspectives," Professor Armand Ruffo challenged his students to consider the various forms in which Indigenous peoples are incarcerated, including literal incarceration in the Canadian prison system. The Correctional Service of Canada (CSC) reports that, "[w]hile Indigenous people represent approximately four per cent of the Canadian adult population; almost twenty-three

---

20. ACRL RBMS-SAA Joint Task Force (2017), "Guidelines for Primary Source Literacy," 5-6.

percent of federally sentenced offenders are Indigenous."[21] The printed work by Indigenous inmates often focuses on either the loss or reconnection with their culture. Students examining the newsletters focused not only on how the newsletters provide a space for the inmate voice, but also a space to share an incarcerated culture. By examining the collection and pursuing critical reading of the texts, students validated the prisoners' writings as an important part of Indigenous literature.

As with all primary sources, the prison newsletter collection provides insight into people's experiences of historical events. Examining the newsletters connected students to the often-undervalued inmate experience. They not only gained primary source research experience, but also recognized these missing voices in the historical record or literary canon. By promoting and teaching with this collection, we chose to share marginalized voices to which students would not otherwise be exposed; this choice resulted in original student research, and provided inspiration for continued use of primary sources.

Back to the Penitentiary

As mentioned, serendipitous discussions in the reading room during the winter of 2016 led to our outreach program at Joyceville Institution. Building on the Prison Sentences exhibit, we reached out to the Institution and jointly developed a plan to bring the newsletters there as part of a pop-up exhibit. Eventually, sharing the publications in a classroom setting, reminiscent of the Archambault Report's recommendation for increased education, became the goal. Ideally, it would have been best to work with a current university program that was already involved in the local prisons, but they were no longer in existence. Projects are typically slow to move through the bureaucratic approval process of any institutional environment, and security concerns (a top priority for the CSC) extended the timeframe.

Each institution has a specific security classification that determines which programs are offered. Joyceville is a minimum-security site with

---

21. Correctional Service Canada, "Indigenous Corrections," last modified January 2017, https://www.csc-scc.gc.ca/publications/092/005007-3001-eng.pdf.

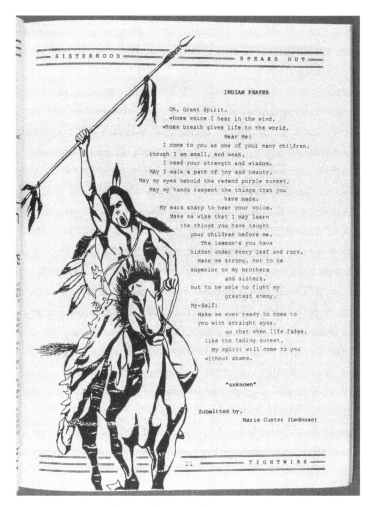

Figure 5. Page from *Tightwire*, Vol. 23, no. 2, Summer 1989.
*Courtesy of W.D. Jordan Rare Books and Special Collections,
Queen's University, Kingston, Ontario.*

a clustered facility based on a residential design model. It consists of small-group accommodation houses in addition to a medium security section. Minimum-security institutions have fewer limitations, which means that correctional staff restrict movement and privileges as little as possible. This environment is meant to prepare inmates for their eventual return to the community (although not all inmates will be released).[22] Inmates spend their days either working at job sites, developing trade skills, or taking classes.

A teacher with the CSC finally replied to our proposal, interested to learn more about the project. Together with the teacher and the Joyceville librarian, we developed a day-long program that combined six teaching sessions supported by a pop-up exhibit. In consultation with the teacher, items were selected for the class, including a number of early newsletters from KP, Collins Bay, Joyceville, and P4W. The inmates had an interest in KP since a number of them had done time there, and photos of inmates in the yard and the print shop were included. Personal narratives written in prisons in Kingston, such as Roger Caron's *Go Boy*, which won the Governor General's Award for English-language nonfiction in 1978, were also displayed. Additionally, we brought a large folio volume of plates from Denis Diderot's *Encyclopédie*, published in 1772, and an 1883 edition of John Bunyan's *Pilgrim's Progress and Other Works*. The latter has split fore-edge paintings with one scene titled "Bunyan's Dream" and the other a portrait of Bunyan. We wanted to expose the inmates to a range of print material, while staying within the themes of censorship and imprisonment.

Prior to the visit, we learned that we would have two spaces: one room for our materials and another for the class session. We set up our items in a large room with tables and prepared for three classes in the morning and another three in the afternoon. Inmates were not required to attend, so others who were interested (e.g., staff and inmates not in the classes) were invited to stop by in between the class visits.[23] We prepared for six small groups with a lesson plan that included a brief introduction to special collections, including care and handling, a general overview of the history of printing, and the history of the penal press in Canada

---

22. Correctional Service of Canada, "Institutional Profiles—Ontario Region—Joyceville Institution—Correctional Service Canada," Last modified September 9, 2012, http://www.csc-scc.gc.ca/institutions/001002-3007-eng.shtml.

23. Announcements were made throughout the day on the institution's PA system. At the end of the day, the teachers reported that almost of the students had participated.

at the beginning of each class. Following this, inmates would have an opportunity to handle the material and complete a prepared hand-out.[24] As it turned out, inmates, staff, and others filtered in and out, and we ended up scrapping our lesson plan in favor of a general announcement about how to handle the material. We distributed hand-outs and asked visitors to respond to whatever they found to be of interest. Luckily, we had prepared brief labels with bibliographical information for each item and, instead of delivering a prepared history of the penal press, we moved amongst the material answering questions and listening to the inmates' own stories.

This unexpected change to our plan worked better for the inmates and for us. By exploring the items in a less structured way, the inmates were better able to respond to the materials and comfortably ask us questions. The rehearsed lecture would have created conversation barriers and could have discouraged them from handling the material. Instead, we were able to discuss the art of printing and some of their own art practices. Others quoted *The Pilgrim's Progress* and connected to the various trades represented in Diderot's *Encyclopédie*.

At the end of the morning and afternoon sessions, we met as one large group. We began each session by going through the questions from the provided hand-out—questions that were designed to help inmates record their thoughts about the material. Responses were as diverse as the group itself, with most of the inmates willing to share their opinions and relate the material to their own current interests and activities.

We had been told that the class was at a high school level, spanning the learning spectrum. While we had anticipated this, we were not prepared for the majority to have English as a second language, and this proved to be a barrier for some of the inmates.

Most of the hand-outs were returned to us, many with thoughtful comments. The hope had been to use the prison newsletters to encourage writing and reflection. Although the inmates were impressed that their predecessors had learned about printing and were interested in *Tightwire*,

---

24. See Appendix.

it was the images from KP and the Diderot volume that excited them the most. They were impressed by the condition of the eighteenth- and nineteenth-century books and the intricacies of producing a fore-edge painting or engraving. Our conversation reflected their interest in art and the visual aspects of the newsletters. In regard to the newsletter content, one inmate wrote, "I live this every day, I don't want to read or write about it." To fully engage the inmates in the newsletters, it was felt that a writing exercise focusing on the newsletters would need to be integrated into the teaching session. Before future visits, the teacher would have the class complete an assignment using downloaded digitized versions of the newsletters from *The Penal Press*.

Conclusion

The exhibit in 2016 focused on the deep and unique ambivalence of being an inmate-author/editor, through analyzing the newsletter printing and editing processes. Initially, the goal of the curator was to raise awareness of the collection in the Queen's community as well as the broader Kingston community. The exhibit's success led to a strong connection with other libraries and museums in Kingston and neighboring cities. Part of the exhibition went on tour to the Lennox and Addington Library, and partnerships were formed with the Canadian Penitentiary Museum and *The Penal Press*.

While it is important to preserve these inmate voices, it is also vital for curators to bring their narratives to light. By exhibiting the newsletters, we wanted to promote the material as significant primary documents that were ripe for research. The fourth-year History students and English graduate students who worked with the newsletters were provided the opportunity to research beyond the traditional historical narrative and literary canon. By engaging with the material, they validated the inmates' voices.

While the exhibit provided students with an in-depth look at inmates' writing, allowing them to appreciate its historical significance, the currently incarcerated were of course unable to visit the exhibit or take part in the instruction process. By bringing the newsletters, some books written by prisoners in Kingston penitentiaries, and a few other rare books and photos from our collection to Joyceville, we were able to reconnect the exhibit with its creative source. Although our hope to inspire a new wave of prison newsletter writers was met with tepid response, we were able to reconnect with the inmate community, learn more about their current modes of creative rehabilitation, and establish an instruction format that will allow us to return to Joyceville and share materials that resonate with them.

As special collections professionals, we aim to engage current and potential users while eliminating barriers to access. From finding the right contact to gaining access to the facility itself, bringing special collections to a prison environment is a difficult process. Perseverance is necessary and flexibility with the logistics and design of the program is key. As a teaching collection, it was rewarding to move beyond these barriers and bring items from the W.D. Jordan Rare Books and Special Collections to this diverse and marginalized community. The experience reminded us that, as curators, we represent many voices in our collections, both loud and whispered. By interacting with the community who created these newsletters, we can better share their stories with students and other users. While many inmates seemed disinterested in the prison newsletters, they were curious about special collections in general. The prison classroom thus became a co-learning space; we learned more about the individuals whose history we steward, and the inmates learned that their creative output has value beyond prison walls.

Appendix

W.D. Jordan Rare Books and Special Collections Visit
Topic: Introduction to Prison Newsletters and Primary Sources

Care and Handling: Please remember that these are rare and unique objects that should be handled with care. Do not use pen near the materials.

1. Meet the document: How is the newsletter printed? In columns? In color? Are there any illustrations? Try to describe the document as if you were explaining it to someone who can't see it.

2. Observe its parts:

What is the full title of the text?	
Who is/are the authors?	
Publisher (name and location)	
Date	
Any other interesting features?	

3. Try to make sense of it: What is it talking about? Who is the intended audience? The inmates? Outside subscribers? A mix of both? Why do you think these newsletters were produced?

4. Reflection: What surprised you? What are your impressions from today's visit? What questions do you want to pursue?

Bibliography

ACRL RBMS-SAA Joint Task Force (2017). *"Guidelines for Primary Source Literacy."* Approved February 12, 2018. http://www.ala.org/acrl/sites/ala.org.acrl/files/content/standards/Primary%20Source%20Literacy2018.pdf.

Canada, and Joseph Archambault. *Report of the Royal Commission to Investigate the Penal System of Canada.* Ottawa: J.O. Patenaude, 1938. http://catalog.hathitrust.org/Record/001135337.

Canada. Office of the Commissioner of Penitentiaries. *Report of the Commissioner of Penitentiaries Canada 1949-1950.* Ottawa: Queen's Printer, 1951. https://www.publicsafety.gc.ca/lbrr/archives/csc-arcp-1950-1951-eng.pdf.

Correctional Service Canada. "Indigenous Corrections." Last modified January 2017. https://www.csc-scc.gc.ca/publications/092/005007-3001-eng.pdf.

Correctional Service Canada. "Institutional Profiles—Ontario Region—Joyceville Institution—Correctional Service Canada," Last modified September 12, 2017. http://www.csc-scc.gc.ca/institutions/001002-3007-eng.shtml.

Dhillon, Sunny. "BC Corrections Rescinds Ban on Two of Three Prisoner Publications." *Globe and Mail.* March 15, 2017. https://www.theglobeandmail.com/news/british-columbia/bc-corrections-rescinds-ban-on-two-of-three-prisoner-publications/article34317966/.

Gaucher, Robert. "Canadian Penal Press: A Documentation and Analysis." *Journal of Prisoners on Prisons* 2, no. 1 (1989): 3-24.

Gendreau, Paul, and Wayne Renke, "Capital Punishment." In *The Canadian Encyclopedia.* Historica Canada. Article published February 6, 2006; last modified December 07, 2017. https://www.thecanadianencyclopedia.ca/en/article/capital-punishment.

Mohandesi, Salar. "Manifesto of the Groupe d'Information Sur Les Prisons (1971)." *Viewpoint Magazine.* February 16, 2016. https://www.viewpointmag.com/2016/02/16/manifesto-of-the-groupe-dinformation-sur-les-prisons-1971/.

Morris, James McGrath. *Jailhouse Journalism: The Fourth Estate Behind Bars*, Reprint ed. New Brunswick, NJ: Transaction Publishers, 2001.

The Penal Press—A History of Prison from Within. Accessed December 31, 2018. http://penalpress.com/.

Chapter 3

GETTING OUT OF THE ARCHIVE: BUILDING POSITIVE COMMUNITY PARTNERSHIPS AND STRONG SOCIAL JUSTICE COLLECTIONS

Elizabeth Call and Miranda Mims

Introduction

The professional field dealing with special collections is in a moment of reflection and response. This transition is causing us to refocus the work we do in regard to archiving and curation – not to emulate prior practices, but to readjust the lens by which we approach our work. Empathy, connection, equity, and trust are becoming our values over processes, standards, and collecting. For many special collection departments, past practices dictated that we build relationships in order to build collections. Changing practices in the field are challenging us to reevaluate how we show up as community partners. If we are no longer entering into "partnerships" as an aspect of our acquisition policies, what then is our role, and how can we justify it to our institutions?

The Rare Books, Special Collections, and Preservation Department (RBSCP) at the University of Rochester (UR) is embracing this shift.[1] Critically examining and rethinking past collection development practices

---

1. Although this piece is focused on RBSCP, the work of this project is now in partnership with Rochester Institute of Technology (RIT) Archives. Together RBSCP and RIT Archives are creating a model that focuses on community building around preserving Rochester's progressive human rights history.

is not a straightforward path in an academic library. RBSCP has been in alignment with both UR's strategic plan that has a strong focus on community engagement[2] and the River Campus Libraries' strategic aims of "Extending Access to Collections"[3] and "Engaging Community."[4] We have been examining our capacity and commitment to being more intentional in how we approach working with the various communities in and around Rochester and Western New York.

A new initiative to redefine the scope of RBSCP's human rights and social justice holdings has been a real impetus for this change. Collections around the concept of human rights encompass not only examples of social justice, but also abuses of those inalienable rights. As we reflected on this reality, we had to then examine our role in building a social justice framework into the work we do as librarians and archivists and rethink how we ensure equitable access to our spaces that have historically been perceived as closed or unwelcoming. Human rights are defined as the fundamental inalienable rights we have as human beings,[5] and social justice is the actions taken by individuals or groups to obtain human rights on behalf of themselves or others.

As we began interrogating some of the issues surrounding traditional methods of archiving and collection development, we remained cognizant of the contention between adding value versus continuing to deepen issues of exploitation and acts of colonization.[6] Many reposi-

---

2. "University Strategic Plan." Strategic Plan. Accessed July 6, 2019, https://www.rochester.edu/strategic-plan/.

3. River Campus Libraries, University of Rochester. "River Campus Libraries Strategic Plan 2018-2025." Accessed July 6, 2019, https://www.library.rochester.edu/files/pdf/strategic_priorities_2018-2025.pdf.

4. River Campus Libraries, "River Campus Libraries Strategic Plan 2018-2025."

5. The United Nations defines "human rights" as rights inherent to all human beings, regardless of race, sex, nationality, ethnicity, language, religion, or any other status. Human rights include the right to life and liberty, freedom from slavery and torture, freedom of opinion and expression, the right to work and education, and many more. Everyone is entitled to these rights without discrimination. "Human Rights." United Nations. Accessed July 6, 2019, http://www.un.org/en/sections/issues-depth/human-rights/.

6. Leigh Patel, *Decolonizing Educational Research: From Ownership to Answerability* (New York: Routledge, 2016).

tories are grounded and sustained in white privilege and historically have been spaces of elitism and exclusivity.[7] As we noticed absences in RBSCP's holdings, particularly around twentieth and twenty-first century local human rights activity, we had to resist the impulse to simply fill the gaps.[8] Past structures around collection development are no longer adequate. Consequently, we decided to embrace the post-custodial model, which stems from, and is built upon, community partnerships and community archiving. The convergence of several factors has made this critical examination and reframing possible and necessary: first, the acknowledgment that special collections/libraries are not neutral spaces;[9] second, the recognition that staffing will never be at the level necessary to adequately and sustainably describe and make accessible all of the cultural heritage that has been—and is being—created, and accepting that physical and digital space is finite; third, acknowledgment of, and respect for, the expertise of our respective communities; and fourth, the focus on building partnerships versus building collections.

---

7. Much has been written about whiteness in higher education. One recent report, "Whiteness in Higher Education: The Invisible Missing Link in Diversity and Racial Analyses" aptly traces the history of colleges in the U.S. to show that the nation's first universities were originally intended explicitly for the "male children of the aristocracy"; the whole ethos behind higher education is one of exclusion rather than inclusion. Nolan L. Cabrera, Jeremy D. Franklin, and Jesse S. Watson, "Whiteness in Higher Education: The Invisible Missing Link in Diversity and Racial Analyses." *ASHE Higher Education Report* 42, no. 6 (2017): 7-125, 58 and 61, doi:10.1002/aehe.20116.

8. Our work initially began by examining our collections' priorities in an attempt to identify gaps in our current collections and to think about ways to document the stories that are not currently represented in order to redefine, reframe, and continue to establish a broadened collecting area around human rights and social justice. Our goal is still to both highlight "hidden" or under-described collections already held by RBSCP and to build in a way that is more engaged in understanding Rochester's diverse and multi-faceted history, especially in the twentieth and twenty-first centuries. It also aims to accept and embrace the current complexities surrounding traditional methods of collection building, which may be a departure from previous collecting norms.

9. Randall C. Jimerson, "Archives for All: Professional Responsibility and Social Justice," *American Archivist* 70, no. 2 (Fall/Winter 2007): 254, doi: 10.17723/aarc.70.2.5n20760751v643m7.

Existing Legacies and New Consciousness

Generally speaking, special collections departments within academic institutions reflect university culture, including the exclusivity, privilege, and lack of diversity. Special collections departments have often done a better job of keeping people out than of creating a culture of inclusion. While the reasons for this vary, the very act of naming spaces "special" and "rare" denotes value and uniqueness, which has justified[10] assumptions that librarians and archivists have sometimes made about their right and power to exclude whomever they choose in the name of preservation and security. Although the culture of exclusion within special collections is changing with the development of policies that extend greater use and access, the tensions between preservation, security, and access are real and ongoing. The perceptions about who does and does not have access only deepens this power divide.[11] The more we acknowledge and accept that special collections and archives have been used as sources of power,[12] the easier it will be for archivists and curators to consciously own our responsibility for providing access to the collections we manage. The work of dismantling the culture of gatekeeping by charting a new and uncomfortable terrain of openness is challenging, yet necessary.

Like many institutions, RBSCP and RIT Archives are trying to address concerns that surround access to our collections. The most arduous of these is changing the perceptions of those from outside of our respective institutions. This is a hurdle shared with many academic special collections and is a nod to our common origin stories, from our beginnings as treasure chests to the evolution toward spaces that allow hands-on access to primary sources. When access to archives is

---

10. Randall C. Jimerson, *Archives Power: Memory, Accountability, and Social Justice* (Chicago, IL: Society of American Archivists, 2010), 294.

11. Anna Robinson-Sweet, "Truth and Reconciliation: Archivists as Reparations Activists," *American Archivist* 81, no. 1 (Spring/Summer 2018): 32, doi: 10.24242/jclis. v1i2.42.

12. Rodney G.S. Carter, "Of Things Said and Unsaid: Power, Archival Silences, and Power in Silence," *Archivaria* 61: Special Section on Archives, Space and Power (Spring 2006): 216.

considered a human right, our discourse must be honest and intentional about who we serve and why. As professionals in this field, we also cannot rest on the assumption that if we simply fill the archive with new voices, perspectives, and experiences, it will automatically attract new users. If it is our intention to be more inclusive, we must do more to open the space to those who have not historically been our main audiences. Part of that is as straightforward as following Michelle Caswell and Marika Cifor's call to "transform the reading room space from a cold, elitist, institutional environment to an effective, user-oriented, community-centered service space."[13]

Nevertheless, there are also real physical, financial, and logistic barriers that many users face in getting onto and then navigating university campuses. For instance, while Rochester is a mid-sized city, it is not very walkable or bike-friendly[14] and only one bus line serves the campus. If potential visitors do not have access to a car, reaching RBSCP can be difficult and, if they do drive, there is a fee to park. Another factor is that most special collections are typically less visible than other areas of the library. One major improvement made to the physical space of RBSCP was to have glass doors installed (the old doors were mostly wood with tiny glass windows). Entering into special collection spaces can be intimidating both to researchers who are familiar with them as well as those who are less so. Even small adjustments can help engender a feeling of safety and belonging.

While the issues around access are important to note, training staff and student employees requires the most attention and intentionality.[15]

---

13. Michelle Caswell and Marika Cifor, "From Human Rights to Feminist Ethics: Radical Empathy in the Archives," *Archivaria* 81 (Spring 2016): 23-43.

14. While there have been attempts at changing this—including giving away bikes, expanding the network of bike lanes, and instituting a bike share program—Rochester's extreme winter weather prevents bicycling from being a completely reliable commuting option.

15. Detailed information on this topic is also available in the recently published "IFLA Guidelines for Library Services to People Experiencing Homelessness," created by the IFLA Library Services to People with Special Needs Section of the International Federation of Library Associations and Institutions (IFLA). While these guidelines are intended for all types of libraries, they do not address the specific issue

A significant component of access involves the ways researchers are treated by staff, i.e., being aware of power dynamics and how they impact our relationships.[16] Caswell and Cifor claim that "radical empathy"[17] is necessary when creating and implementing training for those who work[18] in special collection repositories. If we assert that we are committed to "access for all," we should be ready to deliver on that declaration. Confronting barriers around access was not initially at the forefront as we began to privilege relationships over collecting; however, perceptions of inaccessibility do have an impact on the relationships we build.

Challenging injustice in special collections is a major undertaking. But it is also an opportunity to assess the environment and begin to address the physical and cultural obstacles that may conflict with our abilities to engage with our various communities. The myopic attitude around who is believed to have the right to use our collections is also intrinsically connected to collection development policies. It would be simple and convenient to believe that neutrality of archival practice has been systemic, but this has not been the case. Collection development policies are political, and there are always decisions being made around what has enduring value and what does not. *Perceived* value—what is deemed "worthy" or "special," and what is not—has always played a role in what shows up in a collection. In many ways, these value judgments have been used, as Randall C. Jimerson states, to "bolster the prestige and influence of the powerful elites in societies."[19] It is only recently that more archivists are acknowledging this, and have begun embracing our shared responsibility to engage with and combat this legacy.

---

with regard to training staff and student employees within special collections working with researchers who have been impacted by homelessness. Library Services to People With Special Needs Guidelines Working Group, International Federation of Library Associations and Institutions. "IFLA Guidelines for Library Services to People Experiencing Homelessness," August 2017.

16. Verne Harris, "The Archival Sliver: Power, Memory, and Archives in South Africa," *Archival Science* 2, no. 1-2 (2002): 63-86, doi:10.1007/BF02435631.

17. Caswell and Cifor, "From Human Rights to Feminist Ethics," 25.

18. The "who" would include us too!

19. Jimerson, "Archives for All," 254.

It is frustrating when profound silences are found in the archives,[20] especially in local history collections. When the intention is to represent a specific locale, the history of the majority culture too often rises to the surface and everything else gets lost. Or, what majority culture considers relevant or important, in regards to underrepresented persons, events, or histories does not align with how those they are documenting would appraise and preserve their own cultures. These skewed collections are often a consequence of a profession that is extremely homogeneous.[21] What is the impact regarding our sense of worth when we are underrepresented or misrepresented by those who do not share our identities or our experiences? What is the message being transmitted when one does not show up in a local history collection? Although deeply concerned with silences[22] in the collection and filling them with what has been explicitly or implicitly left out, the discussion around "inclusivity" is tricky, and at times our efforts only further inadequacies. Rodney G.S. Carter states, "Archival power is, in part, the power to allow voices to be heard. … The power of the archive is witnessed in the act of inclusion, but this is only one of its components. The power to exclude is a fundamental aspect of the archive…Not every story is told."[23] Special collections are—in their own essence—memory repositories, yet they can also contribute to forgetting and erasure.[24]

In 1992, Terry Cook noted a major paradigm shift occurring in the archival profession, one that helped archival thinking move away from a

---

20. Michel-Rolph Trouillot and Hazel V. Carby, *Silencing the Past: Power and the Production of History* (Boston, MA: Beacon Press, 2015).

21. Lae'l Hughes-Watkins, "Moving Toward a Reparative Archive: A Roadmap for a Holistic Approach to Disrupting Homogeneous Histories in Academic Repositories and Creating Inclusive Spaces for Marginalized Voices," *Journal of Contemporary Archival Studies* 5, Article 6 (2018), accessed July 6, 2019, https://elischolar.library.yale.edu/jcas/vol5/iss1/6/.

22. Michelle Caswell, "Seeing Yourself in History: Community Archives and the Fight Against Symbolic Annihilation," *The Public Historian* 36, no. 4 (November 2014): 36. Jimerson, "Archives for All," 277.

23. Carter, "Of Things Said and Unsaid," 216.

24. Christina Sharpe, *In the Wake: On Blackness and Being* (Durham: Duke University Press, 2016), 12.

narrow-minded focus on exclusive ownership to an inclusive collaborative partnership. Born out of debates about original order that arose from discussions of how to manage digital records, Cook states that "custodial" and "curatorial" were the past while "post-custodial" and "knowledge-oriented" were future-forward.[25] As early as 1975, collection development was being looked at with a critical eye.[26] However, the collections-centric model—appraisal, acquisition, description, and preservation—has continued to be the traditional modus operandi in the profession, even as it has proven problematic and has resulted in whitewashed collections reflecting dominant cultural values and mistrust in the community. Along with many of our peers and colleagues, we are excited about rethinking this model and moving toward a system of collaboration and cooperation that prioritizes relationships and people. Amalgamating the discourses around community archiving and human rights archives decenters how privilege shows up in the archive.

From Ownership to Partnership

The project to leverage a more structured and intentional social justice and human rights initiative—one that would not simply document people, events, and organizations throughout the Greater Rochester Area, but would be centered on building community partnerships—is extensive and complicated, both in scope and subject matter, and we anticipate it will take several years to fully realize and execute.

RBSCP has strong local history collections that reflect Rochester's rich legacy of progressive social politics and reform. Collections document

25. Terry Cook, "The Concept of the Archival Fonds in the Post-Custodial Era: Theory, Problems and Solutions," *Archivaria* 35: Proceedings of the ACA Seventeenth Annual Conference, Montreal 12-15 September 1992 (Spring 1993): 31.

26. In an article from 1975, F. Gerald Ham outlines five changes that made conditions ripe for archivists to move from custodians to active agents: what is being collected (from personal and family papers to papers of institutions and movements); the sheer volume of material; missing information (phones have made it less likely that "important" information will be written down); the ephemerality of records; and technology. Ham, in 1981, goes on to coin the phrase "Post-Custodial." F. Gerald Ham, "The Archival Edge," *American Archivist* 38, no. 1 (January 1975); "Archival Strategies for the Post-Custodial Era," *American Archivist* 44, no. 3 (Summer 1981).

the legacies of Frederick Douglass and Susan B. Anthony; the Rochester chapter of the National Organization for Women,[27] which fought for women's reproductive rights, welfare, equal rights, and pay equity; the Rochester Feminist Collection, which advocated for the Equal Rights Amendment in the 1970s, reproductive rights, and equal rights for lesbians; the Rochester Socialist Scrapbook Collection;[28] the Rochester Black Freedom Struggle Oral History Project;[29] and the Alternatives for Battered Women Inc.,[30] currently known as Willow Domestic Violence Center. We also have the papers of individuals who were active in their own right, such as Ruth Scott,[31] who championed gender and racial equality; Franklin Florence,[32] who was a leader in the activist group Freedom, Independence, God, Honor, Today, which formed after the 1964 riots; Rabbi Philip S. Bernstein;[33] and Dr. Walter Cooper,[34] who was involved in the Civil Rights movement. These are some of the well-known collections that highlight social justice work spearheaded by Rochesterians. But while these collections, along with other material held by RBSCP, capture aspects of Rochester's struggles toward equality and justice, they are incomplete.

27. National Organization for Women, Rochester chapter records, D.417, Rare Books, Special Collections, and Preservation, River Campus Libraries, University of Rochester.

28. Rochester Social Scrapbook Collection, D.110, Rare Books, Special Collections, and Preservation, River Campus Libraries, University of Rochester.

29. "Rochester Black Freedom Struggle Online Project," Rare Books, Special Collections, and Preservation, River Campus Libraries, University of Rochester.

30. Alternatives for Battered Women Collection, D.237, Rare Books, Special Collections, and Preservation, River Campus Libraries, University of Rochester.

31. Ruth Scott Papers, D.390, Rare Books, Special Collections, and Preservation, River Campus Libraries, University of Rochester.

32. Franklin Florence Papers, D.167, Rare Books, Special Collections, and Preservation, River Campus Libraries, University of Rochester.

33. Philip S. Bernstein Papers, D.269, Rare Books, Special Collections, and Preservation, River Campus Libraries, University of Rochester.

34. Dr. Walter Cooper papers, D.385, Rare Books, Special Collections, and Preservation, River Campus Libraries, University of Rochester.

We are currently in the early stages and are still solidifying our objectives. Because of the scale of the project, and because its success depends on building community partnerships, which takes time and trust, we decided to focus on one area: the ongoing struggle of the homeless in Rochester. After an initial survey of our holdings, we concluded that the voices from those most directly impacted by human rights abuses were few and far between, which is systemic across many repositories. Within RBSCP's collections, an understanding of the issues faced by people impacted by homelessness is primarily gleamed from governmental or charitable records; the perspective of individuals and first-hand accounts of lived experiences are absent.

When the idea to develop an initiative to document twentieth and twenty-first century social justice and human rights activities in and around the Greater Rochester Area was first being discussed, we were thinking in terms of how we could fill the gaps in the existing collections, starting with the stories of those impacted by homelessness. We initially began with an oral history project to capture and preserve the voices of individuals and activists fighting for the essential human right to shelter. We quickly realized that, by going into the larger community with this plan, we would be doing exactly what we did not want to do—assuming that this was how a community wanted to be documented. Rather than treating this as an academic project, we needed to step into this work devoid of any project plan or pre-identified end products.

Some initial considerations that are driving the early stages of our work include:

- understanding the history of homelessness in Rochester;
- establishing trust and transparency as we build community partnerships and community-based archival projects;
- establishing a clearer definition of RBSCP's role as a community partner, and more broadly where archives fit with community partnerships;
- identifying who our community partners are and defining what those partnerships mean;

- defining what a "safe space" in the library is for, and with, various groups within the community;
- identifying all collections in RBSCP that connect to the issues of homelessness in the Greater Rochester Area; and
- identifying gaps in RBSCP's collections with regard to this subject area.

Through one of our community partnerships, we have been able to address these foundational considerations. Outside of UR, we have begun partnering with Kim Smith, the statewide organizer of Voices of Community Activists (VOCAL-NY), a New York statewide membership organization that advocates for the rights of those most impacted by HIV/AIDS, Hepatitis C, drugs, homelessness, and mass incarceration. We first met Smith at Rochester's Activism Fair in the spring of 2018 and quickly formed an ongoing relationship. As stated earlier, we initially planned to embark on an oral history project, which is still very much a possible byproduct of this relationship, but for now we have decided to drop any collection-centered agenda and focus on building the relationship.

An example of one of the programs we are partnering with Smith and Partners Advocating for Community Change on is entitled "Emancipation." Our role will be to develop community sessions that will address healing through archiving personal histories. While Emancipation did not receive funding through the Rochester Monroe County Anti-Poverty Initiative to put on programming that would address trauma within the community, Smith is hopeful that the program will find funding through another source.

Recently, VOCAL-NY has joined forces with the Rochester Tenant Union and the Rochester Homeless Union to form the Rochester Housing Coalition. Through our relationship with Smith and VOCAL-NY, we have been regularly attending the Rochester Housing Coalition rallies and action planning meetings. The group has formed in order to apply pressure to local politicians and to make the public aware of several housing bills[35] that will be up for a vote in the New York State Senate in June 2019. By going to the weekly meetings, we have made a connection with Saint Joseph's House of Hospitality, which has been providing food, shelter, and clothing to those in need in Rochester since 1941. We had not been collecting the organization's quarterly newspaper (published since 1941); however, because of this connection, RBSCP will begin to archive this important publication and hopefully will be able to get back issues to ensure the serial's preservation.

We have also met with key people, like the leaders of the Rochester Homeless Union, Patrick Braswell and Tyrone Hodge; Sister Grace Miller, the founder of the House of Mercy; and Dr. Harry Murray, a sociology professor at Nazareth College and community activist, on a somewhat regular basis. As we began attending meetings, we saw the same faces over and over, which allows for the necessary relationship-building.

As a result of making these connections, we decided that—in order to get a better grasp of the history of homelessness in Rochester—we needed to start with the more recent past. Doing this allows us to gain greater understanding of the context for today, and it allows us access to people currently involved with the crisis. Since 1985, the House of Mercy has been providing food and shelter to members of Rochester's homeless population who have been turned away from the county-run shelters. Murray undertook a significant study that analyzed a collection of obituaries that Miller had been writing and archiving since the 1990s. He found that the higher the poverty rate, the lower the life expectancy of a person—and this was even more so for women who on average live longer than men. In fact, from analyzing these thirty years' worth of obituaries, he found that the life expectancy of a homeless person in Monroe County was significantly shorter than that of any other homeless person in the United States.[36] To put this into perspective,

---

35. Two of these bills are in the Assembly Housing Committee: Eviction Protections Bill (Prohibition of Eviction without a Good Cause) and Expand Rent Stabilization Bill.

36. Harry Murray, "Homelessness as Death Sentence: Findings from the House of Mercy," November 19, 2017.

the report points out that "out of 190 countries reported in the 2016 UN Human Development report, only SIX have a lower life expectancy than homeless Americans in the House of Mercy sample: Ivory Coast, Chad, Central African Republic, Sierra Leone, Lesotho, and Swaziland. No county has a lower life expectancy than the homeless women in the House of Mercy obituaries."[37] In another report that analyzed 2010 U.S. Census data, Rochester was found to be the fifth poorest city out of the seventy-five largest cities in the country.[38]

We must continue to remind ourselves of the important point that we are archivists, not activists, in these relationships. We are not attending community meetings as citizens, but in our professional capacity of archivists. It is part of the work, when we introduce ourselves, to make clear what our roles are and who our employers are. We have come to see our role as multi-dimensional. First, and foremost, we serve as reminders that the work that these activists are doing is important and should be documented; that the work is ephemeral and the memory of it quickly vanishes; that they have options for how this work is documented—and importantly, it can be something they choose to document and preserve and keep within their own communities, or it can be something they choose to have another institution preserve.

Conclusion

As we shift our focus from *ownership* to *partnership*, adopting a post-custodial model[39] is a promising solution. Two existing models to which we are looking are the Southern Historical Collection's community archives project (part of the Wilson Special Collections Library, University of North Carolina Chapel Hills Libraries), and the University of Southern California (USC) Libraries' collaborative "Los Angeles Community

---

37. Murray, "Homelessness as a Death Sentence," 2.

38. Edward Doherty, "Poverty and the Concentration of Poverty in the Nine-County Greater Rochester Area," Rochester Area Community Foundation, December 2013.

39. Christian Kelleher, "Archives Without Archives: (Re)Locating and (Re)Defining the Archive Through Post-Custodial Praxis," *Journal of Critical Library and Information Studies* 1, no. 2 (2017). doi:10.24242/jclis.v1i2.29.

Histories Digitization Project." It is important to note here that both of these initiatives are grant funded.

"Building a Model for All Users: Transforming Archive Collections through Community-Driven Archives,"[40] spearheaded by the Southern Historical Collection, is a community archives project that partners with national community members to document and preserve their own histories. One component of this three-year project, "Archivist in a Backpack," is a kit with the tools needed for someone to plan and conduct an oral history project, including archival materials, a portable scanner, oral history question cards, feedback cards, pencils, audio recorder, etc.[41] The "Los Angeles Community Histories Digitization Project," founded by the National Endowment for the Humanities, is a collaboration between six archives in Southern California[42]: Go for Broke National Education Center, Filipino American Library, First African Methodist Episcopal Church of Los Angeles, USC Center for Religion and Civic Culture, Workman and Temple Family Homestead Museum, and Pasadena Museum of History. The project will allow for free access to a digital archive of over 17,000 items hosted by the USC Digital Library and Digital Public Library of America. One of the pillars of this project is that they are expanding access to archival materials created by underrepresented communities in Los Angeles, but they are not serving as a physical repository.

Collection development defined strictly by the acquisition of physical materials is no longer viable on its own, but there are benefits to the post-custodial model. It addresses the issue of removing cultural heritage items from spaces where material culture has been created,

40. "Community-Drive Archives Overview," Louis Round Wilson Library Special Collections, University of North Carolina Chapel Hill, accessed June 2, 2019. https://library.unc.edu/wilson/shc/community-driven-archives/about/.

41. "Archivist in a Backpack Supply List," Louis Round Wilson Library Special Collections, University of North Carolina Chapel Hill, accessed June 2, 2019. https://library.unc.edu/wp-content/uploads/2018/08/Year2_BackpackSupplies_Print.pdf.

42. "NEH Supports Los Angeles Community Histories Digitization Project," USC Libraries, University of Southern California accessed June 2, 2019. https://libraries.usc.edu/article/neh-supports -los-angeles-community-histories-digitization-project.

and from the people directly related to that legacy.[43] As we began to further question our own role in the realm of social activism and social justice, we could no longer see the issue of addressing absence in such a marginalized way. It is not a matter of simply filling the void with new voices. Although this is necessary in terms of capturing a "lost" or "forgotten" history, conducting oral histories is still centered around traditional definitions of collection development. Our departure from this framework is complicated for many reasons. Centering relationships and community partnerships and decentering collections requires a major cultural change. Even with space and staff limitations, collections are what we know.

Documentation and preservation are still important. We are not seeking to abandon those tasks across the board; we are just exploring alternatives to traditional models to see how they will work for us. And, of course, not all of our views are or will be accepted by our institution, but we are nonetheless committed to opening up dialogue around the changes we are seeing in the profession. We will continue to question and unpack the ethics of our work in building collections around issues of homelessness in the Rochester area. Knowing the complicated history UR has had with the city in this regard, we also had to ensure that the work we are about to embark upon is fully supported by library admin-istration. Our intention to build relationships outside of UR depends on this support. Trust is not easily built, and we must have support from within our own institution in order to build relationships outside it.

As archivists and special collections librarians, we must develop a social consciousness. The more that those of us responsible for man-aging special collections commit to becoming more involved in the communities we document, the more invested the archive becomes in promoting social justice. We believe the new framework we have adopted, to deprioritize collecting in favor of a focus on building relationships and

---

43. Michelle Caswell, "Toward a Survivor-Centered Approach to Records Docu-menting Human Rights Abuse: Lessons from Community Archives," *Archival Science* 14, no. 3-4 (2014): 315. doi:10.1007/s10502-014-9220-6.

forming partnerships, will help us to reconsider professional assumptions and procedures in order to put us on the path to archival justice.

Bibliography

Cabrera, Nolan L., Jeremy D. Franklin, and Jesse S. Watson. "Whiteness in Higher Education: The Invisible Missing Link in Diversity and Racial Analyses." *ASHE Higher Education Report* 42, no. 6 (2017): 7-125. doi:10.1002/aehe.20116.

Carter, Rodney G.S. "Of Things Said and Unsaid: Power, Archival Silences, and Power in Silence." *Archivaria* 61: Special Section on Archives, Space and Power (Spring 2006): 215-33. Accessed July 6, 2019, https://archivaria.ca/index.php/archivaria/article/view-File/12541/13687.

Caswell, Michelle. "Seeing Yourself in History: Community Archives and the Fight Against Symbolic Annihilation." *The Public Historian* 36, no. 4 (November 2014): 26-37. doi :10.1525/tph.2014.36.4.26.

Caswell, Michelle. "Toward a Survivor-Centered Approach to Records Documenting Human Rights Abuse: Lessons from Community Archives." *Archival Science* 14, no. 3-4 (2014): 307-22. doi:10.1007/s10502-014-9220-6.

Caswell, Michelle, and Marika Cifor. "From Human Rights to Feminist Ethics: Radical Empathy in the Archives." *Archivaria* 81 (Spring 2016): 23-43.

Cook, Terry. "The Concept of the Archival Fonds in the Post-Custodial Era: Theory, Problems and Solutions." *Archivaria* 35: Proceedings of the ACA Seventeenth Annual Conference, Montreal 12-15 September 1992 (Spring 1993): 24-37. Accessed January 9, 2019, https://archivaria.ca/archivar/index.php/archivaria/article/view/11882/12835.

Doherty, Edward. "Poverty and the Concentration of Poverty in the Nine-County Greater Rochester Area." Rochester Area Community Foundation, December 2013.

Ham, F. Gerald. "The Archival Edge." *American Archivist* 38, no. 1 (January 1975): 5-13.

Ham, F. Gerald. "Archival Strategies for the Post-Custodial Era." *American Archivist* 44, no. 3 (Summer 1981): 207-16.

Harris, Verne. "The Archival Sliver: Power, Memory, and Archives in South Africa." *Archival Science* 2, no. 1-2 (2002): 63-86.

Hughes-Watkins, Lae'l. "Moving Toward a Reparative Archive: A Roadmap for a Holistic Approach to Disrupting Homogenous Histories in Academic Repositories and Creating Inclusive Spaces for Marginalized Voices." *Journal of Contemporary Archival Studies* 5, Article 6 (2018). Accessed July 6, 2019, https://elischolar.library.yale.edu/jcas/vol5/iss1/6.

Jimerson, Randall C. "Archives for All: Professional Responsibility and Social Justice." *American Archivist* 70, no. 2 (Fall/Winter 2007): 252-81. doi: 10.17723/aarc.70.2.5n20760751v643m7.

Jimerson, Randall C. *Archives Power: Memory, Accountability, and Social Justice.* Chicago, IL: Society of American Archivists, 2010.

Kelleher, Christian. "Archives Without Archives: (Re)Locating and (Re) Defining the Archive Through Post-Custodial Praxis." *Journal of Critical Library and Information Studies* 1, no. 2 (2017). doi:10.24242/jclis.v1i2.29.

Library Services to People with Special Needs Guidelines Working Group, International Federation of Library Associations and Institutions (IFLA). "IFLA Guidelines for Library Services to People Experiencing Homelessness," August 2017.

Murray, Harry. "Homelessness as Death Sentence: Findings from the House of Mercy." November 19, 2017. Accessed July 6, 2019, http://www.saintjoeshouse.org/blog/wp-content/uploads/2017/11/Article.pdf.

Patel, Leigh. *Decolonizing Educational Research: From Ownership to Answerability.* New York: Routledge, 2016.

Robinson-Sweet, Anna. "Truth and Reconciliation: Archivists as Reparations Activists." *American Archivist* 81, no. 1 (Spring/Summer 2018): 23-37. doi:10.17723/0360-9081-81.1.23.

Sharpe, Christina Elizabeth. *In the Wake: On Blackness and Being.* Durham: Duke University Press, 2016.

Trouillot, Michel-Rolph, and Hazel V. Carby. *Silencing the Past: Power and the Production of History.* Boston, MA: Beacon Press, 2015.

Chapter 4

MEN, MASCULINITIES, AND THE ARCHIVES: INTRODUCING THE CONCEPT OF HEGEMONIC MASCULINITY IN ARCHIVAL DISCOURSE

François Dansereau

> No man has been excluded from the historical record because of his sex, yet all women were.[1]—Gerda Lerner

Historian Gerda Lerner's statement in a book exploring the historical evolution of patriarchy suggests that both the prominence of men's narratives and the absence of women's in historical documents originate from particular social configurations. In this chapter, I focus on the first part of Lerner's statement and will attempt to problematize the association of men and masculinity with archival principles and practices. To do so, I will examine the ways in which existing theoretical frameworks articulated in archival literature lead us to discuss men and masculinity's links with archives and archival thinking. First, I will explore the connection between bureaucracy and archival structures and processes. Then, I will examine the literature assessing the power of archives and the contribution of research in community archives. Community archival initiatives, which have contributed substantially

---

1. Gerda Lerner, *The Creation of Patriarchy* (New York: Oxford University Press, 1986), 5.

to developments in archival discourse in recent years, can increase our understanding of power structures in mainstream archives, i.e., government archives, corporate archives, university special collections and archives, hospital archives, and others. The exploration of this literature will provide analytical frameworks to confront mainstream archival notions and practices, as well as their implication with respect to gender and masculinity paradigms. Consequently, I introduce the concept of hegemonic masculinity in the archival field. Developed by the sociologist R.W. Connell, the theoretical model of hegemonic masculinity has been discussed in a diversity of fields.

In this chapter, I position archives and recordkeeping configurations as part of social exchanges and practices that are embedded in cultural and political frameworks. Drawing on recent research in the archival realm, I will advance the argument that traditional archival principles and standardized frameworks have an inherent gendered component. I will also argue that mainstream archives have contributed to the validation and articulation of masculinity. In this chapter, I suggest that the production of knowledge through the documentation of men's activities and relations in the archives have been reinforced by formal and standardized bureaucratic recordkeeping practices, such as appraisal and description. The association of the concept of hegemonic masculinity with archives highlights a multiplicity of elements of power in the archives and will contribute, I hope, to the challenging of dominant archival forces.

Bureaucracy and Archival Apparatuses and Practices

Max Weber's writing about bureaucracy and industry insists on the concept of "rationalization," connecting progress, science, and modernity. Weber discusses the authority of bureaucracy in the formal development of organizations.[2] The rational development of bureaucracy is defined as being inherently tied to capitalism and the nation-state. Moreover,

---

2. Stanislav Andreski, "Introduction" in *Max Weber on Capitalism, Bureaucracy and Religion: A Selection of Texts*, ed. and trans. Stanislav Andreski (London: George Allen & Unwin, 1983), 8–9.

Weber merges rational and standardized bookkeeping with modernity and associates the nation-state with a legal and rationalized structure composed of constitutive documents, organized and managed by trained officers.[3] Rational organization of the law and administrative principles are discussed as drawing on technical means of production and "rational conduct" practices by those who administer these practices in bureaucratic configurations.[4] Weber defines this arrangement as the "rationalization of procedure" that links administrative processes with the development of societal legal frameworks.[5]

The rational principles and practices of bureaucracy are based on the presumed impartiality of administrative functions and the organization of labor. As Beverly H. Burris mentions, "As with technical control, bureaucracy is legitimated on the grounds of impartiality and neutrality: clearly defined rules that ostensibly apply to everyone and allow all to compete fairly and equally."[6] Traditional archival processes are founded on standardized practices that have been elaborated along these modern bureaucratic principles. Michael A. Lutzker discusses the impact of Weber's modern bureaucratic principles on appraisal and archival administrative processes.[7] Lutzker connects administrative frameworks with exercises of authority and hierarchical configurations of bureaucracy.[8] I insist that, despite claims of neutrality, modern bureaucracy, recordkeeping organizations, and provenance of records are always shaped by social, cultural, and political forces. Organizations develop their own languages and paradigms that shape the conceptual structure of their archives.

3. Max Weber, *Max Weber on Capitalism, Bureaucracy and Religion*, 21–26.

4. Weber, *Max Weber on Capitalism, Bureaucracy and Religion*, 28–29.

5. Weber, *Max Weber on Capitalism, Bureaucracy and Religion*, 150.

6. Beverly H. Burris, "Technocracy, Patriarchy and Management," in *Men as Managers, Managers as Men: Critical Perspectives on Men, Masculinities and Managements*, eds. David L. Collinson and Jeff Hearn (London: SAGE Publications, 1996), 67.

7. Michael A. Lutzker, "Max Weber and the Analysis of Modern Bureaucratic Organization: Notes Toward a Theory of Appraisal," *American Archivist* 45, no. 2 (Spring 1982): 119–30, https://doi.org/10.17723/aarc.45.2.n05v8735408776qh.

8. Lutzker, "Max Weber and the Analysis of Modern Bureaucratic Organization."

The administrative structure of mainstream archives developed throughout the twentieth century not only legitimized and standardized the administrative functions of the archivist, but normalized hierarchical frameworks as well: "this routinization [of bureaucratic organizational structures] then embeds social relations structurally, routinizing not only the behaviors but also the subordination of workers within that structure."[9] Archivists have internalized hierarchical frameworks through their positions within the bureaucratic structure and also through their practices. These elements are reminiscent of the theoretical concept of "habitus" elaborated by Pierre Bourdieu. Bourdieu writes about social structures that generate conformity and inequalities for individuals evolving within these structures, even though they might not have been necessarily constructed to generate these conditions.[10] The increasing volume of electronic records from the 1980s onward only enhances the technical characteristics and standardized bureaucratic work of archivists, through the management of increasing amounts of information.

We should not underestimate the relationship between scientific management and the organization of archives. Archival professional paradigms are not exempt from bureaucratic and professional technical control. Characteristics of scientific management have integrated archival principles and practices, thanks in large part to the influence of the early twentieth-century British archivist Hillary Jenkinson's ideas of natural management of records and their emphasis on efficiency, administrative and executive transactions, and measure.[11] The development of standardized processes in the archives is associated with this concept of rationalization of practices. Archivists have been trained

---

9. Marika Cifor and Stacy Wood, "Critical Feminism in the Archives," *Journal of Critical Library and Information Studies* 1, no. 2 (2017): 19. https://doi.org/10.24242/jclis.v1i2.27.

10. Pierre Bourdieu, *Le sens pratique* (Paris: Les Éditions de Minuit, 1980).

11. See Ciaran B. Trace, "On or Off the Record? Notions of Value in the Archive," in *Currents of Archival Thinking*, eds. Heather MacNeil and Terry Eastwood (Santa Barbara, CA: Libraries Unlimited, 2010), 56.

largely to appraise, describe, and give access to documents according to standardized bureaucratic features.

However, while the repetition of standardized scientific frameworks formalizes activities, it also generates knowledge.[12] Documents organized in fonds and collections in traditional archives originate from the subjective organization of information consciously put together by record creators and archivists. Information available in these constructed descriptions is formalized, repetitive, and organized in standardized classification systems, which then become embedded in subjective organizational principles and orders of significance.[13] These standardized descriptions impose uniform approaches and categories on records, and these often simplify narratives or do not necessarily reflect reality.[14] Complex histories are therefore singularized in order to embed records in generalized categories. Archivists have become participants in this construction of reality, enhanced by claims of neutrality through rationalized and bureaucratic principles that categorize human activity. Records described in these categories offer narratives that reflect particular representations, which then become the official version of that orderly enterprise.[15]

12. For parallels with the development of libraries in the United States and their association with business practices and scientific management, see Lua Gregory and Shana Higgins, "In Resistance to a Capitalist Past: Emerging Practices of Critical Librarianship," in *The Politics of Theory and the Practice of Critical Librarianship*, eds. Karen P. Nicholson and Maura Seale (Sacramento, CA: Library Juice Press, 2018), 21–38.

13. Verne Harris, "Archons, Aliens and Angels: Power and Politics in the Archive," in *The Future of Archives and Recordkeeping: A Reader*, ed. Jennie Hill (London: Facet Publishing, 2011), 107.

14. Tom Nesmith, "Reopening Archives: Bringing New Contextualities into Archival Theory and Practice," *Archivaria* 60 (Fall 2005): 268–74; Geoffrey Yeo, "Continuing Debates about Description," in *Currents of Archival Thinking*, 2nd ed., eds. Heather MacNeil and Terry Eastwood (Santa Barbara, CA: Libraries Unlimited, 2017), 172.

15. Ciaran B. Trace, "What Is Recorded Is Never Simply 'What Happened': Record Keeping in Modern Organizational Culture," *Archival Science* 2, nos. 1–2 (2002): 137–59. https://doi.org/10.1007/BF02435634; Brien Brothmen, "Orders of Value: Probing the Theoretical Terms of Archival Practice," *Archivaria* 32 (Summer 1991): 78–100.

Wendy M. Duff and Verne Harris insist that traditional features of archival description simply validate and enhance the worldview of their describers, who are typically in positions of power.[16] Administrative processes of appraisal and description become involved in the normalization of dominant forces and in the elaboration and maintenance of a sense of normalcy.[17] As Gracen Brilmyer writes, "Just as societal norms become embodied within the standardized practices of archives, so too do the definitions and understandings of people produced by archives become ingrained in society."[18] Bureaucratic processes and the rationalization of appraisal and description become directly engaged in normative descriptions and discourses. The manifestation of dominant elements in mainstream archives reflects on cultural norms that, in turn, have an impact on how archives describe human activities and relations. By extension, then, in a Weberian sense, "bureaucracy is seen therefore as not simply a type of organization that is common, increasingly so, within Western society, but as a reflection of the very principles upon which a modern society is based."[19]

Bureaucratic characteristics are reflected in the contemporary configuration of archives, which is closely connected with the neoliberal infiltration of institutional practices. Corporate models of libraries[20] and mainstream archives have largely gone unquestioned under principles of rationality. Marika Cifor and Jamie A. Lee discuss how neoliberalism and

16. Wendy M. Duff and Verne Harris, "Stories and Names: Archival Description as Narrating Records and Constructing Meanings," *Archival Science* 2, nos. 3–4 (2002): 263–85. https://doi.org/10.1007/BF02435625.

17. Michel-Rolph Trouillot, *Silencing the Past: Power and the Production of History* (Boston, MA: Beacon Press, 1995), 84.

18. Gracen Brilmyer, "Archival Assemblages: Applying Disability Studies' Political/ Relational Model to Archival Description," *Archival Science* 18, no. 2 (June 2018): 102. https://doi.org/10.1007/s10502-018-9287-6.

19. David Morgan, "The Gender of Bureaucracy," in *Men as Managers*, eds. Collinson and Hearn, 44.

20. See Karen P. Nicholson, "The McDonaldization of Academic Libraries and the Values of Transformational Change," College and Research Libraries 76, no. 3 (2015): 332, https://doi.org/10.5860/crl.76.3.328.

bureaucratic practices have penetrated the archival professional world.[21] Insisting that neoliberal principles have an impact on archival education, processes, and laborers, they signal that neoliberalism contributes to the production of knowledge in the archives.[22]

The rationality of bureaucratic configurations contributes to the development of hierarchical structures in the workplace that, in turn, allow for the problematization of hierarchical principles from a gendered perspective. "Masculinities" are defined in relation to the history of institutions and are embedded in economic organizations and administrative configurations.[23] Because "men express their dominance in and through hierarchies, formal and informal," bureaucratic frameworks are associated with management structures based on masculinity's reach.[24] These structural effects allow for an expression of masculinity through formal, standardized, and rationalized hierarchies.[25] As Cifor and Stacy Wood assert, "The investment in hierarchy cannot simply be understood as an adherence to rationality, it is a means of creating an order of social relations."[26] Therefore, the passive appraisal and description of institutional records has an inherently gendered component. Embedded in official transactions, archival processes have normalized historical records featuring men and their activities. Administrative configurations of mainstream archives as well as standardized practices of appraisal and description of records of dominant societal forces are associated with masculine endeavors. Simply put, archival practices, including description and the creation of tools to facilitate access to records, have emphasized

---

21. Marika Cifor and Jamie A. Lee, "Towards an Archival Critique: Opening Possibilities for Addressing Neoliberalism in the Archival Field," Journal of Critical Library and Information Studies 1, no. 1 (2017): 1–22. https://doi.org/10.24242/jclis.v1i1.10.

22. Cifor and Lee, "Towards an Archival Critique."

23. R.W. Connell, Masculinities (Berkeley: University of California Press, 1995), 29–36.

24. Morgan, "Gender of Bureaucracy," 49.

25. Morgan, "Gender of Bureaucracy," 43–60.

26. Cifor and Wood, "Critical Feminism in the Archives," 19.

allegedly neutral transactions and have participated in hierarchical management configurations.

Archives and Archival Turns

Since the early 2000s, researchers in the archival realm have recognized that archives are a space of power where political orders and discourses are part of archival processes and practices.[27] Mainstream archives are not neutral in their conception but instead impose order and validate frameworks typically conceived by authorities. Traditional archives are social constructs devised by forces that seek to develop and maintain their power. Jacques Derrida famously highlights that political power finds its source in the control of archives.[28] In the same vein, Joan Schwartz and Terry Cook assert that controlling the archive allows dominant forces to control societal paradigms, and societies' memory and identity.[29] Archives contribute to exercises of power, and this representation of power is maintained through structural and symbolic operations documented in official transactions. Arguing that archives are socially and culturally constructed and processed, Harris specifies that archives "express and are instruments of prevailing relations of power."[30] In addition, Lae'l Hughes-Watkins writes that "mainstream archives are steeped in a tradition that makes decisions about the

---

27. Joan M. Schwartz and Terry Cook, "Archives, Records and Power: The Making of Modern Memory," *Archival Science* 2, nos. 1–2 (2002): 1–19. https://doi.org/10.1007/BF02435628; Verne Harris, "The Archival Sliver: Power, Memory, and Archives in South Africa," *Archival Science* 2, nos. 1–2 (2002): 63–86. https://doi.org/10.1007/BF02435631; Tom Nesmith, "Seeing Archives: Postmodernism and the Changing Intellectual Place of Archives," *American Archivist* 65, no. 1 (Spring/Summer 2002): 24–41. https://doi.org/10.17723/aarc.65.1.rr48450509r0712u; Eric Ketelaar, "Archival Temples, Archival Prisons: Modes of Power and Protection," Archival Science 2, nos. 3–4 (2002): 221–38. https://doi.org/10.1007/BF02435623.

28. Jacques Derrida, *Mal d'archives: une impression freudienne* (Paris: Galilée, 2008).

29. Schwartz and Cook, "Archives, Records and Power."

30. Harris, "Archival Sliver," 63.

existence, preservation, and availability of archives, documents, and records in our society on the basis of the distribution of wealth and power."[31]

Such power can be expressed directly, as exemplified by colonial forces attempting to dominate Indigenous groups through administrative record-creation frameworks, preservation, and use of archives. Ann Laura Stoler's study of the colonial records of the Netherlands Indies insists on the social imaginaries of colonial rule through the production of records and the power ingrained in the production of knowledge by way of official documentation.[32] Stoler asserts that "colonial archives [act] both as a corpus of writing and as a force field that animates political energies and expertise, that pulls on some 'social facts' and converts them into qualified knowledge, that attends to some ways of knowing while repelling and refusing others."[33] Michel-Rolph Trouillot comments on the power vested in those controlling records and highlights that "the production of historical narratives involves the uneven contribution of competing groups and individuals who have unequal access to the means for such production."[34]

Authors have borrowed methodological approaches of critical race theory in order to signal dominant forces and silencing in the archival realm.[35] Mario H. Ramirez discusses the resistance of traditional archives

31. Lae'l Hughes-Watkins, "Moving Toward a Reparative Archive: A Roadmap for a Holistic Approach to Disrupting Homogenous Histories in Academic Repositories and Creating Inclusive Spaces for Marginalized Voices," *Journal of Contemporary Archival Studies* 5, Article 6 (2018): 2.

32. Ann Laura Stoler, *Along the Archival Grain: Epistemic Anxieties and Colonial Common Sense* (Princeton, NJ: Princeton University Press, 2009). See also Jeannette Allis Bastian, "Reading Colonial Records Through an Archival Lens: The Provenance of Place, Space and Creation," *Archival Science* 6, nos. 3–4 (December 2006): 267–84. https://doi.org/10.1007/s10502-006-9019-1.

33. Stoler, *Along the Archival Grain*, 22.

34. Trouillot, *Silencing the Past*, xix.

35. Anthony W. Dunbar, "Introducing Critical Race Theory to Archival Discourse: Getting the Conversation Started," *Archival Science* 6, no. 1 (March 2006): 109–29. https://doi.org/10.1007/s10502-006-9022-6.

to confront their structures of power that draw on white narratives.[36] Further, Tonia Sutherland sheds light on the archival contribution to the particular homogeneity of historical production, predominantly white history, which not only imposes specific orders based on white supremacy, but in doing so silences and marginalizes African-Americans.[37] For example, Sutherland emphasizes the inability of mainstream archives to document the Black Lives Matter movement's activities: "By failing to consistently collect this visual evidence as an intentional counternarrative, American archives have effectively created a master narrative of normativity around Black death."[38] In identifying American archives' privileging of white narratives, Jarret Drake highlights "'the unbearable whiteness and patriarchy' of traditional archives."[39]

Several authors have demonstrated in their studies that archives can serve as instruments of oppression but also, in a complete reversal, they can serve as evidence of this oppression that can be used to confront those in power. From Harris's studies of records of the apartheid regime in South Africa to projects dedicated to contributing to Indigenous peoples' confrontation of colonial records and reclaiming their identities, archival research has transformed how we understand archival records and their conceptual basis.[40] Eric Ketelaar notes that archives are at

---

36. Mario H. Ramirez, "Being Assumed Not to Be: A Critique of Whiteness as an Archival Imperative," *American Archivist* 78, no. 2 (Fall/Winter 2015): 339–56. https://doi.org/10.17723/0360-9081.78.2.339.

37. Tonia Sutherland, "Archival Amnesty: In Search of Black American Transitional and Restorative Justice," *Journal of Critical Library and Information Studies* 1, no. 2 (2017): 1–23. https://doi.org/10.24242/jclis.v1i2.42.

38. Sutherland, "Archival Amnesty," 13.

39. Quoted in Sutherland, "Archival Amnesty," 17. Jarrett M. Drake, "#ArchivesForBlackLives: Building a Community Archives of Police Violence in Cleveland," *On Archivy*, last modified April 22, 2016, https://medium.com/on-archivy/archivesforBlacklives-building-a-community-archives-of-police-violence-in-cleveland-93615d777289#.5ef4n9jgy.

40. Verne Harris, *Archives and Justice: A South African Perspective* (Chicago: Society of American Archivists, 2006); Sue McKemmish, Livia Jacovino, Eric Ketelaar, Melissa Castan, and Lynette Russel, "Resetting Relationships: Archives and Indigenous Human Rights in Australia," *Archives and Manuscripts* 39, no. 1 (2011): 107–44. See also

once temples that hold and validate power and opposition to dominant forces.[41] Kirsten Weld, in a study of more than seventy-five million documents produced by the police during the civil war in Guatemala (1960–1996), signals the power associated with the idea of setting up a community archive from these police records that ultimately allows people to reconstitute their stories in the face of powerful political forces.[42] The archive, as a physical space, then assumes the position of a symbolic and powerful apparatus conceived to resist assimilation. The process of archiving, thus, can itself be a political act.[43] Indeed, the control of records, and the value of archives, can participate in communities' efforts to develop, maintain, or reclaim their identities.[44] Recent literature and archival initiatives have, thus, revealed the potential of archives to denounce structural dominance in the archives and, simultaneously, to empower communities through community archival efforts.[45]

Anne J. Gilliland, "Moving Past: Probing the Agency and Affect of Recordkeeping in Individual and Community Lives in Post-Conflict Croatia," *Archival Science* 14, no. 3–4 (October 2014): 249–74. https://doi.org/10.1007/s10502-014-9231-3.

41. Ketelaar, "Archival Temples, Archival Prisons."

42. Kirsten Weld, *Paper Cadavers: The Archives of Dictatorship in Guatemala* (Durham: Duke University Press, 2014).

43. Ieuan Hopkins, "Places from Which to Speak," *Journal of the Society of Archivists* 29, no. 1 (April 2018): 83–109. https://doi.org/10.1080/00379810802515069; Michelle Caswell, *Archiving the Unspeakable: Silence, Memory, and the Photographic Record in Cambodia* (Madison: University of Wisconsin Press, 2014).

44. Andrew Flinn and Mary Stevens, "'It is noh mistri, wi mekin histri.' Telling Our Own Story: Independent and Community Archives in the UK, Challenging and Subverting the Mainstream," in *Community Archives: The Shaping of Memory*, eds. Jeannette A. Bastian and Ben Alexander (London: Facet Publishing, 2009), 3–28; Huiling Feng, "Identity and Archives: Return and Expansion of the Social Value of Archives," *Archival Science* 17, no. 2 (June 2017): 97–112. https://doi.org/10.1007/s10502-016-9271-y; Andrew Flinn, Mary Stevens, and Elizabeth Shepherd, "Whose Memory, Whose Archives? Independent Community Archives, Autonomy and the Mainstream," *Archival Science* 9, nos. 1–2 (June 2009): 71–86. https://doi.org/10.1007/s10502-009-9105-2.

45. See, for example, Michelle Caswell, "Seeing Yourself in History: Community Archives and the Fight Against Symbolic Annihilation," *The Public Historian* 36, no. 4 (November 2014): 26–37. https://doi.org/10.1525/tph.2014.36.4.26; Stacie M. Williams and Jarrett M. Drake, "Power to the People: Documenting Police Violence in Cleveland," *Journal of Critical Library and Information Studies* 1, no. 2 (2017): 1–27. https://doi.org/10.24242/jclis.v1i2.33.

A direct, yet external, challenge to mainstream archives' conceptual structure is coming from the burgeoning field of studies in community archives. While the term "community archives" itself is subject to debate,[46] community archiving marks an important transition in how we explore archives. Terry Cook discusses this shift in the archival realm, where community archiving has provided important additions to archival postmodern theoretical concepts of power, while also offering clear challenges to traditional appraisal, preservation, and description of records.[47] The emphasis on the contribution of community archives to collective identity is, however, similar to any other type of archival endeavor.[48] The archival processes of community archives do not differ greatly from archiving in mainstream archival institutions. The production of documents and the preservation of records through archival apparatuses are always filled with political, social, and cultural motivations.[49] One element that differentiates community archives from traditional archives is the former's openness about political motivations and their announced archival activism.[50] Emphasis on the production of archives of underrepresented groups certainly stands as a response to traditional archives. As Andrew Flinn writes, "The very existence of these independent archives, operating outside the framework of mainstream, publicly funded, professionally staffed institutions is both a reproach and a challenge to that mainstream."[51] The focus on social

46. See Andrew Flinn, "Archival Activism: Independent and Community-led Archives, Radical Public History and the Heritage Professions," InterActions: *UCLA Journal of Education and Information Studies* 7, no. 2 (2011): 1–21.

47. Terry Cook, "Evidence, Memory, Identity, and Community: Four Shifting Archival Paradigms," *Archival Science* 13, no. 2–3 (June 2013): 95–120. https://doi.org/10.1007/s10502-012-9180-7.

48. Anne J. Gilliland and Sue McKemmish, "The Role of Participatory Archives in Furthering Human Rights, Reconciliation and Recovery," *Atlanti: Review for Modern Archival Theory and Practice* 24 (2014): 81.

49. Schwartz and Cook, "Archives, Records and Power."

50. See Flinn, "Archival Activism."

51. Flinn, "Archival Activism," 5. See also Andrew Flinn, "The Impact of Independent and Community Archives on Professional Archival Thinking and Practice," in

justice makes community archives important in the evolution of archival theory. The association of archives with social justice and human rights, and the resulting future implications for archival studies, have been clearly defined by Ricardo L. Punzalan and Michelle Caswell.[52] Studies and archival initiatives of community archives have led to the question of whether any document created is a human rights archive.[53] Building on the work connecting archives with human rights and social justice, I now turn to a discussion of gender theory and critical studies of men and masculinities.

Hegemonic Masculinity and the Archives

Research on men and masculinity originate from critical theory paradigms and the feminist movement of the 1970s. Rosabeth Kanter's 1977 study of the men and women of corporate America paved the way for men's studies.[54] The theoretical concept of hegemonic masculinity, developed by R.W. Connell, finds its basis in the theory of cultural hegemony elaborated by Antonio Gramsci in his *Prison Notebooks*, written in the early 1930s.[55] Hegemonic masculinity is characterized as being dynamic, relational, ideological, and part of structures and processes. Connell

---

Future of Archives, ed. Hill, 145–69.

52. Ricardo L. Punzalan and Michelle Caswell, "Critical Directions for Archival Approaches to Social Justice," *Library Quarterly* 86, no. 1 (January 2016): 25–42. https://doi.org/10.1086/684145.

53. Noah Geraci and Michelle Caswell, "Developing a Typology of Human Rights Records," *Journal of Contemporary Archival Studies* 3, Article 1 (2016): 1–24. See also Michelle Caswell, "Defining Human Rights Archives: Introduction to the Special Double Issue on Archives and Human Rights," *Archival Science* 14, nos. 3–4 (October 2014): 207–13. https://doi.org/10.1007/s1050.

54. Rosabeth Kanter, *Men and Women of the Corporation* (New York: Basic Books, 1977).

55. R.W. Connell, Gender and Power (Sydney, Australia: Allen & Unwin, 1987); Connell, Masculinities; R.W. Connell and James W. Messerschmidt, "Hegemonic Masculinity: Rethinking the Concept," *Gender and Society* 19, no. 6 (December 2005): 829–59. https://doi.org/10.1177/0891243205278639; Antonio Gramsci, *Prison Notebooks* (New York: Columbia University Press, 1992).

originally defined it as being part of relational practices that construct masculinity in relation to women and other men through systems and practices.[56] Connell indicates that hegemonic masculinity has repercussions on relational matters with what is referred to as "subordinated," "marginalized," or what is defined as "nonhegemonic" masculinity.[57] In this sense, it is suggested that there are different types of masculinity. These masculinities operate according to historical circumstances and social, political, and cultural frames of reference. Accordingly, masculinity studies are compared to, and find theoretical frameworks in association with, concepts of gender, femininity, homophobia, and other types of masculinity.[58]

Hegemonic masculinity and critical studies on men and masculinities are based on social constructionist frameworks and structural inequality theories.[59] Framed as social constructs and cultural forms, conceptions of men and masculinities are produced and reproduced, are constantly evolving, and vary across time, historical configurations, space, and geographic location.[60] The concept of hegemonic masculinity indicates that masculinity cannot be understood as fixed but is, rather, unstable, dynamic, and unable to be fully realized.[61] In revisiting the paradigm

---

56. Connell, *Gender and Power*, 183–86; Connell, *Masculinities*.

57. Connell, *Gender and Power*, 183–86; Connell, *Masculinities*; Connell and Messerschmidt, "Hegemonic Masculinity."

58. Connell, *Gender and Power*; Connell, *Masculinities*; Eric Anderson, *Inclusive Masculinity: The Changing Nature of Masculinities* (New York: Routledge, 2009).

59. See Edward H. Thompson Jr. and Kate M. Bennett, "Measurement of Masculinity Ideologies: A (Critical) Review," *Psychology of Men & Masculinity* 16, no. 2 (April 2015): 115–33. http://dx.doi.org/10.1037/a0038609; Øystein Gullvåg Holter, "Social Theories for Researching Men and Masculinities: Direct Gender Hierarchy and Structural Inequality," in *Handbook of Studies on Men and Masculinities*, eds. Michael S. Kimmel, Jeff Hearn, and R.W. Connell (Thousand Oaks, CA: Sage Publications, 2005), 15–34; Cliff Cheng, "Men and Masculinities Are Not Necessarily Synonymous: Thoughts on Organizational Behavior and Occupational Sociology," in *Masculinities in Organizations*, ed. Cliff Cheng (Thousand Oaks, CA: Sage Publications, 1996), xi–xx.

60. Connell, *Masculinities*.

61. Kimmel, Hearn, and Connell, "Introduction," in *Handbook of Studies on Men and Masculinities*, 3; Wendy Hollway, "Masters and Men in the Transition from Factory

of hegemonic masculinity, Connell and James W. Messerschmidt state, "Masculinities are configurations of practice that are accomplished in social action and, therefore, can differ according to the gender relations in a particular social setting."[62] Candace West and Don H. Zimmerman, who define social differentiations of gender as performative—what they express as "doing gender"—write that "we conceive of gender as an emergent feature of social situations: both as an outcome of and a rationale for various social arrangements and as a means of legitimating one of the most fundamental divisions of society."[63] Gender and masculinity paradigms, thus, surface from social and cultural environments.[64]

Masculinity as a social construct has also resonated in historical studies of men that have integrated conceptions of the body. Christopher E. Forth's historical study of masculinity in the modern West reinforces this notion of the social construction, maintenance, and dynamic reevaluation of masculinity by examining how men's bodies and their place within structures of power are constantly negotiated. Forth explores the tension and potential conflict between concepts of physical prowess, violence, and robustness of the masculine body and notions of self-regulation, "refined" forms of masculinity, and civilization.[65] This opposition between manly vigor and the danger of overcivilization is put forward when he analyzes the managerial concepts and industrial labor of the first part of the twentieth century. Forth highlights that, "while corporate culture tried to sustain some trappings of entrepreneurial manliness [of commercial manhood], it also insisted upon a refinement of manners that seemed antithetical to traditional masculine qualities

---

Hands to Sentimental Workers," in *Men as Managers*, eds. Collinson and Hearn, 25–42.

62. Connell and Messerschmidt, "Hegemonic Masculinity," 836.

63. Candace West and Don H. Zimmerman, "Doing Gender," *Gender and Society* 1, no. 2 (June 1987): 126. https://doi.org/10.1177/0891243287001002002.

64. Richard Howson, *Challenging Hegemonic Masculinity* (New York: Routledge, 2006), 3.

65. Christopher E. Forth, *Masculinity in the Modern West: Gender, Civilization and the Body* (New York: Pallgrave Macmillan, 2008).

like aggressiveness and competitiveness."[66] The concept of masculinity is presented as constantly adapted and adaptable.

The dynamic element of masculinity operates in all sectors of society and is present in everyday life, particularly in economic structures and institutions.[67] Sociological studies on masculinity and management report on the dominance of men in administrative frameworks.[68] Beverly H. Burris advances the term "technocratic patriarchy" to highlight tactics conceived by managers in the workplace that contribute to how male managers shape their own identities—including ideas that refer to socially constructed "technical expertise" as being more "masculine"—and that establish frameworks to gender others.[69] Highly gendered managerial environments have often relied on claims of objective science that measures efficiency and productivity. David L. Collinson and Jeff Hearn discuss how management is considered neutral in dominant discourses due to claims that bureaucratic practices are embedded in impartial scientific management principles.[70] Studies of organizational structures and bureaucracy have reflected on environments that are inherently gendered and normative. I argue that mainstream archival practices have been developed alongside these bureaucratic and gendered structures that have worked toward the representation of dominant societal forces based on frameworks of hegemonic masculinity.

Critiques of traditional archives that largely document men's activities have come from feminist theory and archival initiatives dedicated to the

---

66. Forth, *Masculinity in the Modern West*, 155.

67. Connell, *Gender and Power*; Connell, *Masculinities*; Connell and Messerschmidt, "Hegemonic Masculinity"; Mike Donaldson, "What Is Hegemonic Masculinity?" *Theory and Society* 22, no. 5 (1993): 643–57. https://doi.org/10.1007/BF00993540. For a discussion of masculinity and socially constructed masculine expressions, see James W. Messerschmidt, "Managing to Kill: Masculinities and the Space Shuttle Challenger Explosion," in *Masculinities in Organizations*, ed. Cheng, 30–34.

68. See Burris, "Technocracy, Patriarchy and Management."

69. Burris, "Technocracy, Patriarchy and Management."

70. David L. Collinson and Jeff Hearn, "Breaking the Silence: On Men, Masculinities and Managements," in *Men as Managers, Managers as Men*, 1–24.

creation of women's archives.[71] The 1973 special issue of the *American Archivist*, "Women in Archives," decries the absence of women's achievements and narratives in the archives. Interestingly, this series of articles combines the limited presence, or the neglect, of women's stories in the archives with the lack of opportunities for women archivists to occupy positions of power in the profession.[72] Financial and resource-based struggles regarding the development of women's archives and the collection of records emphasizing women's records is a common theme in the literature.[73] Cifor and Wood point out, however, that efforts to document women have been too limited in scope and have not provided options to confront the power structures that deny them a legitimate entry into the archival spectrum.[74] They insist on the necessity to integrate intersectional feminist theory into archival conceptions and have highlighted the power of positioning archives alongside feminist social movements in order to dismantle "the heteronormative, capitalist, racist patriarchy on many fronts and through many avenues."[75] They discuss

71. See Kate Eichorn, *The Archival Turn in Feminism: Outrage in Order* (Philadelphia: Temple University Press, 2013).

72. Eva Moseley, "Women in Archives: Documenting the History of Women in America," *American Archivist* 36, no. 2 (April 1973): 215–22. https://doi.org/10.17723/aarc.36.2.36744h4q226234j7; Mabel E. Deutrich, "Women in Archives: Ms. Versus Mr. Archivist," *American Archivist* 36, no. 2 (April 1973): 171–81. https://doi.org/10.17723/aarc.36.2.x74vh77270228681; Miriam I. Crawford, "Women in Archives: A Program for Action," *American Archivist* 36, no. 2 (April 1973): 223–32. https://doi.org/10.17723/aarc.36.2.u31m63436432m53g.

73. See, for example, Anke Voss-Hubbard, "'No Documents–No History': Mary Ritter Beard and the Early History of Women's Archives," *American Archivist* 58, no. 1 (Winter 1995): 16–30. https://doi.org/10.17723/aarc.58.1.hr300127g3142157; Honor R. Sachs, "Reconstructing a Life: The Archival Challenges of Women's History," *Library Trends* 56, no. 3 (Winter 2008): 650–66. https://doi.org/10.1353/lib.2008.0018; Maryanne Dever, "Archiving Feminism: Papers, Politics, Posterity," *Archivaria* 77 (Spring 2014): 25–42; Rachel Miller, Danelle Moon, and Anke Voss, "Seventy-Five Years of International Women's Collecting: Legacies, Successes, Obstacles, and New Directions," *American Archivist* 74, no. Supplement 1 (January 2011): 1–21. https://doi.org/10.17723/aarc.74.suppl-1.q413057641513022.

74. Cifor and Wood, "Critical Feminism in the Archives."

75. Cifor and Wood, "Critical Feminism in the Archives," 2.

the association of archives and identity and note that archives "can be understood as critical tools and modes of self-representation and self-historicization."[76]

Other authors have identified challenges associated with archival material outside of the heteronormative framework. Rebecka T. Sheffield emphasizes the urgency to preserve LGBTQ+ historical records in order to represent social realities through a multiplicity of cultural and social identities.[77] Some have posited the inadequacy of mainstream archival practices to describe underrepresented groups, such as LGBTQ+ communities. Exploring archival description of LGBTQ+ material, Erin Baucom insists on the importance of language in the creation and revision of finding aids.[78] Mainstream archival institutions' inability to adequately describe LGBTQ+ history is particularly due to the lack of bonds between mainstream archives and minority communities.[79] Cifor expands on this notion of inadequate language used to describe LGBTQ+ records in traditional archives and highlights the damage mainstream archives can inflict on perceptions and self-perceptions of minority communities. Cifor signals that hatred is a dominant feature of documents found in traditional archives handling LGBTQ+ records.[80]

The challenges encountered in the documentation of women and LGBTQ+ peoples suggest that mainstream archives have been an environment, both physical and structural, that allows for the production and preservation of historical sources mostly reserved for men and highly resistant to other genders. Masculine expressions in the records seem

---

76. Cifor and Wood, "Critical Feminism in the Archives," 3.

77. Rebecka T. Sheffield, "More than Acid-Free Folders: Extending the Concept of Preservation to Include Stewardship of Unexplored Histories," *Library Trends* 64, no. 3 (2016): 572–84. https://doi.org/10.1353/lib.2016.0001.

78. Erin Baucom, "An Exploration into Archival Descriptions of LGBTQ Materials," *American Archivist* 81, no. 1 (Spring/Summer 2018): 65–83. https://doi.org/10.17723/0360-9081-81.1.65.

79. Baucom, "LGBTQ Materials."

80. Marika Cifor, "Aligning Bodies: Collecting, Arranging, and Describing Hatred for a Critical Queer Archives," *Library Trends* 64, no. 4 (Spring 2016): 756–75. https://doi.org/10.1353/lib.2016.0010.

like the normal order of things in traditional archives. If not directly associated with institutional recordkeeping practices, the collection of personal papers, largely based on men's activities, originates from frames of reference that are inherently masculine. For example, Carol Pal examines the challenge that scientific women of the seventeenth century faced while thinking about leaving traces of their scholarly achievements.[81] The masculine and fraternal environment of paper collectors of early modern Britain simply left no room for women's papers.[82] The historical prominence of men in the archives leads us to problematize this phenomenon, to think in critical terms, and to explore ways to allow for a representation of various identities in the archives.

Toward the Integration of Critical Studies on Men and Masculinities in Archival Theory and Practice

While the concept of hegemonic masculinity has been explored, debated, and contested in studies of sports,[83] psychology,[84] academia,[85]

81. Carol Pal, "Accidental Archive: Samuel Hartlib and the Afterlife of Female Scholars," in *Archival Afterlives: Life, Death and Knowledge-Making in Early Modern British Scientific and Medical Archives*, eds. Vera Keller, Anna Marie Roos, and Elizabeth Yale (Boston: Brill, 2018), 120–49.

82. See Pal, "Accidental Archive."

83. Laura Grindstaff and Emily West, "Hegemonic Masculinity on the Sidelines of Sport," *Sociology Compass* 5, no. 10 (October 2011): 859–81. https://doi.org/10.1111/j.1751-9020.2011.00409.x; Colleen English, "Toward Sport Reform: Hegemonic Masculinity and Reconceptualizing Competition," *Journal of the Philosophy of Sport* 44, no. 2 (2017): 183–98. https://doi.org/10.1080/00948705.2017.1300538; Akihiko Hirose and Kay Kei-ho Pih, "Men Who Strike and Men Who Submit: Hegemonic and Marginalized Masculinities in Mixed Martial Arts," *Men and Masculinities* 13, no. 2 (December 2010): 190–201. https://doi.org/10.1177/1097184X09344417.

84. Martha Wetherell and Nigel Edley, "Negotiating Hegemonic Masculinity: Imaginary Positions and Psycho-Discursive Practices," *Feminism & Psychology* 9, no. 3 (1999): 335–56. https://doi.org/10.1177/0959353599009003012.

85. Martin Kilduff and Ajay Mehra, "Hegemonic Masculinity Among the Elite: Power, Identity, and Homophily in Social Networks," in *Masculinities in Organizations*, ed. Cheng, 115–29; James W. Messerschmidt, "Engendering Gendered Knowledge: Assessing the Academic Appropriation of Hegemonic Masculinity," *Men and Masculinities* 15, no. 1 (April 2012): 56–76. https://doi.org/10.1177/1097184X11428384.

the military,[86] and globalization,[87] it has not yet penetrated the field of archives. As archives have been instrumental in the development of political power and historical masculine endeavors, such as modern warfare, colonialism, the consolidation of nation-states, and in the erection of public institutions, it is instrumental to discuss the implication of masculinity in archival discourse. In research on individuals and groups on the margins around the period of the independence of the United States—and those who were participating in their own sense of independence—historian Kathleen DuVal notes bluntly, "Although nearly half of North America's population was female, few women appear in tales of war and nation-building. Surviving documents tend to focus on what the men were doing: fighting, strategizing, and writing."[88] Colonial and Western conceptions of preservation of memory have defined mainstream archival apparatuses and practices based on particular political objectives connected to masculine endeavors.

Integrating gender in the archival realm is crucial because "To recognize gender as a social pattern requires us to see it as a product of history, and also as a *producer* of history."[89] Gender, then, has archival implications. Connell adds that "gender relations, the relations among people and groups organized through the reproductive arena, form one of the major structures of all documented societies."[90] Acknowledging the presence of gender in socially elaborated archival transactions and institutional structures allows us to think about representation and the reproduction of human relations in the production and silencing of

---

86. Claire Duncanson, "Hegemonic Masculinity and the Possibility of Change in Gender Relations," *Men and Masculinities* 18, no. 2 (June 2015): 231–48. https://doi.org/10.1177/1097184X15584912.

87. Christine Beasley, "Rethinking Hegemonic Masculinity in a Globalizing World," *Men and Masculinities* 11, no. 1 (October 2008): 86–103. https://doi.org/10.1177/1097184X08315102.

88. Kathleen DuVal, *Independence Lost: Lives on the Edge of the American Revolution* (New York: Random House, 2016), 43.

89. Connell, *Masculinities*, 81.

90. Connell, *Masculinities*, 72.

recordkeeping activities. The dynamic social components of gender have an impact on human activities and relations that cannot be distanced from the historical record and recordkeeping strategies.

While several authors have offered ways to confront the power of mainstream archives and their institutions, largely through alternative ways to document underrepresented groups in the archives, I integrate the concept of hegemonic masculinity in archival theory in order to examine mainstream archival processes and to provide a conceptual basis to dismantle masculine dominance in traditional archives. Building on a postmodern archival theoretical frame of reference as well as community and participatory archival initiatives oriented toward the representation of a diversity of people and groups, I add to these frameworks the systematic study of masculinity.

Analysis of processes associated with record creation is crucial to resist dominant forces, including institutions, which have the power to produce, describe, organize, give access to, and disseminate historical records. Mainstream archives have contributed to the dynamic articulation of masculinity by providing systems and spaces in which hegemonic masculinity could be expressed, performed, and preserved. Unquestioned reproduction of social contexts through traditional archival processes enhances the hegemonic form of masculinity. The prominence of men in the archives is not only associated with the number of records describing men's activities and relations. Hegemonic masculinity in the archives is developed through formal and systematic record creation structures that are socially and culturally constructed and embedded in claims of neutrality and objectivity of standardized archival practices. The elaboration of men and masculinity in the archives is the result of recordkeeping frameworks that emphasize the collection of traces depicting powerful masculine figures and administrative activities largely conceived of and controlled by masculine configurations of authority. Hegemonic masculinity in the archives is expressed through consciously conceived institutional structures and also by unintentional power paradigms.

The confrontation of hegemonic masculinity in the archives must be executed according to dynamic principles put forward by archivists who are challenging traditional archives. These must include a substantive discussion of archival concepts and practices. Archival activities and principles, including their characteristics of respect des fonds, description, original order, and current definitions of provenance and creatorship, are part of political processes that impose a structural order on records. But these are inadequate for the description of underrepresented groups and for human rights archives.[91] It has been argued that traditional descriptions are "key agents in the oppression, marginalization, silencing, alienation and traumatization of individuals and communities that have been involved in social justice and human rights movements, for example, through how acts and victims are classified, euphemized, or submerged."[92] Moreover, traditional practices of arrangement, description, and creation of finding aids can even create barriers for users.[93] These archival endeavors are not transparent and neutral. Elizabeth Yakel claims that archivists must be conscious of the social construction of archival practices, including past descriptive conceptual structures, and suggests acknowledging the dynamic aspect of processes in the archives in order to think about representation there.[94]

Notions of neutrality in archival practices should now be discarded by archivists.[95] Archivists' interventions and use of records, what Ketelaar

91. Stacy Wood, Kathy Carbone, Marika Cifor, Anne Gilliland, and Ricardo Punzalan, "Mobilizing Records: Re-Framing Archival Description to Support Human Rights," *Archival Science* 14, nos. 3–4 (October 2014): 402. https://doi.org/10.1007/s10502-014-9233-1.

92. Wood, Carbone, Cifor, Gilliland, and Punzalan, "Mobilizing Records," 398.

93. Elizabeth Yakel, "Archival Representation," Archival Science 3, no. 1 (2003): 1–25. https://doi.org/10.1007/BF02438926.

94. Yakel, "Archival Representation," 19. For a discussion of legacy data and issues related to legacy systems and descriptive configurations, see Christian James and Ricardo L. Punzalan, "Legacy Matters: Describing Subject-Based Digital Historical Collections," *Journal of Archival Organization* 12, nos. 3–4 (2015): 198–215. https://doi.org/10.1080/15332748.2015.1150104.

95. For a discussion of ethics, archival pedagogy, and archivists' neutrality, see Anne J. Gilliland, "Neutrality, Social Justice and the Obligations of Archival Education and Educators in the Twenty-First Century," *Archival Science* 11, nos. 3–4 (November 2011): 193–209. https://doi.org/10.1007/s10502-011-9147-0.

refers to as "archival activation," infuses archives with new knowledge and perspectives.[96] The maneuvers of archivists must be considered in order to understand the historical context of archives. Archivists' professional standing and activities play a part in the representation of human transactions and relations, including hierarchical paradigms. Moreover, "the archive can never be a quiet retreat for professionals and scholars and craftspersons. It is a crucible of human experience, a battleground for meaning and significance, a babel of stories, a place and a space of complex and ever-shifting powerplays."[97] Authors have even identified archivists as witnesses to these narratives and archival dynamics, connecting social justice with emotional justice.[98] Along these lines, I position the role of male archivists within the notion of "caring masculinity" put forward by Karla Elliott. Drawing on feminist theory principles, "caring masculinity" is proposed as a critical framework that offers the potential to confront masculine power and envision a transformation in gender relations.[99]

Positioning human beings at the center of archival thinking and practices has brought new frameworks of analysis. Cifor has developed the concept of affect theory in the archives.[100] Connecting archives with human relations, bodies, institutions, time, space, and global connections, Cifor writes that "affect theory provides a theoretical toolkit needed to conceptualize and reinterpret more fully, and to enact change for

---

96. Eric Ketelaar, "Tacit Narratives: The Meaning of Archives," *Archival Science* 1, no. 2 (2001): 131–41. https://doi.org/10.1007/BF02435644.

97. Harris, "Archival Sliver," 85.

98. See Ricardo L. Punzalan, "'All the Things We Cannot Articulate': Colonial Leprosy Archives and Community Commemoration," in *Community Archives*, eds. Bastian and Alexander, 187–219; Caswell, Archiving the Unspeakable; Weld, Paper Cadavers; Marika Cifor, "Affecting Relations: Introducing Affect Theory to Archival Discourse," *Archival Science* 16, no. 1 (March 2016): 7–25. https://doi.org/. 10.1007/s10502-015-9261-5.

99. Karla Elliott, "Caring Masculinities: Theorizing an Emerging Concept," *Men and Masculinities* 19, no. 3 (August 2016): 240–59. https://doi.org/10.1177/1097184X15576203.

100. Cifor, "Affecting Relations."

justice in archival functions and concerns such as appraisal, access, use, responsibility, accountability and service."[101] The archivist is positioned as being deeply involved in these affective relations and implicated in the process of representing people in the archives.[102] Further, Jennifer Douglas and Allison Mills discuss the artificial division in the archival realm between institutional and personal records.[103] Every documented society is characterized by personal involvement in record creation and recordkeeping structural frames. Positioning bodies in the configuration of appraisal and description concepts challenges dominant masculine administrative structures in the archives. Associating affect with participatory archiving toward the objective of respectfully describing records from LGBTQ+ communities, Cifor again argues, "By becoming aware of how bodies and objects are put into relation by affect, and by bringing attention to (bad) affects, we can queer—'radically opening'—the archives to contradictory, contestable, and nonnormative histories and work toward a more just present and future for queer and trans people."[104] Scholarly efforts and intersectional approaches have offered ways to open up the archives and to confront configurations that have typically neglected certain areas of human activities and relations or have reproduced dominant features of archival practices. Caswell brings forward the theme of archival pluralism and highlights the multiplicity of archival realities that archivists must consider in order to contextualize the production of knowledge, and to reflect on how we transmit information and allow access to archives.[105]

---

101. Cifor, "Affecting Relations," 9.

102. Cifor, "Affecting Relations."

103. Jennifer Douglas and Allison Mills, "From the Sidelines to the Center: Reconsidering the Potential of the Personal in Archives," *Archival Science* 18, no. 3 (September 2018): 257–77. https://doi.org/10.1007/s10502-018-9295-6.

104. Cifor, "Aligning Bodies," 772.

105. Michelle Caswell, "On Archival Pluralism: What Religious Pluralism (And Its Critics) Can Teach Us about Archives," *Archival Science* 13, no. 4 (December 2013): 273–92. https://doi.org/10.1007/s10502-012-9197-y.

These approaches have been added to other research in the archival field that has explored and revised notions of appraisal, provenance and records creatorship, and custodialism. Appraisal strategies must consider human relations that are evident in records, including hierarchies in the form and content. This archival mindset allows archival theory to connect with other disciplines to find creative ways to represent, in a dynamic way, records documenting human relations. Terry Eastwood discusses a democratic aspect of appraisal, oriented toward better representation of people and serving the needs of communities.[106] Along these lines, Douglas describes the sociohistorical context of provenance to challenge the ways we think about record creatorship.[107] There is no doubt that arguments about parallel provenance,[108] or thinking about ethnicity when we discuss provenance,[109] are put forward to ensure a multiplicity of representations in the archives. These frameworks confront the traditional conceptions of provenance, which position the record as ingrained in administrative structures rather than being associated with the documentation of people and the overall context of human activities.[110]

These ideas, along with deconstructionist principles, stimulate discussions about the scope of archives.[111] As Harris highlights, "The deconstructive move in relation to binary opposites is not simply to wage battle against them. It is, rather, to expose their provenances and

---

106. Terry Eastwood, "Reflections on the Goal of Archival Appraisal in Democratic Societies," *Archivaria* 54 (Fall 2002): 59–71.

107. Jennifer Douglas, "Origins: Evolving Ideas about the Principle of Provenance," in *Currents*, eds. MacNeil and Eastwood (2010), 23–43.

108. Chris Hurley, "Parallel Provenance: What if Anything Is Archival Description?," *Archives and Manuscripts* 33, no. 1 (2005): 110–45.

109. Joel Wurl, "Ethnicity as Provenance: In Search of Values and Principles for Documenting the Immigrant Experience," *Archival Issues* 29, no. 1 (2005): 65–76.

110. See Stacy Wood, Kathy Carbone, Marika Cifor, Anne Gilliland, and Ricardo Punzalan, "Mobilizing Records," 402.

111. Ketelaar, "Tacit Narratives"; Verne Harris, "Insistering Derrida: Cixous, Deconstruction, and the Work of Archive," *Journal of Critical Library and Information Studies* 1, no. 2 (2017): 1–19. https://doi.org/10.24242/jclis.v1i2.28.

deployments. It is to use them strategically, play with their spectrality—by demonstrating how each 'opposite' opens out of the other, and how each bifurcates endlessly."[112] Building on the position of Brilmyer—who reflects on the preservation or elimination of power structures in the archives—I, by extension, indicate that, while masculine configurations of power in the archives should not be eliminated through archival revision, nor should they be put on the front stage of archival thinking and practices.[113] The exploration of hegemonic masculinity and the archives is put forward to deconstruct its features in order to give space to other archival approaches. The elaboration of archival principles, such as provenance, and archival activities of appraisal and description should then be thought of as a means of investigation conceived to explore structures of power and to find efficient ways to represent human activities and relations in the archival spectrum.

Problematizing the prominence of men and masculinity in the archives through the concept of hegemonic masculinity adds, I believe, another perspective that contributes to an understanding of archives and their dynamic structural configurations. Introducing critical studies on men and masculinities to studies of archives testifies to the relational networks of archives and challenges their configuration. For example, as Sheffield mentions, "just because a university preserves unexplored history does not mean that it is ready to acknowledge or confront any of the structural inequalities that exist in order to create the conditions in which that history remains unexplored to begin with."[114] Dominant structures of power in the archives cannot be confronted if we do not directly question, study, and address the fundamental concepts that support these structures.

---

112. Harris, "Insistering Derrida," 11.

113. Brilmyer, "Archival Assemblages," 111. On the issue of "fixing power" or the question of erasing power frameworks from the archives, see Emily Drabinski, "Queering the Catalog: Queer Theory and the Politics of Correction," *Library Quarterly* 83, no. 2 (April 2013): 94–111. https://doi.org/10.1086/669547.

114. Sheffield, "More than Acid-Free Folders," 580.

Mainstream archives must borrow tactics and actively listen to what community and participatory archives have brought forward, and conceive ways to revisit their frameworks and practices that have allowed for the articulation and maintenance of these dominant paradigms. The work of community archives is crucial but, as Hughes-Watkins asserts, "Mainstream archives, including academic repositories, cannot see the community archive as a type of absolution or emancipation from their debt to society."[115] Studying archives through the principles of hegemonic masculinity addresses notions that have nurtured dominant masculinity in mainstream archives and have marginalized femininity and other types of masculinity and genders. Archives have, then, the potential to bring attention to inequality and oppression as well as to "evidence of wrong-doing and evidence for undoing the wrong."[116]

Hughes-Watkins believes that, by engaging in social justice endeavors, archival initiatives in mainstream archives can contribute to "reparative archival work."[117] In addition, Tonia Sutherland highlights the power extracted from the use of counternarratives for truth and reconciliation processes. Sutherland proposes the concept of archival amnesty based on accountability.[118] It is with this frame of mind that I introduce the concept of hegemonic masculinity in mainstream archives. The ever-evolving archives are then engaged in the questioning of their operations and frameworks, "thinking about what constitutes credible archival knowledge, how such knowledge should be produced, preserved, and interpreted, and who should be imbued with such powers."[119] It is the responsibility of archivists evolving in mainstream archives to find

115. Hughes-Watkins, "Moving Toward a Reparative Archive," 15.

116. Ketelaar, "Archival Temples, Archival Prisons" 231.

117. Hughes-Watkins, "Moving Toward a Reparative Archive," 15.

118. Sutherland, "Archival Amnesty."

119. May Chazan, Melissa Baldwin, and Laura Madokoro, "Aging, Activism, and the Archive: Feminist Perspectives for the 21st Century," *Archivaria* 80 (Fall 2015): 61.

creative ways to break their complicity in the "ongoing silencing of minority groups."[120]

Archivists must pursue involvement in pedagogical and educational activities to discuss men and masculinities' impact on the shaping of traditional archives and to develop new tactics oriented toward social justice. Discussions of archival literacy and archival intelligence bring useful arguments to imagine strategies to contextualize the dynamics of power embedded in primary sources.[121] Analysis of the language of records and pedagogical conceptions of the archives evokes interconnected networks between the historical record, human activities, archival principles and practices, and the users. Duff and Jessica Haskell propose the concept of the "rhizome" that puts forward collaborative approaches and dynamic user engagement in archival processes.[122] Not completely disregarding traditional descriptive techniques, they advance nonhierarchical, collaborative approaches, such as social media technologies, mobile apps, and gamification to increase user involvement and connection with archives.[123] Other initiatives such as digitization, exhibits, and other outreach projects need to integrate this element of a community of users and to think about culturally sensitive material being exposed.[124] Archivists then must problematize the scope of their activities in order to avoid reinforcing structures of power, such as the elaboration of dominant masculine paradigms in the archives.

---

120. Caswell, "Seeing Yourself in History," 36.

121. Elizabeth Yakel and Deborah A. Torres, "AI: Archival Intelligence and User Expertise," *American Archivist* 66, no. 1 (Spring/Summer 2003): 51–77. https://doi.org/10.17723/aarc.66.1.q022h85pn51n5800.

122. Wendy M. Duff and Jennifer Haskell, "New Uses for Old Records: A Rhizomatic Approach to Archival Access," *American Archivist* 78, no. 1 (Spring/Summer 2015): 38–58. https://doi.org/10.17723/0360-9081.78.1.38.

123. Duff and Haskell, "New Uses for Old Records."

124. Zinaida Manžuch, "Ethical Issues in Digitization of Cultural Heritage," *Journal of Contemporary Archival Studies* 4, Article 4 (2017): 1–17.

Conclusion

The prominence of men's activities and their position of power in the archives have been emboldened by archival bureaucratic processes that originally claimed neutrality. As I have highlighted in this chapter, the discussion and integration of critical studies on men and masculinities in the archival realm relies on the current debates in archival theory, largely advanced by the impact of studies on community and participatory archives. In other words, the introduction of the concept of hegemonic masculinity in archival theory would not have been possible without the contribution of recent archival literature regarding notions of representation and identity, and the challenging of traditional archival practices. What the concepts of hegemonic masculinity and critical studies on men and masculinities offer is an understanding of how masculinities operate in the social and political spectrum. The connection between these theoretical frameworks and the archives is oriented toward the confrontation of power dynamics in the archives, the dismantling of hegemonic masculinity in archival structures, and a better representation of women and LGBTQ+ peoples in the archives.

The integration of critical studies on men and masculinity in archival studies, and archivists' practices that include reflections on gender and masculinity will, I hope, address structures of power in the archives and lead to the pursuit of dynamic approaches to archival principles and practices aligned with social change. More research and case studies are needed to problematize the impact of masculinity in the archives. Hopefully, this chapter will initiate further discussions about masculinity and the archives and will lead to examples of how masculinity can be discussed and addressed in the archives field.

Bibliography

Anderson, Eric. *Inclusive Masculinity: The Changing Nature of Masculinities*. New York: Routledge, 2009.

Andreski, Stanislav, ed. and trans. *Max Weber on Capitalism, Bureaucracy and Religion: A Selection of Texts*. London: George Allen & Unwin, 1983.

Bastian, Jeannette A. and Ben Alexander, eds. *Community Archives: The Shaping of Memory*. London: Facet Publishing, 2009.

Bastian, Jeannette Allis. "Reading Colonial Records Through an Archival Lens: The Provenance of Place, Space and Creation." *Archival Science* 6, nos. 3–4 (December 2006): 267–84. https://doi.org/10.1007/s10502-006-9019-1.

Baucom, Erin. "An Exploration into Archival Descriptions of LGBTQ Materials." *American Archivist* 81, no. 1 (Spring/Summer 2018): 65–83. https://doi.org/10.17723/0360-9081-81.1.65.

Beasley, Christine. "Rethinking Hegemonic Masculinity in a Globalizing World." *Men and Masculinities* 11, no. 1 (October 2008): 86–103. https://doi.org/10.1177/1097184X08315102.

Bourdieu, Pierre. *Le sens pratique*. Paris: Les Éditions de Minuit, 1980.

Brilmyer, Gracen. "Archival Assemblages: Applying Disability Studies' Political/Relational Model to Archival Description." *Archival Science* 18, no. 2 (June 2018): 95–118. https://doi.org/10.1007/s10502-018-9287-6.

Brothmen, Brien. "Orders of Value: Probing the Theoretical Terms of Archival Practice." *Archivaria* 32 (Summer 1991): 78–100.

Caswell, Michelle. *Archiving the Unspeakable: Silence, Memory, and the Photographic Record in Cambodia*. Madison: University of Wisconsin Press, 2014.

Caswell, Michelle. "Seeing Yourself in History: Community Archives and the Fight Against Symbolic Annihilation." *The Public Historian* 36, no. 4 (November 2014): 26–37. https://doi.org/10.1525/tph.2014.36.4.26.

Caswell, Michelle. "Defining Human Rights Archives: Introduction to the Special Double Issue on Archives and Human Rights." *Archival Science* 14, nos. 3–4 (October 2014): 207–13. https://doi.org/10.1007/s1050.

Caswell, Michelle. "On Archival Pluralism: What Religious Pluralism (And Its Critics) Can Teach Us about Archives." *Archival Science* 13, no. 4 (December 2013): 273–92. https://doi.org/10.1007/s10502-012-9197-y.

Chazan, May, Melissa Baldwin, and Laura Madokoro. "Aging, Activism, and the Archive: Feminist Perspectives for the 21st Century." *Archivaria* 80 (Fall 2015): 59–87.

Cheng, Cliff, ed. *Masculinities in Organizations*. Thousand Oaks, CA: Sage Publications, 1996.

Cifor, Marika, and Jamie A. Lee. "Towards an Archival Critique: Opening Possibilities for Addressing Neoliberalism in the Archival Field." *Journal of Critical Library and Information Studies* 1, no. 1 (2017): 1–22. https://doi.org/10.24242/jclis.v1i1.10.

Cifor, Marika, and Stacy Wood. "Critical Feminism in the Archives." *Journal of Critical Library and Information Studies* 1, no. 2 (2017): 1–27. https://doi.org/10.24242/jclis.v1i2.27.

Cifor, Marika. "Aligning Bodies: Collecting, Arranging, and Describing Hatred for a Critical Queer Archives." *Library Trends* 64, no. 4 (Spring 2016): 756–75. https://doi.org/10.1353/lib.2016.0010.

Cifor, Marika. "Affecting Relations: Introducing Affect Theory to Archival Discourse." *Archival Science* 16, no. 1 (March 2016): 7–25. https://doi.org/10.1007/s10502-015-9261-5.

Collinson, David L., and Jeff Hearn, eds. *Men as Managers, Managers as Men: Critical Perspectives on Men, Masculinities and Managements*. London: SAGE Publications, 1996.

Connell, R.W., and James W. Messerschmidt. "Hegemonic Masculinity: Rethinking the Concept." *Gender and Society* 19, no. 6 (December 2005): 829–59. https://doi.org/10.1177/0891243205278639.

Connell, R.W. *Masculinities*. Berkeley: University of California Press, 1995.

Connell, R.W. *Gender and Power*. Sydney, Australia: Allen & Unwin, 1987.

Cook, Terry. "Evidence, Memory, Identity, and Community: Four Shifting Archival Paradigms." *Archival Science* 13, no. 2–3 (June 2013): 95–120. https://doi.org/10.1007/s10502-012-9180-7.

Crawford, Miriam I. "Women in Archives: A Program for Action," *American Archivist* 36, no. 2 (April 1973): 223–32. https://doi.org/10.17723/aarc.36.2.u31m63436432m53g.

Derrida, Jacques. *Mal d'archives: une impression freudienne.* Paris, France: Galilée, 2008.

Deutrich, Mabel E. "Women in Archives: Ms. Versus Mr. Archivist." *American Archivist* 36, no. 2 (April 1973): 171–81. https://doi. org/10.17723/aarc.36.2.x74vh77270228681.

Dever, Maryanne. "Archiving Feminism: Papers, Politics, Posterity." *Archivaria* 77 (Spring 2014): 25–42.

Donaldson, Mike. "What Is Hegemonic Masculinity?" *Theory and Society* 22, no. 5 (1993): 643–57. https://doi.org/10.1007/BF00993540.

Douglas, Jennifer, and Allison Mills. "From the Sidelines to the Center: Reconsidering the Potential of the Personal in Archives." *Archival Science* 18, no. 3 (September 2018): 257–77. https://doi.org/10.1007/s10502-018-9295-6.

Drabinski, Emily. "Queering the Catalog: Queer Theory and the Politics of Correction." *Library Quarterly* 83, no. 2 (April 2013): 94–111. https://doi.org/10.1086/669547.

Drake, Jarrett M. On Archivy. "#ArchivesForBlackLives: Building a Community Archives of Police Violence in Cleveland." Last modified April 22, 2016. https://medium.com/on-archivy/archivesforBlack-lives-building-a-community-archives-of-police-violence-in-cleveland-93615d777289#.5ef4n9jgy.

Duff, Wendy M., and Jennifer Haskell. "New Uses for Old Records: A Rhizomatic Approach to Archival Access." *American Archivist* 78, no. 1 (Spring/Summer 2015): 38–58. https://doi.org/10.17723/0360-9081.78.1.38.

Duff, Wendy M., and Verne Harris. "Stories and Names: Archival Description as Narrating Records and Constructing Meanings." *Archival Science* 2, nos. 3–4 (2002): 263–85. https://doi.org/10.1007/BF02435625.

Dunbar, Anthony W. "Introducing Critical Race Theory to Archival Discourse: Getting the Conversation Started." *Archival Science* 6, no. 1 (March 2006): 109–29. https://doi.org/10.1007/s10502-006-9022-6.

Duncanson, Claire. "Hegemonic Masculinity and the Possibility of Change in Gender Relations." *Men and Masculinities* 18, no. 2 (June 2015): 231–48. https://doi.org/10.1177/1097184X15584912.

DuVal, Kathleen. *Independence Lost: Lives on the Edge of the American Revolution.* New York: Random House, 2016.

Eastwood, Terry. "Reflections on the Goal of Archival Appraisal in Democratic Societies." *Archivaria* 54 (Fall 2002): 59–71.

Eichorn, Kate. *The Archival Turn in Feminism: Outrage in Order.* Philadelphia: Temple University Press, 2013.

Elliott, Karla. "Caring Masculinities: Theorizing an Emerging Concept." *Men and Masculinities* 19, no. 3 (August 2016): 240–59. https://doi.org/10.1177/1097184X15576203.

English, Colleen. "Toward Sport Reform: Hegemonic Masculinity and Reconceptualizing Competition," *Journal of the Philosophy of Sport* 44, no. 2 (2017): 183–98. https://doi.org/10.1080/00948705.2017.1300538.

Feng, Huiling. "Identity and Archives: Return and Expansion of the Social Value of Archives." *Archival Science* 17, no. 2 (June 2017): 97–112. https://doi.org/10.1007/s10502-016-9271-y.

Flinn, Andrew. "Archival Activism: Independent and Community-led Archives, Radical Public History and the Heritage Professions." *InterActions: UCLA Journal of Education and Information Studies* 7, no. 2 (2011): 1–21.

Flinn, Andrew, Mary Stevens, and Elizabeth Shepherd. "Whose Memory, Whose Archives? Independent Community Archives, Autonomy and the Mainstream." *Archival Science* 9, nos. 1–2 (June 2009): 71–86. https://doi.org/10.1007/s10502-009-9105-2.

Forth, Christopher E. *Masculinity in the Modern West: Gender, Civilization and the Body.* New York: Pallgrave Macmillan, 2008.

Geraci, Noah, and Michelle Caswell. "Developing a Typology of Human Rights Records." *Journal of Contemporary Archival Studies* 3, Article 1 (2016): 1–24.

Gilliland, Anne J., and Sue McKemmish. "The Role of Participatory Archives in Furthering Human Rights, Reconciliation and Recovery." *Atlanti: Review for Modern Archival Theory and Practice* 24 (2014): 78–88.

Gilliland, Anne J. "Moving Past: Probing the Agency and Affect of Recordkeeping in Individual and Community Lives in Post-Conflict Croatia." *Archival Science* 14, no. 3–4 (October 2014): 249–74. https://doi.org/10.1007/s10502-014-9231-3.

Gilliland, Anne J. "Neutrality, Social Justice and the Obligations of Archival Education and Educators in the Twenty-First Century." *Archival Science* 11, nos. 3–4 (November 2011): 193–209. https://doi.org/10.1007/s10502-011-9147-0.

Gramsci, Antonio. *Prison Notebooks*. New York: Columbia University Press, 1992.

Grindstaff, Laura, and Emily West. "Hegemonic Masculinity on the Sidelines of Sport." *Sociology Compass* 5, no. 10 (October 2011): 859–81. https://doi.org/10.1111/j.1751-9020.2011.00409.x.

Harris, Verne. "Insistering Derrida: Cixous, Deconstruction, and the Work of Archive." *Journal of Critical Library and Information Studies* 1, no. 2 (2017): 1–19. https://doi.org/10.24242/jclis.v1i2.28.

Harris, Verne. *Archives and Justice: A South African Perspective*. Chicago: Society of American Archivists, 2006.

Harris, Verne. "The Archival Sliver: Power, Memory, and Archives in South Africa." *Archival Science* 2, nos. 1–2 (2002): 63–86. https://doi.org/10.1007/BF02435631.

Hill, Jennie, ed. *The Future of Archives and Recordkeeping: A Reader*. London: Facet Publishing, 2011.

Hirose, Akihiko, and Kay Kei-ho Pih. "Men Who Strike and Men Who Submit: Hegemonic and Marginalized Masculinities in Mixed Martial Arts." *Men and Masculinities* 13, no. 2 (December 2010): 190–201. https://doi.org/10.1177/1097184X09344417.

Hopkins, Ieuan. "Places from Which to Speak." *Journal of the Society of Archivists* 29, no. 1 (April 2018): 83–109. https://doi.org/10.1080/00379810802515069.

Howson, Richard. *Challenging Hegemonic Masculinity.* New York: Routledge, 2006.

Hughes-Watkins, Lae'l. "Moving Toward a Reparative Archive: A Roadmap for a Holistic Approach to Disrupting Homogenous Histories in Academic Repositories and Creating Inclusive Spaces for Marginalized Voices." *Journal of Contemporary Archival Studies* 5, Article 6 (2018): 1–17.

Hurley, Chris. "Parallel Provenance: What if Anything Is Archival Description?" *Archives and Manuscripts* 33, no. 1 (2005): 110–45.

James, Christian, and Ricardo L. Punzalan. "Legacy Matters: Describing Subject-Based Digital Historical Collections." *Journal of Archival Organization* 12, no. 3–4 (2015): 198–215. https://doi.org/10.1080/15332748.2015.1150104.

Kanter, Rosabeth. *Men and Women of the Corporation.* New York: Basic Books, 1977.

Ketelaar, Eric. "Archival Temples, Archival Prisons: Modes of Power and Protection." *Archival Science* 2, nos. 3–4 (2002): 221–38. https://doi.org/10.1007/BF02435623.

Ketelaar, Eric. "Tacit Narratives: The Meaning of Archives." *Archival Science* 1, no. 2 (2001): 131–41. https://doi.org/10.1007/BF02435644.

Kimmel, Michael S., Jeff Hearn and R.W. Connell, eds. *Handbook of Studies on Men and Masculinities.* Thousand Oaks, CA: Sage Publications, 2005.

Lerner, Gerda. *The Creation of Patriarchy.* New York: Oxford University Press, 1986.

Lutzker, Michael A. "Max Weber and the Analysis of Modern Bureaucratic Organization: Notes Toward a Theory of Appraisal." *American Archivist* 45, no. 2 (Spring 1982): 119–30. https://doi.org/10.17723/aarc.45.2.n05v8735408776qh.

MacNeil, Heather, and Terry Eastwood, eds. *Currents of Archival Thinking*, 2nd ed. Santa Barbara, CA: Libraries Unlimited, 2017.

MacNeil, Heather, and Terry Eastwood, eds. *Currents of Archival Thinking*. Santa Barbara, CA: Libraries Unlimited, 2010.

Manžuch, Zinaida. "Ethical Issues in Digitization of Cultural Heritage." *Journal of Contemporary Archival Studies* 4, Article 4 (2017): 1–17.

McKemmish, Sue, Livia Jacovino, Eric Ketelaar, Melissa Castan, and Lynette Russel. "Resetting Relationships: Archives and Indigenous Human Rights in Australia." *Archives and Manuscripts* 39, no. 1 (2011): 107–44.

Messerschmidt, James W. "Engendering Gendered Knowledge: Assessing the Academic Appropriation of Hegemonic Masculinity." *Men and Masculinities* 15, no. 1 (April 2012): 56–76. https://doi. org/10.1177/1097184X11428384.

Miller, Rachel, Danelle Moon, and Anke Voss, "Seventy-Five Years of International Women's Collecting: Legacies, Successes, Obstacles, and New Directions." *American Archivist* 74, no. Supplement 1 (January 2011): 1–21. https://doi.org/10.17723/aarc.74.suppl-1. q413057641513022.

Moseley, Eva. "Women in Archives: Documenting the History of Women in America." *American Archivist* 36, no. 2 (April 1973): 215–22. https://doi.org/10.17723/aarc.36.2.36744h4q226234j7.

Nesmith, Tom. "Reopening Archives: Bringing New Contextualities into Archival Theory and Practice." *Archivaria* 60 (Fall 2005): 259–74.

Nesmith, Tom. "Seeing Archives: Postmodernism and the Changing Intellectual Place of Archives." *American Archivist* 65, no. 1 (Spring/Summer 2002): 24–41. https://doi.org/10.17723/ aarc.65.1.rr48450509r0712u.

Nicholson, Karen P., and Maura Seale, eds. *The Politics of Theory and the Practice of Critical Librarianship*. Sacramento, CA: Library Juice Press, 2018.

Nicholson, Karen P. "The McDonaldization of Academic Libraries and the Values of Transformational Change." *College and Research Libraries* 76, no. 3 (2015): 328–38. https://doi.org/10.5860/crl.76.3.328.

Pal, Carol. "Accidental Archive: Samuel Hartlib and the Afterlife of Female Scholars." In *Archival Afterlives: Life, Death and Knowledge-Making in Early Modern British Scientific and Medical Archives*, edited by Vera Keller, Anna Marie Roos, and Elizabeth Yale, 120–49. Boston: Brill, 2018.

Punzalan, Ricardo L., and Michelle Caswell. "Critical Directions for Archival Approaches to Social Justice." *Library Quarterly* 86, no. 1 (January 2016): 25–42. https://doi.org/10.1086/684145.

Ramirez, Mario H. "Being Assumed Not to Be: A Critique of Whiteness as an Archival Imperative." *American Archivist* 78, no. 2 (Fall/Winter 2015): 339–56. https://doi.org/10.17723/0360-9081.78.2.339.

Sachs, Honor R. "Reconstructing a Life: The Archival Challenges of Women's History." *Library Trends* 56, no. 3 (Winter 2008): 650–66. https://doi.org/10.1353/lib.2008.0018.

Schwartz, Joan M., and Terry Cook. "Archives, Records and Power: The Making of Modern Memory." *Archival Science* 2, nos. 1–2 (2002): 1–19. https://doi.org/10.1007/BF02435628.

Sheffield, Rebecka T. "More than Acid-Free Folders: Extending the Concept of Preservation to Include Stewardship of Unexplored Histories." *Library Trends* 64, no. 3 (2016): 572–84. https://doi.org/10.1353/lib.2016.0001.

Stoler, Ann Laura. *Along the Archival Grain: Epistemic Anxieties and Colonial Common Sense*. Princeton, NJ: Princeton University Press, 2009.

Sutherland, Tonia. "Archival Amnesty: In Search of Black American Transitional and Restorative Justice." *Journal of Critical Library and Information Studies* 1, no. 2 (2017): 1–23. https://doi.org/10.24242/jclis.v1i2.42.

Thompson, Edward H. Jr., and Kate M. Bennett. "Measurement of Masculinity Ideologies: A (Critical) Review." *Psychology of Men & Mascu-*

linity 16, no. 2 (April 2015): 115–33. http://dx.doi.org/10.1037/a0038609.

Trace, Ciaran B. "What Is Recorded Is Never Simply 'What Happened': Record Keeping in Modern Organizational Culture." *Archival Science* 2, nos. 1–2 (2002): 137–59. https://doi.org/10.1007/BF02435634.

Trouillot, Michel-Rolph. *Silencing the Past: Power and the Production of History*. Boston, MA: Beacon Press, 1995.

Voss-Hubbard, Anke. "'No Documents-No History': Mary Ritter Beard and the Early History of Women's Archives." *American Archivist* 58, no. 1 (Winter 1995): 16–30. https://doi.org/10.17723/aarc.58.1.hr300127g3142157.

Weld, Kirsten. *Paper Cadavers: The Archives of Dictatorship in Guatemala*. Durham, NC: Duke University Press, 2014.

West, Candace, and Don H. Zimmerman. "Doing Gender." *Gender and Society* 1, no. 2 (June 1987): 125–51. https://doi.org/10.1177/0891243287001002002.

Wetherell, Martha, and Nigel Edley. "Negotiating Hegemonic Masculinity: Imaginary Positions and Psycho-Discursive Practices." *Feminism & Psychology* 9, no. 3 (1999): 335–56. https://doi.org/10.1177/0959353599009003012.

Williams, Stacie M., and Jarrett M. Drake. "Power to the People: Documenting Police Violence in Cleveland." *Journal of Critical Library and Information Studies* 1, no. 2 (2017): 1–27. https://doi.org/10.24242/jclis.v1i2.33.

Wood, Stacy, Kathy Carbone, Marika Cifor, Anne Gilliland, and Ricardo Punzalan. "Mobilizing Records: Re-Framing Archival Description to Support Human Rights." *Archival Science* 14, nos. 3–4 (October 2014): 397–419. https://doi.org/10.1007/s10502-014-9233-1.

Wurl, Joel. "Ethnicity as Provenance: In Search of Values and Principles for Documenting the Immigrant Experience." *Archival Issues* 29, no. 1 (2005): 65–76.

Yakel, Elizabeth. "Archival Representation." *Archival Science* 3, no. 1 (2003): 1–25. https://doi.org/10.1007/BF02438926.

Yakel, Elizabeth, and Deborah A. Torres. "AI: Archival Intelligence and User Expertise." *American Archivist* 66, no. 1 (Spring/Summer 2003): 51–77. https://doi.org/10.17723/aarc.66.1.q022h85pn51n5800.

Chapter 5

THE GENTLEMAN'S GHOST: PATRIARCHAL EUROCENTRIC LEGACIES IN SPECIAL COLLECTIONS DESIGN

Jesse Ryan Erickson

Introduction: Library Neutrality

Special collections reading rooms inherited by research libraries across the Western world were designed for white men. Even as the existence of some of these spaces predate constructions of white masculinity as we understand them today, their interiorities—rooted in the visual language of power and colonialism—have contributed to the processes by which those constructions have been formed. As much as we concern ourselves with promoting diversity in the field and creating research environments that are supportive of greater inclusivity, until we confront this sacred cow head-on, our best efforts to embrace the changing demographics of higher education and scholarship will be ceaselessly marred by this discernable irony. It may not be productive or even possible for us, as institutions, to declare our intent to "decolonize" our spaces without understanding what it means that such spaces are, in essence, living vestiges of the colonial. No, it is not enough for us to simply acknowledge these physical biases in special collections library spatiality. More than that, we must attempt to understand how this condition is a manifestation of years spent mythologizing the intentional rarefication of primary source research. The rarifying of research, or rather the calcification of research practice, is inherently exclusionary.

In his polemical essay, "Is There a Future for Special Collections? And Should There Be? A Polemical Essay," Daniel H. Traister describes this problem in the following terms:

> Our stuff simply cannot be subjected to such risks. Too valuable, too rare, too precious, it is the stuff of scholarship. It exists to be the happy hunting ground of scholars. It should be kept for them, their students, and their work. I agree that this is not an utterly insane point of view. But, contrary to accepted mythologies, it is by no means the only point of view that is conceivable.[1]

Unfortunately, this "point of view" acts as a duplicitous filter intended to weed out the undesirable "other," in part, through affect. Armed with this understanding, there must be recourse to rectification that one can discover in the exploration of the affective dimensions of these spaces. For, on deeper consideration of the nature of affect and its place in reading rooms, we find what Kathleen Stewart has defined as a "bloom-space"—a territory that emerges from the intertwining of bodies with systems of power in the configuration of a refrain. This staccato of affective refrain, in Stewart's understanding, engages with the materiality of space "across real and imaginary social fields and sediments, linking some kind of everything."[2]

In the eyes of some, special collections reading rooms are spaces where bodies interact with things and ideas to produce discoveries and to shed light into the hidden recesses of time. For others, they are places where identities and intellects come to be monitored under the piercing gaze of long-embedded power structures. In an actualization of its own metaphor, reading rooms become performative spaces where white gloves were once worn by their gatekeepers as a symbol of purity. As these gloves were slipped on by these gatekeepers (often with dramatic flourish) under the guise of preservation, the act of doing so

---

1. Daniel H. Traister, "Is There a Future for Special Collections? And Should There Be? A Polemical Essay," *RBM: A Journal of Rare Books, Manuscripts and Cultural Heritage* 1, no. 1 (January 2000): 61, http://repository.upenn.edu/library_papers/22.

2. Kathleen Stewart, "Worlding Refrains," in *The Affect Theory Reader*, ed. by Melissa Gregg and Gregory J. Seigworth (Durham, NC: Duke University Press, 2010), 340.

was closely akin to the performance of a ritual. These gloves, after all, are also the white gloves of the magician. Nevertheless, current trends oblige those working in the field today to rail collectively against this *tradition of the white glove*, also under the guise of preservation. Below the surface, however, this could be yet another one of the field's attempts to divorce itself from its own elitist image. Why? Is our push toward the egalitarian truly in anticipation of a more diverse future? Is it really in the interest of promoting greater access and inclusivity?

The primary assertion underlying the imperative for a recognition of spatial bias in reading rooms is premised upon a notion that libraries are *not*, and *never have been*, neutral entities. The question itself of whether libraries can be neutral is still being debated. At the American Library Association's (ALA) 2018 Midwinter Meeting, former president Jim Neal moderated a conversation around this question. The responsibility of positioning library neutrality as one of the profession's foremost ethical imperatives fell to James LaRue and Em Claire Knowles. "Neutrality," LaRue maintains, "is about the refusal to deny people access to a shared resource just because we don't like the way they think."[3] He concludes, somewhat ahistorically, that neutrality "is enshrined in our values, our laws, and our policies."[4] Chris Bourg and R. David Lankes offered counterarguments to the question. Bourg provided some historical context to the discussion by noting that one cannot call attention to a need for neutrality in libraries without first coming to terms with the reality that "the origin of public libraries in the U.S. is inextricably tied to the fact that the history of the United States is a history of settler colonialism, of slavery, of segregation, and of state-sponsored discrimination."[5] Included in the conversation were a group of panelists—among them, Emily Drabinski and Emily Knox. In articulating their stance against the idea that libraries should or can

---

3. American Library Association. "Are Libraries Neutral?" *American Libraries*, June 2018, 33-34.

4. American Library Association. "Are Libraries Neutral?" 33-34.

5. American Library Association, 34.

be neutral, both Drabinski and Knox argued that libraries as material entities are constantly making choices that are reflective of larger local, national, and global conversations.[6] This set of circumstances, in their view, is particularly resonant with how the library has had to grapple with controversial problems concerning race relations. Accordingly, the decisions made in libraries by staff and professionals at all levels are persistently political, either implicitly or explicitly.

Reading between the lines of this debate, one can extrapolate that libraries, as an institution, encompass an infrastructure that was founded upon hierarchical, colonial, and exclusionary modalities of power. Historically, institutions of this nature have needed to be pushed toward the egalitarian through conscious and unwavering civic activism. The argument for neutrality clearly positions itself from an egalitarian center. But the emphasis on equitable access to "a shared resource" by diverse groups ignores the myriad ways that longstanding institutional disparities have manifested themselves in the materiality of library spaces. It is a position, moreover, that lacks an appreciation of how the spatiality of place can intercede in the complex processes of identity construction and the position of the "self" in relation to the "other." Identities, as Stuart Hall has shown, are not fixed and stable centers from which objectivity can be ascertained through bodily interactions initiated from the internal and directed toward the external.[7] Rather, in a continuous subjective dialogic with the past, Hall argues that "identities are about questions of using the resources of history, language and culture in the process of becoming rather than being: not 'who we are' or 'where we came from,' so much as what we might become, how we have been represented and how that bears on how we might represent ourselves."[8]

Given contemporary understandings of affective subjectivity with respect to processes of identity construction, defenses of the library as

6. American Library Association, 36.

7. Stuart Hall, "Introduction: Who Needs Identity?" in *Questions of Cultural Identity*, ed. Stuart Hall and Paul du Gay (London: SAGE Publications Ltd, 1996), 4.

8. Hall, "Introduction: Who Needs Identity?", 4.

a fundamentally neutral entity silently transform into intellectual arti-facts.[9] A deeply veiled tension between tradition and modernity, rather than conservatism and progressivism, drives the debate, even when the dichotomy itself is based in essentialist fantasy.[10] The same tension pulsates in the patriarchal and Eurocentric impulses of conventional rare book reading rooms. On the one hand, tradition compels stakeholders to adopt the existing historical design conventions of the gentleman's library as the quintessential archetype of what is "proper" for the read-ing room environment. On the other, modernity urges professionals from underrepresented groups and information consumers alike to introduce disruptions to this model in the interest of growth, progress, and sustainability. More tellingly, hypermodernity increasingly pushes the spatial orientation of the nature of identity from an attachment to a collective identity (e.g., nationalism, patriotism, institutionalism, familialism, etc.) to a greater investment in individual identity.[11] This shift is a logical byproduct of individualized, quasi-autonomous acts of globalized capitalistic consumption; it is a new iteration of moder-nity defined, at least in part, by the correspondingly new affordances of internet and communication technologies.[12] Then again, not to fall hopelessly into the trap of technological determinism in perceiving this shift, outlining the contours of this discursive progression should offer a path for us to move beyond the persistence of bibliophilic recursion.

---

9. It should be noted that *Questioning Library Neutrality: Essays from Progressive Librar-ian*, ed. Alison M. Lewis (Duluth, MN: Library Juice Press, 2008) takes up the subject extensively, setting the stage for an activist librarianship that became the subject for subsequent iterations of the debate.

10. Marilyn Strathern makes an analogous argument for how this tension exists in our cultural understandings of temporality, and she describes our relationship with both modernity and tradition as being situated within distinctly "Euro-American" notions of kinship. See Marilyn Strathern, "Enabling Identity? Biology, Choice and the New Reproductive Technologies," in *Questions of Cultural Identity*, 40-44.

11. Although, I should note that more recently a resurgence of polarized and extreme tribalism appears to be on the rise in contemporary political discourse, but one stilled modeled by hyper-individualism.

12. Gilles Lipovetsky and Sébastien Charles, *Hypermodern Times*, trans. Andrew Brown (Cambridge, UK: Polity, 2005), 31-35.

In some ways "real," in other ways "imagined," this recursion extracts a cult-like devotion to a sense of tradition from the implicit legacies of its white male provenance.

In the summer of 2003, the Task Force on Diversity for the Rare Books and Manuscripts Section (RBMS) of the Association of College and Research Libraries (ACRL) submitted its *Diversity Action Plan* to its Executive Committee.[13] This report, which was authored by Julie Grob on behalf of the task force, included a number of alarming findings that outline the depth and scope of the field's diversity problem. The report opens by calling out "ethnic homogeneity" in the field, noting that a 1997 survey of the RBMS' membership revealed that ninety-six percent of its members were white.[14] Having identified some of the more difficult challenges in dealing with this problem, the RBMS made a concerted effort to foster greater diversity within its membership. Since the time of this report's release, a follow-up survey conducted in 2015 showed that at least some modest progress had been made on this front.[15] For the most part, however, the specific issue of white hegemony in special collections library spatiality received comparatively less attention. Grob notes that, historically, "university libraries that received rare book collections created special rooms to house them that incorporated the sumptuous furniture and wood-paneled walls of a gentleman's library."[16] She cites the Doheny Memorial Library of the University of Southern California's Treasure Room as a clear example of the materiality of the field's elitism. Grob leaves the issue there, however, focusing instead on some of the other challenges related to diversity in special collections librarianship.

---

13. A Division of the American Library Association.

14. Julie Grob, "RBMS, Special Collections, and the Challenge of Diversity: The Road to the Diversity Action Plan," *RBM: A Journal of Rare Books, Manuscripts, and Cultural Heritage* 4, no. 2 (2003): 74-107, doi:10.5860/rbm.4.2.219.

15. From approximately ninety-five percent down to eighty-seven percent by 2015. See Elspeth Healey and Melissa Nykanen, "Channeling Janus: Past, Present, and Future in the RBMS Membership Survey," *RBM: A Journal of Rare Books, Manuscripts, and Cultural Heritage* 17, no. 1 (2016): 58, https://doi.org/10.5860/rbm.17.1.461.

16. Grob, "RBMS, Special Collections, and the Challenge of Diversity," 78.

Singling out the absence of an in-depth discussion about the lack of diverse representation in library spatiality in Grob's *Diversity Action Plan* is not the fault of the report itself. The document has made a vital contribution to the field by introducing its members to the broader diversity problem in special collections and setting the general parameters of the discourse. However, recent developments in library and information studies, both in pedagogical and practical terms, have set the stage for us to take a fresh look at our research spaces, particularly within special collections. The emergence of critical librarianship, led by library scholars and professionals such as Safiya U. Noble, Lisa Janicke Hinchliffe, Emily Drabinski, Meghan Sitar, Maura Seale, Rose L. Chou, and Annie Pho, has contributed to intermediations ranging from combatting misrepresentation in the ever-evolving systems of knowledge organization to identify and address microaggressions experienced by professionals of color working in the field.[17] Not unconnected, the maturation of critical bibliography, under the direction of Michael Suarez, Caroline Wigginton, Barbara Heritage and others, has provided a path for exploring how the study of the materiality of texts can support inclusion and social justice. Bibliographic scholarship, it should be stated, is an area of study that is deeply invested in rare book reading rooms as research spaces. New materialism, moreover, considers how a space works to shape its environment in affective non-human agentic instantiations of co-construction.[18] A materialism that accounts for the subjective experience is the connective tissue that cogently binds the pursuit of change.

Taken together, these different streams of development provide us with the language needed to analyze identity in relation to the spaces and the things with which we interact in the process of producing

---

17. Kenny Garcia, "Keeping Up with Critical Librarianship," *Association of College & Research Libraries: A Division of the American Library Association*, accessed December 7, 2018, http://www.ala.org/acrl/publications/keeping_up_with/critlib.

18. Rick Dolphijn and Iris Van Der Tuin, *New Materialism: Interviews & Cartographies, New Metaphysics* (Ann Arbor: Open Humanities Press, 2012), https://quod.lib.umich.edu/o/ohp/11515701.0001.001/1:5.2/--new -materialism-interviews-cartographies?r gn=div2;view=fulltext.

knowledge. The transdisciplinarity of these various schools of thought become essential to the praxis of paradigmatic redirection. Accepting the limitations of its literal temporality being situated in ableism (e.g., sight) and heteronormativity—insofar as it foregrounds an Oedipal complex as a locus of apperception-induced temporal rupture—the Lacanian "mirror stage" argument has had to contend, not only with the mirror in its capacity to reflect the self in that earliest marker in the development of relational subjectivity, but also with the mirror's image as an "object" of apperception. Reflections are altered by visible manipulations ranging from the subtle (e.g., the specific angle or position of the mirror) to the absurd (e.g., the smoothness of the surface, or that which produces the "funhouse" mirror image). Extending the metaphor, so too do the affective dimensions of the spaces where we produce knowledge shape, mold, warp, frame, and distort the subjective experience of *doing* research.[19] This experience, in effect, constitutes the impact of things colliding with bodies.[20]

Desktop Panopticism

The extent of the literature on special collections reading rooms that professionals are likely to consult for their practice comes in the form of field-specific manuals like Steven K. Galbraith and Geoffrey D. Smith's *Rare Book Librarianship: An Introduction and Guide*, Sidney E. Berger's *Rare Books and Special Collections*, and Alison Cullingford's *The Special Collections Handbook*. Of the three listed, Cullingford's book, which is a very effective manual in terms of what it sets out to achieve, was written primarily for readers in the United Kingdom. Still, many of the practical

---

19. Jacques Lacan, "The Mirror Stage as the Formative I Function as Revealed in Psychoanalytic Experience," chap. 1 in *Écrits: A Selection*, trans. Bruce Fink (New York: W.W. Norton, 2004). It seems to me that the awareness of self-consciousness, with respect to the research process, is inextricably tied to the material forces that work in concert with human agency, and through interaction and perception (as much as the apperceptive apriority), produce the "experience."

20. As in Gilles Deleuze and Félix Guattari's reframing of the Oedipal complex in their *Anti-Oedipus: Capitalism and Schizophrenia* (New York: Viking Press, 1977).

instructions it contains are relevant to the field as it is practiced in the United States.

In her chapter covering "user services," Cullingford folds subsections on "visitor experience" and reading room design into a broader section titled, "Managing Special Collections Visitors."[21] The guidelines provided in this text are primarily mundane assessments rooted in the expectation of routine special collections operations. An *ideal visitor* is implied throughout many of the section's listed bullet points, imagined, it seems, as a genderless, neuro-typical person of an unstated racial or ethnic background (though it is difficult for one not to imagine a white male researcher *of a certain age* when reading through the list). It is suggested, for instance, that visitors "will appreciate advice on where to buy food," without a consideration of culturally inflected culinary proclivities or socio-economically determined limitations on spending. We are instructed to provide "lighting that enables readers to see well without strain," implicitly assuming a particular construction of visibility premised upon ableist standards of research practice.[22] Berger's chapter on special collections library spatiality likewise opts to omit reference to the racial demographics or cultural backgrounds of potential visitors.[23] Moreover, the historicity of "old spaces" is virtually stripped out of his section on reading room renovation. Much of the section deals specifically with the challenges of cost, storage, temperature control, and other physical conditions.[24] Questions about existing interior design conventions that privilege Eurocentric histories are also left unaddressed.

Many of the works in this genre contain a chapter or section devoted to security and theft prevention. Theft prevention is typically discussed as a matter of preservation. Under the current model, researchers can never

---

21. Alison Cullingford, *The Special Collections Handbook* (London: Facet Publishing, 2011), 151-52.

22. Cullingford, *The Special Collections Handbook*, 154-55.

23. Sidney E. Berger, *Rare Books and Special Collections* (Chicago: Neal-Schuman, an Imprint of the American Library Association, 2014), 166-68.

24. Berger, *Rare Books and Special Collections*, 167.

be afforded a level of trust that would abolish the need for surveillance. And yet, in order to have a better grasp on the affective dimensions at play in library spaces, we must consider how surveillance can shape the experience of research and contribute to the othering of diverse populations. The professional literature provides no shortage of recommendations for how to conduct surveillance. Cullingford, for example, notes that the positioning of the staff desk "needs to be angled so that staff can see what readers are doing, but readers do not feel oppressed."[25] To put it slightly differently, readers must be watched and they must understand that they are being watched, but they must be treated as if they are not being watched. The casual call for a soft surveillance is illuminative of power relations involved with special collections spaces that are at once visible and invisible. In this case, on the exterior, power can be exercised through a combination of technological and human agency.

The image of the staff member watching from the desk, often on a computer screen that displays closed circuit video surveillance, comports with Michel Foucault's description of Jeremy Bentham's vision of the Panopticon – an experimental building modeled to be an architecturally enabled unit for mass observation.[26] The implicit contract between researcher and staff to agree to the watcher/watched relationship, reinforced by the user registration form, is performed both through staff members' observations of researchers and through the researchers' awareness of being surveilled. Yet it also functions in the Foucauldian sense, in a "concerted distribution of bodies, surfaces, lights, gazes; in an arrangement whose internal mechanisms produce the relation in which individuals are caught up."[27] Framing reading room surveillance within the construct of the Panopticon can be seen as part of the larger effort to employ critical theory for the benefit of library operations. The "postmodern turn" in library and information studies has been

25. Cullingford, *The Special Collections Handbook*, 156.

26. Michel Foucault, *Discipline and Punish: The Birth of the Prison*, trans. Alan Sheridan (New York: Vintage Books, 1995).

27. Foucault, *Discipline and Punish: The Birth of the Prison*, 204.

effective in bringing greater awareness to modalities of power operating at the institutional level. Drawing upon Foucauldian discourse analysis, for instance, Gary P. Radford argues that the "library experience" can be dislodged from positivistic formulations of *arriving at* knowledge to poststructuralist articulations of *producing* knowledge.[28] The production of knowledge, we learn, occurs through a discursive practice that accounts for the interplay of the subjective and the imaginary.[29]

The Derridean method of semiotic analysis known as "deconstruction" has been utilized in the decoding of the field's professional discourse.[30] This discourse, evidently, is populated by platitudes and value-based rhetorical abstractions.[31] David Woolwine notes that, with Derridean deconstruction, there are no "transcendental signifiers," and, consequently, "the meanings of texts only arise within an interpretive act which entails connections to other texts."[32] According to this form of analysis, professional rhetoric, especially a rhetoric steeped in abstraction-based language, much like identity, cannot be fixed. It will change alongside varying interpretations that have unique relevance for different concerns. In this manner, paying closer attention to the way that language is used within the profession can be revelatory of the

---

28. Gary P. Radford, "Flaubert, Foucault, and the Bibliotheque Fantastique: Toward a Postmodern Epistemology for Library Science," *Library Trends* 46, no. 4 (Spring 1998): 616.

29. Radford, "Flaubert, Foucault, and the Bibliotheque Fantastique," 616-18. For a similar discussion on how this paradigmatic shift applies to the experience of library spatiality, see Gary P. Radford, Marie L. Radford., and Jessica Lingel, "The Library as Heterotopia: Michel Foucault and the Experience of Library Space," *Journal of Documentation* 71, no. 4 (2015): 733, doi:10.1108/JD-01-2014-0006.

30. Employing the term "deconstruction," I refer to the method developed by poststructural theorist Jacques Derrida. The term is used to describe the process of using philosophical analysis to destabilize longstanding dichotomies that are foundational to Western language(s) and thought.

31. S.W. Staninger, "Deconstructing Reorganizations in Libraries," *Library Leadership and Management* 28, no. 2 (2014): 2, https://journals.tdl.org/llm/index.php/llm/article/view/7057/6279.

32. David Woolwine, "The Patriot Act and Early ALA Action: Habermas, Strauss, or Derrida?" *Library Philosophy and Practice* (October 2009): 7, http://www.uidaho.edu/~mbolin/lp&p.htm.

fluid power relations that continue to define the practice. The subtitle, "Managing Special Collections Visitors," for example, which Cullingford uses as a paratextual device for engendering a sense of coherence to the instructional content of her book, couches itself within a veil of objectivity to render the language of power and control (i.e., "Managing … Visitors") to a benign state of tacit approval.[33] The interpretation of the operant gerund (i.e., "Managing") in the subtitle will change depending on readers' personal experiences with either managing or being managed. Nevertheless, linguistic abstractions that circulate within the field's professional discourse can support existing power relations, many of which are symptomatically hierarchical.

The strategic employment of "equal protection" and "equal opportunity" rhetoric within the field—like the idea that library neutrality offers "equal access" to a "shared resource"—is a case in point. The idea is incongruous with the reality of institutional racism. The use of such rhetoric is flawed, not only because it ignores the persistence of white supremacy in the deepest fabrics of Western society, but also because it places the responsibility for overcoming it primarily on those who are oppressed within the constructs of its corrosive and restrictive regimes. In the words of Charles R. Lawrence III, "the understanding of this ideology provides valuable insight into the seductive powers of the ideology of equal opportunity as well as into our resistance to abandoning one of its most critical conceptual images: the intent requirement."[34] The question remains: equal opportunity for whom? Racism does not need to take the form of overt acts performed with a conscious intent to promote one's bigotry, express bias, or engage in racial violence. It can be unconscious and silent, though no less malignant. Institutional racism, in particular, functions through a profound cultural embeddedness that has outlasted much of the intentionality of its human agency.

---

33. Cullingford, *The Special Collections Handbook*, 153.

34. Charles R. Lawrence III, "The Id, the Ego, and Equal Protection: Reckoning with Unconscious Racism," in *Critical Race Theory: The Key Writings That Formed the Movement*, ed. Kimberlé Crenshaw, Neil Gotanda, Gary Peller, and Kendall Thomas (New York: New Press, 1995), 239.

Moving from the rhetorical to the experiential, the panoptic qualities that are at work in special collections reading rooms exist in both the symbolic and the material realms. Of course, this phenomenon is not limited to the reading room experience in special collections libraries or even libraries in general. Symbolically, "justice is blind" but the sculptural representations of that symbol standing at the foot of our courthouses enduringly privilege a Eurocentric model of feminine beauty that its blindfold cannot conceal. Similarly, the Eurocentric architectural motifs and interior design features that dominate in special collections reading rooms can activate a deeper layer of the panoptic in the minds of researchers and professionals of color working on either side of the reference desk. It is not only the awareness that we are being watched, or the perception that we are being watched more closely than our white male peers, that is at work here; it is the multitude of subtle aesthetic details that together convey the message that "we do not belong."

The fact that women and racial minorities were barred access to these spaces for so many generations in the history of higher learning still resonates in a way that requires removing oneself from a culturally comfortable space (i.e., one's home or community) to an imposingly menacing one. The remoteness of these archival research spaces, which are often walled off or geographically distant from communities of color, and isolated from the other parts of a parent library, helps to create this atmosphere. Cullingford's *Handbook* alludes to this remoteness with a single word phrased as a question: "Barriers?"[35] Decades earlier, Charles W. Mann implored that rare book reading rooms "must avoid at all costs becoming a last bastion of class differences in the shape of a quiet museum at the top of a stairwell."[36] You can insert race and gender differences alongside class in that sentence to visualize a more accurate picture of this reputation of institutional exclusivity. However, the symbolic forces at work in the materiality of these spaces become

---

35. Cullingford, *The Special Collections Handbook*, 154.

36. Charles W. Mann, "The Role of Rare Books in a University Library," *The Courier* 9, no. 3 (1972): 28, https://surface.syr.edu/cgi/viewcontent.cgi?article=1078&context=libassoc.

literal when it comes to policing bodies of color. Moments of social friction arise when people enter these spaces and are deemed to be "out of place." The judgment typically occurs in relation to predispositions that are nurtured by Eurocentric aesthetic sensibilities. Cultural capital becomes determinant in the silent assessments of whether a visitor's presence is acceptable.[37] Rigid expectations of aesthetic conformity can create an atmosphere where one's fashion choices alone can present barriers to access, especially when the attire integrates aspects of popular culture (e.g., hip hop and "urban contemporary") that have been demonized by negative stereotypes and the reigning standards of social respectability.[38]

Regrettably, external conformity to the acceptable range of aesthetic expression will not guarantee protections from the byproducts of unconscious racism. Consider, for a moment, an incident that occurred at Catholic University of America's Judge Kathryn J. Dufour Law Library. On October 10, 2018, Juán-Pabló González, a student researcher of color, was removed from the premises by the University's law enforcement primarily because Brittany McNurlin, the student library assistant on staff that day, did not believe that he had the right to study in that space. González explained to McNurlin that he was also a library employee and that, as a graduate student at the University's library school, he had, in fact, obtained the necessary permission to study in that building. The incident prompted the coining of the phrase "studying while Black."[39] McNurlin, who reportedly had volunteered for the Veterans Consortium and the Capital Area Immigrant Rights Coalition, has refused to acknowledge that race was a factor in her decision to call the police on González. However, the relatively high frequency with which men and women of color have the police called on them for the

---

37. And here I employ the term "cultural capital" as described in Pierre Bourdieu, "The Forms of Capital," in *Handbook of Theory and Research for the Sociology of Education*, ed. John G. Richardson (Westport, Conn.: Greenwood Press, 1986), 243-48.

38. Lipovetsky, *Hypermodern Times*, 37-38.

39. Michael Harriot, "Video: Librarian Calls Cops on Student for Brazen Attempt at #StudyingWhileBlack [Updated]," WYPIPO, Root, October 24, 2018, https://www.theroot.com/video-librarian-calls-cops-on-student-for-brazen -attem-1829940301.

most quotidian activities suggests that unconscious racial bias remains a pervasive aspect of our daily interactions. Again, we find a case where bodies colliding with a space can provoke instances of unconscious racial exclusion. A reactive approach to policy development that waits for clearer and more unambiguous acts of racial discrimination to occur before addressing the disparities in the library experience among diverse populations completely disregards advancements in critical race theory like Derrick A. Bell Jr.'s "racial realist" approach to jurisprudence.[40] In calling upon the rhetoric of equal opportunity, we ignore the harsh reality with which underrepresented groups must contend in navigating an educational system founded upon white supremacy.

The Status Quo

We live in a world where rare book reading rooms are designed to look like a gentleman's study. But how did we get here? Despite all of the attempts to recreate an artificial aesthetic based on its own historicity, rare book collections and the libraries that house them are largely understood to be products of the twentieth century.[41] However, one must look back to a period beginning around the end of the nineteenth century to locate the historical moment at which these collections and their spaces really start to emerge in the style with which we are familiar today. This period, which focused on acquisitions of the largest and most complete collections of the West's "rarest" editions, continues to be looked upon as the golden age of rare book librarianship. It stretched well into the second half of the twentieth century.[42] The bibliophilic zeal that brought about some of America's most prestigious libraries can be traced to competitive book collecting by familial dynasties and new-money millionaires. These wealthy collectors—most notably,

---

40. Derrick A. Bell Jr., "Racial Realism," in *Critical Race Theory: The Key Writings That Formed the Movement*, ed. Kimberlé Crenshaw, Neil Gotanda, Gary Peller, and Kendall Thomas (New York: New Press, 1995), 302.

41. Steven Kenneth Galbraith and Geoffrey D. Smith, *Rare Book Librarianship: An Introduction and Guide* (Santa Barbara, Calif.: Libraries Unlimited, 2012), 2-9.

42. Galbraith and Smith, *Rare Book Librarianship: An Introduction and Guide*, 5-6.

John Pierpont Morgan, William Andrews Clark, and Henry Edwards Huntington—began building their collections in earnest by the early 1900s, largely by exploiting Europe's post-World War I rare book market. Perhaps as capitalists, as products of the Gilded Age, they needed an infusion of "taste" to complement their growing status as the nation's elite. All the same, by the time these men took up the pursuit of legacy building, librarianship had already started developing, both in the trade of rare books and in the nomenclature of special collections.[43] Across the Atlantic, eighteenth-century antiquarianism—associated with bibliographers, amateur historians, and independent scholars like Thomas Frognall Dibdin, Thomas Phillips, and Samuel Weller Singer—set many of the trends in place that would later be adopted in nascent practices of professional rare book librarianship, both in the U.S. and abroad.[44] A network of bibliographic reciprocities was set in place with reverberations that would intertwine the worlds of private book collectors and booksellers, auctioneers, museum curators, and academics, all involved in some way with a larger mission to advance knowledge and preserve history and culture.[45]

The basic narrative for this spatial ontology is one that is told and retold. The year 1884, for example, witnessed the establishment of Brown University's first special collections library:

> Begun by Albert Gorton Greene, Class of 1820, expanded by Caleb Fiske Harris, class of 1834, and bequeathed to Brown by Senator Henry Brown Anthony, Class of 1833, the Harris Collection had long

---

43. The combined use of "rare books" and "reading room" as professional terminology in nineteenth-century library literature can be found, for example, in David Masson, *The British Museum, Historical and Descriptive* (Chambers's Instructive and Entertaining Library Edinburgh: W. and R. Chambers, 1850), 420-21; and Frederick M. Crunden, "How We Protect Rare and Illustrated Books: St. Louis Public Library," *Library Journal* 15, no. 4 (1890): 104.

44. Eric Holzenberg, "Book Collecting," *Encyclopædia Britannica*, Encyclopædia Britannica, Inc. Last modified May 24, 2017. https://www.britannica.com/topic/book-collecting.

45. This basic network of relationships continues to be relevant in contemporary collection development practices in special collections librarianship. For example, see Vanessa King, "Special Collections: What Are They and How Do We Build Them?" *International Journal of Legal Information* 46, no. 2 (2018): 91, doi:10.1017/jli.2018.12.

been renowned as one of the largest and most important collections of Americana in private hands, its aim being to collect every printed work of American and Canadian poetry and drama from colonial times onward…Recognizing its importance, the library placed the collection in a specially secured room, where over the next twenty years it would be joined by other books identified as rare. The Harris Collection was Brown's first major special collection in the modern sense and the Harris Room the library's first specifically designated rare book room.[46]

This description on the founding of John Hay Library's Harris Room encapsulates the interconnectedness of bibliophilic networks: book-dealers, scholars, and administrators who structure the grounds of modern-day rare book reading rooms. Complete with tautological claims of its own value together with unattainable utopian visions of absolute possession, the narrative is emblematic of an impulse that would drive other research libraries to advance along similar lines. The rare book room's original interior was designed in a style that would closely match the public imagination of an aristocratic household library; this would be the *ideal study*.

As part of the public imagination, the image of the ideal study has been a subject of fascination for bibliophiles across generations. In 1887, the British bibliophile J. Rogers Rees offered his account of the ideal:

> To begin with the room itself. It should be of moderate size, not too large, for I have always considered that an extensive apartment of this kind encourages the mind to wander; in smaller space it is more concentrated, bound down, as it were, to the work it sets itself to accomplish.

> The objects around should be in keeping with the frame of mind a man desires to encourage when alone in his study, and should not be numerous. They should be household gods, loved for their beauty or associations; should have their fixed positions allotted them, and be kept there, so that no seeking with the eye should disturb a course of thought. The pictures and busts, the very furniture and its distribution, must be made subservient to the dreams or work of the occupier of the nook. (85-86)

---

46. Mark N. Brown et al. *Special Collections at Brown University: A History and Guide*, ed. Leslie T. Wendel (Providence, R.I.: Friends of the Library of Brown University, 1988), 22.

There is a familiarity to the ideal as described by Rees. He allows for a certain degree of subjectivity to shape the space, just as he acknowledges, in his own way, that the space will also correspondingly have an impact on the act of studying. Despite that, his imagination limits itself to a conventional range of customary design features. According to this view, the design should complement the occupant of study (ordinarily assumed "male" even if gender is not made explicit). The room's "objects ... should be in keeping with the frame of mind *a man desires*" (emphasis added). He expects these objects will be "pictures and busts."

Modeling spatiality is inevitably an exercise of abstraction. It lacks the specificity of a case study or microanalysis, always verging on the Platonistic. Looking at the subject in the lens of theory, modeling allows us to single out some of the core elements of rare book reading room design. These elements are found in varying instantiations but essentially follow a predetermined template. There are a least three standard models for special collections architecture and interior design that are still relatively commonplace: the historic house museum, the blended, and the assimilative. The models are made up of concentric circles emanating from a center that has the gentleman's study as its nexus (see **Figure 1**). Historic house museum libraries emerged rather organically from the provenances of their collections' founders. Their legacies have formed the basis for some of the more culturally prestigious libraries in the United States – libraries like the Morgan Library, the Huntington Library, the William Andrews Clark Memorial Library, and the Rosenbach.[47] Such collection spaces are designed to fully maintain the look and the feel of the collector's study. They lend the impression of bibliophilic temples devoted less to fresh scholarship and more to the storied legacies of the founding collectors. The enduring, posthumous presence of these collectors is edified in portraits and busts that decorate the walls and corners alongside the standing floor globes and tapestries displayed throughout the spaces. Ethereal gazes emanate

---

47. Eric Holzenberg, "Book Collecting," *Encyclopædia Britannica*, Encyclopædia Britannica, Inc.

from the objects as a perpetual reminder of their exalted place in the histories of these collections.

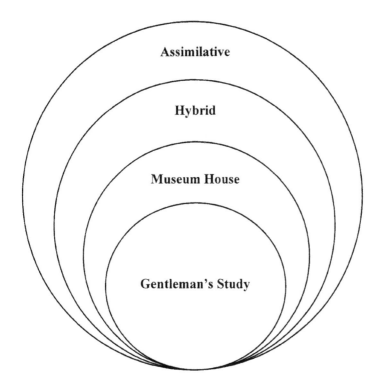

Figure. 1. Current Models for Special Collections Reading Room Design.

Next, the blended model, the most common of the three, is a combination of the traditional library reading room and the gentleman's study. It is most frequently found in university special collections and the archival collections of historical societies. These spaces are characterized by the selective incorporation of many of the design features that define a gentleman's study. This would include mahogany or chestnut-colored furniture, carpets ranging from cool to dark in palette, low lighting, and other decorative features that are evocative of a traditional Western study. In place of founding collectors' portraits and busts, there might be portraits of the institution's historically most celebrated librarians and collection builders, or there could be statuettes and portraits dedicated to notable literary figures representative of the institution's collection strengths. As a blended space, however, an attempt is often made to integrate features of contemporary design. Most often, these features include ergonomically driven choices that accommodate collection use and technological considerations that would enhance efficiency in visitor services. This fusion between tradition and modernity democratizes the space to increasingly diverse populations. However, in the face of overarching security and preservation concerns, it has moved in this direction in a limited capacity.

The assimilative model, the least common of the three, is usually found in research centers for underrepresented groups. It is sometimes used for independent archival collections. Its approach to design adopts Western conventions to serve specific communities. It is assimilative, so instead of any radical divergence from the convention there is only substitution. In other words, Eurocentric portraits and busts are replaced by similar types of art and artifacts more representative of the cultural backgrounds highlighted in the collections. Much like the blended model, many of the familiarities of conventional reading room design are present in these spaces, including the style of furniture, the lighting, and the carpeting. The difference is that, instead of a bust of Shakespeare or Gutenberg, one might find—such as in an Africana studies research center—a West African mask or a painting of Toussaint L'Ouverture.

Collectively, these models represent a status quo that has been in place for well over a century. The radically collaborative, function-oriented shift in interior design that has already occurred in public libraries has been slow to penetrate the present stasis of the rare book reading room. Andrew Carnegie's mahogany dream fades as it succumbs to the rising tide of the sparkling new makerspace. That Carnegie-like vision, rigid and unyielding, survives in special collections. Design features that define the status quo in special collections may seem innocuous to most; in some cases, they may be considered the most appropriate fit for the space. But these features also carry with them the capacity to be deleterious to the advancement of knowledge, particularly as it is understood in the paradigms of intersectional inclusivity.

Coupled with the awareness that special collections as research environments are panoptic spaces, conventional reading room interior design choices can contribute to a previously unnamed phenomenon that I call the "reading room effect." The reading room effect is both cognitive and affective. The affect of the space works to trigger involuntary bodily responses: feelings of nervousness, an increased heart rate when entering special collections spaces, shakiness when handling rare and expensive materials, or a hushed queasiness in the practice and performance of archival research. While I call this phenomenon the "reading room effect," it is actually a range of effects inducing "double consciousness" in elliptical rarefaction.[48] Simultaneous waves of anxiety and wonder subconsciously oscillate within while one works in the space. Anxiety accompanies the intake of the grandiosity, and there is a sense of wonder in seeing the painterly splendor, the classical beauty ascribed to the space through treasures displayed on tables, in cases, and around the room. The effects are intensified when researchers from historically marginalized and oppressed groups handle objects from their own cultural heritages. There is a gnawing awareness that such objects were, at some point, acquired through geopolitical means— a provenance engendered by centuries of global inequality. Elliptical in its ability to generate epistemological affectations of civilizational rootedness, the affectations are fashioned through the tactical use of the historical signifiers of traditional intellectualism (e.g., standing floor globes, antique rugs, and portraits and busts of "great men"). Likewise, it rarefies the intellectual density of knowledge diversity, converting that complexity into a narrow construct of knowledge production. In this way, producing knowledge is subliminally informed by the misguided

---

48. And here I refer, of course, to the Du Boisian "double-consciousness" of experiencing the world both as a person of color and as a person possessing an awareness of the expectation to conform to the standards set by white hegemony. See W.E.B. Du Bois, Souls of Black Folks Essays and Sketches, 1979 ed., *Great Illustrated Classics* (New York: Dodd, Mead, 1979).

notion that Eurocentricity is the principal source of both civilizational antiquity and global modernity.

Remedial Spatialization

In October 2017, Charlottesville's Rare Book School held its first Bibliography Among the Disciplines international conference.[49] During this conference, the American Philosophical Society hosted a roundtable discussion dedicated to starting a conversation about bibliography's complicated relations to its colonialist and imperialist history. Participants spoke at length about bibliography's potential for promoting social justice. Race was an obvious subject that needed to be addressed. The roundtable convened in reaction to an earlier incident that had moved the realities of racism right up to the doorstep of the Rare Book School. The incident in question was the Unite the Right rally, organized to protest plans to remove a statue of Robert E. Lee from Emancipation Park in Charlottesville, Virginia.[50] On August 12, 2017, Charlottesville was the scene of civic unrest when rally marchers—populated mostly by members of various neo-Nazi and white supremacists groups—encountered anti-fascist protesters and social justice activists who were vehemently opposed to their demonstration.[51] The meeting of these two opposing ideologies—one based on racism and bigotry, the other based on diversity and equality—tragically turned from pugilistic to homicidal when James Alex Fields Jr. drove his 2010 Dodge Challenger into a crowd of counter-protesters, killing thirty-two-year-old activist Heather Heyer and injuring at least nineteen others. Charlottesville, which has hosted the

---

49. The event was organized with the support of the Andrew W. Mellon Foundation and the new Mellon Society of Fellows in Critical Bibliography. Caroline Wigginton, "Critical Bibliography and Social Justice," American Philosophical Society (blog), December 21, 2017, https://www.amphilsoc.org/blog/critical-bibliography-and-social-justice.

50. Also called the "Charlottesville rally."

51. Fenit Nirappil, "McAuliffe Has Change of Heart on Confederate Statues," *Washington Post* (Washington, D.C.), August 16, 2017, https://www.washingtonpost.com/local/virginia-politics/following-charlottesville-northam-says-hell-urge-removal-of-confederate-statues/2017/08/16/d6bfc7ea-82aa-11e7-b359-15a3617c767b_story.html?utm_term=.f06e4d9e74b7.

Rare Book School since 1992, resuscitated important questions concerning the state of diversity within the field of book-historical scholarship after this tragic incident. The fact that the materiality of our research spaces continues to contribute to longstanding practices of exclusion shows that we are still a long way from fully embracing diversity.

The Charlottesville rally is a horrific example of bodies colliding with things over space. It led us to question what objects (i.e., things), as symbols within an ideology, represent within a given space. From the Confederate flag to the Liberty Bell, from the "border wall" to the Statue of Liberty, objects and territories can become symbols that permeate the national consciousness and evolve in ways that are largely removed from their original meanings. It is important to look at cultural objects as symbols in relation to spatiality, again and again, and with a perspective that recognizes their susceptibility to post-structural semiotic mutability. In a sense, the imperative to reconsider our special collections reading rooms as the physical embodiment of the field's diversity problem is not extraneous to the debate over the preservation of Confederate monuments. Many of these statues were erected during the Jim Crow era as part of a post-Reconstruction campaign to reassert the status and permanency of white dominance in America's institutions. Others were commissioned during the Civil Rights Movement for the same purpose. Defenders of these monuments have routinely relied on historical revisionism to bolster their claims that the statues are wedded to the preservation of the South's cultural history. As a compulsion to revel in nostalgia, such defenses ignore the fact that the Confederacy was, ultimately, a treasonous enterprise. And yet, up until recently, a deeply embedded institutional racism has enabled these statues to stand in the nation's public spaces for decades without serious, sustained critical scrutiny.

Some may think that looking at the Robert E. Lee statue aspect of the Charlottesville rally in relation to special collections reading room design is an offensive and sophistic misrepresentation, considering the degree to which agents of the most devastating human atrocities are commemorated in the former and champions for the cultivation of knowledge and learning are celebrated in the latter. It is easy for us to distance ourselves from the possibility that the two can exist either in parallel or in syzygy. However, reading this example as a simple one-to-one analogy misses a more crucial point that seeks out the inter-connectedness between historical revisionism, public memory, and the affective dimensions of materiality at play in both. In rejecting rigid ethical dichotomies, one finds that the dividing line separating the history of policing the bodies of racialized others and the history of supporting their intellectual cultivation in the United States may not be so distinct.

Issues of class, race, ethnicity, and gender are inextricably tied to the legacies of America's most prominent book collectors. Huntington, for instance, as the owner of the Pacific Electric Railway Company, relied on local law enforcement to police temporary railway workers from Mexico and put an end to their attempts to unionize and strike under the Unión Federal Mexicanos.[52] In the spring of 1903, Hunting-ton authorized a series of unscrupulous business tactics to ensure that organizers did not succeed in their efforts to secure better wages and sanitary living conditions. This story of migrant exploitation, which was "the first twentieth-century confrontation between Mexican workers and the LAPD," is not reflected in the spaces that house a collection that was, at least in part, acquired through the wealth attained from the exploitation of these laborers.[53] But unlike Confederate monuments, most rare book research spaces cannot simply be removed or taken down as a suitable remedy for contemporary cultural restitution. Prag-matism and the actualities of real-world operations compel us to let the philanthropic underpinnings of these spaces outweigh the possibility of pursuing such drastic measures.

---

52. Jeffrey Marcos Garcilazo, *Traqueros: Mexican Railroad Workers in the United States, 1870 to 1930*, Al Filo: Mexican American Studies Series, no. 6 (Denton, Tex.: UNT Press, 2012), 96-102.

53. "The Los Angeles Police Department," see Edward J. Escobar, *Race, Police, and the Making of a Political Identity: Mexican Americans and the Los Angeles Police Department, 1900-1945*, Latinos in American Society and Culture, vol. 7 (Berkeley: University of California Press, 1999), 37-38.

How then can we account for these histories of socio-political and racial marginalization without resorting to revisionism, sanitization, or eradication? Between these extremes, *transparency in spatial representation* becomes more attractive than concealment or erasure. These histories and provenances have involved the marginalization of people across a range of targeted demographics; correspondingly, the path toward transparency will follow along the lines of what Kimberlé Crenhsaw calls "intersectionality" (a concept that has since seen its own discourse emerge within contemporary feminist praxis and social justice activism).[54] Exposing "power" in one relationship at the expense of suppressing the experiences of others is self-defeating. Rockwood Mansion presents visitors with the opportunity to see Rural Gothic Revival architecture up close, but there is little mention of how Joseph Shipley and the firm Shipley, Welch, and Co. amassed capital through the shipping of cotton during the period of slavery.[55] The standing exhibition of the Thomas Jefferson Library at the Library of Congress says much about the influence his reading had on his evolving views of African enslavement; take the Hemings Family Tour at Monticello to learn more about his sexually abusive relationship with Sally Hemings. Maintaining the legacies of the historic house museum libraries in the twenty-first century inexorably must also require being honest about these aspects of spatial legacies and contextualizing them in a very public way. Otherwise, attempts to foster greater inclusivity will be superficial at best.

The Eurocentric and patriarchal heritage privileged, not only in these collections but also in their spaces, is a vestige of colonialism that is deeply problematic and must be confronted. That alone is not enough to forever mark them as monuments to the history of America's moral failings or seek to erase their existence from the national consciousness. There is value to keeping these spaces and the collections they house

---

54. Kimberlé Crenshaw, "Intersection of Race and Gender," in *Critical Race Theory: The Key Writings That Formed the Movement*, ed. Kimberlé Crenshaw, Neil Gotanda, Gary Peller, and Kendall Thomas (New York: New Press, 1995), 357-58.

55. Thomas J. Mickey, *America's Romance with the English Garden* (Athens, Ohio: Ohio University Press, 2013), 45.

alive and thriving for posterity that goes beyond just the educational. There is a capacity, I think, among the most marginalized in society to appreciate the trappings and conventions of a gentle*person*'s literary taste and artistic aesthetic, even as we strive for something more representative of ethnic and cultural diversity. There is, moreover, an interrelatedness to our shared global and national identities. As much as progressive society seeks to expand, diversify, disregard, and re-conceptualize the Western canon, the works of literature that have come to define it become infused in popular culture as a result of their seemingly infinite capacity for global adaptation. This heritage is one that, for better or worse, is blended through a media environment that extends well beyond books.

Conclusion: Imagining the Alternatives

When dealing with the permanence of well-established historic house museum collections like the Huntington Library, pragmatic contextualization is arguably the most reasonable path to spatial remediation. For these institutions, it is virtually impossible to separate these spaces from their Euro-American legacies. Yet, the institutional rigidity required to work with the house museum spaces should not inhibit current and future library directors and administrators from working with designers to create flexible, more culturally sensitive and adaptable spaces for research in the future. There are real possibilities for change, either when existing spaces are expected to undergo substantial renovations, or when new, independent, community-driven collections or research centers are launched.

There is always a question as to how far such efforts will go in either confronting or embracing countervalent modalities of resistance.[56] Changes can be adopted incrementally, progressively, or radically depending on the nature of the collections housed in the spaces and the stakeholders involved with their locations and their potential for use. Be that as it may, it is important to appreciate that change is more or less

---

56. A detailed analysis of "countervalence" in public opinion relevant to this discussion can be found in John Zaller, *The Nature and Origins of Mass Opinion* (Cambridge, UK: Cambridge University Press, 1992), 121-22.

inevitable. Postmodern sensibilities in the field have bred a greater awareness of how the machinations of power operate within our memory
institutions, but this awareness has yielded to a hypermodernity that
allows individuals to exercise their own autonomy in acts of resistance.
Resistance here manifests itself through the digitally mediated channels of social media threads and viral videos.[57] The relatively recent
proliferation of the use of social media, going back less than a decade,
has created a shift that has effectively reversed the panoptic gaze of a
space back to an individual-to-authority relationship.

Moving forward, then, special collections reading rooms as traditionally exclusive and panoptic spaces must understand this new paradigm
and not only work within it, but support and encourage it as well. The
most incremental approach to shifting this orientation can lead to a
more inclusive research environment. We could begin, for example, to
integrate contemporary interior design aesthetics into our reading room
spaces. Low lighting, dark carpets, and dark wood furniture could be
replaced with the soft lighting, brick walls and concrete, and hardwood
flooring associated with the industrial style of contemporary design
(see **Figure 2)**. There could be a browsable, accessible, non-circulating
collection in the staging area beyond reference materials. Institutional
attachments to the pseudo-historicity of a space can either be reassessed
or abandoned, especially if that historicity is not tied to an individual
collector's legacy. What a space loses in traditional visual signifiers, it
gains back in accessibility and contemporary cultural relevance. The
renovation of the John Hay Library in 2013, which included a new special
collections reading room, made considerable advances in this direction
while remaining within the aesthetic boundaries of the blended model.[58]

57. Simon Gottschalk, *The Terminal Self: Everyday Life in Hypermodern Times. Interactionist Currents* (Milton: Taylor and Francis, 2018), 46-47, https://ebookcentral.proquest.
com/lib/udel-ebooks/reader.action?docID=5254632&query=.

58. Michael Dubin, "John Hay Library to Undergo Renovations: The Hay Will Close
Temporarily While the Library's Reading Room is Expanded," *Brown Daily Herald* (Providence, R.I.), February 22, 2013, http://www.browndailyherald.com/2013/02/22/
john-hay-library-to-undergo-renovations/.

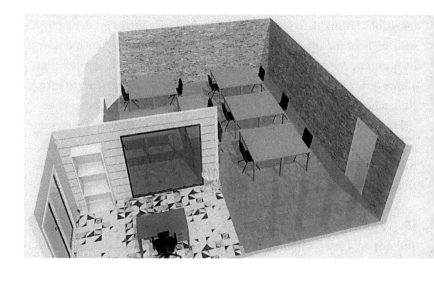

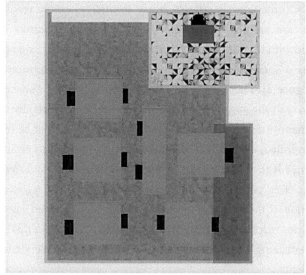

Figure 2. Contemporary Industrial Design for
Special Collections Reading Rooms.

The result offers a reading room that is more open and accessible to its
readers, as well as additional spaces for consultation and conversation.

Moderate changes to the status quo move us forward, but they are still rooted in design conventions that have been developed to support traditionally Eurocentric pedagogies and gendered research practices. Much of what I have covered here deals with the theoretical undercurrents of the impact these design conventions have on affect. Theory opens the door for long-term structural change that should and must occur over time. As bell hooks has rightly maintained, the process of theorization itself can be a form of practice enacted through discourse; it is a process aligned with feminist praxis.[59] "When our lived experience of theorizing is fundamentally linked to processes of self-recovery, of collective liberation, " hooks states, "no gap exists between theory and practice."[60] Further than that, hooks illustrates that a "reciprocal process" binds one to the other. Praxis in this analysis of rare book reading room design enables speculation into the possibilities of emancipating research spatiality from its conventions without being immediately defeated by the structural realities of budgetary constraints, vendor inventories, international trade regulations, and preservation concerns. It is a speculative exploration pitted against the field's history of exclusion, particularly the exclusion of women and feminist theory.

From Estelle Doheny to Bella da Costa Greene, women have been vital to the development of special collections libraries and rare book librarianship; but women's contributions to this history are conspicuously overlooked in the narratives conveyed through conventional reading room design. The sexism of these spaces is not simply exhibited by the faces of men commemorated in the portraits and busts that decorate the spaces; the status quo in reading room design is, above all, set up for research practices that reinforce existing patriarchal structures and power

---

59. bell hooks, "Theory as Liberatory Practice," *Yale Journal of Law and Feminism* 4, no. 1 (1991): 2. See also, Safiya Umoja Noble, foreword to *Critical Library Pedagogy Handbook*, Volume 2: Lesson Plans, ed. Kelly McElroy and Nicole Pagowsky (Chicago: Association of College and Research Libraries, a Division of the American Library Association, 2016), vii.

60. hooks, "Theory as Liberatory Practice," 2.

relations.[61] It perpetuates the myth of the silent, solitary researcher as the purveyor of knowledge, the notion of the "lone genius" searching out "discoveries" in the archives. Human agency in knowledge production becomes framed in a "great men of learning" approach to the underlying pedagogy. Feminist praxis challenges this narrow approach to research. In addition to conventional literacy practices and research methods, women—and women of color in particular—have pioneered effective, alternative ways of producing knowledge and preserving their own history.[62] Contemporary research spaces should promote the ethics of community building and consider feminist pedagogy to be not just legitimate but essential when engaging with primary sources. Truly progressive changes to the current state of design will create new spaces for collaborative learning that are uninhibited by longstanding patriarchal gender constructions.

Likewise, the materialization of decolonized spaces should be premised around notions of multiculturalism rather than Eurocentrism. There may be some truth to the idea that there are aspects of research spaces that are shared across different cultures: book stacks, bookshelves, carpets, maps, charts, writing instruments, relics, curios. Yet, there is hardly a clearer picture of neocolonial spatiality than the presence of the diverse cultural artifacts found in traditional Western research libraries. Such artifacts are often part of a living tradition. The research spaces for multicultural and area studies should be reflective of the collections' cultures of origin.

The histories of diverse populations are ignored in the West when the approach to their cultures is limited to looking at them as "objects

---

61. Important developments in the current paradigm are noted in Jennifer Garland, "Locating Traces of Hidden Visual Culture in Rare Books and Special Collections: A Case Study in Visual Literacy," *Art Documentation: Journal of the Art Libraries Society of North America* 33, no. 2 (2014): 313-15, doi:10.1086/678473.

62. For example, using grangerizing to preserve history, see Ellen Gruber Garvey, *Writing with Scissors: American Scrapbooks from the Civil War to the Harlem Renaissance* (Oxford: Oxford University Press, 2012), 220-25; for a related discussion on friendship albums, see Britt Rusert, "Disappointment in the Archives of Black Freedom," *Social Text* 33, no. 4, 125 (2015): 19-33, doi:10.1215/01642472-3315874.

of study." Sri Lankan libraries can be traced back to the middle of the first century before the Current Era, and reading rooms flourished centuries later under Parakramabahu the Great.[63] Sri Lanka is but one example in a rich library history that is familiar to many regions of East, Southeast, and Western Asia. Other parts of the world are treated as if they were utterly devoid of libraries and literary culture before Western imperial intervention, a commonly held view despite a surplus of material evidence to the contrary. From Ethiopia to Mali, well-established bibliographic systems of knowledge production and cultural preservation existed in Africa well before colonialization. More recently, the Ahmed Baba Institute of Higher Learning and Islamic Research, formerly located in Mali, housed a collection of several hundred thousand historical manuscripts from Timbuktu. Before its destruction in 2013, the Institute was in a building designed by Cape Town's dhk architecture company.[64] It was a modern mud-brick building with reading rooms conversant in the aesthetics of both traditional Malian and Islamic design.[65] When constructing spaces for collections of this nature, designers *should* focus on the cultural autonomy of their users. In research spaces that house a variety of cultural artifacts, decision makers should consider emphasizing diverse cultural heritages in their interior designs as a first step toward creating spaces that support different ways of producing knowledge that are culturally specific.

Perhaps the greatest potential for implementing radical innovations to reading rooms at the conceptual level lies in the intellectual stewardship of counterhegemonic collections. Possibilities for change in such cases rest on our abilities to facilitate the development of mobile spaces with agile design. We have pop-up stores, curated pop-ups in

---

63. T.G. Piyadasa, *Libraries in Sri Lanka: Their Origin and History from Ancient Times to the Present Time*, Studies on Sri Lanka Series, No. 1 (Delhi, India: Sri Satguru Publications, 1985).

64. Al-Qaeda allied, anti-colonial groups burned the library down in 2013.

65. Admin, "Ahmed Baba Institute Library," *Earth Architecture: Architecture, Design, and Culture Using of Mud, Clay, Soil, Dirt & Dust* (blog), April 17, 2011, https://eartharchitecture.org/?p=665.

stores, and pop-up exhibits, so why not pop-up reading rooms? Take, for example, hip hop archives. Instead of limiting access to a "hip hop archive" to a traditional special collections research environment, where its accessibility requires people who actually identify with hip hop culture to conform to an unfamiliar set of aesthetic standards in accordance with visually dissonant spaces, a mobile collection space, or a "pop-up reading room," could be configured to support hip hop as an instrument of technocultural knowledge production.[66] Black technocultural practices, as André Brock points out, involve an "assemblage of artifacts, practice, and cultural beliefs" that are both rooted in, and in constant conversation with, "racial identity."[67] Imagine a reading room space that did not just "make accessible" archived hip hop materials for scholars to research but allowed for remixing collection records, using graffiti black books as calligraphic manuals, and practicing dance as a form of performative knowledge based on collection recordings and works in support of technocultural practice. Imagine a hip hop reading room space that did not display pictures of famous hip hop artists in an assimilative way, but one that entirely mirrored the aesthetic language of hip hop and contemporary fashion. Hip hop culture is often inhibited from refinement in conventional reading room spaces. You can build collections that are pedagogical in nature, and you can build teaching collections that are less attached to their monetary or archival value and intended more for a variety of educational purposes that embrace sampling, remixing, and disassembling of the materials. The approach will always be community oriented, scaled up or down to address the needs of communities and the collections that support them.

Whatever the level of change institutions intend to adopt, the most important factor is the acknowledgment that the status quo is unsustainable. It has only been sustainable up to this point mostly because it has relied on its exclusivity to protect it from outside influences and

66. I focus on hip hop culture here partly because it is the culture that I grew up in as an African American male living in the Los Angeles area during the 1980s and '90s.

67. André Brock, "Critical Technocultural Discourse Analysis," *New Media & Society* 20, no. 3 (2018): 1014, doi:10.1177/1461444816677532.

demands. But we are no longer married to the exclusivity that has defined special collections and rare book reading rooms for over a century. If we embrace the changes now, we will be prepared to meet the demands of an increasingly diverse user population.

Bibliography

American Library Association. "Are Libraries Neutral?" *American Libraries*, June 2018.

Bell, Derrick A. Jr. "Racial Realism." In *Critical Race Theory: The Key Writings That Formed the Movement*, edited by Kimberlé Crenshaw, Neil Gotanda, Gary Peller, and Kendall Thomas, 302-12. New York: New Press, 1995.

Berger, Sidney E. *Rare Books and Special Collections*. Chicago: Neal-Schuman, an Imprint of the American Library Association, 2014.

Bourdieu, Pierre. "The Forms of Capital." In *Handbook of Theory and Research for the Sociology of Education*, edited by John G. Richardson, 241-58. Westport, Conn.: Greenwood Press, 1986.

Brock, André. "Critical Technocultural Discourse Analysis." *New Media & Society* 20, no. 3 (2018): 1012-30. doi:10.1177/1461444816677532.

Brown, Mark N., Jane K. Cabral, Rosemary L. Cullen, Catherine J. Denning, Peter Harrington, Richard B. Harrington, Jennifer B. Lee, Martha L. Mitchell, Jean M. Rainwater, Mary T. Russo, John H. Stanley, and Samuel A. Streit. *Special Collections at Brown University: A History and Guide*. Edited by Leslie T. Wendel. Providence, R.I.: Friends of the Library of Brown University, 1988.

Crenshaw, Kimberlé "Intersection of Race and Gender." In *Critical Race Theory: The Key Writings That Formed the Movement*, edited by Kimberlé Crenshaw, Neil Gotanda, Gary Peller, and Kendall Thomas, 357-77. New York: New Press, 1995.

Crunden, Frederick M. "How We Protect Rare and Illustrated Books: St. Louis Public Library." *The Library Journal* 15, no. 4 (1890): 104.

Cullingford, Alison. *The Special Collections Handbook*. London: Facet Publishing, 2011.

Deleuze, Gilles, and Félix Guattari. *Anti-Oedipus: Capitalism and Schizophrenia*. New York: Viking Press, 1977.

Dolphijn, Rick, and Iris Van Der Tuin. *New Materialism: Interviews & Cartographies*. New Metaphysics. Ann Arbor: Open Humanities Press, 2012. https://quod.lib.umich.edu/o/ohp/11515701.0001.001/1:5.2/--new-materialism-interviews-cartographies?rgn=div2;view=fulltext.

Du Bois, W.E.B. *Souls of Black Folk: Essays and Sketches*. 1979 ed. *Great Illustrated Classics*. New York: Dodd, Mead, 1979.

Dubin, Michael. "John Hay Library to Undergo Renovations: The Hay Will Close Temporarily While the Library's Reading Room is Expanded," *Brown Daily Herald* (Providence, R.I.), February 22, 2013. http://www.browndailyherald.com/2013/02/22/john-hay-library-to-undergo-renovations/.

Escobar, Edward J. *Race, Police, and the Making of a Political Identity: Mexican Americans and the Los Angeles Police Department, 1900-1945*. Latinos in American Society and Culture, Volume 7. Berkeley: University of California Press, 1999.

Foucault, Michel. *Discipline and Punish: The Birth of the Prison*. Translated by Alan Sheridan. New York: Vintage Books, 1995.

Galbraith, Steven Kenneth, and Geoffrey D. Smith. *Rare Book Librarianship: An Introduction and Guide*. Santa Barbara, Calif.: Libraries Unlimited, 2012.

Garcia, Kenny. "Keeping Up with Critical Librarianship." *Association of College & Research Libraries: A Division of the American Library Association*. Accessed December 7, 2018. http://www.ala.org/acrl/publications/keeping_up_with/critlib.

Garcilazo, Jeffrey Marcos. *Traqueros: Mexican Railroad Workers in the United States, 1870 to 1930*. Al Filo: Mexican American Studies Series, Number 6. Denton, Tex.: UNT Press, 2012.

Garland, Jennifer. "Locating Traces of Hidden Visual Culture in Rare Books and Special Collections: A Case Study in Visual Literacy." *Art Documentation: Journal of the Art Libraries Society of North America* 33, no. 2 (2014): 313-26. doi:10.1086/678473.

Garvey, Ellen Gruber. *Writing with Scissors: American Scrapbooks from the Civil War to the Harlem Renaissance*. Oxford: Oxford University Press, 2012.

Gottschalk, Simon. *The Terminal Self: Everyday Life in Hypermodern Times. Interactionist Currents*. Milton: Taylor and Francis, 2018. https://ebookcentral.proquest.com/lib/udel-ebooks/reader. action?docID=5254632&query=.

Grob, Julie. "RBMS, Special Collections, and the Challenge of Diversity: The Road to the Diversity Action Plan." *RBM: A Journal of Rare Books, Manuscripts, and Cultural Heritage* 4, no. 2 (2003): 74-107. doi:10.5860/rbm.4.2.219.

Hall, Stuart. "Introduction: Who Needs Identity?" In *Questions of Cultural Identity*, edited by Stuart Hall and Paul du Gay, 1-17. London: SAGE Publications Ltd, 1996.

Harriot, Michael. "Video: Librarian Calls Cops on Student for Brazen Attempt at #StudyingWhileBlack [Updated]," WYPIPO. *Root*. October 24, 2018. https://www.theroot.com/video-librarian-calls-cops-on-student-for-brazen-attem-1829940301.

Healey, Elspeth, and Melissa Nykanen. "Channeling Janus: Past, Present, and Future in the RBMS Membership Survey." *RBM: A Journal of Rare Books, Manuscripts, and Cultural Heritage* 17, no. 1 (2016): 53-81. https://doi.org/10.5860/rbm.17.1.461.

Holzenberg, Eric. "Book Collecting." *Encyclopædia Britannica*. Encyclopædia Britannica, Inc. Last modified May 24, 2017. https://www.britannica.com/topic/book-collecting.

hooks, bell. "Theory as Liberatory Practice." *Yale Journal of Law and Feminism* 4, no. 1 (1991): 1-12.

King, Vanessa. "Special Collections: What Are They and How Do We Build Them?" *International Journal of Legal Information* 46, no. 2 (2018): 89-92. doi:10.1017/jli.2018.12.

Lacan, Jacques. "The Mirror Stage as the Formative *I* Function as Revealed in Psychoanalytic Experience." In *Écrits: A Selection*. Translated by Bruce Fink, 3-10. New York: W.W. Norton, 2004.

Lawrence, Charles R. III. "The Id, the Ego, and Equal Protection: Reckoning with Unconscious Racism." In *Critical Race Theory: The Key Writings That Formed the Movement*, edited by Kimberlé Crenshaw, Neil Gotanda, Gary Peller, and Kendall Thomas, 235-56. New York: New Press, 1995.

Lewis, Alison M., ed. *Questioning Library Neutrality: Essays from Progressive Librarian*. Duluth, MN: Library Juice Press, 2008.

Lipovetsky, Gilles, and Sébastien Charles. *Hypermodern Times*. Translated by Andrew Brown. Cambridge, UK: Polity, 2005.

Mann, Charles W. "The Role of Rare Books in a University Library." *The Courier* 9, no. 3 (1972): 25-31. https://surface.syr.edu/libassoc.

Masson, David. *The British Museum, Historical and Descriptive*. Chambers's Instructive and Entertaining Library. Edinburgh: W. and R. Chambers, 1850.

Mickey, Thomas J. *America's Romance with the English Garden*. Athens, Ohio: Ohio University Press, 2013.

Nirappil, Fenit. "McAuliffe Has Change of Heart on Confederate Statues." *Washington Post* (Washington, D.C.), August 16, 2017. https://www.washingtonpost.com/local/virginia-politics/following-charlottesville-northam-says-hell-urge-removal-of-confederate-statues/2017/08/16/d6bfc7ea-82aa-11e7-b359-15a3617c767b_story.html?utm_term=.f06e4d9e74b7.

Noble, Safiya Umoja. Foreword to *Critical Library Pedagogy Handbook, Volume 2: Lesson Plans*. Edited by Kelly McElroy and Nicole Pagowsky, vii-xiv. Chicago: Association of College and Research Libraries, a Division of the American Library Association, 2016.

Piyadasa, T.G. *Libraries in Sri Lanka: Their Origin and History from Ancient Times to the Present Time*. Studies on Sri Lanka Series, No. 1. Delhi, India: Sri Satguru Publications, 1985.

Radford, Gary P. "Flaubert, Foucault, and the Bibliotheque Fantastique: Toward a Postmodern Epistemology for Library Science." *Library Trends* 46, no. 4 (spring 1998): 616-34.

Radford Gary P., Marie L. Radford., and Jessica Lingel. "The Library as Heterotopia: Michel Foucault and the Experience of Library Space." *Journal of Documentation* 71, no. 4 (2015): 733-51. doi:10.1108/JD-01-2014-0006.

Rees, J. Rogers. *The Diversions of a Book-Worm*. London: Elliot Stock, 1887.

Rusert, Britt. "Disappointment in the Archives of Black Freedom." *Social Text* 33, no. 4, 125 (2015): 19-33. doi:10.1215/01642472-3315874.

Stewart, Kathleen. "Worlding Refrains." In *The Affect Theory Reader*, edited by Melissa Gregg and Gregory J. Seigworth, 339-54. Durham, NC: Duke University Press, 2010.

Staninger, S.W. "Deconstructing Reorganizations in Libraries." *Library Leadership and Management* 28, no. 2 (2014): 1-4. https://journals.tdl.org/llm/index.php/llm/article/view/7057/6279.

Strathern, Marilyn. "Enabling Identity? Biology, Choice and the New Reproductive Technologies." In *Questions of Cultural Identity*, edited by Stuart Hall and Paul du Gay, 37-52. London: SAGE Publications Ltd, 1996.

Traister, Daniel H. "Is There a Future for Special Collections? And Should There Be? A Polemical Essay." *RBM: A Journal of Rare Books, Manuscripts and Cultural Heritage* 1, no. 1 (January 2000): 54-76. http://repository.upenn.edu/library_papers/22.

Woolwine, David. "The Patriot Act and Early ALA Action: Habermas, Strauss, or Derrida?" *Library Philosophy and Practice* (October 2009): 1-11. http://www.uidaho.edu/~mbolin/lp&p.htm.

Zaller, John. *The Nature and Origins of Mass Opinion*. Cambridge, UK: Cambridge University Press, 1992.

Chapter 6

SENSITIVE MATERIALS IN THE SPECIAL COLLECTION: SOME CONSIDERATIONS

Daniel German

Introduction

Special collections have always included materials that may not "fit" into regular collections, for example, manuscripts, collections on particular subjects, or even items whose connections to a library may seem most tenuous. What is also found in special collections is information/material that may, in some circumstances, be regarded as sensitive, delicate, or potentially dangerous. In fact, such information epitomizes the concept of "special" collections, i.e., materials outside of the norm and materials that hold some form of interest, for whatever reason. The problems that exist, however, are what to do with this information, and how to provide access to material when said access may damage some legitimate interests. At the same time, how do we not provide access? After all, censorship is, generally speaking, outside of a library's social responsibilities—or is it?

In this chapter, I will examine several instances where there may exist legitimate interests in restricting some access, examining the issues both pro and con access, and where possible proposing some methods of mediating between the two points of view.[1] I will look at issues around

---

1. See the examples used in Daniel German, "Who Owns the Archives? A North American Perspective on Issues of Ownership and Control over Holdings of Archival Repositories," *Revista Arhivelor/Archives Review* LXXXV, no. 2 (2008): 9-29. A number

sensitive personal information, obscene material, and government secrets as they are discovered in special collections, suggesting some approaches to handling them while pointing out the pitfalls of not doing so.

In addressing these issues, perhaps the first factor that must be mentioned is: What legislation/rules govern your activities? Many special collections may be tied to institutions that receive public funding. In this event, they may also be subject to access and privacy laws, rules, and guidelines. Always read and try to understand what legislation guides your activities. Remember the old tag: ignorance of the law is no excuse. However, having said that, and assuming that the rules in place allow for some leeway, let us consider some of our options for dealing with sensitive material.

Considerations to be examined:

1. Personal information (both sensitive and commonplace).
2. Information received in confidence—when can it be released?
3. The awkward topic, be it Nazi memorabilia or obscenity—how to handle delicate themes?
4. Dealing with legal requirements—whether through responding to subpoenas or issues of copyright.
5. The acquisition of high market-value materials—can there be too much of a good thing?

1. Pardon Me but That's Awfully Personal

It is one of the constant realities of the information world that some information is considered to be more sensitive than other information; of all sensitive types of information, perhaps the most sensitive, for individuals, is personal information.

There are a number of definitions for what constitutes personal information but, in essence, it is any information related to identifiable individuals. This may relate to their opinions, their history, their ethnicity,

---

of these examples are used elsewhere in this chapter.

their religion, their finances, their health, and even their telephone numbers. All relate to individuals, and there may be varying levels of harm caused if the information is publicly released.

Special collections often receive materials containing personal information. From diaries to correspondence, church records to doctor's files, there are a number of avenues by which personal information may wend its way through to the special collection. Having arrived, though, the question becomes: what to do with it?

It may be trite but, in essence, the key to ameliorating any issues over the presence of personal information is the establishment, early on, of clear and enforceable rules. These rules represent an informed manner of managing this information.

The first thing to do is to establish guidelines by which personal information may be accessed. The most obvious guideline is to only release information that would not harm the interests of identifiable individuals.[2] Other rules governing access are quite straightforward. For example, you might establish a test to determine whether releasing the information would be an unwarranted invasion of privacy. One set of rules with which I am familiar (that of Library and Archives Canada, or LAC, for short) establishes a four-prong test.[3] Generally, the tines of this fork are: 1) the expectations of the individual, 2) the sensitivity of the information, 3) the probability of injury, and 4) the context in which the information is found.

LAC has a test by which personal information must be considered prior to release. But what do we mean when we say that we *consider* the expectations of the individual, the sensitivity of the information, the

---

2. For an excellent discussion of some of the elements inherent in this issue, see Heather MacNeil, *Without Consent: The Ethics of Disclosing Personal Information in Public Archives* (Lanham, Maryland; Society of American Archivists and Scarecrow Press, Inc., 1992).

3. Canada, National Archives of Canada/Archives nationales du Canada, *Guidelines for the disclosure of personal information for historical research at the National Archives of Canada = Lignes directrices relatives à la communication de renseignements personnels aux fins de recherches aux Archives nationales du Canada* (Ottawa: Minister of Supply and Services Canada, ©1995): 3-4.

probability of injury, and its context? That is to say, when considering these factors, what issues come into play?

An Invasion of Privacy Test

Let us look at the first prong of the four-prong test—*expectations* of individuals. When they provided the information, what did they expect would happen with it? For this part of the test, we examine the conditions that governed the collection of the information. Was the information compiled or obtained under guarantees that preclude some or all types of disclosure? Can the information be considered to have been unsolicited or given freely with little expectation of it being maintained in total confidence, or have the individuals made versions of the information public and thus waived their right to privacy? For example, if people write to newspapers to express their opinions, can they then consider those opinions private and personal? Of course not! In such cases, individuals' expectations should be very limited; obviously, they have waived their right to privacy, at least insofar as those opinions are concerned. What about, however, when one sends a letter to the government to discuss, for example, one's criminal record? Obviously, in such a case, there is a greater implicit understanding that the information is to kept confidential, i.e., not to be widely disseminated. That expectation is all the greater if the correspondence is more recent.

Let us now turn to the second prong of the four-prong test—the *sensitivity* of the personal information. Here, we attempt to ascertain whether it is highly sensitive personal information or whether it is innocuous, whether it is current information, and for that reason more sensitive, or whether the passage of time has reduced that sensitivity. When considering what is sensitive, we further take into account whether the information belongs to one of the categories that we could identify as being more sensitive than others: medical information, records related to criminal activities or security, and records related to personal finance. For example, a record related to a serious medical condition may be quite sensitive, and thus should not be released. On the other hand, if the medical problem is relatively minor, e.g., a cold, it would surely be reasonable to consider that information to be innocuous and releasable, just as a ticket for jaywalking in 1945 is of lesser sensitivity than a 2010 arrest for terrorism.

With respect to the third prong of the test, i.e., the *probability of injury*, even though the information being considered falls into one of the "sensitive" categories, that does not in itself mean that the information is sensitive. Remember, current information concerning one's financial situation may be quite sensitive, but information regarding an individual's salary in 1935 is far less likely to cause anyone any harm today. Of course, in making any such determination about the probability of injury, some disagreement is inevitable: what one person feels is sensitive is not necessarily what another person might find to be sensitive. However, for the most part, I think that there is a core, shared understanding of what constitutes truly sensitive personal information.

When considering the probability of injury, we are concerned with assessing whether the release of any personal information, which may, in fact, be "sensitive," could reasonably be expected to result in some form of measurable injury. In this part of the test, "injury" may be defined as any harm or embarrassment that would have a direct negative effect on an individual's career, reputation, financial position, health, or wellbeing. For example, let us take the case of comments in a letter wherein rumors are recounted concerning an individual's use of illicit drugs. If the information were released, it would probably cause embarrassment, and depending on the individual's position, may, in fact, cause harm to that person's career. On the other hand, general personal information, such as that found in a CV sent along with a 1970s job application, may be relatively innocuous—its release may have no discernable effect on the person's career, provided there are no other factors (such as its context) that may give added weight to the information.

Finally, let's consider the fourth prong of the test—the *context* in which the information is found. Context of information may seem to be a curious factor to take into account, since we are, after all, dealing with information that is either sensitive or innocuous. There is little point in withholding access to innocuous information, just as there seems no good to come from releasing sensitive personal material. Perhaps what we are looking at here is the fact that the context of a file—the placement of some information—may make even the most innocuous of information become sensitive.

For example, let us take someone's name, perhaps alone on a piece of paper, with no other information included—something that is of no real sensitivity and can surely be released, even if no other information in the file can be. Ah, but let us look at the file it is in, the context: if the file is entitled "Nice People," the personal information—that is to say, the name on the otherwise blank piece of paper—may be released. But let us change the name of the file to "Drug Dealers" and suddenly the innocuous information is transmuted, purely by the context in which it is found, into being extremely sensitive.

2. When We Get Information in Confidence, Just How Confidential Is It?

Frequently, special collections may acquire, or be offered, information that they are told should be held in confidence—for example, trade secrets of a local company: a recipe of special herbs and spices used by a chain of chicken restaurants (Louisiana Fried Chicken, or LFC, for short). How long should the special collection keep the information confidential?

Obviously, the answer here must be: as long as necessary. If releasing the information will harm the legitimate interests of the donors/ depositors, then do not release it. Of course, if it turns out that a crucial part of the recipe is something unsafe, then perhaps you will need to discuss it further, but always, ALWAYS, think before you act. Remember—you may be governed by external rules, and you may have signed an agreement that legally binds you to keeping the material confidential. Know and understand how and why you are keeping the information confidential.

You should also consider whether there actually is a need to keep it confidential. If LFC published a cookbook describing its recipe, then the fact that your copy is marked "confidential" should not govern all of your actions. There should always be an objective reason for confidentiality, not simply because someone once said it should be.

On the other hand, if the information acquired has a government origin, then the "confidential" stamp might have greater significance. According to the policies of various agencies, information that they have deemed to be classified may not be examined until such time as the originating agency indicates that the information is unclassified – no matter how long said material may have been publicly available. Perhaps one of the best examples of this is found on the website of the Lyndon Baines Johnson Presidential Library (a branch of the United States National Archives and Records Administration). On June 13, 2011, the website proudly announced that the Pentagon Papers, a collection of classified materials that had been stolen and published in the national press, would be officially released, forty years to the day after the Papers were first made publicly available.[4] However, until such time as the American government itself released the information, possession of it by an unauthorized individual was contrary to federal law.

3. To Whom Did This Used to Belong and Why Does It Have That Strange Cover?

Other areas of sensitivity in special collections may be external to the content but directly connected to issues around the format of the material or even its past owners. Of course, one of the common issues around format in the modern era is related to the dominance of digital records. The problems of handling, migrating, and otherwise maintaining the viability of digital records are well known, even if long-term answers are still tenuous. (If this is your greatest concern, then look elsewhere, as that topic is far too broad for this chapter.) Instead, the format being questioned is the material from which the collection has been created. This material can range from the ephemeral to the morbid, and may include quite delicate and easily damaged materials, as well as materials that can raise problematic concerns.

---

4. See http://www.lbjlibrary.org/press/pentagon-papers as accessed 24 May 2019.

For example, let us imagine that a special collection has obtained a book or codex with a curious binding. If the binding is merely a normal, or even an abnormal, form of leather, preservationists should examine the binding to ensure its viability. On the other hand, if the leather is quite rare—made from the skin or other parts of an extinct animal for example—those who are offended by it may challenge its inclusion in the special collection.

This problem may be greatly exacerbated if the leather in question originated from a source less rare, but far more problematic, such as a human being. For some odd reason, there exist a number of items that were bound in human skin.[5] Disgusting as this may be, if the special collection holds something of such an odd nature and it has decided to retain the material, it is incumbent upon the managers to ensure that it is safe. Such items create problems that range from handling, sensitivities, general dislike, and other factors, which I would suggest fall into the general category of "squick."[6] Into this category may be placed shrunken heads, scalps, mummies, and any other human remains. If you have any of these types of items in your special collection, or you are offered any, check your policies quite carefully. If you do not have any policies covering such items, then be prepared to draft some—what you hold depends very much on your special collection's mandate, but be ready to respond when the squick factor appears.

It is clear that special collections should also be both aware and wary of issues surrounding records related to Indigenous peoples. These often involve ethical conundrums regarding access and ownership, not to mention provenance. The history of Western civilization's dealings

---

5. Rigby Graham, "Bookbinding with Human Skin," *The Private Library. Series* 1. Volume 6, no. 1 (1965): 14-18.

6. A researcher at Harvard University when asked about the presence of human-bound books in the University collections is quoted in the University newspaper as saying, "Given the many pressures on library purchasing these days ... I wouldn't want to prioritize this kind of book; the text rather than the binding of a book is what matters to most students and scholars." Ann Blair, quoted in Samuel P. Jacobs' "The Skinny on Harvard's Rare Book Collection: Human Flesh-Bound Volumes R.I.P. on Library Shelves," *Harvard Crimson*, 2 February 2006.

with Indigenous peoples has been fraught with theft, violence, and bad faith, and the avenues by which Indigenous materials have found their ways into special collections have frequently been unsuitable for close examination. If an institution has acquired such material in the past, whether it be artifacts, memorabilia, or even human remains, it is incumbent upon a wise administrator to be prepared: understand the laws that now govern such materials, and be ready to act in a manner that will not embarrass your institution.[7]

There also exist a number of publications or other materials which are associated with individuals or movements of questionable morality. If a special collection has, for instance, as part of its research mandate, the study of social or political movements, it would not be unusual for the collection to include publications or ephemera related to such movements, or possibly having belonged to such groups.[8] If a special collection holds the private papers of a local politician, that's not likely a problem. However, should the materials be related to an organization such as the Nazi party, that may very well be challenged. The acquisition of a book that previously belonged to a political leader may be of interest, but if the leader is the head of a group that is linked to illegal, criminal, or immoral activities, that's another matter altogether. Again, what you hold should depend on your collection's mandate; so, if you want to collect the propaganda of the Ku Klux Klan or the Aryan Brotherhood, be prepared[9]—it's not only the motto for the Boy Scouts. (By the way, the founder of the Boy Scouts, Robert Baden-Powell, made his name as commander of a besieged community. I am just saying.)

---

7. Richard Cox et al., "A Different Kind of Archival Security: Three Cases," *Library & Archival Security* 22, no. 1 (2009): 33-60.

8. See, for example, the acquisition by Library and Archives Canada of a report from Adolph Hitler's personal library – David Brennan's "What If the Nazis Won? Rare Book Suggests Hitler's Plans for North American Holocaust," *Newsweek*, 25 January 2019.

9. An online search for North American special collections holding Ku Klux Klan materials shows a surprising amount available, reflecting no doubt the impact this group has had. See, for example, the Ku Klux Klan Collection in the Michigan State University Special Collections, as described at https://lib.msu.edu/spc/collections/kkk/ as accessed 24 May 2019.

4. But, Seriously, Do We Need to Be Lawyers?

We may not all need to be lawyers, but we should have at least a cursory knowledge of the laws governing our collections. From copyright to privacy, and access to legal agreements, know what binds your collection. Regardless of your circumstances, a number of laws can affect your collection; be aware of them and again be prepared.

When acquiring material on deposit, avoid accepting collections "on permanent loan" if at all possible. It sounds fine, but even if it binds donors, does it bind their heirs?

If you accept a collection of letters and the donor wants it open immediately and the letters are full of scurrilous tales, are you on the hook for any complaints?

The answer to both questions is a definite maybe. The answer really depends on the terms of your agreement, the jurisdiction in which you operate, and above all, what laws govern your activities. Few special collections have lawyers on staff, but everyone should be aware of who in the institution can be called on for legal advice.

In a well-known case at the University of Texas, the University had acquired, "on permanent loan," the manuscript of a memoir called the de la Peña diary. The de la Peña diary was quite controversial in Texas. Among other events, it recounted the experiences of a Mexican official during the rebellion that resulted in an independent Texas. A key element to this rebellion occurred during a siege of the Alamo, an old mission which the rebels used as a fort. According to the traditional mythos, all of the defenders died fighting when the Alamo fell. But, according to de la Peña, this was not quite accurate and it even suggests that one of the great American and Texan heroes, Davy Crockett, was actually captured and later executed. Whether the manuscript was correct is debatable, but there was no question as to the financial value of the material. Once the owner who loaned the manuscript died, his heir quickly placed it on the open market. Fortunately, the purchasers donated the de la Peña diary to the University of Texas, but there are few guarantees that another institution would be as lucky.[10]

---

10. Rick Lyman, "Story of Davy Crockett's Execution Hits the Auction Block," *New*

If you acquire the collected papers of a local group and the police want to consult that group, do you know your legal rights? A number of special collections and archives have found themselves fighting in court to defend promises of confidentiality against police subpoenas[11]—only join such a fight if it is important to your institution, or perhaps to your own ethics. If you are not prepared for a legal battle, then perhaps such a collection should be refused or directed to another institution. Either way, know where you stand under the law that governs your jurisdiction.

It is clear that not all institutions truly understand some of the legal issues surrounding the acquisition of some "special" collections. Boston College in Massachusetts has, as part of its mandate, the documentation of the Irish American and Irish experience. Since political strife in Ireland, particularly Northern Ireland, has dominated that area during the last half of the twentieth century, it is not surprising that Boston College attempted to document some of the political actors. In a particularly innovative program, past participants in some of the political strife were interviewed, with the promise that the contents of the tapes would not be released during their lifetimes. As Boston College eventually found out, such a promise may not be legally enforceable. The restrictions to access were challenged by those who wished to use the tapes immediately as evidence in trials.[12] Had they better considered the legal quagmire into which they plunged, Boston College may have been better prepared for the problems that emerged. Making a promise is not the same as having the legal wherewithal to support said promise.

5. Are There Hidden Costs to Acquiring Some Materials?

In this chapter, we have considered material possessing certain inherent sensitivities. I now turn to sensitivities involving high market-value

York Times, 18 November 1998; Christopher Lee, "A Legendary Gift: Hicks, Partner Give Diary to UT that Disputes Traditional Tale of Crockett's Alamo Death," *Dallas Morning News*, 16 December 1998.

11. See, for example, Harold L. Miller, "Will Access Restrictions Hold Up in Court? The FBI's Attempt to Use the Braden Papers at the State Historical Society of Wisconsin," *American Archivist* 52, no. 2 (Spring 1989): 180-90.

12. Patrick Keefe, "Who Killed Jean McConville? Did a Secret Archive at Boston College Hold Clues?" *Globe Magazine*, 9 February 2019.

content. It should readily become apparent that the answer to issues around sensitivity is normally based on a solid understanding of the issues under consideration. Generally, knowledge trumps most difficulties.

Most institutional collections welcome the addition of items of high market value. Certainly, there don't *seem to be* any obvious problems when someone donates valuable items—a Faberge egg, for example, or an original copy of the US Constitution. Nonetheless, one of the realities of life is that money (or, in this case, fiscal value) does not always buy happiness.

Let us imagine that some kindly individual approaches a special collection offering to donate an item of great market value. At first glance, this looks like a wonderful opportunity. The donor offers the item at no cost. Why should this be an issue? Why shouldn't the institution embrace the gift and happily advertise its new acquisition? In fact, such an offer should be considered with all of its attendant potential issues.

Issue one: does the item meet the acquisition criteria/mandate of the special collection? If not—if the only reasons to take the item are that it has financial value or intellectual prestige attached to the ownership—do those reasons necessarily outweigh some of the pragmatic issues surrounding any item of great financial value?

Issue two: most special collections operate under limited budgets. Even if the item under discussion is a no-cost donation, there are certain ancillary costs to any such acquisition. Does the institution's insurance policy cover such material? Does the special collection have sufficient security to guard such a valuable item? Is there a secured location available to hold such an item? And, finally, is the special collection prepared to expend the necessary funds to provide care for such an item?

In 2012, Patricia and Michael Mounce published a survey of theft in American academic special collections in which the levels of security commonly utilized were examined. It was clear from the results of this survey that there are serious gaps in both special collections' security and their knowledge of attendant security issues. According to the survey results, more security measures are required, although there is often a difference of opinion as to relative priorities.[13] No doubt, a number of the issues related to the response were related to the financial capabilities of the institution, but theft has been taking a greater and greater toll on resources.[14]

In the best of all possible worlds, nothing will go wrong, but the existence of insurance companies is predicated on the reality that sometimes things do go wrong. If the special collection acquires this item of high market value, even if the acquisition appears to be free, the ancillary costs are obvious and substantive.

Conclusion

BE PREPARED—it is obvious, repetitive, and yet far too few pay attention. The old saying is: know your enemy. I'm not suggesting that we should view the rules, laws, and guidelines that govern our special collections as enemies, but know them nonetheless.

BE PREPARED—what are your rights and your obligations? Under what agreements have you obtained material, and what did those materials contain?

BE PREPARED— accept the wondrous materials and take those items that make your collections "special." Don't turn them away if they are problematic, but do consider whether they are worth the problems. There are many items that are sensitive, whether they contain personal information, are bound in dodo skin, once belonged to a dictator, or include the secret LFC recipe. Look them over, consider them carefully, but be aware and knowledgeable. Recognize why you might want them, and why you might not. Above all:

BE PREPARED.

---

13. Michael Mounce and Patricia Mounce, "An Investigation of Special Collections Library Theft," *Library & Archival Security* 25, no. 2 (2012): 99-118.

14. Ross Griffiths and Andrew Krol, "Insider Theft: Reviews and Recommendations from the Archive and Library Professional Literature," *Library & Archival Security* 22, no. 1 (2009): 5-18.

Bibliography

Brennan, David. "What If the Nazis Won? Rare Book Suggests Hitler's Plans for North American Holocaust." *Newsweek*, 25 January 2019.

Canada, National Archives of Canada/Archives nationales du Canada. *Guidelines for the disclosure of personal information for historical research at the National Archives of Canada = Lignes directrices relatives à la communication de renseignements personnels aux fins de recherches aux Archives nationales du Canada* Ottawa: Minister of Supply and Services Canada, ©1995.

Cox, Richard, Abigail Middleton, Rachel Grove Rohrbaugh, and Daniel Scholzen. "A Different Kind of Archival Security: Three Cases." *Library & Archival Security* 22, no. 1 (2009): 33-60.

German, Daniel. "Who Owns the Archives? A North American Perspective on Issues of Ownership and Control over Holdings of Archival Repositories." *Revista Arhivelor/Archives Review* LXXXV, no. 2 (2008): 9-29.

Graham, Rigby. "Bookbinding with Human Skin." *The Private Library*. Series 1. Volume 6, no. 1 (1965): 14-18.

Griffiths, Ross, and Andrew Krol. "Insider Theft: Reviews and Recommendations from the Archive and Library Professional Literature." *Library & Archival Security* 22, no. 1 (2009): 5-18.

Jacobs, Samuel P. "The Skinny on Harvard's Rare Book Collection: Human Flesh-Bound Volumes R.I.P. on Library Shelves." *Harvard Crimson*, 2 February 2006.

Keefe, Patrick. "Who Killed Jean McConville? Did a Secret Archive at Boston College Hold Clues?" *Globe Magazine*, 9 February 2019.

Ku Klux Klan Collection, Michigan State University Special Collections, as accessed 24 May 2019, https://lib.msu.edu/spc/collections/kkk/.

Lee, Christopher. "A Legendary Gift: Hicks, Partner Give Diary to UT that Disputes Traditional Tale of Crockett's Alamo Death." *Dallas Morning News*, 16 December 1998.

Lyndon Baines Johnson Presidential Library, Pentagon Papers News Release, 13 June 2011, as accessed 24 May 2019, http://www.lbjlibrary.org/press/pentagon-papers.

Lyman, Rick. "Story of Davy Crockett's Execution Hits the Auction Block." *New York Times*, 18 November 1998.

MacNeil, Heather. *Without Consent: The Ethics of Disclosing Personal Information in Public Archives.* Lanham, Maryland: Society of American Archivists and Scarecrow Press, Inc., 1992.

Miller, Harold L. "Will Access Restrictions Hold Up in Court? The FBI's Attempt to Use the Braden Papers at the State Historical Society of Wisconsin." *American Archivist* 52, no. 2 (Spring 1989): 180-90.

Mounce, Michael, and Patricia Mounce. "An Investigation of Special Collections Library Theft." *Library & Archival Security* 25, no. 2 (2012): 99-118.

Chapter 7

HEALING THROUGH INCLUSION: PRESERVING
COMMUNITY PERSPECTIVES ON THE KOMAGATA MARU
INCIDENT

Melanie Hardbattle

28-11-1913	39 men came from Homeland (India) by ship. After a long struggle with immigration, 35 men were allowed to disembark. Four men were not allowed due to sickness.
18-05-1914	Raja Singh was sent by boat to anchor Komagata Maru at Port Alberni dock.
20-05-1914	An attempt was made to go near Komagata Maru by small boat but the Canadian Government did not permit it. Following gentlemen went – Bhai Bhag Singh, Balwant Singh, Mitt Singh, Rahim, Babu Harnam Singh, Rattan Singh and Uttam Singh Hans.
23-05-1914	Komagata Maru ship arrived in Vancouver at 11 A.M.[1]

---

1. Khalsa Diwan Society [Diary], Vancouver, B.C. [: Volume 1 – English translation], [ca. 1926], Arjan Singh Brar Collection, Simon Fraser University Library Special Collections and Rare Books, Burnaby, British Columbia, Canada, http://komagatamarujourney.ca/node/15901.

Introduction

Our understanding of history and ability to reconstruct it is shaped by the gaps as well as the records that remain, by whatever was deemed important to collect or include, and by whatever was excluded, deliberately or inadvertently, from the official documentary record. Those who have suffered injustices are often those who are most vulnerable to exclusion.

Until recent years, the contemporary archival record pertaining to South Asian immigrants and would-be immigrants to British Columbia, Canada in the early 1900s that was most accessible to the ordinary researcher was overwhelmingly created and shaped by those from outside of the community. It was molded by the language and opinions of the government officials and media of the time, and often by the viewpoints of the individuals who determined which records should be preserved for posterity. Research in this area has involved interpreting the gaps in documentation and sifting through the biases of the records creators. As a result, we know a lot about the attitudes and prejudices faced by the early South Asian Canadian population, but less about who these first immigrants really were and how historically significant events were seen from their perspectives and documented in their own words.

The words quoted at the beginning of this chapter, recorded neatly in a blue-lined notebook by Arjan Singh Brar in the late 1920s, begin his documentation of the Komagata Maru incident of 1914 and the struggles faced by South Asian immigrants to Canada in the early twentieth century, from the local South Asian Canadian community's perspective. For decades, these words lay carefully protected inside an old metal chest in the home of Brar's family, coming out only occasionally by request to those aware of the material and its significance. In 2012, ninety-eight years after the incident, the diary containing these words, along with related documents, photographs, and sound recordings, was brought out of storage, digitized, and made available online to the world through the *Komagata Maru: Continuing the Journey* website.

In this chapter, I will examine how Simon Fraser University (SFU) Library leveraged opportunities provided by a Citizenship and

Immigration Canada grant to create partnerships with the local South Asian Canadian community to develop and make accessible a significant group of holdings relating to a sensitive subject—the Komagata Maru incident—and the community's continued fight for justice and for equal rights as Canadian citizens, including the right to vote. Using the resulting website as a vehicle for engaging the South Asian Canadian community, the project led to a much more balanced archive and a better understanding of the Komagata Maru incident one hundred years later.

The Komagata Maru Incident

In the early hours of May 23, 1914, a Japanese ship named Komagata Maru, carrying 376 passengers, mostly immigrants from Punjab, India, came to the end of a long journey from Hong Kong, arriving at its intended destination—Burrard Inlet in Vancouver, BC, Canada. The passengers, all British subjects, were challenging the "continuous journey regulation," a recent amendment to Canada's *Immigration Act*, which stated that immigrants must come to Canada "by continuous journey from the country of which they are natives or citizens and upon through tickets purchased in that country."[2] The regulation, enacted in 1908, was part of an effort to curb Indian immigration to Canada, despite the fact that India was also part of the British Empire. At that time, there were few shipping agencies that came directly from India without a stopover. The Canadian Pacific Steamship Company was an exception and was asked to stop selling tickets from India to Canada. This made it difficult, if not impossible, for individuals born in India to immigrate to Canada. As an additional deterrent, a regulation was passed later that same year requiring potential Indian immigrants to have $200.00 in their possession at the time of their arrival in Canada.[3]

---

2. Library and Archives Canada, Statutes of Canada, *An Act to Amend the Immigration Act, 1908*, Ottawa: SC 7-8 Edward VII, Chapter 33.

3. Hugh Johnston, *Voyage of the Komagata Maru* (Vancouver, BC: University of British Columbia Press, 2014), 16-17.

Immigrants from India first arrived in Canada at the turn of the last century and, by the end of 1908, the population had reached 5,209.[4] These early pioneers faced overt racism and anti-Asian immigration sentiments, culminating in the formation of the Asiatic Exclusion League and the disenfranchisement of South Asian Canadians in April 1907. This was followed on September 7, 1907 by the Vancouver race riots, which resulted in businesses and homes owned by Chinese and Japanese Canadians being vandalized. As a result of the Continuous Journey Regulation, the South Asian population in Canada dramatically dropped to 2,342 by 1911, a decline of approximately 55% from 1908.[5]

In October 1913, thirty-nine Indian-born passengers aboard the Panama Maru—a ship carrying fifty-six passengers from Yokohama, Japan to Victoria, BC—successfully challenged the regulation with the assistance of lawyer Edward J. Bird and gained entry to Canada. Seeking a similar outcome, passengers led by Gurdit Singh, an Indian-born business man living in Singapore and Malaya who chartered the ship in Hong Kong, boarded the Komagata Maru bound for Canada where they hoped to establish new lives in Canada by pursuing work as laborers and farmers. The June 1, 1914 issue of *The Hindustanee* reported that "The ship was arranged to be brought in with the cooperation of many men, the majority of who are farmers seeking to secure, as British subjects, a little of the millions of fertile acres of British Columbian soil now lying wastefully idle, so that they might till them and eke out a living in the same ways that hundreds of thousands of white men are making a living in different capacities in India."[6]

Even though the passengers on board the Komagata Maru understood the obstacles they faced in their search for a new life, they made

---

4. Norman Buchignani, "South Asian Canadians," Canadian Encyclopedia, May 12, 2010, accessed December 10, 2018, https://www.thecanadianencyclopedia.ca/en/article/south-asians.

5. Canada. Statistics Canada. *Census and Statistics Office, Fifth Census of Canada 1911*, 1913, accessed January 2, 2019, http://publications.gc.ca/collections/collection_2016/statcan/CS98-1911-2.pdf.

6. Husain Rahim, "Welcome Komagata Maru," *Hindustanee*, June 1, 1914, accessed December 10, 2018, http://komagatamarujourney.ca/node/10263.

the long and uncomfortable journey to challenge this discrimination nonetheless. This time, however, government officials were prepared for the ship's arrival and there was a much different outcome; despite the fact that they were all British subjects, the passengers, with the exception of the ship's doctor and his family and a handful of returning passengers, were unable to disembark. They were forced to remain on board the crowded ship with rapidly dwindling supplies of food and water. Sustained only by the benevolent efforts of the sympathetic local South Asian Canadian community rallying on their behalf, the passengers battled with immigration officials for two months. On July 23, 1914, the Komagata Maru and its remaining passengers were forcibly sent back to India under threat of gunfire from the Canadian military vessel, the S.S. Rainbow. When the ship arrived in Budge-Budge, India after a six-month journey, nineteen of the passengers were killed in a skirmish with police, and many of the survivors were imprisoned or confined to their villages for many years.[7] During all stages of the incident, stacks of bureaucratic paperwork and correspondence documenting the actions and attitudes of the government officials involved were generated by these individuals and have been carefully preserved by institutions, such as Library and Archives Canada (LAC) and the City of Vancouver Archives (CoV Archives).

Exclusion and Erasure

Located at the CoV Archives, the fonds of Henry Herbert (H.H.) Stevens, a Member of Parliament for Vancouver at the time of the incident and an outspoken opponent of Asian immigration and an ardent proponent for a "white Canada," includes correspondence, reports, newspaper clippings, and other material documenting in great detail the incident from not only his perspective, but from that of the federal government and the key immigration officials involved, such as Malcolm Reid and

---

7. Simon Fraser University Library, Komagata Maru: Continuing the Journey, accessed December 1, 2018, http://komagatamarujourney.ca.

William Hopkinson.[8] In the documents they authored, these officials recorded information about the passengers and the local South Asian Canadian community, interviewing some in depth and noting their testimonies. The records in his fonds are a key primary source for information about interactions between the officials and the South Asian community in the years surrounding the incident; however, it is all documented from the viewpoint of the officials upholding the legislation intended to keep South Asians out of Canada. While they provide detailed and important evidence of the opinions, attitudes, and machinery behind the forces working against the passengers, they raise the following questions: How did the perspectives and roles of officials in the incident color the way in which they recorded these events or the actions and words of the passengers? Can we trust the accounts of those bent on keeping these immigrants out of the country as accurate representations? In spite of these significant concerns, the documents, preserved and made available by government institutions, along with contemporary newspaper reports, have been the records most accessible to those doing research in this area and constructing the narrative about the episode, leaving significant gaps.

Despite the fact that Vancouver's first archivist, Major J.S. Matthews, lived only blocks from the Sikh temple in Kitsilano, early records of the community do not appear to have made their way into the collection of the City of Vancouver Archives. I can locate only two mentions of "hindoos" in Matthews' seminal work *Early Vancouver*, published in 1956, including one sentence pertaining to the Komagata Maru incident, and each is framed by the context and viewpoint of the British- or Canadian-born pioneer whose story Matthews is recording.[9]

In the photographic record, we see rare glimpses of South Asians captured by photographers who documented the city. A well-known

---

8. Henry Herbert Stevens fonds, AM69, City of Vancouver Archives, Vancouver, British Columbia, Canada.

9. Major James Skitt Matthews, *Early Vancouver* (Vancouver, BC: City of Vancouver, 2011), http://former.vancouver.ca/ctyclerk/archives/digitized/EarlyVan/index.htm.

Philip Timms photograph, taken on Granville Street in 1907,[10] and a 1909 photograph of the crowd at the opening of the Granville Street Bridge, show that early South Asian immigrants were participating in the daily life of the city, but details about their identity have proven elusive due to other gaps in the contemporary documentary record—city directories, for example.[11]

Although I had lived in the Kitsilano neighborhood of Vancouver for several years, I had no idea that the neighborhood had once been home to many South Asian and Japanese immigrants in the early twentieth century, until I looked through old directories for the city in 2012. The directories are a significant source of information regarding those inhabitants of Vancouver who are not captured elsewhere in the archives. They list the names of the primary residents of each property along with other valuable information, such as occupation, place of employment and, in some cases, the names of spouses and/or children. The directories first show that individuals of South Asian origin lived in the Kitsilano and Fairview areas in 1908, the same year that the first Sikh gurdwara (temple) in North America was built at 1866 West Second Avenue. It was also the year that the government was actively trying to persuade the South Asian Canadian population to relocate to British Honduras.[12]

In addition to making this discovery, I was struck by the fact that, while all of the residents of a presumably British or European heritage were identified and recorded by name, and sometimes by occupation, their neighbors of South Asian or Asian origin were for the most part completely anonymous and devoid of names, recorded only by their perceived ethnicity, for which the derogatory terms "Hindoos" or "Hindu"

10. People and business along the 500 to 300 blocks of Granville, 1907, VPL6781, Historical Photographs Collection, Vancouver Public Library, Vancouver, British Columbia, Canada.

11. Crowd at the opening of the Granville Street Bridge, 1909, VPL8342, Historical Photographs Collection, Vancouver Public Library, Vancouver, British Columbia, Canada.

12. Henderson Publishing Company, Henderson's *City of Vancouver Directory*, (Vancouver, BC: Henderson Publishing, 1908).

or "Japanese," and sometimes simply "foreigners," were used. For example, the 1914 directory listing for West Second Avenue between Cedar and Cypress reads as follows:

> 1804: Vacant; 1819: Boyd John A.; 1822: Donaldson Wm; 1822 (rear): Vacant; 1827: Vacant; 1828: Hind Mrs Jean; 1831: Harrison Arthur; 1831 (rear): Butler John; 1832: Gibbs Chas E.; 1833: 1 Vacant, 2 Evans Thos W, 3 Wing Manley E., 4 Vacant; 1836: Burns Edw; 1842: Jacobs Mrs Alice; 1843: Vacant; 1846: Hindoos; 1847: Hindoos; 1856: Norman Percy E; 1866: Sikh Temple; 1867: Martin Geo; 1872: Sikh Committee; 1874: Cox Herbt C.; 1882: Vacant; 1890: Bestland Chas; 1892: Collins Robt; 1897: Sailes Joseph.

An effort has been made to identify and list the name of the man or woman at each address, with the exceptions of the only addresses containing inhabitants of South Asian origin (e.g., 1846 and 1847).[13]

As such, those controlling the documentation of this information reinforce the general sentiment that these individuals are to be viewed as interlopers or outsiders who do not merit individual entries. The use of the term "foreigners" within some directories further suggests a refusal to recognize these individuals as part of society—they are to be viewed as undesirable "aliens" or visitors from another country purely on the basis of their ethnicity.[14] In the alphabetical index for 1907, only two "Singhs" are listed in the entire city.[15] Over the next few years—although the labels of "Hindu," "Hindoos," or "Japanese" still dominate—there is a small growth in the number of individual names that make it into the street directory as well, such as S. Singh, laborer at Rat Portage Lumber Mill in False Creek and resident of 1678 West Second Avenue.[16] In the years immediately preceding and following the

---

13. Henderson Publishing Company, *Henderson's Greater Vancouver City Directory Part 1* (Vancouver, BC: Henderson Publishing, 1914).

14. Henderson Publishing Company, *Henderson's Greater Vancouver City Directory,* (Vancouver, BC: Henderson Publishing, 1917).

15. Henderson Publishing Company, *Henderson's City of Vancouver Directory,* (Vancouver, BC: Henderson Publishing, 1907).

16. Henderson Publishing Company, *Henderson's City of Vancouver and North Vancouver Directory Part 2* (Vancouver, BC: Henderson Publishing, 1910).

Komagata Maru incident in 1914, however, there is evidence of a shift back to identifying these residents solely by their ethnicity. Interestingly, this appears to coincide with the economic downturn of 1912, which led to an increasing fear of new immigrants competing for jobs. In a *Vancouver Sun* article published on December 2, 1913, Premier Robert McBride comments on the "hindoo question," claiming that opposition to "alien immigration" was "not based on grounds of racial animosity, but purely on social and economic grounds."[17] Not only did these decisions to exclude individuals from these records neglect to acknowledge their existence at the time, it has also helped to erase many of them from the historical record.

At the time of the Komagata Maru incident, the media also promulgated the idea that South Asian immigrants were to be considered as foreigners and not genuine in their desire to develop new lives in Canada. When the Komagata Maru arrived in Vancouver, headlines stoked fears of being overrun with South Asian immigrants through the use of phrases such as "Hindu Invaders."[18] Words such as "tourists" and "excursion" were also used to describe the passengers and their journeys to Canada, serving to make light of their experiences and to encourage the notion that the passengers and as well as past immigrants were foreigners only temporarily visiting Canada.[19] While these articles document the information, attitudes, and opinions about the Komagata Maru and its passengers to which Vancouverites were exposed at the time of the episode, they cannot be considered objective accounts of the incident or the motivations of the passengers. *The Hindustanee*, published in Chinatown for a brief time in 1914 by Husain Rahim, stood alone amongst the Vancouver press as an advocate for the passengers. In his

---

17. "Hindu Deportation Stated to Assume Very Grave Aspect," *Vancouver Sun*, December 2, 1913, accessed December 10, 2018, http://digital.lib.sfu.ca/km-5125/newsclipping-vancouver-sun-hindu-deportation-stated-assume-very-grave-aspect.

18. "Hindu Invaders Now in the City Harbor on Komagata Maru," *Vancouver Sun*, May 23, 1914, accessed December 10, 2018, http://komagatamarujourney.ca/node/8194.

19. "A Hindu Excursion," *Vancouver Daily Province*, May 27, 1914, accessed December 10, 2018, http://komagatamarujourney.ca/node/8288.

June 1, 1914 editorial titled "Welcome to the Komagata Maru," Rahim wrote: "We extend a cordial welcome to Bhai Gurdit Singh and his party of 375 Hindustanees on board the S.S. Komagata Maru, which arrived in this harbor on the morning of the 22nd [sic] of last month. All kinds of spectacular and alarming stories in which the arrival of this ship has been termed a Hindu invasion have been indulged in by the local press day after day, in their sensation mongering dailies…"[20]

Although Gurdit Singh later published his own version of events,[21] the majority of passengers aboard the Komagata Maru, and even the community onshore, did not have access to the same tools or channels as the government officials to document and preserve their own view of events. Faced with such obstacles, it is easy to assume that, nearly a hundred years after the incident, all relevant records should have already made their way into institutions or have been lost or destroyed.

The Project Begins

Over the past decade, SFU Library has built up a strong digital presence, with over 130 digital collections featured on its website, including many of a multicultural nature. In 2011, the Library received $350,000 in funding from Citizenship and Immigration Canada as part of the Community Historical Recognition Program to build a website of resources related to the Komagata Maru incident of 1914. With in-kind and other funding from the Library, the total budget for the project was nearly $500,000. The team dedicated to this project at the Library included administrators, librarians, archivists, library systems staff, and students. Brian Owen, then the Associate Dean of Libraries for Processing and Systems, served as project manager. My own role in the project was two-fold: I served as the project coordinator and I contributed in my capacity as an archivist.

20. Rahim, "Welcome Komagata Maru."

21. Gurdit Singh, *Voyage of Komagatamaru or India's Slavery Abroad* (Calcutta: Gurdit Singh, [1928]).

Half a million dollars is a daunting amount for one institution to spend on a major digitization project without extensive holdings of relevant material. Special Collections had begun collecting in the area of South Asian Canadian history but, at the time, the division had only one collection of primary documents, photographs, and sound recordings pertaining to the very early community in British Columbia. We would later discover, however, that this included some very significant items. We had also recently acquired the very large archives of the Canadian Farmworkers Union and had collaborated with the SFU Archives in digitizing their Indo-Canadian Oral History Collection. Our first step was to involve Hugh Johnston, SFU professor emeritus of History and author of the seminal text *The Voyage of the Komagata Maru*, as a consultant. He and his publisher generously allowed us to make a digital copy of the entire 1989 edition of his book available online, which became an important anchor to our site. I spent an entire afternoon with Johnston poring over his original research files, which were still fully intact. With the permission of LAC, the CoV Archives, and the Government of India, we were able to digitize and make available the entire content of the research files.

A partnership was established with the CoV Archives that enabled them to scan all of the files relating to the Komagata Maru and Asian immigration to Canada in the H.H. Stevens fonds. Relevant photographs from their collection and from that of the Vancouver Public Library were also acquired. These collaborations were key to providing the digital archives with a strong foundation, particularly in terms of the "official" government record, but what really made this project unique was its ability to engage the community and to locate records that had rarely been seen outside of it.

Engaging the Community

With the tagline "Engaging the World," SFU's strategic vision is "To be the leading engaged university defined by its dynamic integration of innovative education, cutting-edge research, and far-reaching community engagement."[22] That, in many ways, is the vision of community engagement this project has embodied. A decision was made at the outset that, in order to increase its accessibility among the community that was most affected by the event, the website text would not only be made available in the required English and French, but in Hindi and Punjabi as well. In addition, we decided that the website should be as accessible to members of the general public seeking to learn more about the incident and the history of the community as it would be to scholarly researchers, so we provided sufficient background and contextual information to the records being presented and used less academic language throughout the website. We also sought to make the website itself as engaging as possible by creating interactive features such as a timeline and passenger list to encourage users to explore the site and its contents.

As we began the project, SFU librarian Moninder Lalli took on the role of Community Liaison Librarian. She immediately connected with the community and acquired items relating to the Komagata Maru for digitization from local South Asian Canadian poets, authors, and historians. By connecting with these individuals, we began to generate interest, publicity, and excitement for the project within the community. The response we received was overwhelmingly positive, despite the fact that, as a government-funded institution from outside of the community, our motivations could reasonably have been questioned. Many within the community welcomed SFU's involvement in the project, since we were respected and viewed as a neutral party. That was important in a community that has been politically divided over the incident, most particularly about whether a proper apology had been made by the Canadian government under the leadership of Prime Minister Stephen Harper. While we added contextual information to provide a more curated experience through the website, we were careful to ensure that it was presented in a very neutral manner and could accommodate several perspectives.

---

22. "Strategic Vision," Simon Fraser University, accessed December 20, 2018, http://www.sfu.ca/content/dam/sfu/engage/StrategicVision.pdf.

A couple of months into the project, something happened that I believe had a dramatic impact on its level of success: we hired two students from the community, Naveen Girn and Milan Singh, who were involved in academic projects relating to the South Asian Canadian experience—the Air India bombing and the Komagata Maru incident. They brought enthusiasm, deep subject expertise, passion, perspective, and a knowledge of how to navigate the community politically and with the correct protocols. With established relationships and trust within the community, Girn and Singh were invaluable in connecting us with key individuals and organizations with archival material, knowledge, ideas, and resources to contribute. They ensured that the content created for the website—most particularly the text, lessons plans, and video interviews—was created in a manner that was balanced, respectful, and sensitive to the community, and they ensured that the social justice and educational significance of the event was not lost.

We created an Indian Scholarly Advisory Committee early on to suggest possible content for digitization and to advise us on more sensitive issues regarding community relations. Similarly, we benefited from the wisdom of the SFU-India Advisory Council, a body set up to further the University's relationships with India, and to encourage engagement with BC's South Asian community. Significantly, the feedback that we consistently received from these groups was that the website should not focus solely on the Komagata Maru incident but that it should demonstrate how the community was able to overcome the obstacles that had been put in its way and to develop and prosper in subsequent years.

As a result, we were able to develop a strong community component for the website, including video interviews with scholars, youth, and community members descended from passengers, which provided varying contexts and perspectives through which to view the archival content. Also included were: published books on the history of the local South Asian Canadian community by leading South Asian Canadian scholars; records of playwrights and poets who have written about the Komagata Maru; records pertaining to the struggle to regain the vote for South Asians; and primary documents, photographs, and sound recordings relating to the incident and the early history of South Asians in Vancouver.

Another unexpected outcome of this outreach work was the development of a collaborative relationship with the Vancouver Khalsa Diwan Society (KDS), an organization that was intimately involved in providing support for the passengers on the ship in 1914 and whose history figures prominently in many of the records digitized for the website. The members gladly shared with us the items that they had developed for their own displays, such as Johnston's biographies of one hundred people involved in the incident. This proved to be an important contextual anchor for the website. Having the biographies available on the website ensured that they reached an even greater audience. The KDS also helped to identify content for the website and supported and promoted our project extensively in the community. In return, we advised its members professionally on their own activities, which included the establishment of a museum relating to the event and the community's history. Two years later, in 2014, we were again able to collaborate with the KDS to plan events commemorating the centenary of the incident.

Throughout the project, many individuals commented that they had not learned about the Komagata Maru incident at school and had only become aware of it as adults. Thus, an important component of the website is lesson plans, targeting students from Grade 4 to high school, which are framed around the digitized material and encourage engagement with the records. The number of lesson plan downloads has increased on an annual basis, with approximately nine hundred downloads in 2017.

When the website was completed in May 2012, we had two events: a website launch to thank everyone who had been involved with the project and a day-long symposium that featured discussion panels with community historians, writers, artists, poets, filmmakers, and youth. The symposium truly began a dialogue with the community in terms of exploring the roots of the incident, its lasting impact on the South Asian Canadian community and Canadian society as a whole, and the lessons to be learned to prevent such an injustice from occurring in the future.

Documenting the Community

The combination of technology with records from the South Asian Canadian community has been powerful. As academic institutions begin to focus "on the truly unique materials that are out there," Brian Owen sees the SFU Library's Komagata Maru project as reflecting a trend towards "focusing on local and community-based topics and material that up until recently were dismissed as not being germane to academic research or discussions…more and more, institutions realize just how rich that content is now." Engaging with the local community and working "with the actual creators, owners, or people who are the stewards" to make their records openly and freely available enabled us "to make [the content] available in ways that is sensitive to some of their concerns or their perspectives on it and ultimately it means we are making content available not even just to the local community and our academic institution…[but] to a wider [community]."[23]

When the project was initiated in 2012, members from the community came forward with records relating to the incident, and beyond, from a multitude of perspectives. For instance, Aruna Pandia loaned us her family's archives relating to the work of her father, Dr. Durai Pal Pandia, so they could be digitized for the website. A lawyer and activist, Dr. Pandia was instrumental in helping the South Asian community in Canada regain the right to vote in 1947 and in advocating for significant improvements to the rights of immigrants in Canada. In addition, individuals who had participated on the committee for the commemoration of the 75th anniversary of the incident in 1989 loaned us their records documenting the activities that had taken place.

In 2012, we made contact with the family of Arjan Singh Brar. Arriving in Canada in 1926, Brar was an active member of the pioneer South Asian Canadian community in Vancouver. He had held numerous roles within the KDS at Vancouver's first Sikh temple and was at the center of the religious, political, economic, and social life of the community.

---

23. Brian Owen, interview by author, Simon Fraser University Library, September 13, 2018.

Brar had a keen interest in local history and, as secretary of the society for many years, recorded in great detail the activities of the community dating back to the early 1900s. All of the records that he had collected documenting the early history of the community were stored in an old metal chest. This included scrapbooks of original, and in many cases rare, newspaper clippings documenting the local South Asian community for the period from 1913 to 1921, including an entire scrapbook devoted to the Komagata Maru incident and several issues of *The Hindustanee*.

In two thin, DIY-looking notebooks, Arjan had carefully recorded by hand, in Punjabi, the history and activities of the Vancouver KDS and the local South Asian Canadian community between 1906 and 1947. Significantly, the diary includes an extremely rare account of the Komagata Maru incident and related events from the local community's perspective. The diary is filled with the names of individuals who participated in events, which demonstrates that there was indeed an active and thriving local community at the time. Also included were several original letters from the passengers' lawyer, Edward J. Bird, documents relating to the struggle to regain the right to vote, and a rare recording of Prime Minister Jawaharlal Nehru's visit to the temple in 1949. A surprise not only to us during this process, but to the Brar family itself, was the discovery in the chest of the original minute book for the United India Home Rule League and its successor organization located in Kitsilano. The minute book documents the origins of the Indian independence movement in Vancouver and the local community's contribution to the fight against British rule in India. It also records the activities of the group and all of the members by name. Since the minute book was written in Punjabi, it was not until community historian Kalwant Nadeem Parmar read the text while preparing the items for the project that its significance came to light. The family happily loaned all of the material to us for digitization and to make it available online. With the digitization of this material, the history of the community began to emerge in its own words and to become a part of the known historical record.

Figure 1. Arjan Singh Brar Collection, Simon Fraser University Library, Special Collections and Rare Books Division.

Significantly, the chest also contained an alternate passenger list for the Komagata Maru (in Punjabi) that Brar had created close to the time of the incident. Brar's list contained information that was not captured, or different—or arguably more accurate than what was in the official ship's manifest. We hired an SFU student to consolidate the information from the two lists and, with input from Hugh Johnston and Parmar, to create the most comprehensive and accurate passenger list to date. Integrating information from official reports made once the ship returned to India with hard-to-find monographs, the list also includes any known information concerning the fate of each passenger. To make the list interactive, a record for each passenger was linked from his or her entry in a digital copy of the original ship's manifest, and we linked any digitized documents related to a particular passenger with his or her record. All of the original source documents are available online and we recognize that the passenger list will continue to develop over time, particularly as new information from descendants of the passengers becomes available. With all of this additional information and with the correction of known errors, the identities of the passengers are becoming clearer and are now in a highly accessible format.

Experiencing the extremely positive response to the records being accessible online, just prior to the 100th anniversary of the incident in 2014, the Brar family gifted the chest and all of its contents to the Library. Arjan Singh Brar had passed away while his son Amarjit was still a young man. The chest full of his father's carefully prepared documents and newspaper clippings was one of the items Amarjit inherited; he knew that the items were very meaningful to his father and he kept them as a memento of him, but he did not really understand their value until years later. Amarjit was unable to read Punjabi, so he did not know what the passenger list was or why it mattered; his mother, also, did not have any knowledge of the material or its significance. Nobody knew about the significance of the records sitting in the chest, and they might easily have been thrown out.

When I asked Amarjit why he decided to donate his father's papers that meant so much to him to the SFU Library, he responded that it was "not a difficult decision" and gave three reasons.[24] First, he knew that SFU would take care of the items and that they would be safe and preserved. The family had had a flood in recent years that nearly destroyed the documents. Over the years, some items had gone missing and he did not want to risk the material being discarded at a future date. The family had grown to trust the Library, and had visited Special Collections and felt comfortable with the space and the staff. His sons agreed that the material would be safer in the secure, climate-controlled vault in Special Collections.

Second, the material would be accessible both online and in the Library for anyone to look at and to learn from. During his lifetime, Arjan had taken great pride in showing the documents to visiting scholars with an interest in learning the history recorded within them. In contrast, prior to the material being digitized and then donated, "It was just sitting here, in a trunk, no one knew about it and it might be thrown out." Amarjit feels that his father would have appreciated having the material widely available for research and that he would have been honored to know that interest in it had "reached this height."

24. Amarjit Brar, interview by author, Brar residence, September 21, 2018.

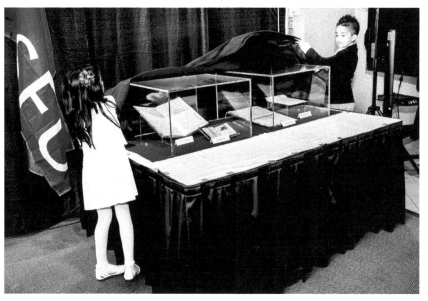

Figure 2. Arjan Singh Brar's great-grandchildren unveil items from his collection pertaining to the Komagata Maru incident, May 23, 2014.

Third, Amarjit considered himself to be the custodian of the material, and he wanted recognition and a legacy for his father. At the 2014 commemoration event, Arjan's great-grandchildren unveiled a case containing items from the collection as part of the formal program. His great-grandson in particular was very proud of the records and of being a part of their donation.

Through the connections made during the project and the positive reputation of the website, we have also received donations from other families within the community. In 2015, the records of Ajaib Sidhoo, a Vancouver businessman and philanthropist who emigrated from India as a small child in the 1920s, were donated to Special Collections and Rare Books by his children. His archives document the experiences of a young South Asian Canadian man growing up near the sawmills of Vancouver Island and in the neighborhood of Kitsilano, primarily through the candid photographs he took long before the days of Instagram and Facebook.

With current technologies and the Internet, why should family members donate the physical items that mean so much to them? Why not lend them for scanning and keep the material within the family? While some access is certainly better than none and, as previously discussed, there are many benefits to having the material digitized, there is no replacement for viewing the original documents in person, to touch them, and to see the ink on the page. We have had scholars very familiar with the digitized documents travel long distances just to view them in person and experience them firsthand. To see the indent that Arjan's pen made in the paper as he painstakingly wrote out the information for each of the 376 passengers on the list and to hear the swish of the paper as one scans through the diary in its three-dimensional form create connections that just cannot be replicated online.

Although digitization affords tremendous access, it is not without its pitfalls. It is not unusual to hear stories about original archival records that were microfilmed many years ago and the originals destroyed only to discover later that the job was sloppily done with edges of text cut off or pages missed. In some cases, the quality of the microfilm or the original itself is terrible and the text or important pieces of information are obscured, leading to gaps and questions that could be answered if the original was still accessible. For instance, the microfilmed copy of the Komagata Maru manifest contains many blemishes that obscure information which might still be possible to recover if one had access to the original document. Scanning quality has improved significantly since the early days of microfilm, yet sometimes the quality of the digital copy does not always capture all of the detail that exists in the original item and it is necessary to have access to the original record to accurately determine the information that it contains.

In addition, maintaining the digital files and the website that hosts them is expensive and difficult over time. Websites require maintenance to keep them working and to keep the content accessible, which can be expensive and resource intensive. While many projects get an initial infusion of cash from a grant, there may not be ongoing resources in terms of budget or staff to keep the site going and the content accessible once it is gone. Another important consideration is whether the organization digitizing the material has the ability to preserve the digital files. All of this adds up to the very real possibility that long-term digital access may not always be possible and these resources are at risk of becoming inaccessible and once again lost to the historical record. While paper sitting in acid free boxes in a vault with a stable temperature and perfect humidity may last for hundreds of years, we don't yet have the same confidence in digital content.

Drawing on the expert knowledge of community members and scholars, the project also helped us to identify several significant and unique items that were in our own collection, such as an original 1913 photograph of the passengers from the Panama Maru ship in custody in Victoria, BC, with members of the local community (including Husain Rahim) in the foreground. There is also an original photograph of Mewa Singh's funeral.

In the months following the incident, several murders took place within the Vancouver South Asian community. These were related to hostilities that had developed in the community as a result of actions taken by immigration officer William Hopkinson, who had been one of the key characters in the Komagata Maru incident. In October 1914, Mewa Singh shot and killed Hopkinson at the Vancouver court house, an action for which he was executed in January 1915. He has been commemorated as a martyr in the community ever since. Although Hopkinson's funeral procession—which consisted of 2,000 men and saw thousands of Vancouverites lining crowded streets—was extensively covered by the media, there had been no known published photographs of Singh's funeral procession. Despite the procession being much humbler in size than Hopkinson's, the photograph shows a united and strong community presence. The community in 2014 was extremely excited to learn of the resurfacing of this photographic document—this side of the story is now accessible and has relevance. The photograph has been widely shared online, in social media posts, and in publications. Most importantly, it was used extensively during the commemoration of the 100th anniversary of Singh's death in January 2015 and informed the re-enactment of the procession in its original location. As such, the image is already filling in the gaps and informing our understanding of this story that is so sacred to the community.

The Academic Institution as Custodian

Why should an academic institution take on the role of custodian? Would it not be better if records remained within the community that created them? Would they not be better able to provide context for them and to maintain control over their access and how they are used? Community-based archives and academic institutions each offer advantages and disadvantages. Community-based archives often have very strong connections with the communities they are documenting, and those organizations will be aware of existing collections. Due to these connections, they will often have the implicit trust of potential donors, which might take academic institutions much longer to build. Since it is their own communities' histories that they are preserving, community-based archives and their staff tend to have a deep knowledge of the people and events represented in the material with which they are working. However, such organizations are often under-funded or may have an unstable funding base. As such, they may not have the resources needed to keep the archives open and accessible full time. Their hours may be limited, which could have an impact on accessibility. Likewise, although they may have a keen interest in making the material accessible online, they may not have the equipment or technical resources necessary to digitize the material and host it online.

On the other hand, archives in academic institutions are more likely to have stability in terms of financial and staffing resources, regular hours and the ability to provide unrestricted public access to collections. Such stability also guarantees that they can commit to indefinite preservation of the records that they acquire in all formats and that donors can feel confident that their archives will be safe. They are also more likely to have highly trained full-time staff to work with the collections, access to more funding, and a robust infrastructure for digitization and other special projects, as well as a purpose-built, climate-controlled physical location for storing the material. In those cases where a community is divided on certain issues, an academic institution may be viewed as more neutral, causing fewer concerns with regard to accessing material. The ability to digitize material and make it accessible on a wide scale so that it can be viewed freely anywhere, anytime, and by anyone further flattens the ability to have access to records. It guarantees that knowledge is open to a broad audience and that it is not limited to privileged access by scholars and researchers who have connections or who can travel to view it in person. As one who handles reference requests for the website, I know first-hand that the records online are contributing to scholarship that is taking place in Canada, Europe, and even Kuala Lumpur. Renisa Mawani, author of *Across Oceans of Law: The Komagata Maru and Jurisdiction in the Time of Empire* and professor in the Department of Sociology at the University of British Columbia concurs that

> the website has been invaluable to researchers interested in the Komagata Maru and working in the fields of Punjabi, Canadian, and BC history. My own work draws from archives in Vancouver, Ottawa, London, Glasgow and Delhi, however, the site has provided a shorthand for looking up details on the passengers, authorities, and the voyage. The digitized records and photographs have been incredibly useful for teaching as well, giving students opportunities to think critically about archives and the making of history.[25]

The work done by community and academic archives does not have to be mutually exclusive. Collaboration between the two can be tremendously advantageous for both parties. For example, larger institutions can provide support by signing on to grant proposals and, if necessary, by providing technical training and expertise. They can also benefit from the passion and profound knowledge of the community held by community-based archives. The challenge is to establish strong communication with each other and to discover how best to complement each other's activities so that together they build a stronger network.

May 23, 2014 marked the 100th anniversary of the Komagata Maru's arrival in Vancouver. The Library was part of a consortia of eight organizations across the Lower Mainland that scheduled exhibits and events to commemorate the anniversary. For our part in the activities, the Library added additional materials to the website, and planned and

---

25. Renisa Mawani, email message to author, January 2, 2019.

hosted a commemoration event with nearly 300 guests. Physically situated in a room overlooking the area of Burrard Inlet that had been inhabited by the ship and its 376 passengers a century earlier to the day, we had an incredible opportunity to connect with and recognize the community and to reflect on the significance of the incident and its legacies. In addition to pioneers, descendants of passengers, and other members of the community, attendees included elected government officials, members of the SFU administration, and project partners. The event was livestreamed on the Canadian Broadcasting Corporation television network and featured on local news broadcasts. It also provided an opportunity to publicly recognize the Brar family for its contribution to the Komagata Maru archive. During the anniversary events, material from the website was used extensively in blog posts, publicity and promotional materials, as well as by academics and the media as they wrote on the subject. Since much of this material had come directly from the community, it was possible to have a far more balanced and complete story surrounding the incident than would ever have been the case only a few years prior.

Conclusion

Since its launch in March 2012, traffic to the website has continued to increase. In 2017, for example, there were nearly 95,000 visits and over 135,000 page views from users all over the world. On May 18, 2016, when Canadian Prime Minister Justin Trudeau delivered an official apology for the incident in Parliament, the number of site views spiked at 2,500 for that day alone. When considering this continued growth in use, Owen reflected that "In some ways, the site is a victim of its own success; we can't just say that the project is over and we met the [grant] requirements for the five years…we have to keep this one up for the long-haul…with successes come obligations and responsibilities…but it's a good problem to have."[26]

---

26. Owen, interview.

The website continues to be a living entity, and we continue to add new material as further funding becomes available. In 2015, the Library received funding from the Government of India to digitize and make more material available through the website. With this assistance, we were able to locate some previously little-known records and to publish full English translations of Arjan Singh Brar's diary, increasing access to an even broader audience. Events hosted by the Consul General of India provided opportunities to reconnect with the community and with so many of the individuals who had been involved with the project over the years.

My own experiences working with the community and donors on this project and beyond affected me tremendously in terms of developing my personal research interests and professional passions. Above all, it taught me that it is important to keep challenging the notions about what we consider to be the "official" historical record and our responsibilities as memory-keepers to ensure that the record is as complete as possible. As archives of the community become more accessible, our ability to reconstruct history is continually evolving and shifting; our understanding becomes more inclusive and multidimensional, providing us with the opportunity to better understand the early South Asian Canadian community through new contexts. With every new record that is added, more than one hundred years after the ship left Canada, new and more complex perspectives on the Komagata Maru incident and the community's fight for equality and justice continue to emerge. Early South Asian Canadian pioneers had names, families, and an active community, and their role in shaping this province in the face of considerable adversity should be acknowledged. As a result, the website has contributed to a much richer awareness of the incident and the history of South Asians in Canada. Having the community's account of the incident and subsequent events online and accessible further legitimized these records and the community's experiences. Most importantly, it empowered the community to come to terms with past injustices and it helped to propel forward new calls for social justice—for all Canadians.

Bibliography

Brar, Amarjit. Interview by author. September 21, 2018.

Buchignani, Norman. "South Asian Canadians." *Canadian Encyclopedia.* May 12, 2010. https://www.thecanadianencyclopedia.ca/en/article/south-asians.

Canada. Statistics Canada. Census and Statistics Office. "Fifth census of Canada 1911." 1913. Accessed January 2, 2019. http://publications.gc.ca/collections/collection_2016/statcan/CS98-1911-2.pdf.

Henderson Publishing Company. *Henderson's City of Vancouver Directory.* Vancouver, BC: Henderson Publishing, 1907.

Henderson Publishing Company. *Henderson's City of Vancouver Directory.* Vancouver, BC: Henderson Publishing, 1908.

Henderson Publishing Company. *Henderson's City of Vancouver and North Vancouver Directory Part 2.* Vancouver, BC: Henderson Publishing, 1910.

Henderson Publishing Company. *Henderson's Greater Vancouver City Directory Part 1.* Vancouver, BC: Henderson Publishing, 1914.

Henderson Publishing Company Limited. *Henderson's Greater Vancouver City Directory.* Vancouver, BC: Henderson Publishing, 1917.

Johnston, Hugh. *Voyage of the Komagata Maru.* Vancouver, BC: University of British Columbia Press, 2014.

Library and Archives Canada. Statutes of Canada. *An Act to Amend the Immigration Act,* 1908. Ottawa: SC 7-8 Edward VII, Chapter 33.

Matthews, Major James Skitt. *Early Vancouver.* Vancouver, BC: City of Vancouver, 2011. http://former.vancouver.ca/ctyclerk/archives/digitized/EarlyVan/index.htm.

Owen, Brian. Interview by author. September 13, 2018.

Rahim, Husain. "Welcome Komagata Maru." Vancouver, BC: *Hindustanee,* June 1, 1914.

Simon Fraser University. "Strategic Vision." SFU.ca. Accessed December 20, 2018. http://www.sfu.ca/content/dam/sfu/engage/StrategicVision.pdf.

Simon Fraser University Library. "Komagata Maru: Continuing the Journey." Accessed December 1, 2018. http://komagatamarujourney.ca.

Singh, Gurdit. *Voyage of Komagatamaru or India's Slavery Abroad.* Calcutta: Gurdit Singh, [1928].

Vancouver Daily Province. "A Hindu Excursion." May 27, 1914. http://komagatamarujourney.ca/node/8288.

Vancouver Sun. "Hindu Deportation Stated to Assume Very Grave Aspect." December 2, 1913. http://digital.lib.sfu.ca/km-5125/newsclipping-vancouver-sun-hindu-deportation-stated-assume-very-grave-aspect.

Vancouver Sun. "Hindu Invaders Now in the City Harbor on Komagata Maru." May 23, 1914. http://komagatamarujourney.ca/node/8194.

Chapter 8

ETHICAL CATALOGING AND RACISM IN SPECIAL COLLECTIONS

Elizabeth Hobart

Introduction

Cataloging is an ethical act, ensuring the discoverability of library resources regardless of content. If an item is uncataloged, or cataloged at a minimal level, the item risks being overlooked by researchers. In an open stack library, there is always a chance that an item might be discovered by serendipity, but in special collections, where materials are in closed stacks, cataloging is even more important. Without a detailed, accurate record, items literally remain hidden.

Cataloging decisions are governed in part by standards, such as "Resource Description and Access," "Descriptive Cataloging of Rare Materials," and the "Library of Congress Subject Headings" (LCSH), but applying these standards requires catalogers' judgment. To represent materials ethically, catalogers must ask questions in the course of their work, such as: how much information is necessary for discovery? How many access points and subject headings should be added? How much detail should be included in notes? Are we risking censorship by including certain subject headings or flagging the presence of slurs? And, finally, how do catalogers balance these concerns with the need to move quickly?

These ethical challenges become more pronounced when cataloging items that espouse ideas with which the cataloger disagrees. Materials expressing racist viewpoints frequently appear in special collections. In some cases, content about race will be apparent from the nature of the material. Researchers can expect to encounter racism in, for example, the papers of the Ku Klux Klan. Works with subtler racism, such as fiction with stereotypical descriptions of people of color or magazines with cartoons containing racist caricatures, are more difficult, and catalogers may be tempted to avoid these items or minimize racist aspects. Although facing racism can be uncomfortable for catalogers, the potential harm caused by minimizing racism should outweigh this discomfort. In special collections, which often hold historical collections, minimizing racism risks presenting a whitewashed version of history. While some materials will still be findable, others will be hidden, which in turn can contribute to a limited understanding of the history of racism.

In this essay, I will describe my own experiences cataloging items containing racism in special collections. First, I will provide historical framing, including a discussion of colorblind racism and its effects on cataloging. Second, I will discuss three examples drawn from my own work cataloging special collections, including decisions made and the effects of those decisions. Third, I will conclude by providing advice for others cataloging similar materials.

Colorblind Racism and Librarianship

In the 1960s, the idea of racial colorblindness emerged as an attempt to end segregation. Whereas the Jim Crow laws segregated by race, proponents of racial colorblindness believed that colorblindness would lead to equality.[1] In the decades since, this idea has spread widely, to the extent that the phrase "I don't see color; I just see people" has almost become a stereotype. Regardless, racial disparities continue. Median income for non-Hispanic white American households in 2017 was $68,000,

---

1. Michael K. Brown et al., *Whitewashing Race: The Myth of a Color-Blind Society* (Berkeley: University of California Press, 2003), 3.

compared to $40,500 for black households.[2] In 2015/2016, 88 percent of white students in the United States graduated from high school within four years, compared to only 76 percent of black students.[3] At the state level, white graduation rates range from 76 to 94 percent, while black graduation rates range from 57 to 88 percent.[4] Black students' college completion rate within six years is 45.9 percent, compared to 67.2 percent for white students.[5] Approximately one third of all black males will be imprisoned during their lifetimes, and roughly 8 percent of all black people are arrested annually.[6] African American homeowners are more likely to have high-interest mortgages, and the median listing price of homes in majority-black neighborhoods is over $150,000 less than neighborhoods with less than 1 percent black population.[7]

Despite these disparities, nearly 75 percent of white Americans claim to be racially colorblind.[8] The insistence that no significant difference exists between races represents a form of racism that differs significantly from the Jim Crow-era: colorblind racism. Although scholars' definitions of "colorblind racism" vary, they share two key aspects:

2. "Historical Income Tables: Households," United States Census Bureau, last updated August 28, 2018, https://www.census.gov/data/tables/time-series/demo/income-poverty/historical-income-households.html.

3. "Public High School Graduation Rates," *National Center for Education Statistics*, updated May 2018, https://nces.ed.gov/programs/coe/indicator_coi.asp.

4. "Public High School Graduation Rates."

5. Doug Shapiro et al., *A National View of Student Attainment Rates by Race and Ethnicity: Fall 2010 Cohort*, Signature Report no. 12b (Herndon, VA: National Student Clearinghouse Research Center, 2017), https://nscresearchcenter.org/wp-content/uploads/Signature12-RaceEthnicity.pdf.

6. Eduardo Bonilla-Silva, *Racism without Racists: Color-Blind Racism and the Persistence of Racial Inequality in America*, 5th ed. (Lanham: Rowman & Littlefield, 2018), 34.

7. Joseph P. Williams, "Segregation's Legacy: Fifty Years After the Fair Housing Act was Signed, America is Nearly as Segregated as When President Lyndon Johnson Signed the Law," *U.S. News*, April 20, 2018, https://www.usnews.com/news/the-report/articles/2018-04-20/us-is-still-segregated-even-after-fair-housing-act; Christopher Ingraham, "How White Racism Destroys Black Wealth," *Washington Post*, November 28, 2018, https://www.washingtonpost.com/business/2018/11/28/how-white-racism-destroys-black-wealth/.

8. Philip J. Mazzocco, *The Psychology of Racial Colorblindness: A Critical Review* (New York: Palgrave Macmillan, 2017), 45.

1) race is not the cause of current racial disparities; and 2) individual behavior is emphasized over group identification.[9] Or, as summarized by Meghan Burke, "colorblind racism typically refers to an assertion of equal opportunity that minimizes the reality of racism in favor of individual or cultural explanations for inequality."[10] However, racial privilege, in which white people receive group-based advantages while people of color are placed at a disadvantage, continues to affect society. As a result, when the burden of racial disparities is shifted from groups to individuals, white people benefit, receiving individual credit for achievements, while people of color are individually held responsible for failing to achieve at the same level.[11]

The call for equality without recognition of underlying power structures is echoed in discourse around libraries and librarianship. Notably, the "Core Values of Librarianship of the American Library Association" states that "the publicly supported library provides free and equal access to information for *all people* of the community."[12] This statement, however, emphasizes the ideal of equality over the reality of existing power structures and, as a result, fails to engage with discussions around race and inequality.[13] In the past, these power structures were more apparent in libraries, but libraries' attempts at neutrality have obscured this. Jonathan Furner divides the history of public libraries in the United States into two eras: from 1850-1945, libraries chiefly served a minority of elite scholars while providing entertainment to the masses.[14] Since 1945, however, the conception of libraries as guardians of democracy has become more predominant. While this has opened the library to

---

9. Bonilla-Silva, *Racism without Racists*, 2; Meghan Burke, *Colorblind Racism* (Cambridge: Polity Press, 2019), 2; Brown et al., *Whitewashing Race*, 7.

10. Burke, *Colorblind Racism*, 2.

11. Bonilla-Silva, *Racism without Racists*, 63.

12. "Core Values of Librarianship," American Library Association, adopted June 29, 2004, http://www.ala.org/advocacy/intfreedom/corevalues (emphasis added).

13. Maura Seale, "Compliant Trust: The Public Good and Democracy in the ALA's 'Core Values of Librarianship,'" *Library Trends* 64, no. 3 (2016): 592.

14. Jonathan Furner, "Dewey Deracialized: A Critical Race-Theoretic Perspective," *Knowledge Organization* 34, no. 3 (2007): 151.

more users, oppression is rarely replaced immediately by democracy. Instead, librarians have been placed in a position of "remain[ing] stoically neutral and indifferent to conflicting interests."[15] Ideally, this neutrality would lead to equality, but the existing power structures instead can lead to an environment that continues to privilege white people over people of color.

These attempts at neutrality and colorblindness have spilled into the library catalog, with catalogers trying to remain "stoically neutral," even in the face of racism.[16] Too often, rather than noting racism in a resource, the catalog record is silent. Sometimes, catalogers simply fail to catalog racist materials, making these items undiscoverable. Colorblind practices can also lead catalogers to minimize racism in descriptions. For instance, Maurice Wheeler cites examples of libraries that label collections of minstrel music as "Ragtime" or "African American Music," despite the white, racist origin of these compositions.[17] In addition, racist content is often omitted from catalog records. For example, since cover art and lyrics don't need to be described, catalogers often decide simply not to describe them.[18]

Historical collections and archives reflect the history of racism. Cataloging these materials allows researchers to locate them, rather than hiding them in backlogs or behind comfortable terminology. To do otherwise risks hiding or obscuring the darker parts of our history. As long as racial differences exist, we must likewise acknowledge that race exists, and that eliminating or avoiding the language of race does not remove the underlying racism.[19] Rather, colorblind approaches can become an excuse for avoiding discussions around race, which in turn leads to continued policies of racial colorblindness and, in Furner's

---

15. Furner, "Dewey Deracialized," 151.

16. Furner, "Dewey Deracialized," 151.

17. Maurice B. Wheeler, "Politics and Race in American Historical Popular Music: Contextualized Access and Minstrel Music Archives," *Archival Science* 11, no. 1/2 (March 2011): 61.

18. Wheeler, "Politics and Race in American Historical Popular Music," 67.

19. Furner, "Dewey Deracialized," 165.

words, "continued adherence to a policy of 'neutrality' or 'colorblind-ness' merely serves to preserve the status quo in which the interests of the currently dominant group are ministered above all others."[20]

To demonstrate the effects of cataloging on racist materials, I will share three examples from my own experience cataloging special collections: a high school yearbook, a biography of Nancy Astor, and a letter describing a race riot. I will describe the items, cataloging decisions made, and successes and failures.

Example 1: Gastonia High School Yearbook

In a prior job, I cataloged a collection of North Carolina education materials, which included pamphlets defending segregation and course catalogs listing advanced courses for white students while only offer-ing schooling through the fifth grade for black students. Racism will be obvious in these materials without special effort from the cataloger. The 1922 issue of *The Spinner*, the Gastonia High School yearbook, however, is not as obviously racist.[21] Each section of the yearbook opens with a cover page with a humorous illustration. The "Senior" section, for instance, features a picture of an owl wearing a cap and gown and holding a diploma. The end of the volume, however, features a cartoon depicting a lynching bearing the text "The End."

Cataloging rules require noting the presence of illustrations, but not detailed descriptions of their content. Reacting to the illustration with horror, my impulse was to finish the item quickly, so I omitted mention-ing the image, which, at the time, was the easy and comfortable thing to do. As a more experienced cataloger, however, I now recognize this as an act of erasure. Six years later, while writing this chapter, I needed to find this yearbook again, but could no longer recall the title or the creator. To find the illustration, I needed to search through volumes of scanned yearbooks page by page. If I had added a note when cata-loging the item, retrieval would have been much easier. Instead, the

---

20. Furner, "Dewey Deracialized," 153.
21. Gastonia High School, *The Spinner* vol. 3 (1922).

record contains only basic bibliographical information, including title
and publication information, and a few notes and subject headings:

Label	Content
Frequency:	Annual
Note:	Description based on: Vol. 3 (1922).
Note:	Latest issue consulted: Vol. 3 (1922).
Subject:	Gastonia High School (N.C.) – Periodicals.
Subject:	Gastonia High School (N.C.) – Students – Yearbooks.
Subject:	School yearbooks – North Carolina – Gastonia.

If I were to catalog this item now, I would, at minimum, include a
note describing the illustration:

Label	Content
Note:	1922 issue includes a cartoon depiction of a lynching.

Or provide some added detail:

Label	Content
Note:	1922 issue includes illustrations on section divider pages. The ending section includes a depiction of a lynching, with the caption "The End."

I would also consider including a subject heading. LCSH, the most
frequently used controlled vocabulary for subject access, has long been
criticized for failing to reflect the diversity of library users, sometimes
"othering" certain groups or even including pejorative terminology.
Sanford Berman was one of the early critics of LCSH. His book, *Prejudices and Antipathies*, identifies a number of problematic headings and

proposes "remedies," such as canceling a heading or replacing it with a less problematic term.[22]

"Lynching" was one of the problematic headings identified by Berman. In this case, the problem wasn't the heading itself, but the inclusion of a cross-reference to "Criminal Justice, Administration of," while omitting other cross-references.[23] His suggested remedies included removing the cross-reference, and adding instead references to "Homicide," "Murder," "Offenses against the person," "Terrorism," and "Violent deaths."[24] He further suggested adding a sub-heading for "Afro-Americans – Persecutions," with a cross-reference to "Lynching."[25] Subsequently, the cross-reference to "Criminal Justice" has been replaced with "Homicide" as a broader term. The current authority record, however, makes no mention of race. As a result, while the worst aspects of the record have been corrected, the authority record for "Lynching" takes a colorblind approach. While not ideal, the heading itself is not inaccurate. As a result, I would consider adding this subject heading to the record:

Label	Content
Subject:	Lynching – Pictorial works.

My cataloging of *The Spinner* is a misstep from early in my career. By failing to mention the illustration, I have hidden it. This was comfortable for me at the time, but failed to serve library patrons, which is particularly notable in light of recent events. Following the surfacing of blackface photographs of Virginia Governor Ralph Northam in

---

22. Sanford Berman, *Prejudices and Antipathies: A Tract on the LC Subject Heads Concerning People*, 1993 ed. (Jefferson, NC: McFarland, 1993).

23. Berman, *Prejudices and Antipathies*, 59-60.

24. Berman, *Prejudices and Antipathies*, 60-61.

25. Berman, *Prejudices and Antipathies*, 61. Note: at the time of Berman's writing, the authorized subject heading for African Americans was "Negroes." He suggested substituting the term "Afro-Americans," and uses this term throughout. When the Library of Congress updated this subject heading, they used the term "African Americans."

a yearbook, journalists have conducted research on racist imagery in yearbooks. Brett Murphy, for instance, found a "stunning number" of racist images in a review of 900 college and university yearbooks.[26] As a high school yearbook, *The Spinner* would have been excluded from his study, but subsequent researchers may wish to include high school yearbooks. Without reference to the racial content, this item is much harder to find.

Perhaps more importantly, failing to note a potentially triggering illustration also does a disservice to users who might not wish to see it. Instead, I have left future researchers to stumble upon it without warning. To quote Michael Gorman: "No librarian would insist on someone reading a text that she or [he] found offensive."[27] To my mind, flagging the presence of offensive content is not censorship. It prevents users from accidentally reading or viewing something they may find offensive. The catalog record I prepared for this item failed to protect researchers, while also failing to make the item discoverable. As a more experienced and socially aware cataloger, I now make a greater effort to consider the needs of all users.

Example 2: My Miss Nancy

My Miss Nancy is a biography of Lady Nancy Astor, written by Ruby Vaughan Bigger in the voice of Astor's mammy, Veenie.[28] Bigger describes visiting Veenie's home, where she witnesses Veenie telling her grandchildren the story of Miss Nancy's childhood. The story is told in dialect, including a glossary at the end of the volume to explain Bigger's phonetic spellings (e.g., "De: The," "Gwine: Going").[29] Bigger

26. Brett Murphy, "Blackface, KKK Hoods and Mock Lynchings: Review of 900 Yearbooks Finds Blatant Racism," *USA Today*, February 20, 2019, https://www.usatoday.com/in-depth/news/investigations/2019/02/20/blackface-racist-photos-yearbooks-colleges-kkk-lynching-mockery-fraternities-black-70-s-80-s/2858921002/.

27. Michael Gorman, "Revisiting Enduring Values," *JLIS*.it 6, no. 2 (May 2015): 18.

28. Ruby Vaughan Bigger, *My Miss Nancy: Nancy Astor's Virginia "Mammy" Tells Why 'Her Littl' Mistis Ain't Neber Gwine Lose her 'Sition Ober Dar in Inglan',"* 3rd ed. (Macon, GA: J.W. Burke, 1925).

29. Bigger, *My Miss Nancy*, 52.

illustrates her account with a photograph of Veenie and her family on the porch of their house, and uses slurs and stereotypes to describe Veenie's family, calling her grandchildren "little pickaninnies, with kinky plaits."[30]

This book did have copy cataloging available in OCLC Connexion, but the record was minimal:

Label	Content
Author:	Bigger, Ruby Vaughan.
Title:	My Miss Nancy : Nancy Astor's Virginia "mammy" tells why "her littl' mistis ain't ne- ber gwine lose her 'sition ober dar in Inglan' / by Ruby Vaughan Bigger.
Edition:	3rd ed.
Publication:	Macon, Ga. : J.W. Burke, 1925, ©1924.
Description:	43 pages, [4] leaves of plates: illustrations ; 18 cm
Subject:	Astor, Nancy Witcher Langhorne Astor, Vis- countess, 1879-1964.

Little mention was made of Veenie, even though she was the purported narrator. Although the book opens with a paean to mammies ("Mammy, dear to the hearts of all Southerners – both young and old, belongs to a fast vanishing type, who are rapidly becoming mere tradition, and in their passing, the entire Southland is losing something very precious and vital"), the subject headings make no mention of race relations or of nursemaids.[31] Only the subtitle ("Nancy Astor's Virginia 'mammy' tells why 'her littl' mistis ain't neber gwine lose her 'sition ober dar in Inglan'") hints at Veenie.

Re-cataloging this book, I wanted to bring more attention to both race relations and to Veenie. First, I added a summary:

---

30. Bigger, *My Miss Nancy*, 13.

31. Bigger, *My Miss Nancy*, 5.

Label	Content
Summary:	Biography of Lady Astor (née Nancy Witcher Langhorne), the first woman to sit on the British Parliament, narrated from the perspective of her African American nursemaid, Mammy Veenie, as written by Ruby Vaughan Bigger. Dialect story; Bigger employs phonetic spelling to capture Veenie's speech. Includes photographs of Veenie and her grandchildren at their cabin, located near the Langhorne family's Mirador estate; Lady Astor; and locations around Albemarle, Virginia.

This summary introduces both Veenie and race relations into the description. Second, I added subject headings to better describe the racial content of the work, including:

Label	Content
Subject:	Nannies – Virginia – Albemarle County.
Subject:	Albemarle County (Va.) – Race relations – History – 19th century.
Subject:	Albemarle County (Va.) – Race relations – History – 20th century.

While "Nannies" is not an exact synonym for "Mammies," it is the closest terminology currently available in LCSH. "Mammies" was formerly authorized as a subject heading, and was one of the problematic terms identified by Berman. Berman states: "An Afro-American woman, when asked what she thought of the word, responded unhesitatingly, 'I wouldn't want to be called one.'"[32] Berman's suggested remedy was to substitute another heading, such as "Child nurses, Afro-American."[33] Subsequent to the publication of *Prejudices and Antipathies*, "Mammies"

---

32. Berman, *Prejudices and Antipathies*, 72.

33. Berman, *Prejudices and Antipathies*, 72.

has been removed from LCSH, both as a heading and as a cross-reference. As a result, the closest term available is "Nannies," although LCSH does not include an "African American" subdivision, instead leaving race out of the heading entirely.

To wrap up the record, I added a subject heading for Veenie herself. Although Bigger wrote this book as a biography of Astor, the work is largely about Veenie and her family, including photographs of Veenie and of her home. Acknowledging her as a subject of the work seemed appropriate. These edits make the item more discoverable, highlight the racial content, and bring focus to Veenie, all of which had been previously lacking.

Example 3: Autograph Letter Signed from Emily Wilmarth

Race relations in the North during Reconstruction bears study. There is a common misapprehension that racism was a distinctly Southern problem. While the North and West did pass civil rights laws during Reconstruction, Desmond King and Stephen Tuck found that the progression of white supremacy was not limited to the South, but rather occurred nationwide.[34] However, studies on the development of white supremacy in the United States focus on the South, giving only passing reference to other regions.[35] Although New York had abolished slavery in 1827, the races were not equal; although legally free, an African American "could pass an entire life without any but the most superficial contacts with whites."[36]

These racial tensions are reflected in a letter written by Emily Wilmarth in October 1866 to her friend Annie Trembly, recounting a race

---

34. Desmond King and Stephen Tuck, "De-Centring the South: America's Nationwide White Supremacist Order After Reconstruction," *Past & Present* 194, no. 1 (February 2007): 216.

35. King and Tuck, "De-Centring the South," 218.

36. James V. Carmichael Jr., "Southern Librarianship and the Culture of Resentment," *Libraries & Culture* 40, no. 3 (Summer 2005): 327.

riot that occurred in Amityville, New York, on October 20, 1866.[37]
As a historical account, this letter is important. I have been unable to
locate other descriptions of this event, which seems to have largely
been forgotten. This letter could contribute to a better understanding
of race relations in New York in the immediate post-Civil War period.
However, my first attempt at cataloging the letter was anemic:[38]

Label	Content
Author:	Wilmarth, Emily, author.
Title:	Letter from Emily Wilmarth, Amityville, New York, to Annie E. Trembly, Hudson City, New Jersey, 1866 October 23, about a race riot : autograph manuscript.
Production:	Amityville, New York, 1866 October 23.
Note:	Written on lined paper, folded for mailing.
Summary:	Letter describing a race riot in Amityville, New York. The riot occurred on October 20, 1866, at a Political Republican meeting. Wilmarth recounts the event, including descriptions of weapons used, and mentions several people by name.
Subject:	Race riots – New York (State) – Amityville.
Subject:	Reconstruction (U.S. history, 1865-1877) – New York (State) – Amityville.
Subject:	Amityville (N.Y.) – Race relations.
Genre:	Correspondence.

While this record is accurate and does include information on race,
it shies away from describing the racist aspects of the letter, which are
blatant in the original. Wilmarth uses racial slurs ten times in her brief

---

37. Emily Wilmarth to Annie E. Trembly, October 23, 1866, Special Collections
Library, Pennsylvania State University.

38. Letter cataloged according to *Descriptive Cataloging of Rare Materials (Manuscripts)*.

four-page letter. She expresses fear of the rioters, saying that she has "a loaded gun in my room that I keep by the head of the bed every night."[39] The catalog record I had prepared omitted Wilmarth's own viewpoints, and failed to mention the slurs. With the description as it stood, I risked "insist[ing] on someone reading a text that she or [he] found offensive."[40] After some consideration, I expanded the summary to include additional information:

Label	Content
Summary:	Letter describing a race riot in Amityville, New York. The riot occurred on October 20, 1866, at a Political Republican meeting. Wilmarth recounts the event, including descriptions of weapons used, and mentions several people by name. The author employs racial slurs and mentions a rumor that the rioters will return, assuring her correspondent that "the boys are prepared for them" and that she is sleeping with a rifle at the head of her bed.

Although I added only a single sentence, I flagged the presence of racial slurs and provided context for the author's views. I believe that anyone choosing to read the letter will now be forearmed with information about the contents and the context of the document.

Conclusion and Advice for Catalogers

Cataloging racism forces us to reckon with the darkest parts our history and to carefully read and describe documents that express viewpoints that may run counter to our deepest convictions. Nevertheless, this work is crucial. Ignoring race is an act of erasure. Ignoring racism, or treating it as a "private matter," risks hiding a history of suppression that

---

39. Wilmarth to Trembly, October 23, 1866, 3.

40. Gorman, "Revisiting Enduring Values," 18.

continues to affect us.[41] Minimizing racism risks presenting a version of history that does not reflect reality. I do acknowledge the discomfort that accompanies this work, but also believe that discomfort does not outweigh others' pain. With that in mind, I have several suggestions for catalogers facing these challenges:

1. **Learn about bias and discrimination**. Ultimately, ethical cataloging should center our users. Activist Kayla Reed posted this acronym for "ally" on Twitter: "A—always center the impacted, L—listen & learn from those who live in the oppression, L—leverage your privilege, Y—yield the floor."[42] If we want to make the catalog more equitable, the first step is centering oppressed people and learning from them. Learning about bias and discrimination is a lifelong process. Start by talking to people from diverse backgrounds and listen to what they say, no matter how uncomfortable. If you work for a university, your institution may offer free courses on diversity and inclusion. If not, consider asking your supervisor to fund your attendance. There are also abundant resources for reading and study. You might start with some of the works cited in this chapter, or with guides, such as the "Racial Equity Resource Guide" or resources compiled by Black Lives Matter.[43]

2. **Catalog the items**. While it is easy to allow racist items to languish in backlogs, the effect is to keep them hidden. They should be discoverable, and the only way to ensure their discoverability is to catalog them.

3. **Take your time**. Approach problematic items thoughtfully, thinking through potential impacts. My first impulse with the Wilmarth letter, for instance, was to catalog it quickly. If I had, the record

---

41. Seale, "Compliant Trust," 595.

42. Kayla Reed, Twitter, June 12, 2016, https://twitter.com/ikaylareed/status/7422 43143030972416?lang=en.

43. "Racial Equity Resource Guide," W.K. Kellogg Foundation, accessed December 15, 2018, http://www.racialequityresourceguide.org; "Resources," Black Lives Matter, accessed December 15, 2018, https://blacklivesmatter.com/resources.

would have lacked essential information. Taking a few extra days to think through potential impacts will help to ensure better description without significantly delaying cataloging.

4. **Establish local policies**. Consult with colleagues, including catalogers, archivists, public service librarians, and curators. If available, include diversity experts, and consider getting input from library users, particularly members of affected groups. Work together to establish local policies about cataloging these items. No one should have to make these decisions in a vacuum. Make your policies available to library staff, and plan to revise them periodically. If necessary, provide training sessions to catalogers, so everyone knows and understands the policies, and knows where to find assistance if needed.

5. **Take advantage of your local catalog**. You may not want to make substantial changes to OCLC master records, which will be shared and may be edited by others. You may, however, feel freer to make substantial changes in your local catalog. For instance, the illustration in *The Spinner* appeared only in the 1922 issue, but the yearbook was published into the 1950s. Because of this, I might hesitate to add notes about the illustration to the master record, since the note applies to only one issue. However, I would feel freer to add these notes in the local catalog. Decide which approach you will use, and include this information in your documentation.

Catalogers play a powerful role; their work can either expose a resource, or hide it. Racism is present throughout history, and special collections libraries focus on collecting historic materials. As a result, special collections catalogers are almost guaranteed to encounter racism in the course of their work. The legacy of colorblind racism can lead us to hide or minimize these materials, which in turn hides history. By taking our time with these resources and thinking through the impacts of our cataloging, we can better serve our researchers and our collections.

Bibliography

American Library Association. "Core Values of Librarianship." Adopted June 29, 2004. http://www.ala.org/advocacy/intfreedom/coreval-ues.

Berman, Sanford. *Prejudices and Antipathies: A Tract on the LC Subject Heads Concerning People.* 1993 ed. Jefferson, NC: McFarland, 1993.

Bigger, Ruby Vaughan. *My Miss Nancy: Nancy Astor's Virginia "Mammy" Tells Why "Her Littl' Mistis Ain't Neber Gwine Lose her 'Sition Ober Dar in Inglan.'"* 3rd ed. Macon, GA: J.W. Burke, 1925.

Black Lives Matter. "Resources." Accessed December 15, 2018. https://blacklivesmatter.com/resources.

Bonilla-Silva, Eduardo. *Racism without Racists: Color-Blind Racism and the Persistence of Racial Inequality in America.* 5th ed. Lanham: Rowman & Littlefield, 2018.

Brown, Michael K., Martin Carnoy, Elliott Currie, Troy Duster, David B. Oppenheimer, Marjorie M. Shultz, and David Wellman. *Whitewashing Race: The Myth of a Color-Blind Society.* Berkeley: University of California Press, 2003.

Burke, Meghan. *Colorblind Racism.* Cambridge: Polity Press, 2019.

Carmichael, James V., Jr. "Southern Librarianship and the Culture of Resentment." *Libraries & Culture* 40, no. 3 (Summer 2005): 324-53.

Furner, Jonathan. "Dewey Deracialized: A Critical Race-Theoretic Perspective." *Knowledge Organization* 34, no. 3 (2007): 144-68.

Gastonia High School. *The Spinner* vol. 3 (1922).

Gorman, Michael. "Revisiting Enduring Values." *JLIS.it* 6, no. 2 (May 2015): 13-33.

Ingraham, Christopher. "How White Racism Destroys Black Wealth." *Washington Post*, November 28, 2018. https://www.washingtonpost.com/business/2018/11/28/how-white-racism-destroys-black-wealth/.

King, Desmond, and Stephen Tuck. "De-Centring the South: America's Nationwide White Supremacist Order After Reconstruction." *Past & Present* 194, no. 1 (February 2007): 213-53.

Mazzocco, Philip J. *The Psychology of Racial Colorblindness: A Critical Review*. New York: Palgrave Macmillan, 2017.

Murphy, Brett. "Blackface, KKK Hoods and Mock Lynchings: Review of 900 Yearbooks Finds Blatant Racism." *USA Today*, February 20, 2019. https://www.usatoday.com/in-depth/news/investigations/2019/02/20/blackface-racist-photos-yearbooks-colleges-kkk-lynching-mockery-fraternities-black-70-s-80-s/2858921002/.

National Center for Education Statistics. "Public High School Graduation Rates." Updated May 2018. https://nces.ed.gov/programs/coe/indicator_coi.asp.

Reed, Kayla. "A–always center the impacted, L–listen & learn from those who live in the oppression, L–leverage your privilege, Y–yield the floor." Twitter, June 12, 2016. https://twitter.com/ikaylareed/status/742243143030972416?lang=en.

Seale, Maura. "Compliant Trust: The Public Good and Democracy in the ALA's 'Core Values of Librarianship.'" *Library Trends* 64, no. 3 (2016): 585-603.

Shapiro, Doug, Afet Dundar, Faye Huie, Phoebe Khasiala Wakhungu, Xin Yuan, Angel Nathan, and Youngsik Hwang. *A National View of Student Attainment Rates by Race and Ethnicity: Fall 2010 Cohort*. Signature Report no. 12b. Herndon, VA: National Student Clearinghouse Research Center, 2017. https://nscresearchcenter.org/wp-content/uploads/Signature12-RaceEthnicity.pdf.

United States Census Bureau. "Historical Income Tables: Households." Updated August 28, 2018. https://www.census.gov/data/tables/time-series/demo/income-poverty/historical-income-households.html.

Wheeler, Maurice B. "Politics and Race in American Historical Popular Music: Contextualized Access and Minstrel Music Archives." *Archival Science* 11, no. 1/2 (March 2011): 47-75.

Williams, Joseph P. "Segregation's Legacy: Fifty Years After the Fair Housing Act was Signed, America is Nearly as Segregated as When President Lyndon Johnson Signed the Law." *U.S. News*, April 20, 2018. https://www.usnews.com/news/the-report/articles/2018-04-20/us-is-still-segregated-even-after-fair-housing-act.

Wilmarth, Emily to Annie E. Trembly, October 23, 1866. Special Collections Library. Pennsylvania State University.

W.K. Kellogg Foundation. "Racial Equity Resource Guide." Accessed December 15, 2018. http://www.racialequityresourceguide.org.

Chapter 9

INVISIBLE IN PLAIN VIEW: LIBRARIES, ARCHIVES, DIGITIZATION, MEMORY, AND THE 1934 CHATHAM COLOURED ALL-STARS

Heidi L.M. Jacobs

There is a small stretch of railway along the Windsor-Québec City corridor that contains a remarkable piece of Canadian history. Although I had taken the train through Chatham, Ontario hundreds of times, I had never noticed Stirling Park until one June afternoon in 2016, when I stood alone in the ballpark with my feet on home plate and saw the VIA train pass by. Now, whenever I take the train through Chatham, I wonder how I had missed something so obvious so many times. Stirling Park has been there for at least eighty-five years, but it is hidden in plain view to many, myself included, who simply pass by.[1]

If you know where to look, however, you can see Stirling Park from the train, just past a thin row of trees. It was there, in the summer and fall of 1934, that Chatham's Black community gathered by the hundreds

1. I am grateful to the University of Windsor's Humanities Research group for awarding me a Humanities Research Group Fellowship to research and write this article and to the Faculty of Arts, Humanities and Social Sciences and Leddy Library for facilitating my acceptance of the fellowship. I would also like to thank Devon Fraser for her assistance in preparing this manuscript. I would especially like to acknowledge my gratitude to the Harding Project team: Miriam Wright and Dave Johnston, Blake and Pat Harding, Don Bruner and Mike Murphy from the Chatham Sports Hall of Fame, and Dorothy Wright Wallace and Samantha Meredith from the Chatham-Kent Black Historical Society.

to cheer on the Chatham Coloured All-Stars, the first Black team to win the Ontario Baseball Amateur Association championship. This is the ballpark where Earl "Flat" Chase hit home run balls "so hard, they're still looking for them" and where left-handed shortstop Kingsley Terrell dazzled fans with improbable—near impossible—plays that people remembered decades later. Stirling Park's home plate is less than one hundred feet from the Scane Street house where Wilfred "Boomer" Harding and his siblings grew up and where his mother Sarah collected material to make scrapbooks for each of her eight children.

Like Stirling Park, there are many things about and within libraries, archives, and digital projects that are also "hidden in plain view": questions about the work we do as librarians and archivists, about the choices we make, and the assumptions that guide our decisions. In this article, I use our *Breaking the Colour Barrier* digitization and public history project as a way to engage with pressing questions and issues related to history, memory, archival documents, community, preservation, and librarianship.[2] In so doing, I hope to highlight questions that I believe we must—both as individual librarians and as a profession—consider in more depth and through a range of critical lenses. In particular, I want to engage with the conversations held within archival studies about power and the past and argue that these are also urgent issues for the field of librarianship to consider. Critical archival studies offer a particularly useful model for how we might go about having these conversations.

Before proceeding, it will be useful to describe the larger endeavor that we've come to call the Harding Project and the smaller subsection of the project called *Breaking the Colour Barrier*. In May 2015, my University of Windsor colleague in History, Miriam Wright, presented a local history award to a group in Chatham, Ontario and offered a brief overview of how public history was changing due to digital developments. After her talk, Wright was approached by Pat Harding, who told her about the scrapbooks she had assembled to document the life of

---

2. University of Windsor Leddy Library, *Breaking the Colour Barrier*, last modified February 15, 2018, http://cdigs.uwindsor.ca/BreakingColourBarrier/.

her late father-in-law, Wilfred "Boomer" Harding (1915-1991), focusing on his life-long athletic activity in a racially divided world. Pat Harding was hopeful that Wright and the University of Windsor could help her build a website so this important story could be both preserved and made accessible. Wright's interest was immediately piqued because she realized that the Boomer Harding story offered vital insights into the often overlooked history of race and racism in Southern Ontario. Wright contacted me and my librarian colleague Dave Johnston, asking if our then-new Centre for Digital Scholarship would be interested in partnering to develop a website based on the materials. We were equally excited.

When Boomer Harding's son Blake brought the scrapbooks to the library, we were all shocked to see that the scrapbooks Pat Harding had described were, in fact, three very thick binders, brimming with documents. As we examined them, we saw photographs of Boomer Harding standing with an otherwise all-white high school basketball team, headlines from the *Chatham Daily News* recounting how a Black baseball team played and beat white teams thirteen years before Jackie Robinson started with the Brooklyn Dodgers, and a newspaper photograph of Boomer with a hockey stick and headlines that read: "Boomer Harding Makes Hockey History at Olympia. Becomes First Negro to Play on Local Rink. May be 'First' in Pro Hockey."[3] There were letters Boomer had written while serving in the Canadian military during World War Two, a story about Boomer being Chatham's first Black mail carrier, and evidence that Boomer was a formidable athlete for his entire life. Our project team agreed with the Harding family that the stories contained in the scrapbooks had rarely been conveyed in Canadian history and we were in awe of the meticulousness and comprehensiveness of the historical record that Pat Harding had preserved. We knew that we had something rare and vital and that we needed to do something with it.

---

3. "Boomer Harding Makes Hockey History at Olympia. Becomes First Negro to Play on Local Rink. May be 'First' in Pro Hockey." *Michigan Gazette*, November 16, 1946.

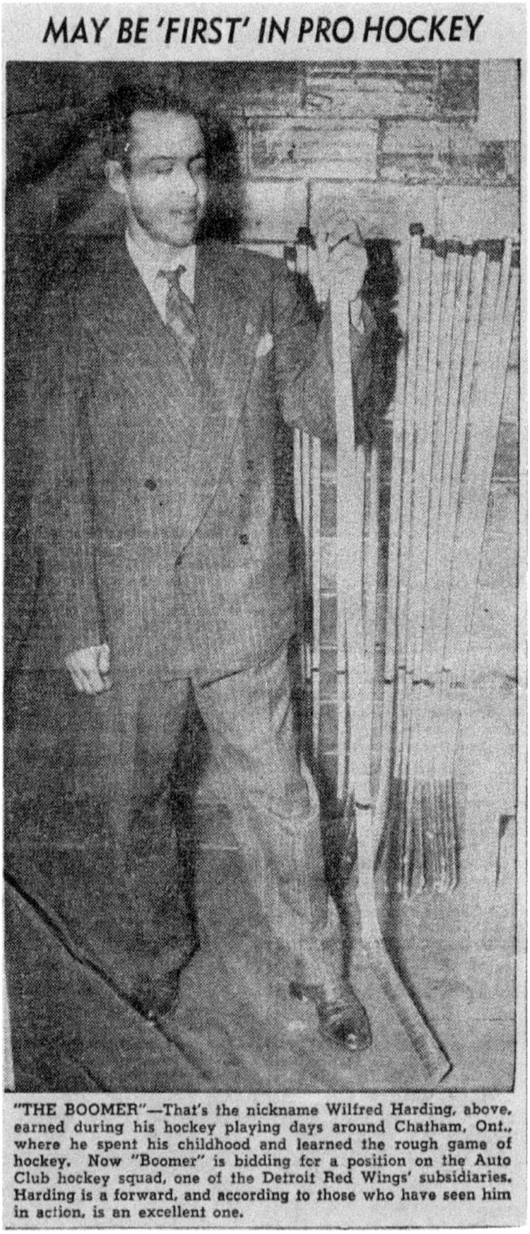

MAY BE 'FIRST' IN PRO HOCKEY

"THE BOOMER"—That's the nickname Wilfred Harding, above, earned during his hockey playing days around Chatham, Ont., where he spent his childhood and learned the rough game of hockey. Now "Boomer" is bidding for a position on the Auto Club hockey squad, one of the Detroit Red Wings' subsidiaries. Harding is a forward, and according to those who have seen him in action, is an excellent one.

Figure 1. "Boomer Harding Makes Hockey History at Olympia. Becomes First Negro to Play on Local Rink. May be 'First' in Pro Hockey." *Michigan Gazette*, 16 November 1946

The Hardings wanted Boomer's story to reach as many people as possible and thought we should target the following audiences: race, sport, and history scholars; friends and descendants of the team; local and regional communities; and kindergarten through post-secondary students. As our project team looked through the binders, we understood that the scale, scope, and importance of Boomer's story could not properly be told in its entirety and that it would be best for us to, initially, focus on one aspect of it and do it well. From there, we believed that we, or future scholars, could add further aspects of the story over time. To this end, we decided to focus on the Chatham Coloured All-Stars' championship winning season in 1934 and we partnered with the Harding Family and the Chatham Sports Hall of Fame to secure an Ontario Trillium Foundation grant. The grant allowed us to develop and launch our website[4] and to engage in a wide range of public outreach activities.[5] Although the Chatham-Kent Black Historical Society was

---

4. It will be useful here to distinguish between two terms—digital archive and digital exhibit—that are often used inter-changeably, and erroneously so. A digital archive is, in many ways, the digital equivalent of a physical archive: materials are "raw" and are an un-curated collection of materials that can be explored by users in a range of ways. A digital exhibit is a highly curated selection of materials that are arranged to tell a particular narrative or to engage users or readers in particular ways. The Harding Project, for example, created both a digital archive (where the team digitized every artifact in high resolution, created detailed metadata and records for each item, created a finding aid, and established protocols for long-term storage and preservation) and a digital exhibit (where we selected items and wrote accompanying text to tell a particular narrative based on the materials we received as a way of introducing scholars and members of the public to the materials and to the story of the Chatham Coloured All-Stars).

5. The Harding Project team is grateful to the Ontario Trillium Foundation for its support of this project through a seed grant. This grant allowed us to digitize and preserve well over a thousand items and create searchable metadata records; conduct and transcribe over a dozen interviews with descendants and friends of the team; find and digitize local press coverage about the 1934 season and place it on an interactive timeline; develop and curate a website with contextual essays; commission the award-winning teacher, Shantelle Browning-Morgan, to write curricular activities for grades 1-12 based on the Ontario curriculum; design and build storyboard exhibits to travel to schools and public libraries; commission a single-page cartoon by Eisner Award nominated cartoonist Scott Chantler; create a set of vintage-looking baseball cards that tell the story of the Chatham Coloured All-Stars players and that are sold as a fund-raising venture for the Chatham-Kent Black Historical Museum; and host a project launch event in Chatham where over three hundred people attended. We also

not a formal partner, the project could not have progressed without its support and assistance.

On the whole, our library was supportive of this project; still, a few comments were made in discussion that revealed several often-unquestioned assumptions about the nature of librarianship and the scope of a librarian's purview. One colleague thought that we should not digitize the material unless our Archives and Special Collections could possess the physical artifacts. Once we possessed the scrapbooks, only then, my colleague argued, should we digitize them as a means of preservation and perhaps access for distant scholars. Another colleague thought that we should simply digitize the material and make the files available in a form that replicated the original scrapbooks. Another colleague suggested that "meddling" with these historic documents was a very "un-librarian" practice. I mention these comments because, taken together, they raise fundamental questions about the nature of librarians' work and reveal assumptions about what a librarian is supposed to be and do. Moreover, these comments suggest a couple of underlying assumptions about historic and archival documents: 1. that there is a "pure" and untainted historical record that must be preserved, and 2. that digitization projects can be neutral.

Libraries, some might argue, are about collecting and facilitating access to knowledge, not about creating it. While some might find this "collecting and facilitating" versus "creating" knowledge question one of mere semantics, I am intrigued with it because it raises an issue that is at the core of librarianship: do we merely collect and provide access to materials or do we, in fact, shape knowledge? To suggest that we do not shape the knowledge our users access overlooks a very obvious practical reality of librarianship: we can only spend money once. And, if we can only spend money once, we must make decisions. As the

began work on a comprehensive site called "Wilfred 'Boomer' Harding: A Barrier Breaking Life," which more closely resembles a digital archive (of all three scrapbook binders) than a digital exhibit. This project has won several awards, including a 2018 Lieutenant Governor's Ontario Heritage Award for Excellence in Conservation and an Ontario Council of University Libraries Outstanding Contribution Award (2017).

English librarian, I am routinely faced with difficult decisions like, should I spend $600 on scholarly editions of several Sir Walter Scott novels, or should I purchase twenty books by emerging and diverse Canadian poets, novelists, and playwrights? The choices I make about how to spend that $600 shapes what future English students will find on the shelves and thus how they, quite literally, see the literary traditions in English. My $600 question is a variant of a question that librarians answer daily, if not hourly, in their everyday work: how should we allocate resources, be they of a monetary, spatial, or human resources nature? Every single choice we make helps to shape our library for present and future users.

When I reflect on the work my colleagues and I have done with the Harding Project, I am frequently reminded of my favorite high school math teacher, Mr. Yeske, who spent countless hours helping me pass his courses. He was insistent that we "show our work," since the final result or answer was only part of any solution. In showing our work, he could trace the journey we made from problem to solution, the logic we followed, and the assumptions and choices we made. For him, the steps we took to arrive at our answer were equally, if not more, important than the final right answer. I see deep connections between the way that Mr. Yeske taught me math and the way I think about libraries and librarianship.

In libraries, we often focus on articulating a final answer and in so doing neglect to "show our work" regarding how we arrived at that answer. Often, we will summon user statistics or other forms of evidence as a way of justifying a renewal or a cancelation, but we rarely articulate to ourselves or to others what assumptions inform the choice of statistics or our interpretation of them. Justifying decisions, however, is not necessarily the only reason to show our work. Sometimes, the final answer at which we arrive might not be quite right, but the assumptions leading up to solving the problem are sound. Or, the decision may be fine, but there are deep flaws in the logic used to make those decisions. It is for this reason that computer programmers show and share their code: people can see the assumptions, help solve potential problems, and build upon what exists to make it better. Or, consider an exhibit I recently saw at the Museum at the Fashion Institute of Technology in New York. The curators displayed several dresses inside out to emphasize that sometimes it's not what the dress looks like from the outside that is important or innovative but, rather, how the inner structure, stitches, and seams work together that is worth considering. Again, it's not always about the final result—it's about the assumptions and principles that guide the work.

Unless our decision-making work is shown—be it in library collections, archival acquisitions, digitization projects, or any other kind of project—we're left with a partial understanding of the work we've done and no rationale or explanation for the decisions we've made. To be sure, there are times when librarianship must provide concrete answers. For example, "Do you have the Merck Index?" or "Should we renew our subscription to the Modern Language Association database?" are not questions we can answer with "perhaps" or "yes and no are equally valid answers." We know how to answer those questions and we are comfortable answering them with confidence. There are times, however, when we must ask difficult questions that lack obvious or definitive answers. These kinds of questions can make us feel uncomfortable. When we're uncomfortable, we are likely to gravitate toward questions we can answer comfortably. In so doing, we put off asking the uncomfortable questions we cannot answer but should be asking.

There are many ways that we could consider the questions related to what is at stake and at play when we make those decisions for our libraries. I would like us as a profession to consider these questions in greater detail and in relation to specific contexts. The scope of this chapter allows me to consider just one aspect of this question: how digitization projects are informed by many material and ideological assumptions related to power and representation.

In researching this project, I was struck by the relative dearth of librarians writing reflectively about academic libraries writ large and asking the difficult questions about the spaces that librarians and libraries occupy in the world. There has been a bourgeoning of excellent, reflective work within the area of critical librarianship written about aspects of academic librarianship such as information literacy and cataloging, or about the impact of neoliberal practices upon academic libraries, yet not much about academic librarianship as a whole and our multi-pronged and interrelated navigation of power structures. Some of the most rigorous, reflective, and praxis-based scholarship I have seen in recent years has come out of critical archives studies. This body of scholarship has much to offer librarians, particularly those engaged in digitization projects. Critical archives scholarship provides questions and a model of inquiry that can help us think reflectively about librarianship and the work we do, pushing our inquiries in new directions so that we can ask new questions about our work—or, at least reframe existing questions in new ways.

In the discussion that follows, I explore how current writing and thinking within archival studies provide us with modes of inquiry that can help us confront, acknowledge, and reconsider our biases and their relation to existing power structures. I will first provide an overview of some of the recent discussions about archives work that could be useful in reconceiving how librarians might think about their work. I will then discuss how this line of thinking influenced our approach to the Harding Project.

Within most scholarship about libraries and librarians, archives and archivists, there is often a careful and understandable drawing of boundaries between these two disciplines. However, in the public eye, they are often seen as interchangeable. The Society of American Archivists offers this distinction: libraries "can generally be defined as collections of books and/or other print or nonprint materials organized and maintained for use…Libraries exist to make their collections available to the people they serve."[6] Like libraries, archives "also exist to make their collections available to people, but differ from libraries in both the types of materials they hold, and the way materials are accessed."[7] Archival

6. "What Are Archives and How Do They Differ from Libraries?" Society of American Archivists, https://www2.archivists.org/usingarchives/whatarearchives.

7. "What Are Archives?" Society of American Archivists, https://www2.archivists.org/usingarchives/whatarearchives.

materials, they go on to argue, "are often unique, specialized, or rare objects, meaning very few of them exist in the world, or they are the only ones of their kind."[8] The nature of the materials determines, to a great extent, the kind of access allowed: "Since materials in archival collections are unique, [archivists] strive to preserve them for use today, and for future generations of researchers."[9] It is important to see the distinctions and demarcations between the two professions but, as we navigate similar terrain, we should be mindful not to let these differences interfere with conversations that could be mutually advantageous.

For a myriad of logical reasons, we often hold onto these distinctions within librarianship: librarians do library work and archivists do archival work. A recent book published by the American Library Association entitled *Archives in Libraries: What Librarians and Archivists Need to Know to Work Together*, is particularly revealing of this professional distinction and/or disciplinary split. It aims to "narrow the divide" between libraries and archives and "build shared understandings between archivists and librarians and library directors while helping archivists working within libraries to better negotiate their relationships with the institution and with their library colleagues."[10] The suggestion that libraries and archives are separate and separated is even apparent on the book's cover, which shows parallel lines of library books on the far left and boxes of archival holdings on the far right, with a rigid corridor in between. Even the non-italicized "Archives" in yellow and italicized "Libraries" in red on the cover suggests a "farmers and ranchers" type of relationship between the professions.

The scope of this article won't allow an in-depth discussion about how or why those distinctions exist, nor how we might overcome them.

---

8. "What Are Archives?" Society of American Archivists, https://www2.archivists. org/usingarchives/whatarearchives.

9. "What Are Archives?" Society of American Archivists, https://www2.archivists. org/usingarchives/whatarearchives.

10. Jeanette A. Bastien, Megan Sniffen-Marinoff, and Donna Webber, *Archives in Libraries: What Librarians and Archivists Need to Know to Work Together* (Chicago: Society of American Archivists, 2018).

Additionally, I do not want to elide or dismiss the vital and distinct professional differences between archivists and librarians. Instead, I want to argue that librarians, especially those engaged in digital projects, have much to gain and learn from engaging in the conversations that archivists are having about their work. Many archivists, especially those engaged in critical archives studies, are currently asking urgent and deeply relevant questions that can problematize our own thinking in libraries and thus push us to complicate our understanding of our work and broaden our professional discussions. Of particular interest to me are the ways in which some archivists have taken on questions related to power and inclusion within archival work.

The material and cultural records we have of the past are, quite simply, an amalgamation of artifacts and documents that, serendipitously or deliberately, have survived. Libraries, archives, and special collections are filled with items that did not befall misfortune at the hands of natural forces or human intervention: letters that were kept in an attic that did not leak or a basement that did not flood; diaries that were saved and not burned; newspaper stories that were published and not tossed into an editor's wastepaper bin; articles that were saved; pictures that were put into albums; and newspapers that were microfilmed. The preservation of the historical record is made possible by chance, choice, and/or careful neglect.

When one thinks of archivists and scholars doing archival research, one often thinks of the white gloves worn so our fingers don't leave dangerous oils on fragile pages. The white gloves can also be a generative metaphor for thinking about how we see our interactions with historic documents. We might, for example, want to believe that—as librarians and archivists—we have metaphoric white gloves on and that we leave no trace of ourselves on the collections we accession, preserve, maintain, and/or digitize. The Harding Project, like most other archival or digital collections, is covered in fingerprints—real and metaphoric—of those who assembled and created this collection of documents and who ensured—actively or passively—that this material record would exist for future generations. Boomer's mother, Sarah Holmes Harding, for example, collected and saved documents and newspaper clippings about all of her children and gave them to each child. Boomer's wife, Joy, saw these stacks of papers as junk and clutter and would have tossed them all out but was persuaded to let Boomer keep them in his shed. When Pat Harding saw these clippings, she saw them as treasures worth saving. One does wonder what the legacy of Boomer Harding and the Chatham Coloured All-Stars would have been had Joy Harding gotten her way and taken the piles of paper to the burning barrel or if Pat Harding hadn't seen the value in them and made scrapbooks. We must also be thankful that these documents weren't victims of floods, mice, or fire. Thinking of the collection of documents that we have digitized for the Harding Project reminds us not only of the precarious nature of the material record, but also of the continuous level of evaluation and choice within a document's lifespan. Decisions are made at multiple junctures in a document's existence about whether to consider it part of an historical record and preserve it or discard it as extraneous or inconsequential. The chance encounter between Pat Harding and Miriam Wright and our collective decision to digitize the material is just the latest in a long stream of events and decisions that determined whether these documents and the stories they tell would survive, and who would be able to see and hear them. As technology evolves, it will be up to future librarians and archivists to decide whether to retain the physical scrapbooks and steward the digital files.

If we consider the ways in which decisions—whether deliberate and methodical or serendipitous and haphazard—inform what gets preserved in the material historical record, we can see how power-laden archival choices are. What gets preserved, stored, displayed, or maintained determines what stories are told and what voices are heard. Joan H. Schwartz and Terry Cook consider the notion of archives and power and write that

> [a]rchivists have long been viewed from outside the profes-
> sion as "hewers of wood and drawers of water," as those who
> received records from their creators and passed them on to
> researchers. Inside the profession, archivists have perceived

themselves as neutral, objective, impartial. From both perspectives, archivists and their materials seem to be the very antithesis of power.[11]

But archives, they continue, are much more complex sites than these notions reveal, since records

> wield power over the shape and direction of historical scholarship, collective memory, and national identity, over how we know ourselves as individuals, groups, and societies. And ultimately, in the pursuit of their professional responsibilities, archivists – as keepers of archives – wield power over those very records central to memory and identity formation through active management of records before they come to archives, their appraisal and selection as archives, and afterwards their constantly evolving description, preservation, and use.[12]

In the same way, librarians engaged in digitization or digital projects also wield power over records, shaping memory and identity formation. In both instances, the metaphor of the white gloves that leave no trace of ourselves on the documents falls apart, since our fingerprints are all over the records we select and privilege.

It would be easy for our Harding Project team to say that we made no choices—that we simply digitized what we were given and then made a website of items reflecting the Harding scrapbooks. The reality of this project, and indeed, the study of history, is that there is no "pure," untouched historical record free of bias. Individuals and institutions continually make active and passive decisions that shape the historical narrative we inherit. The Harding scrapbooks are a highly mediated collection of documents. Boomer's mother, and others along the way, clipped certain articles that told and illustrated the story they wanted to tell about the Harding family. Pat Harding created the scrapbooks as part of the nomination package she submitted to get Boomer Harding into the Chatham Sports Hall of Fame and thus she shaped them to tell a particular story. Similarly, when we saw the scrapbooks, they aligned

---

11. Joan M. Schwartz, and Terry Cook, "Archives, Records, and Power: The Making of Modern Memory," *Archival Science* 2, nos. 1-2 (2002): 1-2.

12. Joan M. Schwartz, and Terry Cook, "Archives, Records, and Power: The Making of Modern Memory," *Archival Science* 2, nos. 1-2 (2002): 2.

with stories that we thought needed to be told, particularly those stories that reflected southern Ontario's history of racial discrimination and that have been left out of Canadian history far too often. The resultant *Breaking the Colour Barrier* site and project is an amalgamation of the choices that Sarah Holmes Harding, Boomer Harding, Pat and Blake Harding, and the Harding Project team made about what we thought should be preserved, shared, acknowledged, remembered, or, through choices of omission, forgotten. There are metaphoric fingerprints of judgments, beliefs, values, and assumptions all over this project.

Schwartz and Cook argue that it is "essential to reconsider the relationship between archives and the societies that create and use them."[13] For those reasons, it's important to acknowledge several other layers of fingerprints indelibly shaping this project. Several granting agencies provided nearly $80,000 to make the Harding Project a reality, because it told a story that these agencies believed was valid and worth preserving and sharing. This site has won awards because various committees saw value in this story and the project. We are grateful for every grant dollar and award we received, but we also recognize that there were other equally important historical projects that did not get funding or projects that were not recognized because our project was selected instead. There were layers of evaluation and judgment hidden in plain view at every level of the Harding Project that allowed its story to be told instead of another.

Katharine Hodgkin and Susannah Radstone have noted, "history and memory are not abstract forces: they are located in specific contexts, instances and narratives, and decisions have always to be taken about what story is to be told."[14] As we considered various ways to share and convey the stories contained in the three Harding scrapbooks, we knew we could not tell the entire Boomer Harding story in one project. We knew we had to make decisions about the scope and scale of the

---

13. Schwartz and Cook, "Modern Memory," 2.

14. Katharine Hodgkin, and Susannah Radstone, eds., *Contested Pasts: The Politics of Memory* (London: Routledge, 2003), 5.

project. We decided to pick one aspect—baseball—and one team—the 1934 Chatham Coloured All-Stars—as our focus. Our project team then "created" or highlighted a particular narrative from the wealth of materials in the same way that Scott Chantler, the cartoonist we commissioned to draw a single-page comic strip for our project, selected the most compelling and representative scenes to tell the story of the Chatham Coloured All-Stars.

To state the obvious: archives and library collections are not found pre-existing in nature; they are, of course, social constructs. As much as we would like to downplay this fact and as much as we feel disempowered by a range of forces, libraries and archives, too, are about power. Every choice we make—about collecting, about accessioning or deaccessioning, about providing or withholding access—is an exercise in power over what is and what will be known. As Schwartz and Cook further contend, archives "have the power to privilege and to marginalize. They can be a tool of hegemony; they can be a tool of resistance. They both reflect and constitute power relations."[15] Certain voices, they continue, "thus will be heard loudly and some not at all,…[and that] certain views and ideas about society will in turn be privileged and others marginalized."[16] Michelle Caswell, Ricardo Punzalan and T-Kay Sangwand take Schwartz and Cook's ideas about archives and power a few steps further. They write,

> there has been an explosion of efforts to examine the ways in which records and archives serve as tools for both oppression and liberation. This recent scholarship and some community-based archival initiatives critically interrogate the role of archives, records and archival actions and practices in bringing about or impeding social justice, in understanding and coming to terms with past wrongs or permitting continued silences, or empowering historically or contemporarily marginalized and displaced communities.[17]

---

15. Schwartz and Cook, "Modern Memory," 13.

16. Schwartz and Cook, "Modern Memory," 14.

17. Michelle Caswell, Ricardo Punzalan, and T-Kay Sangwand, "Critical Archival Studies: An Introduction," Journal of Critical Library and Information Studies 1, no. 2 (2017): 1.

Caswell et al. have argued for an embracing of the term and intent behind "critical archival studies," which is "emancipatory in nature, with the ultimate goal of transforming archival practice and society writ large."[18] In this way, scholarship concerning archives connects well with parallel concerns within librarianship and offers additional insights into how librarians might engage with critical praxis in our work and thinking.

Other areas related to cultural heritage have also been considering how to make visible the often invisible or "white glove" work of the scholars and researchers behind heritage work. In 2006, "The London Charter for the Computer-Based Visualisation of Cultural Heritage" emerged from a need to "reconcile heritage visualization with professional norms of research, particularly the standards of argument and evidence."[19] Of particular interest to me are the London Charter's fourth principle, "Documentation" and sub-principle 4.6 "Documentation of Process ('Paradata')."[20] Documentation is outlined in this way: "Sufficient information should be documented and disseminated to allow computer-based visualisation methods and outcomes to be understood and evaluated in relation to the contexts and purposes for which they are deployed."[21] The documentation of process, or paradata, is a way to reveal the "fingerprints" of those who created the heritage object and the choices and assumptions that led to its creation. As Hugh Denard describes,

> [n]o matter how thoughtfully a research question is posed in relation to the existing field of knowledge, how painstakingly available sources are researched and interpreted, how discerningly or creatively an argument is elaborated visually, to the viewer, a finished image alone does not reveal the process by which it was created. Even a real-time model,

---

18. Caswell, Punzalan, and Sangwand, "Archival Studies," 2.

19. Hugh Denard, "A New Introduction to The London Charter," in *Paradata and Transparency in Virtual Heritage*, eds. Anna Bentkowska-Kafel, Hugh Denard, and Drew Baker (Burlington, VT: Ashgate, 2012): 57-58.

20. The six principles described within "The London Charter" include: Implementation; Aims and Methods; Research Sources; Documentation; Sustainability; and Access.

21. Denard, "London Charter," 66.

while it allows the user to explore a space in linear time, if it lacks an account of the evaluation of sources or of the process of interpretation, does not, in itself, render the research process visible to the visitor and thus fails to allow the viewer to assess it as part of an argument.[22]

"At the heart of The London Charter," Denard argues, "is the principle that heritage visualizations: 'should accurately convey to users the status of the knowledge that they represent, such as distinctions between evidence and hypothesis, and between different levels of probability.'"[23] The concept of paradata—the documentation of the "evaluative, analytical, deductive, interpretative and creative decisions" that make visible the "relationship between research sources, implicit knowledge, explicit reasoning, and visualisation-based outcomes"—is a useful concept for librarians working with digital collections and exhibits to consider. Paradata is an example of how we might "show our work" by reflecting upon, revealing, documenting, and sharing the choices and assumptions that guide our work and our decisions.[24]

Just as Chantler selected key moments from the Chatham Coloured All-Stars' story to build his four-panel cartoon, we knew that telling a compelling story with a relatable narrative arc would not only pique people's interest, it would make them want to learn more. We fully understood how easy it would be to overwhelm people with too much information, yet we also wanted to offer portals to additional material for those wanting more information. For our web exhibit, we consciously chose a concise narrative arc with a clear beginning, middle, and end, and we looked for opportunities to raise issues of race, racism, and the All-Stars' struggles to defy expectations. Understanding that it would be impossible to accurately convey the whole story of race in Chatham in the 1930s, we hoped that the 1934 season would not only be seen as an engaging narrative but would also be read metonymically for the larger issues of race and racism in Canadian society.

---

22. Denard, "London Charter," 60.

23. Denard, "London Charter," 60.

24. I am grateful to Devon Mordell for drawing my attention to this document and the potential uses of paradata for this project.

The 1934 Chatham Coloured All-Stars: A Story in Four Panels
© Scott Chantler (2016)

Figure 2. The 1934 Chatham Coloured All-Stars: A Story in Four Panels
by Scott Chantler (2016).

Selecting this particular narrative arc meant that we did not focus on Boomer Harding's hockey story, which was, perhaps, even more revealing of the racial barriers that Black Canadians faced and still face in Canada. Harding's hockey story had no decisive victory at the end: no 13-7 score, no parade, no banquet, no headlines. It was difficult to leave that story out of our initial project, but we did so hoping that, by telling the story of the 1934 baseball season well, we could branch out and tell other stories related to Boomer Harding's life, as well as those of other team and community members that were noteworthy. At present, we are currently undertaking several other large-scale projects that not only begin to tell the fuller story of Boomer Harding, but also of sports, race, and racism in Canada. It was, and remains, our project team's hope that the story of the Chatham Coloured All-Stars can generate discussions that bring other stories and documents to the fore. Whether we made the best choices remains to be seen: we made choices and have attempted at each juncture to articulate why and how we made the ones we did.

Focusing our time and resources on the baseball stories has meant that other stories remain untold. Like the $600 I can spend only once on books for my library's literature collection, my time and that of my colleagues is also limited and finite. Every moment we spend on the Harding Project is time we cannot spend on other projects. Every time I see Dorothy Wright Wallace, President of the Chatham-Kent Black Historical Society and a tremendous supporter of the Harding Project, she always asks me, as she should, "But Heidi, what about the girls?" Wright Wallace remembers Black girls' baseball teams in Chatham and Japanese girls' teams from farm camps that few people talk about and has urged us to look at this history. For reasons worth considering, the history of women's sports was not as well documented nor as conveniently preserved as that of men's sports. The history of Japanese farm camps in this part of southern Ontario are just starting to get the attention they have long merited.[25] Focusing our efforts and time on

---

25. Another project at the University of Windsor's Leddy Library is Art Rhyno's work on the Nisei farm camps of Southwestern Ontario: https://cdigs.uwindsor.ca/omeka-s/s/nisei/page/welcome.

Boomer Harding and the All-Stars has meant that we cannot devote that time to recovering girls' and women's history. As someone whose early career was all about trying to find lost and silenced women's literary historical voices, I admit that I am troubled by letting the girls' stories sit silent, but there are simply too many projects and too few hours to do all the work we would like to do. In addition to research into girls' sports, there are also other equally fascinating and important heritage projects that we turn down, put on the back burner, leave on the shelves, or politely decline because, while they are valid and fascinating, we lack the time to get the grants we need to get them off the ground. Again, all of this digital preservation and storytelling work is rooted in choices and decisions.

Fobazi Ettarh describes "vocational awe" as "the set of ideas, values, and assumptions librarians have about themselves and the profession that result in beliefs that libraries as institutions are inherently good and sacred, and therefore beyond critique."[26] The "stereotypical library," Ettarh writes, "is often portrayed as a grandiose and silent space where people can be guided to find answers."[27] In this iteration, librarians are a conduit between knowledge and the users: they are acquirers, organizers, preservers, and facilitators of information. Or, considered another way, librarians are invisible, passive, staid, and static, a conduit between questions and answers.

But a library is not a democratic institution simply because it has "Library" on the front of the building. A library is a democratic institution only when it actively and decisively works to preserve, defend, and enable democratic ideals. Similarly, an archive or a digital exhibit is not inherently democratic or emancipatory simply by existing. In all cases, we must examine our intents and actions, our assumptions and ellipses, in the choices we make. We must ask ourselves the difficult questions about the work we are doing and the work we are not doing. As Schwartz

---

26. Fobazi Ettarh, "Vocational Awe and Librarianship: The Lies We Tell Ourselves," *In the Library with the Lead Pipe* (January 10, 2018), http://www.inthelibrarywiththelead-pipe.org/2018/vocational-awe/.

27. Ettarh, "Vocational Awe," January 10, 2018.

and Cook note, "The point is for archivists to (re)search thoroughly for the missing voices, for the complexity of the human or organizational functional activities under study during appraisal, description, or outreach activities, so that archives can acquire and reflect multiple voices, and not, by default, only the voices of the powerful."[28] Further, as Kellee E. Warren compellingly argues, "When archives ignore or emphasize one narrative over another, it influences how people see themselves and how others see them. When the powerful have control of archives, they can establish narratives of their choosing."[29] Libraries, like archives, must consider and work to enact concrete ways to move in the direction of greater diversity and inclusivity on a range of fronts and in multiple ways.

As Rabia Gibbs cautions, "Incorporating diversity into the historical record does not mean blindly accessioning records related to a specific race or ethnicity...we must see ethnic communities as independent, complex social groups instead of presuming that our diversity agenda is in alignment with minority documentary needs and histories simply because it addresses the issues of diversity."[30] The aim, she argues, is to "initiate a discussion about how to make our diversity initiatives more authentic and meaningful."[31] These are vital questions to consider, especially for those of us working with collections of materials from communities distinct from those to which we belong. In short, it's simply not enough to digitize "lost," "endangered," or "marginalized" voices; we must consider a range of vital questions. For example, how are the voices represented? How are the communities or individuals that produced these voices involved in the decision-making process? Punzalan and Caswell contend that "the challenge is not just how to

28. Schwartz and Cook, "Modern Memory," 17.

29. Kellee E. Warren, "We Need These Bodies, But Not Their Knowledge: Black Women in the Archival Science Professions and Their Connection to the Archives of Enslaved Black Women in the French Antilles," *Library Trends* 64, no. 4 (Spring 2016): 786.

30. Rabia Gibbs, "The Heart of the Matter: The Developmental History of African American Archives," *American Archivist* 75, no. 1 (Spring/Summer 2012): 203.

31. Gibbs, "Heart of the Matter," 204.

get more faces of color at the table, but to interrogate the cultural foundations and accompanying power structures upon which the table is built."[32] Moreover, as Warren argues, changes in our libraries and archives must happen at multiple levels in multiple ways: "the state of archives on enslaved black women and the current data on the recruitment of underrepresented groups in the archives and LIS professions demand the incorporation of concepts from black feminist thought, critical race theory, and cognitive justice into archival science and LIS curriculums. These frameworks will introduce future archivists and librarians to inclusive concepts and practices – practices that not only increase bodies but also create a cosmos of knowledge."[33] Again, librarians can look to the work of critical archival studies scholars as a way to start these conversations and work toward a more inclusive praxis.

As white scholars, none of us from Chatham, we have been constantly aware of the fine line that exists between facilitating a community's efforts to tell their own stories and appropriating those stories. Some members of the Chatham community wondered if it might be best for the community to undertake this digitization project themselves. Had this been the will of our community partners, we would have stepped away. As a result of many open and sincere conversations, we and our community partners came to understood that all parties involved in this project shared a deeply held belief in the importance of the voices and memories, and that each group had various skills and unique resources we could leverage to achieve our shared goals. The Harding family, other team members' families, and various Chatham community groups had documents, varied and vivid stories to tell, community connections, and a passion for history. At the University of Windsor, we had access to grant money, skilled students we could hire, technological equipment and expertise, server space, and a passion for history. In short, we offered the community the support and infrastructure we had access to through

---

32. Ricardo L. Punzalan, and Michelle Caswell, "Critical Directions for Archival Approaches to Social Justice," Library Quarterly: Information, Community, Policy 86, no. 1 (2016): 34.

33. Warren, "Bodies," 789.

the University, so that the community could tell its stories and that those stories could be preserved in their own voices.

Nevertheless, our roles as outsiders in this project were constantly in our minds and probably in the minds of our partners. As with all relationships, we made mistakes; some, we are aware of, and of others, we remain ignorant. We tried, at every step of our project, to consult with our community partners and make sure to have the difficult conversations when they arose. Our community partners did the same. We are often asked whether white scholars should have taken on this project and we understand where that question comes from. We know that, on the one hand, there are legitimate concerns about appropriation and the silencing of voices. On the other hand, there is the potential for the fear of appropriation to dominate so fully that it leads to inaction, which is another form of silencing or exclusion.

None of this work is easy.

Nor should it be.

When it starts seeming easy, we need to stop and consider whether we are asking the difficult questions of ourselves, our work, and our profession. If not, we need to have those conversations and "show our work." Scholarship within librarianship has, in many instances, been guilty of what Michelle Caswell has articulated regarding humanities scholars' refusal to engage with the scholarship of archival studies. Like the humanities, librarianship can benefit tremendously from engaging in this work, since critical archival studies "calls into question fundamental humanities assumptions about how we exist in the world, how we know what we know, and how we transmit that knowledge."[34] If, as Caswell posits,

> critical theory is that which explains what is wrong with the world, how we can change it, and who should change it, then archival studies can

---

34. Michelle Caswell offers this overview of critical archival studies: "It 1. Explains what is wrong with the current state of archival and recordkeeping practice and research and identifies who can change it and how; 2. Posits achievable goals for how archives and recordkeeping practice and research in archival studies can and should change; 3. Provides norms and strategies and mechanisms for forming such critique." Michelle Caswell, "Owning Critical Archival Studies: A Plea," (2016), 6.

add a crucial records-centered component to this configuration; archival studies can interrogate how records contribute to what is wrong with the world, how records can be used to change it, and by whom. Archival studies can help critical theorists conceive of what "a real democracy" is (using Horkheimer's term) by adding our century-long discussion of representation, evidence, accountability, and memory.[35]

These are questions and concerns with which librarianship must engage as we envision what our profession and our broader work should look like today and in the future, and how we might move toward that vision.

In closing, I return to what Mr. Yeske, my patient math teacher, told me as I struggled with a problem I could not solve: "tell me the story of what you're trying to do with this problem." From there, I talked through what I was trying to do and he listened. He validated my thinking but also showed me alternative ways to proceed. Although I couldn't articulate what he was doing then, I now realize that his approach showed a respect for process – an openness to talking about things other than the "right" answer. I came to translate his insistent "show your work" as "I may not like your answer, but show me where you wanted to go, what you were trying to do, what assumptions you were making as you moved through the problem, and we can have a discussion." Perhaps my history with math classes explains a lot about how I approach librarianship. It's not about the one "right" answer but it is about "showing our work." It's about talking through what we're trying to do and working together to find the best ways to proceed. And, it's also about being open to making mistakes, talking them through, and learning from others.

Novelist Arundhati Roy has said, "We know of course there's really no such thing as the 'voiceless.' There are only the deliberately silenced, or the preferably unheard."[36] Librarianship, digital humanities, and history are about choices—about what we tell, what we preserve, what we make accessible, what we highlight, and what we, regardless of our best intentions, silence, neglect, forget, or repress. Who are we not listening

---

35. Caswell, "Owning Critical Archival Studies," 6.

36. "Arundhati Roy: Sydney Peace Prize," November 4, 2004, http://sydney.edu.au/news/84.html?newsstoryid=279.

to when we're listening to others? What stories and voices are hidden in plain view right in front of us that we either cannot or do not see? We cannot do everything but we do make choices about what we do and what we do not do. We must carefully consider and articulate what we're not doing alongside of what we are doing.

Bibliography

"Arundhati Roy: Sydney Peace Prize." Last modified November 4, 2004. http://sydney.edu.au/news/84.html?newsstoryid=279.

Bastien, Jeanette A., Megan Sniffen-Marinoff, and Donna Webber. *Archives in Libraries: What Librarians and Archivists Need to Know to Work Together.* Chicago: Society of American Archivists, 2018.

"Boomer Harding Makes Hockey History at Olympia. Becomes First Negro to Play on Local Rink. May be 'First' in Pro Hockey." *Michigan Gazette.* 16 November 1946.

Caswell, Michelle. "Owning Critical Archival Studies: A Plea." (2016). Retrieved from https://escholarship.org/uc/item/75x090df.

Caswell, Michelle, Ricardo Punzalan, and T-Kay Sangwand. "Critical Archival Studies: An Introduction." *Journal of Critical Library and Information Studies* 1, no. 2 (2017): 1-8.

Denard, Hugh. "A New Introduction to The London Charter." In *Paradata and Transparency in Virtual Heritage*, edited by Anna Bentkowska-Kafel, Hugh Denard, and Drew Baker, pp. 57-71. Burlington, VT: Ashgate, 2012.

Ettarh, Fobazi. "Vocational Awe and Librarianship: The Lies We Tell Ourselves." Last modified 10 January 2018. http://www.inthelibrary-withtheleadpipe.org/2018/vocational-awe/.

Gibbs, Rabia. "The Heart of the Matter: The Developmental History of African American Archives." *American Archivist* 75, no. 1 (Spring/Summer 2012): 195-204.

Hodgkin, Katharine and Susannah Radstone, eds. *Contested Pasts: The Politics of Memory.* London: Routledge, 2003.

Punzalan, Ricardo L., and Michelle Caswell. "Critical Directions for Archival Approaches to Social Justice." *Library Quarterly: Information, Community, Policy* 86, no. 1 (2016): 25-42.

Rhyno, Art. "The Nisei Farm Camps of Southwestern Ontario (1942-1944)." https://cdigs.uwindsor.ca/omeka-s/s/nisei/page/welcome.

Schwartz, Joan M., and Terry Cook. "Archives, Records, and Power: The Making of Modern Memory." *Archival Science* 2, nos. 1-2 (2002): 1-19.

University of Windsor Leddy Library. *Breaking the Colour Barrier.* Last modified 15 February 2018. http://cdigs.uwindsor.ca/BreakingColourBarrier/.

Warren, Kellee E. "We Need These Bodies, But Not Their Knowledge: Black Women in the Archival Science Professions and Their Connection to the Archives of Enslaved Black Women in the French Antilles." *Library Trends* 64, no. 4 (Spring 2016): 776-94.

"What Are Archives and How Do They Differ from Libraries?" *Society of American Archivists.* https://www2.archivists.org/usingarchives/whatarearchives.

Chapter 10

Refocusing the Lens: Creating Social Justice Encounters for Students in the Archives

Peggy Keeran, Katherine Crowe, and Jennifer Bowers

The University of Denver Special Collections and Archives has historically collected archival materials that reflect the institution's largely hegemonic narratives. In order to address the lack of gender and racial/ethnic diversity in our physical archives, the librarians and curators at the University of Denver Libraries incorporate a social justice perspective into our instructional classes, encouraging students to critically examine the documentary record.

The Arts & Humanities librarian, the Social Sciences librarian, and the Special Collections and Archives curators began collaborating with teaching faculty several years ago to integrate physical and digital primary sources into the curriculum. Although the goal of many classes was to teach students to understand both the differences between and potential uses of primary and secondary sources, we realized that students also need to learn how to address the gaps in the archives and to devise strategies for recognizing and giving voice and visibility to those who have been marginalized. To achieve this goal, we have developed four thematic social justice archival experiences (which often merge and overlap): Silenced Voices; Resistance, Protest, and Activism; Reading Against the Grain; and Social Inequity.

We offer several instructional experiences to highlight "Silenced Voices" in the archives. For this challenge, we've primarily chosen to ask students to interrogate records created about a community by non-community members, potentially without the knowledge or consent of that community. Exercises address the University's problematic history with Native Americans, specifically the Cheyenne and Arapaho nations. Our physical archives holds virtually nothing of this history, much of which concerns the role played by University of Denver's founders in the Sand Creek Massacre in 1864, the year the University of Denver was established. This gap requires creative and critical use of our existing collections that document Native Americans, like Edward Curtis' *The North American Indian,* in order to generate discussions with students about the reasons for this silence in the archives and the different values placed on textual and oral traditions.

Classes that adopt a "Resistance, Protest, and Activism" approach draw upon records related to the student experience, including newspapers, yearbooks, and student organization papers. Students research events from Vietnam War protests at the University of Denver to campus feminist and environmental movements over time, sometimes in conversation with current student activist movements, many of which have corresponding social media hashtags, such as NoDAPL, BlackLivesMatter, MarchForOurLives, DACA, the Women's March, and fossil fuel divestment.

In "Reading Against the Grain" archival sessions, students question historical narratives by studying digital primary source materials, such as American newspaper reports related to the invasion of Belgium in 1914 or Poland in 1939, or student publications and newspaper accounts related to the persecution of Jews in Germany both prior to and during World War II. Students critically examine texts to determine what was reported contemporaneously as opposed to the national myths created since.

Finally, classes that investigate the archives through a "Social Inequity" perspective provide opportunities for students to consider the idea of difference, particularly as manifested in the experiences of underrepresented students at the University of Denver, whether that be through gender, sexual orientation, race and ethnicity, religion, ability, socioeconomic status, or other categories of historically marginalized identity. In these sessions, students analyze visual and textual evidence in the student newspaper to trace historical antecedents to current issues about diversity, equity, and inclusion in higher education.

Our research instruction is informed by the intersection between Critical Information Literacy (CIL) and archival social justice, in which archives are framed as inherently political rather than neutral, and as sites of contestation where narratives can be disrupted to find alternative realities. To help develop agency in students-as-scholars, we center their lived experiences so they don't enter the classroom as static vessels receiving information, but rather as active participants who bring their whole selves into the learning process. Students interrogate physical and digital primary sources individually or in small groups in order to assess who is present/absent/overlooked, and how race and gender are represented. Librarians, curators, and teaching faculty work collaboratively with students on the research process and critical evaluation, rather than directing them through a series of rote tasks. We build exercises into the sessions to allow students to reflect upon what they have learned. What social justice and CIL look like and how they manifest are complex and constantly changing; our interest is in how these changing frameworks inform and are reflected in our instruction and interactions with students researching in the physical and digital archives.

Literature Review

The complexities and multidimensional nature of social justice and CIL within libraries and archives may be attributable to the fact that their definitions and practices grew out of grassroots movements in response to standardized ways of viewing and teaching collections. Emerging from the social upheavals of the 1960s, curators and archivists began to question the ways in which their hegemonic collections were providing commemorative, dominant narratives about society and culture. The prescriptive nature of the Association of College and Research

Librarians (ACRL) Information Literacy Competency Standards, established in 2000, focused on teaching students skills that were largely outcomes-based and measurable rather than on active and reflective lifelong learning. Archivists and librarians began to look outside their professions to find discussions that would inform their practices, and social justice, critical theory, and critical pedagogy offered ways to re-envision how we view, build, and teach with collections. By incorporating theories and approaches from other disciplines, archivists and librarians who were questioning the established methods were free to bring in a wider array of viewpoints from various fields of study. The definitions we use for social justice and CIL are fluid and the applications we employ in teaching are not standardized and concrete, but are an evolving and "complicated set of interwoven practices."[1]

In their 2016 article, Ricardo L. Punzalan and Michelle Caswell trace the importance of social justice in the archives literature since 1970, from Howard Zinn questioning the concept of archival neutrality, to today, when the authors claim that "social justice has become a central, if under-acknowledged, archival value."[2] The authors sift through the literature to define social justice, but acknowledge that it is a complex concept that addresses and works to improve inequalities in building, accessing, and understanding archives. They identify five areas in the archives literature where social justice discussions occur: inclusion of underrepresented and marginalized sectors of society; reinterpretation and expansion of foundational archival concepts; development of community archives; rethinking archival education and training; and efforts to document human rights abuses. Examples offered within these categories include ensuring that both the document creator and the subjects of the records are both present/accounted for, using collective/social memory

---

1. James Elmborg, "Critical Information Literacy: Definitions and Challenges," in *Transforming Information Literacy Programs: Intersecting Frontiers of Self, Library Culture, and Campus Community*, eds. Carroll Wetzel Wilkinson and Courtney Bruch (Chicago: Association of College and Research Libraries, 2012), 77.

2. Ricardo L. Punzalan and Michelle Caswell, "Critical Directions for Archival Approaches to Social Justice," *Library Quarterly: Information, Community, Policy* 86, no. 4 (2016): 37.

to recover silenced voices and discover counternarratives, developing community or grassroots archives to write, correct, or amend dominant narratives, and advocating for archival pluralism within the profession and within the archives. The authors also highlight several areas for future research: alternatives to the legalistic, rights-based framework; diversification of the profession, as well as an increased focus on white privilege, which they identify as the root of the hegemonic problem; economics that negatively impact archives and access, from neoliberalism to defunding archives to corporate funding of commercial digital projects from the archives; and implementing ethical methods for digitizing cultural heritage and assessing the subsequent benefits to the source community. Punzalan and Caswell point to the importance of pluralism in the archives, where "assumptions based on dominant cultures are so prevalent in practice that they are essentially hidden in plain sight," such as the initial resistance to the Protocols for the Native American Archival Materials.[3] This overview of the literature and possible future directions for research illustrate that social justice is vital to understanding how archives, whether physical or digital, are constructed and why they should be viewed as sites of contestation.

Punzalan and Caswell also used Anthony W. Dunbar's characterization of social justice as the criteria for the literature they reviewed. They recommend Dunbar's approach to viewing the archives through a Critical Race Theory (CRT) lens, for "critical race theory's framework for interrogating, challenging, and eliminating the predominance of white supremacy can provide a crucial way forward."[4] Dunbar articulates four goals of social justice in the archives: the equitable distribution of resources; establishing ways for individuals to seek their own agency, reality, or representation; creating dialogue between communities with differing cultural viewpoints; and developing frameworks that recognize

---

3. Punzalan and Caswell, "Critical Directions for Archival Approaches to Social Justice," 33. The Protocols were endorsed by the Society of American Archivists on August 13, 2018. https://www2.archivists.org/statements/saa-council-endorsement-of-protocols-for-native-american-archival-materials.

4. Punzalan and Caswell, 33.

and scrutinize oppression and how it operates.[5] He argues that CRT can "assist in establishing a voice and identity for underrepresented and marginalized populations that can be expressed through an agency of self-empowerment based on issues of significance to them."[6] CRT can help recover voices in the archives, those who are not present and don't have agency, by "creating and recreating identities that are expressive of the lived experiences of marginalized populations" documented in the archives, and by allowing the "dominant culture to fill the role of the objectified or documented."[7] Through these counternarratives, "the introduction of CRT and archives has endless possibilities to raise the collective consciousness about social bias."[8]

David A. Wallace claims that social justice is part of the ethics of archival work, for archives are inherently political, not neutral. He references two professional meetings in 2005 and 2008 where archivists advocated for connecting archives and social justice as critically necessary, and to look externally for models that, for example, embrace "ambiguity over clarity," accept "that social memory is always contestable and reconfigurable," and acknowledge "that social justice itself is ambiguous and contingent on dissimilar space, time, and cultural contexts."[9] The challenge for archivists is "to utilize the past to inform and change the present through concrete action"[10]—social justice must be more than just a concept or a philosophy, it must lead to actual change. Wallace joined Wendy M. Duff, Andrew Flinn, and Karen Emily Suurtamm to study the social justice impact of archives, identify common concepts for social justice derived from definitions found in encyclopedias in the social sciences and sciences, and develop a conceptualization framework

5. Anthony W. Dunbar, "Introducing Critical Race Theory to Archival Discourse: Getting the Conversation Started," *Archival Science* 6, no. 1 (2006): 117.

6. Dunbar, "Introducing Critical Race Theory to Archival Discourse," 127.

7. Dunbar, "Introducing Critical Race Theory to Archival Discourse," 125.

8. Dunbar, "Introducing Critical Race Theory to Archival Discourse," 126.

9. David A. Wallace, "Locating Agency: Interdisciplinary Perspectives on Professional Ethics and Archival Morality," *Journal of Information Ethics* 19, no. 1 (2010): 184.

10. Wallace, "Locating Agency," 186.

for understanding social justice. Their vision is that individuals, communities, and cultural groups are equal and valued, entitled to the same standards of freedom and respect, that violations must be recognized and challenged, that some are privileged at the expense of others through inequalities of power, and that "social justice is always a process and can never be fully achieved."[11] Their article concludes with a list of questions that lead to narratives about human rights violations in order to illustrate the social justice impact of archives. As examples, they create narratives in response to the questions about how concrete actions led to change in the *Los Archivos del Cardenal* project on torture and disappearances in Pinochet's Chile from 1973-1990 and for the Japanese American World War II internment and reparations.

Although the research our students do in class does not necessarily result in action, particularly to the degree discussed by Duff et al., it can be transformative and impactful, providing support for them to become critical thinkers.[12] In our instruction sessions for physical and digital primary sources, CIL allows us to raise issues about social justice in the archives, centering the students as the investigators, and providing them with space and time to examine and reflect upon the artifacts they encounter. The literature related to CIL is still growing and ever evolving. James Elmborg, an early proponent for incorporating critical theory and critical pedagogy into library instruction, promoted rethinking the positioning of students as "objects" or receptacles of knowledge, into students who take active roles in developing agency,[13] later asserting that "librarians should leave their 'expert hat at the door,' thereby abandoning the 'library knows best' model that underlies the

---

11. Wendy M. Duff, Andrew Flinn, Karen Emily Suurtamm, and David A. Wallace, "Social Justice Impact of Archives: A Preliminary Investigation," *Archival Science* 13, no. 4 (2013): 324-325.

12. Transformation of the classroom and of the student is a theme throughout Eamon Tewell's literature review of critical information literacy. Eamon Tewell, "A Decade of Critical Information Literacy: A Review of the Literature," *Communications in Information Literacy* 9, no. 1 (2015): 24-43.

13. Elmborg, "Critical Information Literacy," 2012, 90.

traditional, knowledge-transfer approach to information literacy."[14] In this way, "by developing critical consciousness, students learn to take control of their lives and their own learning to become active agents, asking and answering questions that matter to them and to the world around them."[15] Bringing social justice to the fore of information literacy, Lua Gregory and Shana Higgins describe social justice's most basic values as being the fair, equitable, and respectful treatment of people and their human rights, and aver that "teaching and learning require reflexivity, a shared experience such that we learn from and with each other, and a focus on process toward transformative understanding."[16] Nicole Pagowsky and Kelly McElroy echo this in their evaluation of critical pedagogy, a companion framework to CIL, stating that it "does not diminish the role of the teacher, but rather should enhance it, where learning is viewed as a partnership between teachers and students."[17] Throughout the CIL and social justice literature, it is evident how both can transform teaching and student learning.

Eamon C. Tewell surveyed and interviewed librarians practicing CIL, and identified teaching methods used to promote agency and engagement: discussion and dialogue; group work; skipping database demonstrations; reflection; and problem posing[18] – methods also rel-

---

14. James Elmborg, "Foreword," in *Critical Library Pedagogy: Essays and Workbook Activities*, vol. 1, eds. Nicole Pagowsky and Kelly McElroy (Chicago: Association of College and Research Libraries, 2016), xii.

15. James Elmborg, "Critical Information Literacy: Implications for Instructional Practice," *Journal of Academic Librarianship* 32, no. 2 (2006): 193.

16. Lua Gregory and Shana Higgins, "Introduction," in *Information Literacy and Social Justice: Radical Professional Practice*, eds. Lua Gregory and Shana Higgins (Sacramento, CA: Library Juice, 2013), 4. Lua and Higgins refer to the influence of Paolo Freire's Pedagogy of the Oppressed on the definitions and practices of critical information literacy, and derive their brief definition of social justice from Ozlem Sensoy and Robin DiAngelo's 2012 volume, *Is Everyone Really Equal? An Introduction to Key Concepts in Social Justice Education.*

17. Nicole Pagowsky and Kelly McElroy, "Introduction," in *Critical Library Pedagogy: Essays and Workbook Activities*, vol. 1, eds. Nicole Pagowsky and Kelly McElroy (Chicago: Association of College and Research Libraries, 2016), xvii.

18. Eamon C. Tewell, "The Practice and Promise of Critical Information Literacy: Academic Librarians' Involvement in Critical Library Instruction," *College & Research Libraries* 79, no. 1 (2018): 18-19.

evant for bringing social justice into archival instruction sessions. When selecting items from the archives for teaching or exhibits, Lisa Hooper advises, "in the classroom setting particularly, the need to advance beyond showing commemorative documents of an unchallenged history is of great presence." Instead, she suggests intentionally offering an array of artifacts from differing perspectives that "provide insight into events from the perspective of the subaltern and Other in addition to that of the dominant force."[19] Patrick Williams finds that "the gaps and overlaps among the concepts of archival intelligence and information literacy create a tension that positions archival spaces as ideal sites for critical inquiry and reflection around how we understand and experience information."[20] Following Hooper's advice, Williams works with professors, curators, and archivists to select materials that allow students to encounter silenced voices and imbalances of power; in the physical archives, students explore, read, take notes, and talk about what they are seeing and thinking, and Williams co-explores with them. In one session, students spontaneously gathered around two volumes of early twentieth-century Sanborn Fire Insurance Maps of the area, and began making personal connections to them, noting what was gone (sorority and fraternity houses replaced by a university complex; working class and African American neighborhoods razed when the Interstate bisected the city) and what they knew had replaced the buildings and neighborhoods. "Observations and questions that arose out of this impromptu geography discussion made palpable the interactions in the spaces between these hundred-year-old books and the young people using them; each student's perspective and experience overlaid on the map of our city in complementary, personal ways."[21]

---

19. Lisa Hooper, "Breaking the Ontological Mold: Bringing Postmodernism and Critical Pedagogy into Archival Educational Programming," in *Critical Library Instruction: Theories and Methods*, eds. Maria T. Accardi, Emily Drabinski, and Alana Kumbier (Duluth, MN: Library Juice Press, 2010), 36.

20. Patrick Williams, "What Is Possible: Setting the Stage for Co-Exploration in Archives and Special Collections," in *Critical Library Pedagogy: Essays and Workbook Activities*, vol. 1, eds. Nicole Pagowsky and Kelly McElroy (Chicago: Association of College and Research Libraries, 2016), 113.

21. Williams, "What Is Possible," 112.

Throughout the literature on CIL and social justice in the library and archives, there are references to the value of lived experiences, memory making, agency, problem posing, reflection, and transformation, as well as acknowledgements about the gaps in and hegemony of the archives that provide challenges for finding silenced voices, for discovering activism, for reading against the grain, and for identifying instances of social inequality. In this chapter, we will discuss employing CIL strategies for centering students, active engagement, interrogation of artifacts, and reflection. Further, we will delve into representative primary source class sessions, where we collaborated with professors, either in one-shot classes or multiple visits, to guide students towards examining the physical and digital archives through a social justice lens.

Silenced Voices

The archives is a potent place—a collection of memories and voices from the past that also look ahead to the future. When students first work with archival materials, however, they often need help understanding that the archives, as both a symbol and a materially real place, does not equally represent all members of society. Frequently overwhelmed or enamored with the opportunity to interact with the tangible past, students may not think to question the power implicit in an archival collection, nor consider the contested and political process that determines who is included and excluded from the archives and the impact such privilege or invisibility might have on different communities. Therefore, as instructors, it is critical for us to guide students through deconstructing the issues of power and representation manifest in the archives and in the students' archival experience.

Following the recommendations presented by Duff et al. in their investigation of the social justice impact of archives, we have developed archival sessions centered on a "Silenced Voices" theme that examines archives as structures which perpetuate "non-recognition and marginalization."[22] To this effect, these classes either enable students

---

22. Duff, et al., "Social Justice Impact of Archives: A Preliminary Investigation," 319.

to work with archival materials in our collections created by traditionally marginalized members of society, in this case with Russian and
other Eastern European Jewish immigrants, or with records that were
created by non-community members, specifically those records about
the Cheyenne, Arapaho, and other Native American nations created by
non-Natives. In both classes, students are provided with the opportunity
to question how archives, as mirrors of existing societal structures and
inequality, can both represent and misrepresent, as well as empower and
disempower, individual people and communities.

Our first example, "Sociological Imagination and Inquiry," is a qualitative research methods class required of all Sociology and Criminology
majors that lays the foundation for advanced classes and research projects in the discipline. The Social Sciences librarian and the curator of
the Beck Archives have partnered over the last several years with one
Sociology faculty member to incorporate an intensive, multiple-part,
archival experience into her course. Although we introduce students
to both physical and digital archival materials, our main focus is on
the Jewish Consumptives' Relief Society (JCRS) patient records, which
are part of the Ira M. and Peryle Hayutin Beck Memorial Archives of
Rocky Mountain Jewish history. Founded in 1904 in Denver, Colorado
by Eastern European Jewish immigrants, the JCRS was a non-sectarian
tuberculosis sanatorium that cared, free of charge, for its primarily Jewish
patients, in all stages of the disease, in a culturally sensitive environment that included kosher food, the observance of Jewish holidays, and
a synagogue.[23] The majority of the patients were poor, working class
immigrants, not dissimilar from the founders who were "proud of the
humble and lowly origins of our Society…[and who rejoiced] in the fact
that our beginning was distinctly a movement from below, not initiated
by men of high economic or social standing."[24]

------

23. American Jewish Historical Society, "Guide to the Jewish Consumptives' Relief
Society (Denver, Colo.) Collection, undated, 1905-1955," accessed November 20,
2018, http://digifindingaids.cjh.org/?pID=365605#a2.

24. Philip Hillkowitz, "President's Report," *First Annual Report of the JCRS, 1905,*
12, Beck Archives. Quoted in Jeanne Abrams, Dr. Charles David Spivak: A Jewish

We begin our archival session with an introduction to the JCRS collection by the Beck Archives curator, who presents the historical and social context of the sanatorium, covering such topics as contemporary medical knowledge about tuberculosis and its treatment, working conditions for immigrants who were afflicted, and the reasons for Jewish immigration from Eastern Europe during the late nineteenth and early twentieth centuries. Then, students are encouraged to explore patient records on their own. As they become acquainted with different patients' folders and the records therein, the students begin to piece together details from family letters, sponsoring organization and society letters, and official medical records that document country of origin, occupation, and release or death, to create a portrait of the individual admitted.

During their second session in the archives, the students choose three patients to compare, and, based on the existing material record, they develop sociologically framed research questions that could be answered by their textual analysis. Such questions might concern gender, economic, or national differences. Reading the records closely gives students a very direct encounter with the lived experiences of these patients, who were often marginalized in the United States by their poverty, health, and immigrant status. They can see firsthand, for example, the prevalence of common occupations linked to tuberculosis at that time, such as seamstresses, milliners, and tailors. Students come to empathize with patients who were ill and often died, even though many were only in their early twenties. In other cases, students find the lack of information about patients' lives to be compelling, even when there may be nothing in the folders aside from official admittance forms, which leaves students wondering about who these people were and what happened to them after they left the sanatorium. Such examples reinforce, for students, how arbitrary archival preservation can be, how significant gaps might exist within a collection, and how important it is for all voices, not just those of the privileged, to be represented in the archives.

Immigrant and the American Tuberculosis Movement (Boulder, CO: University Press of Colorado, 2009), 84.

Duff et al. emphasize the value of linking historical to contemporary struggles, cautioning that, through "its traditional focus on 'the past,' and a narrowing focus on archival exposure of past injustices, archives safely stay *one step behind* recognizing and addressing present injustices."[25] The JCRS archival sessions not only lay the groundwork for the students' life course interviews that they conduct later in the quarter (the University of Denver is on the quarter system), but they also enable students to make connections between early twentieth-century and early twenty-first century immigrant experiences and current national debate, drawing attention to such ongoing issues as working conditions, health care opportunities, xenophobia, and community support and resilience.

The JCRS collection represents the history of a particular community comprised of records created by the community about itself, through its patients, family members, religious organizations, and doctors. In sharp contrast, our second class, a first-year seminar taught by a Communications professor, titled "Memory, History, and Contemporary Native Identity," presents a very different challenge and archival experience. Our physical archives hold very few materials about Native Americans. Although we have been working to redress this significant gap, the historical materials that we have about Native Americans were created by people outside the community. This absence of Native perspectives and records in our archives is especially troubling given the role played by the University of Denver's founder, John Evans (who was territorial governor and superintendent of Indian Affairs at the time), and Colonel John Chivington (a member of the executive committee of the University's original Board of Directors) in the Sand Creek Massacre of 1864, the same year the University was established. During the Massacre, an estimated 160 women, children, and elderly members of the Cheyenne and Arapaho nations were attacked and killed.[26] To understand this complicated and problematic history, as a university and a nation, it is

---

25. Duff, et al., "Social Justice Impact of Archives: A Preliminary Investigation," 319.

26. University of Denver, "History & Traditions," accessed November 30, 2018, https://www.du.edu/about/history-traditions.

critical that our instruction, if not our physical archives, represent those impacted by this event. By making students aware of the absence of Cheyenne and Arapaho voices in our archives, we can underscore Julie D. Shayne et al.'s point that "the power to define, populate, and frame the contents of an archive is literally the power to control an historical narrative."[27] Without representation in the archives, the narrative of the Sand Creek Massacre in particular, but also other historical events, is shaped entirely by non-Native perspectives, articulated through those figures with power: the army, the U.S. government and its officials, and the press, among others.

For the "Memory, History, and Contemporary Native Identity" class, we talked with the faculty member in advance about using the absence of records in our archives generated by the Native American community as a learning opportunity. We decided to focus our session with students on the "Silenced Voices" theme in order to discuss the critical issues of bias and representation in the existing documentary record. We also wanted to address how memories and/or the historical record are preserved in different cultures, noting the values placed on and roles served by printed materials and oral traditions. Since the students were studying the Sand Creek Massacre specifically at the time, we could demonstrate not only how and why Cheyenne and Arapaho perspectives were missing from our physical archives but, through a separate session based on subscription and freely available digital sources, we could also illustrate how our digital archival collections of newspapers, government documents, and testimony by those involved perpetuate, for the most part, an unbalanced narrative of Sand Creek.[28]

---

27. Julie D. Shayne, Denise Hattwig, Dave Ellenwood, and Taylor Hiner, "Creating Counter Archives: The University of Washington Bothell's Feminist Community Archive of Washington Project," *Feminist Teacher* 27, no. 1 (2016): 60.

28. One notable exception is George Bent/Ho-my-ike, the son of Owl Woman and a White trader, William Bent, whose description of the Massacre was recorded in letters to and printed by George Hyde in Hyde's biography, *Life of George Bent, Written from His Letters*, published in 1968. After the archive sessions, we also discovered the "Sand Creek Massacre Site Location Study Oral History Project," which provides oral traditions about the Massacre from the Cheyenne and Arapaho descendants, https://www.nps.gov/sand/learn/management/upload/site-location-study_volume-1.pdf.

In addition to the discussion about silence and exclusion, the archival session built on the course themes of Native American memory, identity, and representation by focusing on two Native American sources in our collection—Edward Curtis' *The North American Indian* photogravures (a twenty-volume, twenty-portfolio set) and Aaron Carapella's "Plains Indians and the Way West" map. The Curtis' photogravures fall within the "romanticized West" tradition and were taken primarily in the early twentieth century to document the "vanishing" Native Americans, described by Shamoon Zamir as "narratives of Native demise, or vanishing, as well as the historical self-assurance of white culture."[29] Carapella's Tribal Nations Maps series uses original Indigenous tribal names and records their homelands pre- and post-contact with Europeans; as well, he incorporates reproductions of Curtis's photogravures to denote their ancestral and migratory locations. These two resources provided students an opportunity to examine visual forms of Native American representation created by a White American photographer and an Indigenous cartographer respectively, at different points in time and with very different goals.[30]

After an introduction to the sources, students worked in small groups to select one of Curtis's photogravures to consider how Native Americans were represented in it, taking into account historical perspective and context, such as Curtis' aim to capture timeless, rather than accurate, portraits of his subjects.[31] Then, we concluded the session with

---

29. Shamoon Zamir, "Native Agency and the Making of The North American Indian: Alexander B. Upshaw and Edward S. Curtis," *American Indian Quarterly* 31, no. 4 (2007): 615.

30. Aaron Carapella is a self-taught cartographer and identifies as a "mixed-blood Cherokee." Hansi Lo Wang, "The Map of Native American Tribes You've Never Seen Before," National Public Radio, June 24, 2014, accessed November 30, 2018, https://www.npr.org/sections/codeswitch/2014/06/24/323665644/the-map-of-native-american-tribes-youve-never-seen-before.

31. For example, the photogravure, *In a Piegan Lodge*, 1910a, in which Curtis erased the alarm clock from the final print. See Jennifer Bowers, Katherine Crowe, and Peggy Keeran, "'If You Want the History of a White Man, You Go to the Library': Critiquing Our Legacy, Addressing Our Library Collections Gaps," *Collection Management* 42, no. 3-4 (2017): 166.

a faculty-led group discussion about Carapella's appropriation of the Curtis material and other Native American rewriting of the hegemonic documentary record. We also addressed the controversy within Native American communities about Carapella's project, including the maps series' inaccuracies, the lack of clear source documentation, and the lack of representation of urban Native Americans, among other concerns.[32]

Our "Silenced Voices" sessions have enabled us to use our existing collections to highlight the experiences of marginalized communities, whether documented by the community itself or by outsiders. The sessions have supported our goal of honing students' attention in on issues of representation and on recognizing the archives' unheard voices, aiming, in the process, to foster critically informed readers of archival records who are aware of how power and privilege impact the historical record. Through this social justice lens, we hope that students will begin to understand how our (re)collection of the past shapes our present.

Resistance, Protest, and Activism

The "Resistance, Protest, and Activism" sessions leverage our student-centered archival materials to trace social justice and other related activist movements on campus over time. In these sessions, students work with the student newspaper, yearbooks, and student organization papers for an intimate look at how student affinity groups, environmental groups, war protesters, and others have shaped and responded to University and national conversations.

Like many of our archival instruction partnerships, we arranged for the first-year seminar "Looking Beyond Beyoncé: Millennial Feminism and a New Fourth Wave" to visit the Special Collections reading room to initially examine physical archival sources, and then the students returned later for another session with our relevant digital subscription and open access primary source collections. The seminar was designed

---

32. See Debbie Reese, "A Second Look at Carapella's Tribal Nations Maps," *American Indians in Children's Literature*, August 15, 2016, accessed November 30, 2018, https://americanindiansinchildrensliterature.blogspot.com/2016/08/a-second-look-at-carapellas-tribal.html.

to introduce students to contemporary feminism, as well as to ground them in the historical legacy of women's rights movements in the U.S. The Gender and Women's Studies faculty member was very enthusiastic about incorporating an archival experience into her course, and we met beforehand to discuss which sources to use in our session. We decided that the students would review selected issues of the *Clarion*, our student newspaper, in order to compare the campus dialogue with national media discussion in the feminist magazine *Ms.* We have found that students readily engage with the *Clarion*, as it reflects student experience at the University.

We provided students with issues of both publications from the 1970s to supplement their study of second wave feminism, which was occurring at that point in the quarter. Also, since students would be thinking ahead to their final group projects, in which they would investigate a current issue on campus from various thematic perspectives, we encouraged them to select *Clarion* and *Ms.* articles that were specifically focused on their particular population or topic: LGBTQ students; men as allies; women of color; women in the media; and women and reproductive and educational policy. After reviewing the newspaper and magazine issues, students then worked together in small groups based on their topics to select one *Clarion* and one *Ms.* article to analyze. The students were intrigued by this window into the past for the insight it provided into feminist movements and activism on campus and nationwide, as well as how the articles highlighted the persistence of perennial problems, such as sexual assault. Comparing the local and national articles from the 1970s confirmed some of the students' worst expectations about sexism during that time period but also offered some positive surprises, such as discovering that there were vocal male allies on campus. Overall, the archival experience inspired students to see that, although some challenges still persist forty years later, positive change has occurred and that student activism can make a difference toward creating a more just world.

The "Resistance, Protest, and Activism" theme was also a natural fit for the "Past, Present, and Future of Sustainability in Higher Education" class required of students in the Environmental Sustainability Living and Learning community. The faculty member for this class partnered with the Social Sciences librarian, the curator of Special Collections and Archives, and the Exhibitions and Program manager on a project that spanned two quarters in order to enable students to plan, research, and create exhibits that were displayed in the library as their final projects. The class was framed around environmental justice and students were asked to consider such issues as: "How can we be more inclusive and resilient communities in the face of future challenges? How are university communities confronting the challenges of climate change? What role does higher education play in making the world more just and sustainable?"[33]

Students worked in groups for their exhibit projects and had the freedom to choose a topic of interest, as long as it was related to the aims of the course and its content. As part of researching their sustainability exhibits, we arranged for them to visit the Special Collections and Archives. During the archival session, students perused materials selected by the curator based on the list of potential exhibit topics provided by the professor and in keeping with our social justice goals. Since the groups decided to create physical rather than online exhibits, the session gave them the opportunity not only to research the history of sustainability on campus but also to identify particular items from the archives that they could use in their exhibits. The archival session served an additional purpose beyond its immediate focus by exposing students, more generally, to the range of environmental activity at the University of Denver, as represented in the archival record. To this effect, students explored historical issues of the *Clarion* and *Kynewisbok*, the student yearbook, to find examples of activism related to environmental and social justice topics, such as early campus leaders, Earth Day celebrations, and pollution concerns as expressed both on campus and across the nation. Students also examined files from past student groups, such as

33. Megan Kelly, "The Past, Present, & Future of Sustainability in Higher Education Syllabus," University of Denver, Winter & Spring, 2018.

the Student Environmental Action Coalition, the Environmental Team, and the Environmental Awareness Group, which included ephemera like meeting minutes, pamphlets, newsletters, and event posters. In addition, we made current materials available, ranging from student-generated signs and photographs from the Dakota Access Pipeline protest on campus to papers from the DivestDU group, who are advocating for the University to commit to fossil fuel divestment.

Although not every student group ended up using archival sources for their exhibits, those who did featured newspaper articles and images for the Arboretum exhibit, *Clarion* articles and protest materials in the Activism in Higher Education exhibit, and student organization pamphlets in the Greenwashing exhibit and Influential Students exhibit. Students found the process of researching and creating sustainability exhibits that they could share with the campus community to be empowering. And their experience in the archives, in particular, enabled them to connect to and find their place within the legacy of environmental activism at the University.

We have also worked directly with some library science graduate students on independent studies that focused on collaborative collection development, documentation, and exhibition design related to student resistance and activism. The resulting physical and online exhibits, entitled #RESIST, have become useful tools to teach undergraduates in the first-year writing sequence about text-based interpretation of primary sources. All first-year students at the University of Denver are required to take a two-course college composition sequence, one of which requires them to learn about and utilize different research traditions, including the text-based/interpretive tradition. Several instructors interested in an archival approach to teaching this research tradition have structured classroom sessions in the archives, which wrap up with a tour of the exhibition. Concluding the session with a visit to the exhibition allows students to experience more contemporary examples (NoDAPL, DACA protests, BlackLivesMatter, etc.) than are present in our physical archives. First-year composition classes often see thematic similarities between the language, concerns, and demands of students in the past and those of their own era, particularly students who are members of historically marginalized communities.

Anti-war activism, particularly Vietnam War protests, are well documented in the archives, and have been used in multiple Writing, Sociology, and other undergraduate courses. Woodstock West, a protest held at the University of Denver in response to the Kent State shootings on May 4, 1970, in Ohio, is among the most well-known, largely because, despite a National Guard presence and significant tension between the administration and the students, the protest concluded peacefully and even the administration's role is remembered fondly by many alumni of the era. Many students, faculty, and community members participated, wrote to newspapers and the administration, and created chronologies, fliers and ephemera, and even journal entries documenting minute-by-minute actions. These fliers and ephemera, in addition to coverage in student and national newspapers, provide a much more multi-faceted documentary record than is available for almost any other event in the University's history, making it ideal for instruction sessions. The protest's records cover feminist-focused "rap sessions," as well as a list of demands by the Black Student Alliance that lamented the University of Denver student leadership's refusal to recognize injustices done to the Black community during this period. The demands drew attention to the non-inclusive nature of Woodstock West, such as the lack of response to the killings on May 14, 1970 of multiple Black students at Jackson State who were protesting the killings at Kent State. During these fifty-minute instruction sessions, students are not always provided with contextually appropriate secondary sources. As a result, they can come away with a shallow understanding of the events themselves. We do our best to combat this by ensuring that the document analysis prompts and in-class discussions point students toward as critical a lens as possible.

Students who work with archival materials in collections that document resistance and activism, particularly students who are members of historically marginalized communities reflected in the records, seem to find not only scholarly applications for the materials, but a kind of kinship bond with their predecessors. In more contemporary documentation, students can see themselves in the historical record and in photographs included in our physical and online exhibits. For students new to archival research, the excitement of working with student-created historical records, as well as a validation of their own lived experiences as legitimate forms of evidence, has the potential to build confidence and a sense of wonder in the research process. Our goal is to translate this confidence and newfound archival skillset into critical reflection on secondary sources and the scholars and disciplinary lenses that use archives in their own work.

Reading Against the Grain

Joan M. Schwartz and Terry Cook used the phrase "against the grain" to describe the act of finding that "views of the powerful, for the very same 'mainstream' records, created by the privileged, can be deconstructed by new thinkers 'against the grain' to bring out voices which speak in opposition to power, or that insert irony or sarcasm or doubt."[34] In this section, we discuss two classes in which students examined different types of artifacts in order to question the dominant narrative and to articulate counternarratives that reveal social justice issues related to race, gender, national identity, and more. The records considered are as diverse and ordinary as cookbooks and newspapers, objects that may be familiar to students, although in different formats from those encountered in special collections or digital collections.

The University of Denver Libraries offer grants to faculty who overhaul classes and syllabi to integrate information literacy into courses. We have worked with several faculty members on these changes, and strive to incorporate CIL strategies into the information literacy component. In 2017, two History faculty applied for and received grants to revamp the "Immigrant Voices in Modern America" and "World War II in Europe" classes. The professors had separate goals for the first primary source sessions, where they wanted to have students explore

---

34. Joan M. Schwartz and Terry Cook, "Archives, Records, and Power: The Making of Modern Memory," *Archival Science* 2, no. 1 (2002): 15.

digital collections. When both classes began studying World War II, the classes met together in Special Collections and Archives to examine the student newspaper and various University of Denver-related materials. There, they shared their findings and reflected upon the University of Denver students' lived experiences and campus climate during that war. We focus here specifically on the early work students did with digital newspaper collections for the World War II course.

As part of the learning outcomes, students were to interpret Hitler's military agenda and the persecution of Jews and others as an integral part of waging war, and not viewed or understood separately. By using newspapers, students would learn how historians find suitable primary sources to explore their research questions and how to critically analyze these primary sources, including heeding the unique ways newspaper articles operate as sources for historical study. During the quarter, students were to complete two short writing assignments: one on the invasion of Poland and one on the killing of Jews in Nazi-occupied territories in 1942. In the first session, students were to search for and evaluate how the invasion of Poland was reported in American newspapers published in September 1939, in order to assess what they discovered there in comparison to their secondary readings on the topic. Although we did center the students to actively engage, reflect, and learn, we began by selecting specific digital newspaper collections (national: *New York Times*, *Wall Street Journal*; ethnic: African American newspapers, Jewish American newspapers; and local: Colorado historical newspapers) and demonstrating how best to navigate through them. From experience, we knew that very few students would be well acquainted with physical newspapers, so we brought samples to show features of the paper version, such as headlines, articles that appear above the fold on the front page, and the different sections and paging systems. Students were then free to use the resources we introduced or to explore additional digital American newspapers available. Given worksheets, they researched individually during the rest of the two-hour session to identify three separate accounts of the invasion based on themes they discovered during the research process. Students were to think about how the newspapers related to each other, reflect upon why they chose the three articles, determine (if possible and if time) the background and intended audience of the newspaper, and then write a long paragraph on the back of the worksheet describing and contrasting the coverage.

It was through the close collaboration with the teaching faculty member that such sessions were successful, at that moment and throughout the rest of the quarter. In the first session, students learned the basic skills to navigate, sort, and display articles, had time to work independently while the professor and the librarian were available to address questions about strategies and interpretation, and made decisions based on their own research questions that fell within the parameters of the assignment. Students found a wide variety of responses in local, regional, national, and ethnic newspapers from across the country, from those who voiced loud concerns over German aggression to those who blamed Poland for the invasion. In the confusing days at the very beginning of the war, there wasn't one clear narrative that emerged, but a spectrum that reflected the uncertainty and anxiety in September 1939. Historians may take such evidence and either synthesize it, or favor one narrative over another to create a national narrative, and the students were to question those secondary sources about the invasion based on their own investigations and class discussions.

The History faculty member disclosed that the second newspaper assignment had an even more profound impact on the students. Although the librarian's role at this point was over, students built upon the critical searching and evaluation skills developed in that first class to then turn their attention to the murder of Jews in 1942. Students were instructed to find reports in American newspapers about the Holocaust, to determine whether it was explicit or downplayed, to evaluate whether the account was buried or placed prominently in the paper, and to collectively discuss their discoveries in class. In the report for the information literacy grant, the History faculty member stated that "the class discussion was particularly moving: students determined or realized that there was indeed coverage of the extermination of Jews and others throughout 1942…it was clear to many students that the 'average American' would have known about mass extermination early on in the war…a disturbing finding to many students, who had assumed US citizens knew very little about the events of the Holocaust during the war."[35] The class then had extensive conversations about national myths, such as the Holocaust only being discovered when the Allies reached the camps at the end of the war. This second assignment was transformative for the students.

DU's Special Collections and Archives cookery collection has been used in a variety of classes exploring issues of culture and identity. The collection was established in 1985, when the Boettcher Foundation donated the Husted Culinary Collection, which contained more than 14,000 volumes spanning almost 400 years. The collection, built by Margaret Husted of Alexandria, Virginia, is primarily in English and strong in American regional cookery, including a large number of privately published fund-raising cookbooks from churches and other community groups. Although there are cookbooks on international cuisine, many are by Western authors. The faculty member of an Advanced Standing seminar class (classes that are taken by upper division undergraduates from all fields of study) employed the cookbooks as primary sources in the "Think, Eat, Write: Food History" course, asking students to investigate how different aspects of culture are revealed through this genre. In the first class, students in small groups discussed and answered worksheet questions that guided them on how to interrogate a cookbook "against the grain"—in this case, reading the text not as it was intended, but as a source for understanding the cultural context of food in terms of race, gender, economics, and more. The cookbooks pulled by the curator for the class were based on five themes, which were developed from the collections strengths: special diets (physical culture, food for invalids, baby food, meatless, etc.); mid-twentieth century cooking; food and war (World War I and World War II); food as a cultural bridge (Jewish and Israeli identity, immigrant cooking, Mexican food in the Southwest,

---

35. Carol Helstosky, "Moreland Report," University of Denver Libraries, 2018, 2.

Israeli-British chef Ottolenghi); and domestic economy/household manuals and recipes (Mrs. Beeton and The Kentucky Housewife).

Students visited the Special Collections and Archives four times in order to allow enough space and time to find sources in one of the themes that engaged them. They were shown how to find cookbooks in the library catalog that were located in either Special Collections and Archives or in the circulating stacks, and they were allowed to browse the cookbooks by call number in the closed rare book shelves. The curator found mid-twentieth century barbeque cookbooks to be especially rich in revealing gender roles and stereotypes within this subgenre. The books were marketed to men as a masculinized way of cooking—for, stereotypically, barbequing belongs to that gender—with heavy emphasis on gadgets, putting together grills, being outdoors, and being manly. Cartoons often accompany the recipes—one shows a husband dressed as a doctor and his wife, dressed as a nurse, handing him the implements as he cooks. The intent of these sources is clear and easy for undergraduates unfamiliar with roles related to cooking or cookbooks to understand: this is the cooking that men, specifically husbands, do.

Reading against the grain can be a powerful tool when working with everyday texts, such as newspapers and cookbooks. By examining these types of materials as primary sources, rather than as a means of keeping up on current events or learning how to cook, students begin to decipher and understand the clues that reveal evidence of racism, gender stereotypes, national narratives and myths, and national identity. Students can find counternarratives that reveal social injustices, whether on the macro level of human extermination, or the heteronormative stereotypes of marriage and gender roles found in mid-twentieth century barbeque cookbooks.

Social Inequity

Social inequity manifests in numerous ways in the historical record, offering archivists and librarians opportunities to engage with students around this specific form of systemic oppression through guided instruction in document analysis. Classes across the disciplines examined the records documenting University of Denver students who experienced social inequity: early LGBTQ students, Japanese-Americans, early twentieth-century Black women, and women in higher education overall, as well as changing perspectives on the University's former mascot, Denver Boone. In several cases, we chose the records for their potential to resonate as proxies, showing the consistency with which systemic oppression and social inequity shows up in records held by archives. These records echo Wallace's call "to utilize the past to inform and change the present through concrete action,"[36] and therefore allow for an easier entry into a CIL-focused instruction session.

The records we hold that document the University of Denver's relationship to Japanese internment are particularly relevant to this purpose. Though the University's track record during periods of racism and genocide in American history is poor overall, Colorado and the University's actions pertaining to Executive Order 9066, which confiscated the property of hundreds of thousands of Japanese and Japanese-American people from the U.S. West Coast and interned them in camps in the American West, at least attempted to mitigate harm to those affected by the Order. Governor Ralph Carr, in a decision unusual among Western governors, opposed internment of American citizens of Japanese descent and worked to find placements in Colorado universities for impacted college students.[37] As a result, Colorado colleges, including the University of Denver, took on a number of students who had been displaced. These students are documented in yearbooks, the student newspaper, and in a new acquisition, photographic scrapbooks and personal documents from an alum, Floyd Tanaka, who was interned in Manzanar and then served in the U.S. Army before attending the University of Denver.

We have included these records in two different Sociology courses to meet course outcomes. In an undergraduate course called "Deviance

---

36. Wallace, "Locating Agency," 186.

37. William Wei, *Asians in Colorado: A History of Persecution and Perseverance in the Centennial State* (Seattle, WA: University of Washington Press, 2016), 226.

and Society," we used a variety of records supporting outcomes, but focused on one particular article in the *Clarion* student newspaper with the headline "Japanese Student Says D.U. Is Tops, Nick is Interested in Politics."[38] The articles served as an example of the multiple ways the student attempted "stigma management," a strategy employed by members of social groups thought by the dominant culture to be "deviant" in some way. The student, Nick Iyoya, over the course of the 250-word article, mentions his Christian faith, his love of jazz and American authors, and the loyalty of both the Nisei (first-generation Americans of Japanese descent born in the U.S.) and his father (who was Issei, born in Japan), to the American government. These records connected directly to the readings that the class had already discussed about strategies used by communities facing social stigma, as did records documenting the University's responses to concerns about the safety of Middle Eastern students following the Iranian hostage crisis and the Iraqi invasion of Kuwait. The Sociology instructor also pointed out that records covering early LGBTQ student groups used anonymity to subvert social control, a topic covered earlier in the class. Records detailing the Latinx/Chicanx and Black student experience in the 1970s reflected racial solidarity, and sometimes rebellion, in the face of societal "othering." The 1970s student newspapers also included a number of articles that recorded feminist actions and student groups on campus, in particular related to the issues of sexual assault and rape culture, and an increasing desire among female students to raise the visibility of these issues. Following the Social Inequity instruction session, students incorporated some of the archival research into their projects; as well, the instructor has committed to working with us on future iterations of this course.

The second class to use the archival records covering the University of Denver student experience of Japanese internment was in the context of a multi-part "Sociological Imagination and Inquiry" qualitative research methods class, the same course mentioned in the "Silenced

---

38. Mary Ann Newman, "Japanese Student Says D.U. Is Tops, Nick is Interested in Politics," *Clarion* 46, no. 26 (April 24, 1942): 4.

Voices" section, but with a different instructor. In addition to the records documenting the experience of students displaced by internment, the class reviewed other materials related to World War II and its impact on the college campus—yearbooks, newspapers, photographs, and freshman orientation handbooks. Prior to the session, students read a brief history of this period of time on the University of Denver campus and, with the documents in front of them, were asked to respond to a series of prompts, paying specific attention to how inductive and deductive reasoning both play into the research process. The class discussed the following topics: the changing nature of gender roles for female students on campus; student groups (fraternities, sororities, social clubs); examples of racial inequality; and the impact of returning veterans on campus culture.

The "Seeking Grace: Black Alumnae at the University of Denver" project, which has an accompanying exhibition, is another example of how text-based interpretation through exhibits can highlight social inequity in the historical record. The project, which covers the history of early Black women graduates (1900-1945), served as the basis for two instruction sessions: an undergraduate first year seminar, "20th Century Race and Ethnicity," and a graduate course, "History of Higher Education." In both courses, the professors used the exhibition as a jumping-off point for in-class discussion, with prompts from text and images about the region, higher education, class, internal migration, and the impact of race and social class on Black women in Western colleges and universities. The students in the first year seminar were asked to focus more on the complexities of racial and ethnic categories in the U.S.; we discussed, for example, the concept of "hypodescent."[39] Colloquially known as the "one-drop rule," hypodescent is a form of racial categorization that defines anyone with a known Black ancestor as Black. The "Seeking Grace" project and exhibit provided a series of real-world examples that shed light on the evolving structure of racial

---

39. Christine B. Hickman, "The Devil and the One Drop Rule: Racial Categories, African Americans, and the U.S. Census," *Michigan Law Review* 95, no. 5 (1997): 1163.

categorization in documents like the census, according to changing
political and social times. We also considered how the shifting nature
of racial minoritization can, and should, complicate the "reading" of
photographic or other images of potentially non-White individuals,
and other ways researchers might locate evidence (for example, in addition to the census, Black newspapers) to properly contextualize these
kinds of sources. This discussion proved to be particularly rich, as the
exhibition incorporated yearbook images of forty-three of the early
Black graduates; some of the students remarked that they might not
have "read" some of the women included as Black. The "History of
Higher Education" course utilized the exhibit in different ways, as the
students were all graduate Higher Education majors, and were all planning to become university administrators or researchers. Very few of
these students had ever conducted archival research in the context of
their undergraduate or graduate studies. While they were interested in
the experiences of contemporary students of color, several commented
that they hadn't considered contextualizing or grounding their own
experiences in administration (Higher Education students are also often
employed as graduate assistants throughout the University, often working directly with undergraduate students) by trying to understand the
lived experiences of past students and alumnae. The curator also gave a
brief overview of the project's research design, as all Higher Education
masters students are required to take research methods coursework. The
class learned that, since the project's revival in 2017, the research work
has been directed by questions from the project's research assistants,
all of whom are members of the Sistah Network (a student group
focused on supporting Black women graduate students) with research
interests related to experiences of Black women at Predominantly White
Institutions.

Records that document the lives of those experiencing social inequity—especially when the subjects of the records were themselves
students—can provide researchers who are unfamiliar with critical
analysis with a bridge to this way of thinking about research. Undergraduate and graduate students across multiple disciplines can benefit

from applying this kind of critical lens to their work, especially when there is an added dimension of shared meaning, as in the records of fellow students. Faculty members whose students have worked with archival records have, in many cases, said that their classes experience a deep sense of engagement and wonder in this kind of research, and that they come away from the instruction sessions with greater confidence. In addition, we hope that the students begin to develop a sense of empathy and kinship with their predecessors, a personal connection not always present during the research process.

Conclusion

Information literacy cannot remain static in a world of constant change where new developments are found at the multidisciplinary intersections of theory and practice. CIL was a response, in part, to the 2000 ACRL Standards, as librarians sought to move instruction away from being prescriptive and towards providing a more flexible, responsive means of engaging students. CIL was informed by disciplines outside our profession that incorporated social justice, critical pedagogy, and critical theory as frameworks. The librarians and curators at the University of Denver have been inspired by the 2015 ACRL Information Literacy Framework for Higher Education as a way of discussing and implementing student-centered, collaborative, reflective instruction sessions for courses that have social justice goals. Nonetheless, the Framework has drawn criticism for a variety of reasons, among them for not more explicitly addressing social justice. By their very nature of being standards, the frames can be seen as reinforcing "hegemonic knowledge and an underlying political ideology consistent with neoliberalism."[40] Ian Beilin argues that, while

---

40. Andrew Battista, Dave Ellenwood, Lua Gregory, Shana Higgins, Jeff Lilburn, Yasmin Sokkar Harker, and Christopher Sweet, "Seeking Social Justice in the ACRL Framework," *Communications in Information Literacy* 9, no. 2 (2015): 120. Gregory and Higgins found that, by mapping the ALA Core Values of Librarianship (such as democracy, diversity, the public good, and social responsibility) to the ACRL Framework, social justice values can be aligned with the frames and instructional practices. Lua Gregory and Shana Higgins, "Reorienting an Information Literacy Program toward Social Justice: Mapping the Core Values of Librarianship to the ACRL Framework," *Communications in Information Literacy* 11, no. 1 (2017): 42-54. Although she

the Framework offers students the opportunity to learn to question the power structures that "shape information production and consumption, it nonetheless rests on a theoretical foundation at odds with that goal. [Beilin] urges librarians to embrace the Framework yet also resist it, in the tradition of critical librarians who have practiced resistance to the instrumentalization of the library for neoliberal ends."[41] Curators and librarians should continue to question and resist directives from professional associations that can be seen or interpreted as authoritative. In our opinion, the Framework is flexible enough for us to establish our instructional practices in the physical and digital archives, but, as we have mentioned throughout this chapter, such practices must respond and evolve, given new ideas and different contexts. We need to continue to critique our instructional work going forward, and to develop methods for assessing student success in ways that capture the transformative experience rather than evaluating our instructional programs through statistics alone.

In our physical and digital primary source instruction sessions, we seek to empower students to learn about and reflect upon the voices encountered or omitted in the archives and how these voices offer insights into race, gender, socioeconomic status, culture, identity, and more. Students working in the archives for the first time can be overwhelmed or fascinated by the experience of interacting with the past, and may not think to question the hegemonic powers that have built the buildings and the collections they house; some students have asserted that if these artifacts are preserved, they must represent truth. In order

---

acknowledges that the Framework does integrate social justice into some frames, and discusses its advantages and limits, Laura Saunders proposes a new frame, "Information Social Justice," that can serve as a model for those who wish for a more explicit social justice information literacy frame from which to work. Laura Saunders, "Connecting Information Literacy and Social Justice: Why and How," *Communications in Information Literacy* 11, no. 1 (2017): 55-75.

41. Ian Beilin, "Beyond the Threshold: Conformity, Resistance, and the ACRL Information Literacy Framework for Higher Education," *In the Library with the Lead Pipe* February 25, 2015. http://www.inthelibrarywiththeleadpipe.org/2015/beyond-the-threshold-conformity-resistance-and-the-aclr-information-literacy-framework-for-higher-education/.

to overcome such perceptions, to help students gain agency in order to interrogate primary sources with confidence, to address the gaps in the archives, and to develop strategies for giving voice and visibility to those who have been marginalized, we provide thematic social justice instructional frames that can make the archival experience transformative for students. By using our physical archives innovatively, addressing the gaps and employing social justice perspectives, we collaborate with faculty to immerse students in the physical and digital archives. As the University of Denver archives are rich in student records, instruction can successfully be tied to students' lived experiences, which engages them in the research process by connecting it to their own lived experiences. The University of Denver curators and librarians have long-term goals to diversify the archives by building relationships with underrepresented student, alumni, and community groups in order to find ways to bring their voices into the archives for future generations. Even as these goals are in process, we acknowledge that the archives are reflective of an institutional history fraught with practices that continue to reinforce hegemony—and that the examination of these issues, too, should be incorporated into our instructional exercises. We hope that our model will benefit other institutions lacking representational diversity in their archives by showing ways to creatively use existing collections.

Bibliography

Abrams, Jeanne. *Dr. Charles David Spivak: A Jewish Immigrant and the American Tuberculosis Movement.* Boulder, CO: University Press of Colorado, 2009.

American Jewish Historical Society. "Guide to the Jewish Consumptives' Relief Society (Denver, Colo.) Collection, undated, 1905-1955." Accessed November 20, 2018. http://digifindingaids.cjh.org/?pID=365605#a2.

Battista, Andrew, Dave Ellenwood, Lua Gregory, Shana Higgins, Jeff Lilburn, Yasmin Sokkar Harker, and Christopher Sweet. "Seeking Social Justice in the ACRL Framework." *Communications in Information Literacy* 9, no. 2 (2015): 111-25.

Beilin, Ian. "Beyond the Threshold: Conformity, Resistance, and the ACRL Information Literacy Framework for Higher Education." *In the Library with the Lead Pipe*, February 25, 2015. http://www.inthelibrarywiththeleadpipe.org/2015/beyond-the-threshold-conformity-resistance-and-the-aclr-information-literacy-framework-for-higher-education/.

Duff, Wendy M., Andrew Flinn, Karen Emily Suurtamm, and David A. Wallace. "Social Justice Impact of Archives: A Preliminary Investigation." *Archival Science* 13, no. 4 (2013): 317-48.

Dunbar, Anthony W. "Introducing Critical Race Theory to Archival Discourse: Getting the Conversation Started." *Archival Science* 6, no. 1 (2006): 109-29.

Elmborg, James. "Critical Information Literacy: Implications for Instructional Practice." *The Journal of Academic Librarianship* 32, no. 2 (2006): 192-99.

Elmborg, James. "Critical Information Literacy: Definitions and Challenges." In *Transforming Information Literacy Programs: Intersecting Frontiers of Self, Library Culture, and Campus Community*, edited by Carroll Wetzel Wilkinson and Courtney Bruch, 75-95. Chicago, IL: Association of College and Research Libraries, 2012.

Elmborg, James. "Foreword." In *Critical Library Pedagogy: Essays and Workbook Activities*, vol. 1, edited by Nicole Pagowsky and Kelly McElroy, vii-xiii. Chicago, IL: Association of College and Research Libraries, 2016.

Gregory, Lua and Shana Higgins. "Introduction." In *Information Literacy and Social Justice: Radical Professional Practice*, edited by Lua Gregory and Shana Higgins, 1-11. Sacramento, CA: Library Juice Press, 2013.

Gregory, Lua and Shana Higgins. "Reorienting an Information Literacy Program toward Social Justice: Mapping the Core Values of Librarianship to the ACRL Framework." *Communications in Information Literacy* 11, no. 1 (2017): 42-54.

Helstosky, Carol. "Moreland Report." University of Denver Libraries, 2018.

Hickman, Christine B. "The Devil and the One Drop Rule: Racial Categories, African Americans, and the U.S. Census." *Michigan Law Review* 95, no. 5 (1997): 1161-265.

Hooper, Lisa. "Breaking the Ontological Mold: Bringing Postmodernism and Critical Pedagogy into Archival Educational Programming." In *Critical Library Instruction: Theories and Methods*, edited by Maria T. Accardi, Emily Drabinski, and Alana Kumbier, 29-42. Duluth, MN: Library Juice Press, 2010.

Kelly, Megan. "The Past, Present, & Future of Sustainability in Higher Education Syllabus." University of Denver. Winter & Spring, 2018.

Newman, Mary Ann. "Japanese Student Says D.U. Is Tops, Nick is Interested in Politics." *Clarion* 46, no. 26 (April 24, 1942): 4.

Pagowsky, Nicole and Kelly McElroy. "Introduction." In *Critical Library Pedagogy: Essays and Workbook Activities*, vol. 1, edited by Nicole Pagowsky and Kelly McElroy, xvii-xxi. Chicago, IL: Association of College and Research Libraries, 2016.

Punzalan, Ricardo L. and Michelle Caswell. "Critical Directions for Archival Approaches to Social Justice." *Library Quarterly: Information, Community, Policy* 86, no. 4 (2016): 25-42.

Saunders, Laura. "Connecting Information Literacy and Social Justice: Why and How." *Communications in Information Literacy* 11, no. 1 (2017): 55-75.

Schwartz, Joan M. and Terry Cook. "Archives, Records, and Power: The Making of Modern Memory." *Archival Science* 2, no. 1 (2002): 1-19.

Shayne, Julie D., Denise Hattwig, Dave Ellenwood, and Taylor Hiner. "Creating Counter Archives: The University of Washington Bothell's Feminist Community Archive of Washington Project." *Feminist Teacher* 27, no. 1 (2016): 47-65.

Tewell, Eamon. "A Decade of Critical Information Literacy: A Review of the Literature." *Communications in Information Literacy* 9, no. 1 (2015): 24-43.

Tewell, Eamon C. "The Practice and Promise of Critical Information Literacy: Academic Librarians' Involvement in Critical Library Instruction." *College & Research Libraries* 79, no. 1 (2018): 10-34.

University of Denver. "History & Traditions." Accessed November 30, 2018. https://www.du.edu/about/history-traditions.

Wallace, David A. "Locating Agency: Interdisciplinary Perspectives on Professional Ethics and Archival Morality." *Journal of Information Ethics* 19, no. 1 (2010): 172-89.

Wei, William. *Asians in Colorado: A History of Persecution and Perseverance in the Centennial State.* Seattle, WA: University of Washington Press, 2016.

Williams, Patrick. "What Is Possible: Setting the Stage for Co-Exploration in Archives and Special Collections." In *Critical Library Pedagogy: Essays and Workbook Activities*, vol. 1, edited by Nicole Pagowsky and Kelly McElroy, 111-20. Chicago: Association of College and Research Libraries, 2016.

Zamir, Shamoon. "Native Agency and the Making of *The North American Indian*: Alexander B. Upshaw and Edward S. Curtis." *American Indian Quarterly* 31, no. 4 (2007): 613-53.

Chapter 11

WHITE FOLKS IN THE BLACK ARCHIVE: QUESTIONS OF POWER, ETHICS, AND RACE AROUND A DIGITAL EDITING PROJECT

Clayton McCarl

Introduction

This study considers the implications of pursuing a digital humanities project focused on archival materials that have been decontextualized in geographical, social, and racial terms. I first provide an overview of recent scholarship on the ethics of archival, editorial, and digital humanities work, as well as on the intersections of race with these fields of practice. I then describe the project in question and examine some of the specific challenges involved. Lastly, I reflect upon possible strategies for constructing an approach that accounts for, or at least acknowledges, our limitations as editors, as we try to understand and transmit archival material across social and cultural divides.

Context: Scholarship on Archival, Editorial, and Digital Humanities Ethics

Since the second half of the twentieth century, scholars in fields across the humanities and social sciences have studied the ways that dynamics of power play out in cultural production and in our interactions with each other. Marxist, feminist, post-colonial, and queer theory, as well as other critical tendencies, have informed vast amounts of scholarship questioning social and aesthetic norms, reshaping our understandings of literature and art, and dismantling long-standing structures of power within the intellectual sphere and beyond. Much of this work, explicitly or implicitly, weighs the ethical implications of how we as individuals perceive, construct, speak for, or silence others. Some scholarship on these topics has reflected more specifically on what it means for scholars to do so.

Research within library and information science intersects with the humanities and social sciences, but stands apart by taking information itself, and the tools and methods of its dissemination and curation, as foremost objects of study. In an age in which identities are contested and truth itself is negotiable, the implications of how we manage information are enormous. This is true, not just in terms of digital data, but also in terms of the archival material on which our understanding of the past is constructed.

Perhaps not surprisingly then, scholarship on the ethics of archives, archival processes, and archival research is plentiful.[1] In recent years, for example, Marek Tesar has considered "ethics and truth in archival research," Constantine Sandis has examined "cultural heritage ethics," and Richard J. Cox has proposed criteria for "rethinking archival ethics." Douglas Cox has studied the ethical and legal implications of the destruction of data, and Ronald Houston has argued for clearer "principal precepts" to assist archivists in their work and increase public respect for the profession.[2]

---

1. In literary and cultural studies, "the archive" was at the center of much critical work in the first two decades of this century, largely due to the theorizing of Michel Foucault. However, such scholarship has tended to address the archive more as a concept or metaphor than as a physical repository of tangible materials and the processes around their organization and curation. See, for instance, Antoinette M. Burton, *Dwelling in the Archive: Women Writing House, Home, and History in Late Colonial India* (New York: Oxford University Press, 2003); Roberto González Echevarría, *Myth and Archive: A Theory of Latin American Narrative* (Cambridge: Cambridge University Press, 2006); and Stephen Silverstein, *The Merchant of Havana: The Jew in the Cuban Abolitionist Archive* (Nashville: Vanderbilt University Press, [2016]).

2. Marek Tesar, "Ethics and Truth in Archival Research," *History of Education* 44, no. 1 (2015): 101-14, doi:10.1080/0046760X.2014.918185; Constantine Sandis, *Cultural Heritage Ethics: Between Theory and Practice* (Cambridge, England: Open Book Publishers,

In contrast, scholarship on ethical questions surrounding scholarly editing is relatively scant. Michelle R. Warren takes a broad look at the politics of textual scholarship in a chapter of the *Cambridge Companion to Textual Scholarship*, examining the "power dynamics" involved in editorial processes and their products. Recent articles have also considered the ethical implications or interpretive ramifications of particular editorial decisions or practices. For example, George Bornstein studies the criteria surrounding the inclusion or exclusion of antisemitic passages in different editions of W.E.B. Du Bois's *The Souls of Black Folk*. Jordan Alexander Stein examines the role that editing, among other practices, played in altering the sexual meaning of the work of Edward Taylor.[3]

Scholarship on ethics in digital humanities practice is even scarcer today. Four recent guides to the field—*Digital Humanities* by Anne Burdick, et al.; *Defining Digital Humanities: A Reader*, edited by Melissa Terras, et al.; *Digital Humanities Pedagogy: Practices, Principles and Politics*, edited by Brett Hirsch; and *Digital Humanities in Practice*, edited by Claire Warwick et al.—do not directly address such considerations.[4] Perhaps this is understandable since, to a large extent, scholars have been focused

2014); Richard J. Cox, "Rethinking Archival Ethics," *Journal of Information Ethics* 22, no. 2 (2013): 13-20; Richard J. Cox, "Teaching, Researching, and Preaching Archival Ethics: Or, How These New Views Came to Be," *Journal of Information Ethics* 19, no. 1 (2010): 20-32; Douglas Cox, "In the Trenches: Archival Ethics, Law and the Case of the Destroyed CIA Tapes," *Journal of Information Ethics* 22, no. 2 (2013): 90-101; Ronald D. Houston, "Archival Ethics and the Professionalization of Archival Enterprise," *Journal of Information Ethics* 22, no. 2 (2013): 46-60.

3. Michelle R. Warren, "The Politics of Textual Scholarship," in *Cambridge Companion to Textual Scholarship*, eds. Neil Fraistat and Julia Flanders (Cambridge: Cambridge University Press, 2013), 119-33; George Bornstein, "W. E. B. Du Bois and the Jews: Ethics, Editing, and *The Souls of Black Folk*," *Textual Cultures: Texts, Contexts, Interpretation* 1, no. 1 (2006): 64-74; and Jordan Alexander Stein, "How to Undo the History of Sexuality: Editing Edward Taylor's *Meditations*," *American Literature* 90, no. 4 (2018): 753-84.

4. Anne Burdick et al., *Digital Humanities* (Cambridge, MA: The MIT Press: 2012); Melissa Terras, Julianne Nyhan, and Edward Vanhoutte, eds., *Defining Digital Humanities: A Reader* (Farnham, England: Ashgate, 2013); Brett D. Hirsch, ed., *Digital Humanities Pedagogy: Practices, Principles and Politics* ([Cambridge, England]: Open Book Publishers, 2012); and Claire Warwick, Melissa Terras, and Julianne Nyhan, eds., *Digital Humanities in Practice* (London: Facet, 2012).

on defining this emerging field in terms of objectives, methodologies, and practical approaches.[5]

While often not directed primarily or explicitly at ethical consider-ations, recent scholarship does exist that reflects on the intersection of race and the digital humanities. Genevieve Carpio has looked at "digital ethnic studies," examining ways to utilize digital methods to engage students in the study of African American history. Miriam Posner and Marika Cifor have written about tensions involved in a student-led proj-ect to create a database about African American film. Tara McPherson and Amy E. Earhart have both considered ways that race must be part of conversations within the digital humanities.[6] Perhaps most notably, in the fall of 2018, the African American Digital Humanities Initia-tive at the University of Maryland held a three-day conference titled "Intentionally Digital, Intentionally Black," exploring ways that "digital studies and digital humanities-based research, teaching, and community projects can center African American history and culture."[7]

This article emerges in the context of these conversations about archival and editorial practice, digital humanities, race, and ethics. I consider here what it means to do a digital humanities project, based

---

5. Alexander Reid examines ethical questions surrounding digital humanities and graduate-level education in a chapter of *Debates in the Digital Humanities*, ed. Matthew K. Gold (Minneapolis: University of Minnesota Press, 2012), 350-67.

6. Tara McPherson, "Why Are the Digital Humanities So White? or Thinking the Histories of Race and Computation," in *Debates in the Digital Humanities*, ed. Matthew K. Gold (Minneapolis: University of Minnesota Press, 2012), 139-60; and Amy E. Ear-hart, "Can Information Be Unfettered? Race and the New Digital Humanities Canon," in *Debates in the Digital Humanities*, ed. Matthew K. Gold (Minneapolis: University of Minnesota Press, 2012), 309-18.

7. Genevieve Carpio, "Toward a Digital Ethnic Studies: Race, Technology, and the Classroom," *American Quarterly* 70, no. 3 (2018): 613-17, doi:10.1353/aq.2018.0042; Miriam Posner and Marika Cifor, "Generative Tensions: Building a Digital Project on Early African American Race Film," *American Quarterly* 70, no. 3 (2018): 709-14, doi:10.1353/aq.2018.0056; African American Digital Humanities Initiative, "African American History, Culture and Digital Humanities Conference: Call for Proposals," African American Digital Humanities Initiative, accessed December 18, 2018, https://aadhum.umd.edu/conference/cfp2018; and African American Digital Humanities Initiative, "African American History, Culture and Digital Humanities Conference: Conference Agenda," African American Digital Humanities Initiative, accessed December 18, 2018, https://www.conftool.pro/aadhum2018/sessions.php.

on archival materials and processes of textual editing, when the objects in question exist on the other side of racial, cultural, and social barriers. While in some ways it may be unproductive to racialize scholarly work or emphasize otherness, our academic labors take place in specific social and historical contexts in which dynamics of race and power are present, regardless of whether we acknowledge them. This study offers little in the way of answers, focusing instead on formulating questions, or types of questions, that might be considered when undertaking a project of the sort I describe.

The Project and Its Context

Editing the Eartha M.M. White Collection is an ongoing experiment in collaborative digital editing at the University of North Florida (UNF) in Jacksonville.[8] The project engages members of the campus community in the transcription and TEI-XML encoding of selected materials from the letters and personal papers of local leader, philanthropist, and humanitarian Eartha M.M. White (1876-1974).[9] The project began in 2016 in the context of a summer-semester digital editing course that I taught in partnership with Dr. Aisha Johnson-Jones, at that time head of Special Collections and Archives. Since Johnson-Jones's departure from UNF in early 2017, I have continued the project through occasional workshops, collaborating with a rotating group of student, faculty, and staff volunteers and, in the spring of 2018, a student intern.[10]

Obtained in 1975, the Eartha M.M. White Collection comprised the foundational acquisition of UNF's Special Collections and Archives,

8. Clayton McCarl, ed., *An Interactive Edition of Selected Materials from the Eartha M.M. White Collection*, UNF Digital Humanities Institute, accessed December 18, 2018, https://unfdhi.org/ewproject.

9. TEI-XML is the standard for text markup developed and maintained by the Text Encoding Initiative (TEI) Consortium, and implemented in Extensible Markup Language (known as XML).

10. These phases of the project are described in Clayton McCarl, "Editing the Eartha M.M. White Collection: An Experiment in Engaging Students in Archival Research and Editorial Practice," *Journal of Academic Librarianship* 44, no. 4 (2018). My student intern in the spring of 2018 was UNF History major Susan Williams.

located in the Thomas G. Carpenter Library. To this day, the White Collection continues to be one of UNF's most prized holdings. It is an essential resource for understanding the life and work of White, as well as the African American history of Jacksonville more broadly. As a consequence, it possesses value as a tool to help us reconstruct a past that has been largely erased, and to grapple with matters related to race and inequality in Jacksonville today.[11]

Fundamental contradictions exist, however, surrounding the White Collection's presence at UNF. The University articulates a formal commitment to diversity and inclusion, and maintains a university-level commission dedicated to these topics.[12] Arguably an appropriate goal in any setting, this may be particularly so in Jacksonville, a city with a sizeable African American community (30.1%), a growing Hispanic population (9.7%), and smaller groups of people from around the

---

11. For general information on the White Collection, including year of acquisition, see UNF Thomas G. Carpenter Library, "Eartha M. M. White Collection," UNF, accessed December 18, 2018, https://www.unf.edu/library/specialcollections/manuscripts/eartha-white/Eartha_White.aspx; and Eileen D. Brady, "The Eartha M. M. White Collection at the Thomas G. Carpenter Library, University of North Florida," *Florida Libraries* 38, no. 2 (1995): 28-33. An online exhibit is found on the Library's website: "Eartha M. M. White Collection," UNF, accessed December 18, 2018, https://www.unf.edu/library/specialcollections/manuscripts/collections/Eartha_M__M__White.aspx (a different page, with the same name, from that cited above). Additional items from the White Collection are available on the UNF Digital Commons; see UNF Thomas G. Carpenter Library, "Eartha M. M. White Collection," UNF Digital Commons, accessed December 18, 2018, https://digitalcommons.unf.edu/eartha_white (again, a different page, with the same name, from those cited above). As part of the web materials related to the White Collection, Thomas G. Carpenter Library provides both a general bibliography for White and a listing of holdings in Special Collections related Jacksonville's African American history. See UNF Thomas G. Carpenter Library, "Eartha M. M. White Collection Bibliography," UNF, accessed December 18, 2018, https://www.unf.edu/library/specialcollections/manuscripts/eartha-white/Eartha_White_Bibligraphy.aspx; and UNF Thomas G. Carpenter Library, "Resources in Special Collections: African American Life in Jacksonville, Florida," UNF, accessed December 18, 2018, https://www.unf.edu/library/specialcollections/Resources_-_African_American_Life.aspx.

12. See UNF, "Commission on Diversity and Inclusion (CODI)," UNF, accessed April 9, 2019, https://www.unf.edu/diversity; and UNF Commission on Diversity and Inclusion, "UNF Statement of Unity," UNF, accessed April 9, 2019, http://www.unf.edu/committee/diversity/statement_of_unity.aspx.

world, a fact due in part to the city's history as a primary location for refugee resettlement in Florida.[13]

Despite the University's commitment to diversity, the African American population of Jacksonville is noticeably underrepresented on campus. In the fall of 2018, UNF had 1,618 students identified as "Black or African American," out of a total of 17,002 (9.5%).[14] In spite of the institution's efforts to diversify its employees, the percentages of African American professors and staff members are also disproportionately low. In the fall of 2017, UNF had nineteen tenured or tenure-track faculty members and thirteen others in non-tenure-track positions identified in the demographic data as "Black," out of 600 faculty members overall (5.3%). For the same semester, UNF had 257 staff members identified as "Black" in the system, out of a total of 1,816 (14.2%).[15]

The campus itself presents a sharp contrast to the world evoked by the materials in the White Collection. The University's grounds include the Sawmill Slough Preserve, a wetland habitat conservation area, and are bordered by new shopping malls and residential development. The closest of the city's historic African American neighborhoods is approximately fourteen miles away, which is usually about a twenty-minute drive. Intersected decades ago by the construction of interstate highways I-95 and I-10, and decimated over time by economic and

---

13. This is 2017 data provided by the City of Jacksonville, which cites as its source "U.S. Census Bureau, 2017 American Community Survey." See City of Jacksonville Office of Economic Development, "Demographics," City of Jacksonville, accessed April 9, 2019, http://www.coj.net/departments/office-of-economic-development/about-jacksonville/demographics.

14. See UNF Office of Institutional Research, "Fall 2018 Student Data," UNF, accessed April 9, 2019, https://www.unf.edu/ir/student-data/Fall_2018.aspx.

15. See UNF Commission on Diversity and Inclusion, "Diverse Faculty Recruitment," UNF, accessed April 9, 2019, http://www.unf.edu/committee/diversity/diverse-faculty-recruitment.aspx; UNF Office of Institutional Research, "Headcounts by Rank, Tenure Status, and Ethnicity Fall 2013 to Fall 2017," UNF, accessed April 9, 2019, https://www.unf.edu/ir/inst-research/Faculty-Ethnicity.aspx; and UNF Office of Institutional Research, "Fall Staff Headcounts by Ethnicity Fall 2013 to Fall 2017," UNF, accessed April 9, 2019, https://www.unf.edu/ir/inst-research/Staff-Ethnicity.aspx. These numbers do not include those identified as belonging to "[t]wo or more races."

social forces, the central parts of Jacksonville referenced in the White Collection are largely unknown to most students at UNF. The majority of faculty and staff members are probably most familiar with those areas through the urban renewal and gentrification that is today subsuming many traditionally African American neighborhoods.

To a large extent, the African American history of Jacksonville has been overlooked or neglected, despite the city being home at one time to James Weldon Johnson, Zora Neale Hurston, and A. Philip Randolph, among other major figures. Peter Dunbaugh Smith begins his 2015 study of Jacksonville's late nineteenth- and early twentieth-century jazz and blues communities with the observation by historian Russ Rymer that the city's history "stays invisible because the prominence resides almost exclusively on the black side of town."[16] Only recently have coordinated efforts been made to recover that past, both through the work of scholars like Smith, and through projects like Jacksonville's African American History Trail, undertaken as part of the larger Florida's African American History Trail.[17]

As an institution of higher learning, UNF is surely an appropriate place for these documents to reside. The Thomas G. Carpenter Library has, since the 1970s, provided access to the researchers who have written most of the biographical scholarship through which White is known

---

16. Peter Dunbaugh Smith, *A Cultural History of the First Jazz and Blues Communities in Jacksonville, Florida, 1896-1916: A Contribution of African Americans to American Theatre* (Lewiston, NY: The Edwin Mellen Press, 2015), 1. Smith's citation is to Russ Rymer, *American Beach: A Saga of Race, Wealth, and Memory* (New York: Harper Collins, 1998), 114.

17. Another recent work on Jacksonville's African American history is Robert Cassanello, *To Render Invisible: Jim Crow and Public Life in New South Jacksonville* (Gainesville: University Press of Florida, 2013). See also Mary F.M. Jameson, *Remembering Neighborhoods of Jacksonville, Florida: Oakland, Campbell's Addition, East Jacksonville, Fairfield: The African-American Influence* (St. Louis: Mira Digital Publishing, 2010). For the Heritage Trail, see "African-American Heritage Trail, Jacksonville Historic People and Places," accessed April 9, 2019, http://www.jaxheritagetrail.com; and City of Jacksonville, "Jacksonville's Legacy, African-American Heritage Trail, Jacksonville Historic People and Places, First Edition," City of Jacksonville, September 2013, accessed April 9, 2019, http://www.coj.net/welcome/docs/cvb13-008848-1-afriamericanherittrail(m) lorez.aspx.

today.[18] Perhaps symbolically, though, UNF holds only one-half of White's papers, with the remainder in the possession of the Clara White Mission—which White founded in 1904—precisely in the part of town where White lived and worked.[19]

Problems

Questions of power, ethics, and race can perhaps arise at any of the phases of a project like *Editing the Eartha M.M. White Collection*. For purposes of this discussion, I will consider those stages to include the selection, representation, and interpretation of the materials, as well as the publication and curation of the resulting digital edition.[20] Because this project is still in an experimental phase, I will focus mainly on the earliest stages in this model.

One of the first steps is the selection of the items to be included. Since the project began as a small-scale experiment, I never envisioned editing the entire White Collection.[21] Rather, to date, two primary factors

18. See Daniel L. Schafer, "Eartha M.M. White: The Early Years of a Jacksonville Humanitarian," unpublished paper presented at UNF, 1976; and "Eartha Mary Magdalene White," in *Notable American Women: The Modern Period: A Biographical Dictionary*, edited by Barbara Sicherman and Carol Hurd Green (Cambridge, MA: Belknap Press, 1980), 726-28; Carmen Godwin, "'To Serve God and Humanity': Jacksonville's Eartha Mary Magdalene White (1876-1974)" (master's thesis, University of Florida, 2001). Tim Gilmore, *In Search of Eartha White, Storehouse for the People* ([Jacksonville, FL]: [CreateSpace Independent Publishing], 2014) is a reflection on the author's research into White's life and work. See also the biographical sketch provided by the UNF Thomas G. Carpenter Library: "Eartha M. M. White: Biographical Highlights," UNF, accessed December 18, 2018, https://www.unf.edu/library/specialcollections/manuscripts/eartha-white/Eartha_White_Biography.aspx. One item that predates the arrival of the White Collection at UNF is Leedell W. Neyland's, "Eartha M. White: Jacksonville's 'Angel of Mercy'" in *Twelve Black Floridians* (Tallahassee, FL: Florida Agricultural and Mechanical University Foundation, 1970), 33-41, http://purl.fcla.edu/fcla/dl/AM00000064.pdf.

19. The Clara White Mission is located at 613 West Ashley Street. Ashley Street was the "central thoroughfare" of LaVilla, a predominantly African-American city founded in 1866 and incorporated into Jacksonville in 1887. Ashley Street was "the first street in any of Jacksonville's African-American neighborhoods to be paved." See Smith, A Cultural History, 21-22.

20. Such a model is not intended to be exhaustive, or even necessarily accurate in conceptual terms, but rather merely a way to structure the reflections that follow.

21. Whether we could even do so if we desired is not certain. Approval by the Thomas G. Carpenter Library, and likely other administrative entities, would be required.

have driven the selection of items. During the 2016 summer-session editing course, participants chose their own materials. Under the guidance of Johnson-Jones, they viewed the finding aid and container list, and requested documents that provoked their curiosity. After reviewing the documents in the Special Collections Reading Room, both during class sessions and through individual consultations, they ordered reproductions of the items they desired to edit.[22] For the subsequent workshops, I took a different approach, selecting (or having my student intern select) the materials and requesting the reproductions in advance. This was primarily due to time limitations, and our choices of documents were driven by practical considerations. We needed items that were short enough for participants to edit in the time allotted and that also presented self-contained, closed pieces of discourse (as opposed to, for instance, distributing fragments of some larger work among various participants).

While both of these approaches to identifying materials functioned well for the purposes of the respective experiments, they were inadequate in terms of overall project design. If our work continues in this fashion, the end product promises to be an eclectic and potentially incoherent selection of items that either respond to the interests of individual researchers or conform to a certain standard in terms of length, irrespective of content. Obvious questions arise about what has been left out and whether such a largely random selection of materials presents a false impression of the physical archive it represents.

Do questions of race and power apply here? Perhaps so, if indeed the documents that interest us today, or that are short enough to meet our criteria, present a limited or distorted view of White's life and work in some way. These are, after all, the papers of an actual person. Do we commit an injustice by presenting her textual existence in such an undeliberate, potentially incomplete fashion? To what extent have we edited items that, from the perspective of White, might actually have been relatively insignificant? For example, do these papers contain administrative records that she may not have viewed as having lasting value?

22. See McCarl, "Editing the Eartha M.M. White Collection," 528.

By focusing on these or other types of material, do we overlook other categories of documents she might have deemed more representative or worthy of preservation and dissemination?

Perhaps we are under no obligation to imagine White's possible wishes. Even if we are absolved of such responsibility, we should nonetheless consider how our selection of documents reflects upon, or distorts, Jacksonville's African American past. Are we presenting a vision of that history that is driven by, or that plays into, stereotypes about the city's African American communities today?

For instance, some of the items that have most interested us are the many "letters of appeal" contained in the White Collection. These are generally short communications, often written by individuals with presumably little education, calling on White for help in solving economic, familial, and legal problems. These materials have appealed to us for the humanity they represent and the window they offer into everyday life. They also illustrate White's standing in her community as a respected and charitable leader. At the same time, foregrounding these documents could present an unbalanced view of African American life in Jacksonville during White's day, highlighting the circumstances of some of the most needy and vulnerable.

As scholarship makes clear, Jacksonville's African American neighborhoods around the turn of the twentieth century were vibrant communities in cultural and economic terms.[23] By showcasing these documents that are focused on hardship, we potentially reinforce negative ideas about poverty and lack of educational achievement in inner-city neighborhoods today. As scholars removed from those areas of the city, we may not be troubled by such a limited or potentially misleading view. Surely a goal of our project, however, must be to break down stereotypes, not reinforce them.

If we were to design a more deliberate approach to the selection of materials, what would it look like? We could, of course, attempt to edit

---

23. Herman "Skip" Mason, Jr., *African-American Life in Jacksonville* (Dover, NH: Arcadia Publishing, 1997) gathers numerous images of African American life in Jacksonville in the late nineteenth and early twentieth centuries.

the entire archive, or to handle a sampling of items representing all the different types of documents. In the case of the White Collection, however, we would still face two difficulties. First, as UNF possesses only half of White's papers, the Collection itself is incomplete. Second, even if we had access to the other half, we do not know whether White considered the papers in their totality to in some way represent her life. What, in other words, would be missing?

Likewise, we can encounter problems in deciding how to represent these materials. How do we handle, for instance, misspellings or non-standard aspects of speech in the aforementioned letters of appeal? What do we assert when we reproduce language as is, or alternatively, what are the assumptions present in any regularization that we might implement? In either case, what does it mean to annotate or not to annotate such features? Is presenting both original and standardized readings together an adequate solution, or does such side-by-side juxtapositions only emphasize the distance we find between the original writings and the norm as we perceive it?

We face problems as well in interpreting these documents. If we propose to annotate salient features of a historical nature, for instance, on what do we base our judgments about what is significant? Does every named entity—whether person, organization, building, or otherwise—merit explanation? If not, how do we decide what gets annotated and what does not? We could address just those named entities that have direct relevance to the African American history of Jacksonville. Would such a criterion make sense, however, and even if it did, how would we make such judgments without relying on assumptions that could well be erroneous?

We could run into similar problems if we attempted to map the documents in the archive. Should every place name mentioned in any document be mapped? Perhaps handling only place names within Jacksonville would be a reasonable approach. What does it mean to do this, however? Are we correlating references within the archive to current locations in the city, or are we attempting to reconstruct the geography of the city during the time in question? Perhaps we could connect the documents to historical maps of the city, possibly in some way layering those over the current urban geography.[24] In either case, we must deal with the legacy of segregation in Jacksonville, and must make determinations about how race plays out in the physical space of the city. In a historical sense, this can perhaps be done somewhat objectively, but to make assertions about race and urban space today could be highly problematic.

An attempt at mapping might also raise questions about objectives. In correlating the archival materials to locations on maps of the physical realities of Jacksonville, what exactly would we be trying to achieve? The urban landscape of the city in which White lived and worked can perhaps to some degree be reconstructed in spatial terms. Does this, however, provide a sort of illusion, or allow space to stand in as a proxy for lived experience? No map can show what a place was, how life was lived and experienced there, or the social networks and interactions that made it a place to those who inhabited that space, at that time.

The manner in which we publish our project also may have implications for how we understand and assert relationships of power. What would it mean to publish the edition online under the auspices of UNF, whether through the Thomas G. Carpenter Library or the UNF Digital Humanities Institute? UNF owns the documents, so why should the institution not "own" our edition?

Perhaps there is no controversy here, but for UNF to be the sole stakeholder in the publication of the edition might be a missed opportunity. The fact that the physical materials must "belong" to someone is understandable—they must be curated and preserved. In a sense, however, these documents belong to no one, or to all of Jacksonville, and, in particular, its African American population. Shouldn't our project attempt in some way to "re-patriate" the data, or return ownership in some meaningful way, to those communities?

---

24. In the case of Jacksonville, we also must address the fact that the city was largely destroyed by fire in 1901 and that, in geographical terms, there is a clear before and after surrounding that date.

A similar set of questions pertains to the curation of the data in the future. If the files comprising our edition were to become part of the institutional repository, alongside the source material itself, that might help guarantee their longevity. However, what would it mean for the library itself to assume ownership of the data, or ongoing responsibility for the results of the project? If we conceive of our work as merely the transcription and editing of the documents, then perhaps no reason exists to not reincorporate these materials into the archive itself, or position them alongside it. However, as this study suggests, the outcome of our work is something more, resulting from processes of selection, representation, and interpretation. Our edited materials are not neutral, in other words, and cannot reside innocently next to the sources themselves.

Do all of these questions have implications for how we understand the dynamics of race and power in our project? In some cases, perhaps not. One basic, if tentative, conclusion presents itself, however: when conducting a project of this sort, we may be faced with the problem of not knowing the limits of our own knowledge or perception. We may not know what our assumptions and biases may be, and we may not know how to go about identifying them.

Possible Strategies

How might we account for the potential problems imagined in this paper? First, we might at least be careful not to project onto the past any assumptions or attitudes we may have that are based on the present. To do so would require an honest reckoning with the role that race plays in Jacksonville today. Finding ways to make the *Editing the Eartha M.M. White Collection* project part of larger discussions around issues of race in Jacksonville would help us to better understand such dynamics.

Second, we might minimize some of the issues proposed here by involving Jacksonville's African American communities in the project. This could perhaps be done by conducting our editing workshops not only on campus, but also at schools, libraries, and community centers across the city. Likewise, we might pursue possibilities to partner with community organizations, the local historically black institution Edward Waters College, or the city itself, in the creation and publication of the project. Such an approach might allow us to turn our limitations into strengths. By acknowledging our restricted ability to see how race may play out in the project, we can seize an opportunity to envision the project as a community-based digital endeavor.

Such a process might, of course, best begin on the campus itself, by seeking out ways to increase participation in the project by African-American students, faculty, and staff at UNF. We might reach out, for instance, to students in the African-American/African Diaspora Studies minor and to extracurricular groups including the Black Student Union. Likewise, we should investigate ways to potentially partner with the African-American Faculty and Staff Association.[25] This outreach, however, must be done in a manner that involves these constituencies as true partners in shaping the objectives and design of the project, avoiding the tokenism that at times surrounds the recruitment of minorities to participate in university committees.

Lastly, we must be explicit in the introduction to our digital edition about the limitations we have faced. Even if we cannot fully see or understand how issues of race and inequality might play out in the preparation of our project, an honest reckoning with such an inability is surely a positive step. Indeed, the process of formulating this language could be an important part of how our project creates value—both for participants and for the community. The development of such a text might, therefore, best be done in collaboration with the groups of students, faculty, staff, and community members and organizations discussed above.

Conclusion

To some extent, the reflections in this article may amount to the overthinking of questions that have obvious answers. While this may be,

---

25. Such a possibility first suggested itself in the spring of 2016, when I was preparing for our summer editing experiment. A member of the University Police Department saw me with a stack of posters promoting the course and remarked, "Eartha White—she was my godmother."

these are questions that we do not always ask when undertaking scholarly projects. Often as researchers we exist outside the world of the materials we study in temporal, cultural, and social terms. In this chapter, I propose that we may be best advised, in such situations, to consider the biases we bring to our work, or the ways that the products of our efforts may come to enshrine the limits of our understanding.

In the context of a project like *Editing the Eartha M.M. White Collection*, stark contrasts present themselves between the world of the documents and the environment in which they reside today. Likewise, notable differences exist, in terms of privilege and social power, between most of us who have worked on the project and the people whose writings we transmit. As a U.S. city—particularly one in the South with a history of racial division like that of Jacksonville—such dynamics cannot be considered without taking race into account. It is, furthermore, not a project that deals with a remote, obsolete past, but rather one that connects directly to controversies around structural inequalities in the city of Jacksonville today.

As scholars, we do not often have ethical guidelines to follow, beyond those dealing with academic integrity and appropriate stewardship of resources, as well as the basic societal rules of how we treat students, colleagues, and the other people with whom we work on a day-to-day basis. When faced with projects in which we intentionally or otherwise position ourselves as the mediators, across time or cultural lines, of realities that are not our own, we would benefit from paradigms to follow, or sets of questions we can ask ourselves. Such frameworks might allow us to function more effectively as scholars, and might improve the quality of the work we can produce. They might also help us to better understand the larger roles that our efforts can potentially play in raising awareness, supporting communities, and encouraging change.

Bibliography

African American Digital Humanities Initiative. "African American History, Culture and Digital Humanities Conference: Call for Proposals." African American Digital Humanities Initiative. Accessed December 18, 2018. https://aadhum.umd.edu/conference/cfp2018.

African American Digital Humanities Initiative. "African American History, Culture and Digital Humanities Conference: Conference Agenda." African American Digital Humanities Initiative. Accessed December 18, 2018. https://www.conftool.pro/aadhum2018/sessions.php.

"African-American Heritage Trail, Jacksonville Historic People and Places." Accessed April 4, 2019. http://www.jaxheritagetrail.com.

Bornstein, George. "W. E. B. Du Bois and the Jews: Ethics, Editing, and The Souls of Black Folk." *Textual Cultures: Texts, Contexts, Interpretation* 1, no. 1 (2006): 64-74.

Brady, Eileen D. "The Eartha M. M. White Collection at the Thomas G. Carpenter Library, University of North Florida." *Florida Libraries* 38, no. 2 (1995): 28-33.

Burdick, Anne, Johanna Drucker, Peter Lunenfeld, Todd Presner, and Jeffrey Schnapp. *Digital Humanities.* Cambridge, MA: The MIT Press, 2012.

Burton, Antoinette M. *Dwelling in the Archive: Women Writing House, Home, and History in Late Colonial India.* New York: Oxford University Press, 2003.

Carpio, Genevieve. "Toward a Digital Ethnic Studies: Race, Technology, and the Classroom." *American Quarterly* 70, no. 3 (2018): 613-17. doi:10.1353/aq.2018.0042.

Cassanello, Robert. *To Render Invisible: Jim Crow and Public Life in New South Jacksonville.* Gainesville: University Press of Florida, 2013.

City of Jacksonville. "Jacksonville's Legacy, African-American Heritage Trail, Jacksonville Historic People and Places, First Edition." City of Jacksonville. September 2013. Accessed April 9, 2019. http://www.coj.net/welcome/docs/cvb13-008848-1-afriamericanherittrail(m)lorez.aspx.

City of Jacksonville Office of Economic Development. "Demographics." City of Jacksonville. Accessed April 9, 2019. http://www.coj.net/departments/office-of-economic-development/about-jacksonville/demographics.

Cox, Douglas. "In the Trenches: Archival Ethics, Law and the Case of the Destroyed CIA Tapes." *Journal of Information Ethics* 22, no. 2 (2013): 90-101.

Cox, Richard J. "Rethinking Archival Ethics." *Journal of Information Ethics* 22, no. 2 (2013): 13-20.

Cox, Richard J. "Teaching, Researching, and Preaching Archival Ethics: Or, How These New Views Came to Be." *Journal of Information Ethics* 19, no. 1 (2010): 20-32.

Earhart, Amy E. "Can Information Be Unfettered? Race and the New Digital Humanities Canon." In *Debates in the Digital Humanities,* edited by Matthew K. Gold, 309-18. Minneapolis: University of Minnesota Press, 2012.

Gilmore, Tim. *In Search of Eartha White, Storehouse for the People* [Jacksonville, FL]: [CreateSpace Independent Publishing], 2014.

Godwin, Carmen. "'To Serve God and Humanity': Jacksonville's Eartha Mary Magdalene White (1876-1974)." Master's thesis, University of Florida. 2001.

González Echevarría, Roberto. *Myth and Archive: A Theory of Latin American Narrative.* Cambridge: Cambridge University Press, 2006.

Hirsch, Brett D., editor. *Digital Humanities Pedagogy: Practices, Principles and Politics.* [Cambridge, England]: Open Book Publishers, 2012.

Houston, Ronald D. "Archival Ethics and the Professionalization of Archival Enterprise." *Journal of Information Ethics* 22, no. 2 (2013): 46-60.

Jameson, Mary F.M. *Remembering Neighborhoods of Jacksonville, Florida: Oakland, Campbell's Addition, East Jacksonville, Fairfield: The African-American Influence.* St. Louis: Mira Digital Publishing, 2010.

Mason, Jr., Herman "Skip." *African-American Life in Jacksonville.* Dover, NH: Arcadia Publishing, 1997.

McCarl, Clayton. "Editing the Eartha M.M. White Collection: An Experiment in Engaging Students in Archival Research and Editorial Practice." *The Journal of Academic Librarianship* 44, no. 4 (2018): 527-37.

McCarl, Clayton, ed. *An Interactive Edition of Selected Materials from the Eartha M.M. White Collection.* UNF Digital Humanities Institute. Accessed December 18, 2018. https://unfdhi.org/ewproject.

McPherson, Tara. "Why Are the Digital Humanities So White? or Thinking the Histories of Race and Computation." In *Debates in the Digital Humanities,* edited by Matthew K. Gold, 139-60. Minneapolis: University of Minnesota Press, 2012.

Neyland, Leedell W. "Eartha M. White: Jacksonville's 'Angel of Mercy.'" In *Twelve Black Floridians,* 33-41. Tallahassee, Florida: Florida Agricultural and Mechanical University Foundation, 1970. Accessed December 18, 2018. http://purl.fcla.edu/fcla/dl/AM00000064.pdf.

Posner, Miriam, and Marika Cifor. "Generative Tensions: Building a Digital Project on Early African American Race Film." *American Quarterly* 70, no. 3 (2018): 709-14. doi:10.1353/aq.2018.0056.

Reid, Alexander. "Graduate Education and the Ethics of the Digital Humanities." In *Debates in the Digital Humanities,* edited by Matthew K. Gold, 350-67. Minneapolis: University of Minnesota Press, 2012.

Rymer, Russ. *American Beach: A Saga of Race, Wealth, and Memory.* New York: Harper Collins, 1998.

Sandis, Constantine. *Cultural Heritage Ethics: Between Theory and Practice.* Cambridge, England: Open Book Publishers, 2014.

Schafer, Daniel L. "Eartha M.M. White: The Early Years of a Jacksonville Humanitarian." Unpublished paper presented at UNF, 1976.

Schafer, Daniel L. "Eartha Mary Magdalene White." In *Notable American Women: The Modern Period: A Biographical Dictionary,* edited by Barbara Sicherman and Carol Hurd Green, 726-28. Cambridge, MA: Belknap Press, 1980.

Silverstein, Stephen. *The Merchant of Havana: The Jew in the Cuban Abolitionist Archive.* Nashville: Vanderbilt University Press, [2016].

Smith, Peter Dunbaugh. *A Cultural History of the First Jazz and Blues Communities in Jacksonville, Florida, 1896-1916: A Contribution of African Americans to American Theatre.* Lewiston, NY: The Edwin Mellen Press, 2015.

Stein, Jordan Alexander. "How to Undo the History of Sexuality: Editing Edward Taylor's Meditations." *American Literature* 90, no. 4 (2018): 753-84.

Terras, Melissa, Julianne Nyhan, and Edward Vanhoutte, editors. *Defining Digital Humanities: A Reader.* Farnham, England: Ashgate, 2013.

Tesar, Marek. "Ethics and Truth in Archival Research." *History of Education* 44, no. 1 (2015): 101-14. doi:10.1080/0046760X.2014.918185.

University of North Florida. "Commission on Diversity and Inclusion (CODI)." UNF. Accessed April 9, 2019. https://www.unf.edu/diversity.

University of North Florida Commission on Diversity and Inclusion. "Diverse Faculty Recruitment." UNF. Accessed April 9, 2019. http://www.unf.edu/committee/diversity/diverse-faculty-recruitment.aspx.

University of North Florida Commission on Diversity and Inclusion."UNF Statement of Unity." UNF. Accessed April 9, 2019. http://www.unf.edu/committee/diversity/statement_of_unity.aspx.

University of North Florida Office of Institutional Research. "Fall 2018 Student Data." UNF. Accessed April 9, 2019. https://www.unf.edu/ir/student-data/Fall_2018.aspx.

University of North Florida Office of Institutional Research. "Fall Staff Headcounts by Ethnicity Fall 2013 to Fall 2017." UNF. Accessed April 9, 2019. https://www.unf.edu/ir/inst-research/Staff-Ethnicity.aspx.

University of North Florida Office of Institutional Research. "Headcounts by Rank, Tenure Status, and Ethnicity Fall 2013 to Fall 2017." UNF. Accessed April 9, 2019. https://www.unf.edu/ir/inst-research/Faculty-Ethnicity.aspx.

University of North Florida, Thomas G. Carpenter Library. "Eartha M. M. White: Biographical Highlights." UNF. Accessed December

18, 2018. https://www.unf.edu/library/specialcollections/manuscripts/eartha-white/Eartha_White_Biography.aspx.

University of North Florida, Thomas G. Carpenter Library. "Eartha M. M. White Collection." UNF. Accessed December 18, 2018. https://www.unf.edu/library/specialcollections/manuscripts/eartha-white/Eartha_White.aspx.

University of North Florida, Thomas G. Carpenter Library. "Eartha M. M. White Collection." UNF. Accessed December 18, 2018. https://www.unf.edu/library/specialcollections/manuscripts/collections/Eartha_M__M__White.aspx.

University of North Florida, Thomas G. Carpenter Library. "Eartha M. M. White Collection." UNF Digital Commons. Accessed December 18, 2018. https://digitalcommons.unf.edu/eartha_white.

University of North Florida, Thomas G. Carpenter Library. "Eartha M. M. White Collection Bibliography." UNF. Accessed December 18, 2018. https://www.unf.edu/library/specialcollections/manuscripts/eartha-white/Eartha_White_Bibligraphy.aspx.

University of North Florida, Thomas G. Carpenter Library. "Resources in Special Collections: African American Life in Jacksonville, Florida." UNF. Accessed December 18, 2018. https://www.unf.edu/library/specialcollections/Resources_-_African_American_Life.aspx.

Warren, Michelle R. "The Politics of Textual Scholarship." In *Cambridge Companion to Textual Scholarship*, edited by Neil Fraistat and Julia Flanders, 119-33. Cambridge: Cambridge University Press, 2013.

Warwick, Claire, Melissa Terras, and Julianne Nyhan, editors. *Digital Humanities in Practice*. London: Facet, 2012.

Chapter 12

BREAKING BARRIERS THROUGH DECOLONIAL COMMUNITY-BASED ARCHIVAL PRACTICE

Krista McCracken and Skylee-Storm Hogan

Introduction

Decolonization means being accountable to Indigenous peoples and is directly connected to Indigenous sovereignty and Indigenous concepts of knowledge; it offers a way out of colonization and moves beyond existing structures of colonialism.[1] Decolonization within Canadian archives involves the acceptance of Indigenous worldviews and the inclusion of Indigenous voices in the development and implementation of archival best practices. It also involves transforming archival standards to incorporate diverse perspectives. This transformation should include new metadata practices that allow for Indigenous worldviews, and the use of participatory archival practices that facilitate Indigenous knowledge contributions to archival descriptions. Likewise, a nuanced understanding of the long-term implications of Canada's Truth and Reconciliation Commission's (TRC) Calls to Action is imperative for the archival community's approach to building better relations with Indigenous peoples.

---

1. Eve Tuck and Wayne K. Yang, "Decolonization Is Not a Metaphor," *Decolonization: Indigeneity, Education & Society* 1, no. 1 (2012): 1-40.

In December 2015, the TRC released its final report. Looking at several sectors of society, the TRC made recommendations aimed at making services more accessible, employees better informed, and organizations more committed to honoring the legacy of the Residential Schools[2] system. Heritage and cultural institutions in Canada were highlighted as having key roles in both truth and reconciliation due to their role in "Aboriginal peoples' inalienable right to know the truth about what happened and why, with regard to human rights violations committed against them in the residential schools."[3] The TRC called on heritage organizations, including archives, to create historically literate Canadian citizens who not only understand the events of history, but also grasp how and why the history of Residential Schools connects to the everyday lives of settlers of Canada.[4] The TRC described reconciliation as the establishment of a mutually respectful relationship between Indigenous and non-Indigenous peoples. The process of reconciliation begins with an awareness of the past, acknowledgment of the lasting harms caused by the past, atonement for the causes of those harms, and action to change future behaviors. The very first step of that long process of reconciliation starts—in heritage spaces, museums, and archives—by making accessible a truthful account of the past.

There is a fundamental disconnect between Western archival arrangement principles and the archival needs of many Indigenous community members. Archival concepts of original order, provenance, and access

---

2. Residential Schools in the Canadian context are known as a formal system that has been acknowledged by the Canadian federal and provincial governments, Indigenous peoples, and some Church organizations. The terms "Residential School," "Survivor" and "Indigenous" are capitalized out of respect. For further information see, the *Final Report of the Truth and Reconciliation Commission of Canada* (2015) and *Elements of Indigenous Style: A Guide for Writing By and About Indigenous Peoples* (2018) by Gregory Younging.

3. Truth and Reconciliation Commission of Canada, *The Truth and Reconciliation Commission of Canada: Calls to Action* (Montreal & Kingston: McGill-Queen's University Press, 2015): 8.

4. Truth and Reconciliation Commission of Canada, *The Final Report of the Truth and Reconciliation Commission of Canada*, Vol. 6, Canada's Residential Schools: Reconciliation, (Montreal & Kingston: McGill-Queen's University Press, 2015): 137.

often create barriers for Indigenous peoples looking to utilize archival records. Crystal Fraser and Zoe Todd have argued that, "To reclaim, reshape, and transform the archives to meet the needs of Indigenous peoples requires an honest and blunt engagement with the bureaucratic and arcane structures that govern and shape research today."[5] Archives must consider dramatically transforming their practices to make archives more accessible spaces to Indigenous communities. Community archives, such as the Shingwauk Residential Schools Centre (SRSC), are examples of archival organizations that are decolonizing archival practice beyond the steps outlined in the TRC's Calls to Action. Recognizing the importance of involving the people whom the historical documents represent has contributed to the SRSC actively engaging Residential School Survivors, families, and communities in collection development, archival description, and education programming.

We begin this chapter by exploring the history of archives as colonial spaces, the history of Residential School archival records, and the role of Indigenous community archives in creating new forms of archival understanding. We will then examine the founding of the SRSC, the importance of community engaged archival practice at the SRSC, and the ways in which digital technology has facilitated participatory description and allowed the SRSC to expand its outreach to Survivor communities across the world. Lastly, we will explore the SRSC's approach to decolonizing archival description and archival arrangement practices.

Archives as Colonial Spaces

Mainstream archival spaces and archival description practices are extensions of the colonial relationships that settler states have with Indigenous communities. Archives are entrenched in Western traditions and archival theory, which make decisions about what is valuable, what is erased,

---

5. Crystal Fraser and Zoe Todd, "Decolonial Sensibilities: Indigenous Research and Engaging with Archives in Contemporary Colonial Canada," *L'internationale*, February 15, 2016 http://www.internationaleonline.org/research/decolonising_practices/54_decolonial_sensibilities_indigenous_research_and_engaging_with_archives_in_contemporary_colonial_canada.

and whose narratives are worth preserving. For years, archives actively marginalized Indigenous narratives and played a central role in controlling how Indigenous history was presented and preserved. Archives are never neutral, and many archives continue to reinforce existing colonial hierarchies as inevitable and natural by classifying some individuals (settlers) as observers and others as observed (Indigenous peoples).[6] The place currently known as Canada has been largely documented by settlers, viewing the world through a colonial lens and describing Indigenous communities using non-Indigenous worldviews.

For many Indigenous researchers, archives are spaces of trauma, with archival records reflecting both historical human rights abuses and contemporary harmful colonial relationships that still exist in Canada. Historian Mary Jane Logan McCallum has argued that Indigenous scholars face unique challenges accessing records that are related to their own communities, with many Indigenous community records being situated in Ottawa at Library and Archives Canada. Engaging in archival research can be challenging for Indigenous scholars for numerous reasons. As McCallum notes:

> our work involves reading correspondence, mostly between people who clearly dislike Indigenous people or at best see them as a problem to be solved. They wrote documents that they never intended to share with the people they were writing about, even while they were making decisions that would intimately affect the lives of the people they were discussing....In short, reading DIA [Department of Indian Affairs] records—and the archive itself—can be emotionally and intellectually exhausting, exacerbating the physical strain of archival research.[7]

Archives and the records they hold can be reminders of historical and contemporary violence against Indigenous peoples. Archives can

6. L.L. Terrance, "Resisting Colonial Education: Zitkala-Sa and Native Feminist Archival Refusal," *International Journal of Qualitative Studies in Education* 24, no. 6 (2011): 625.

7. Mary Jane Logan McCallum, "Indigenous People, Archives and History," *Shekon Neechie*, June 21, 2018, https://shekonneechie.ca/2018/06/21/indigenous-people-archives-and-history/.

also be spaces where Indigenous peoples are over-researched by academics and yet made invisible through lack of archival records written from Indigenous perspectives.[8] However, archives can also be spaces of knowledge and healing. Records in archives can assist in the recovery of Indigenous history and revitalization of cultural knowledge. Likewise, access to historical knowledge has the potential to be healing at both the individual and community level.[9] Records that document the abuses and harm inflicted by Residential Schools can provide insight into intergenerational trauma and validate Survivor understandings of their own experiences. In order to better serve Indigenous communities and scholars, archivists must understand the ways in which archival records can be explored and used beyond their original colonial purposes.[10]

In general, archival records relating to Residential Schools are artefacts from the day-to-day administration of the Residential School system. There are very few archival records that are written from the student perspective, and the student-authored documents that do exist often feature a heavy administrative voice. For example, though archives do hold letters written by Residential School students, they are usually form letters, showing little emotion, and they were censored by staff. The views of government authorities, school staff, and religious organizations are evident in monthly reports, correspondence, and general operational records of the schools. Administrative perspectives are evident in the photographs and newsletters created to promote and record the efficacy of Residential Schools.[11] These records were not created to document individual student experience at Residential Schools, yet, in many cases,

---

8. Eve Tuck, "Suspending Damage: A Letter to Communities," *Harvard Educational Review* 79, no. 3 (2009): 412-15.

9. Kimberly L. Lawson, "Precious Fragments: First Nations Materials in Archives, Libraries, and Museums," (Master's thesis, University of Victoria, 2004), 70, https://open.library.ubc.ca/cIRcle/collections/ubctheses/831/items/1.0091657.

10. For more information on the cultural subversion of colonial archival records, see Margot Francis, *Creative Subversions: Whiteness, Indigeneity, and the National Imaginary*, (Vancouver: UBC Press, 2012).

11. Krista McCracken, "Archival Photographs in Perspective: Indian Residential School Images of Health," *British Journal of Canadian Studies* 30, no. 2 (2017): 163-82.

they are the only archival evidence of a student's attendance and the daily routine of Residential School life. The lack of information from the student perspective has implications on our current ability to understand the Residential School system. Missing context and sparse student perspectives impairs the work of those seeking to analyze the "average" student experience at Residential Schools. The narrative gaps in archival records can be filled by reading against the grain, incorporating the analysis of Residential School photographs into historical interpretation, and by the use of oral history or other Indigenous-created records.[12] Community archives, such as the SRSC, which house a combination of colonial archival records and community-generated material provide unique opportunities to examine the history of Residential Schools beyond their colonial paper trail.

Situating the Shingwauk Residential Schools Centre

The Shingwauk Indian Residential School was operated by the Anglican Church of Canada in partnership with the Canadian government in Sault Ste. Marie, Ontario from 1874-1970. The programming at Shingwauk, like the other Residential Schools across Canada, was designed to remove the language, culture, and identities of First Nations, Inuit, and Métis children. Children came to Shingwauk from across Canada, many of them traveling hundreds of miles away from their communities and spending many years away from their families. In the spring of 1970, the Shingwauk School closed its doors. The closure was part of the Canadian government's wider movement in the 1960s and 1970s to phase out Residential Schools across the country. Following Shingwauk's closure and the vacancy of the Shingwauk Hall building, Algoma University, in partnership with the Keewaitnung Institute,[13] moved onto the

---

12. Jennifer S.H. Brown and Elizabeth Vibert, eds., *Reading Beyond Words: Contexts for Native History*, 2nd ed., (Peterborough: Broadview Press, 2003).

13. The Keewatinung Anishinaabe Institute was an Indigenous-operated educational organization founded by community members and former Shingwauk Indian Residential School students in the 1970s in Garden River First Nation. Inspired by the American Indian Movement, the Institute was dedicated to the preservation of Indigenous knowledge and fulfilling the vision of Chief Shingwauk through Indigenous culture-based education.

Shingwauk site in 1971. Algoma University is one of only a few universities in North America located in a former Residential School building. The uniqueness of this location came with responsibilities—Algoma is called upon to do better, to respect the heritage of the land upon which it sits, and to reflect on what it means to inhabit a space that is directly connected to the intergenerational trauma of Residential Schools. Since its relocation to the Shingwauk campus, Algoma University has undertaken many initiatives in cross-cultural education and prides itself on working with local Indigenous communities to create an inclusive and multicultural education environment. The undertaking of cross-cultural programming is directly tied to the Residential School legacy of which Algoma became part upon relocation. One of the most enduring and significant cross-cultural efforts at Algoma has been the establishment and development of the SRSC in 1979. The SRSC, previously known as the Shingwauk Project, is a cross-cultural research and educational development initiative of Algoma University and the Children of Shingwauk Alumni Association (CSAA).

The Shingwauk Project was founded by Professor Don Jackson in collaboration with Dr. Lloyd Bannerman of Algoma University, Chief Ron Boissoneau of Garden River First Nation, and Shingwauk alumni and elder Dr. Dan Pine Sr. of Garden River First Nation. The Project was founded to preserve the history of the Shingwauk Indian Residential School, acknowledge and honor the long history of Indigenous life on the land, and educate the local community about Residential Schools. The first major initiative undertaken by the Shingwauk Project was to host a Residential School Survivor reunion for former students of the Shingwauk School. In 1981, over 400 students, family, staff, and community members gathered on the Shingwauk site for a reunion and to begin to address their communal past. After attending the 1981 reunion, many students, families, and former staff felt compelled to share photographs, scrapbooks, and documents with each other. As a means of facilitating this sharing, Jackson established the Shingwauk archives to promote the sharing of Residential School records and resources. The archives were established with joint governance between the CSAA and Algoma University.

The SRSC is an example of a community archive borne out of a desire to see the history of Residential Schools told from the Survivor perspective. Recognizing the importance of involving the people whom the historical documents represent has contributed to the SRSC programming that actively engages Residential School Survivors, families, and communities in collection development, description, and education programming. As Michelle Caswell et al. have noted, many individuals view "community archives metaphorically as home … home is a space where their experiences and those of their ancestors are validated. For others, still it is a space where intergenerational dialog—sometimes difficult and unsettling—occurs."[14] The work engaged in by the SRSC is informed by intergenerational connections to the Shingwauk site and the need to provide space for truth-telling in relation to Residential Schools. The community-based approach to archival management used by the SRSC has aided it in becoming a trusted archival space among Survivor communities in Canada. The SRSC continues to prioritize telling the history of Residential Schools from a Survivor perspective and aims to extend its archival resources beyond the colonial words and images captured by Residential School records.

From 1981 to 2008, the archives were staffed by volunteers and coordinated by Jackson. Funding for the project was minimal and it initially had no dedicated space. The archives had no governing policies, no real organizational system existed for the collections, and no one with archival experience was associated with the initiative. Its focus was to provide copies of materials to Indigenous communities and act as a community repository for materials relating to Residential Schools.[15] The SRSC was being guided by community needs during this phase

14. Michelle Caswell et al., "Imagining Transformative Spaces: The Personal-Political Sites of Community Archives," *Archival Science* 18, no. 1 (2018): 82.

15. Krista McCracken, "Community Archival Practice: Indigenous Grassroots Collaboration at the Shingwauk Residential Schools Centre," *American Archivist* 78, no. 1 (2015): 181-91.

and was responding to community needs as best as possible, but with limited staff and funding. The professionalization of the SRSC began in 2008 when operational funding was secured from the Aboriginal Healing Foundation. The period from 2010 to 2012 also marked the hiring of a professionally trained archives technician and several student assistants. A formal governance structure was established with the SRSC being jointly governed by the CSAA and Algoma University. A heritage committee comprised of members from both organizations provides guidance on archival best practices, outreach programming, and policy development. During this time, the SRSC's archival collection was made compliant with the Canadian Rules for Archival Description, digitization of the archival holdings was started, and file-level description of archival material began being placed online. Decisions around what material was placed online and how it should be described was informed by guidance from the Shingwauk Survivor community.

Online Access to Residential School Records

Digital archival platforms provide new opportunities for archives to drastically change how Indigenous archival material is described and arranged. There are three major iterations of the SRSC website—early 2000s, 2011, and 2015—each of which has used technology to reach communities and Survivors. Archives can use technology to disrupt colonial historical narratives and shift toward the integration of Indigenous ways of knowing within archival description and arrangement. Since the early 2000s, the SRSC has been posting Residential School photographs online to serve Survivors, intergenerational Survivors, and communities who are unable to travel to Sault Ste. Marie to engage with the SRSC's collections in person.

The earliest iteration of this online outreach decontextualized records from their archival fonds and emphasized organizing photographs by geographic location, time period, or theme. Static photo galleries were created online via the now defunct Shingwauk.auc.ca website. These galleries featured images from Residential Schools across Ontario. These images were sometimes accompanied by captions but often were just grouped together under titles such as "Shingwauk in the 1960s." This early version of the SRSC website also included a "Talking Circle Forum" featuring feedback and reflections submitted by Survivors and Residential School staff. The forum was most active between 2001 and 2002, with nineteen messages being posted during that time. Of those nineteen messages, 32% were written by Survivor Donald Sands, and many of the other messages responded to Sands' comments.[16] Sands passed away in June 2002 and following his death the forum ceased to be a place of sustained community dialogue. The "Talking Circle Forum" is representative of an early attempt by the SRSC to use technology to engage Survivors in dialogue and capture important contextual information about the history of Residential Schools.

In 2011, the SRSC migrated its website to a custom-built Drupal database, which organized material based on archival arrangement principles. This was a significant shift in how material was organized and made accessible on a digital platform. For example, no longer were all the photographs from the Shingwauk Indian Residential School located in one spot. Rather, images and documents were organized based on their creator and according to the archival principle of respect des fonds.[17] This iteration of the SRSC website included a search function that allowed users to narrow what records they were searching. However, the thematic browsing and grouping of images that dominated the previous version of the website was not replicated on this new online platform. The change in website organization represented an increased need for archival staff intervention, in order to teach about how the website worked and to help users use the search function more effectively. The Drupal website also allowed for the attachment of PDFs, a larger number of images to be shared, and larger file sizes

16. Shingwauk Project, "Talking Circle Forum—INDEX," December 14, 2002, *Internet Archive* https://web.archive.org/web/*/http://www.shingwauk.auc.ca/.

17. For more information on this archival principle, see Nancy Bartlett, "Respect Des Fonds: The Origins of the Modern Archival Principle of Provenance," *Primary Sources & Original Works* 1, no. 1-2 (1992): 107-15; and Laura A. Millar, Archives: Principles and Practices (London: Facet Publishing, 2017).

to be uploaded. These technological improvements allowed the SRSC to expand the type and quantity of archival records it provided online.

Currently, the SRSC website includes over 100 distinct archival fonds/collections, thousands of digitized photographs, and hundreds of thousands of pages of digitized textual records.[18] Photographs are available in JPEG format and are attached to their corresponding archival file-level description. For cases where there are over twenty-five images associated with one file, these images are also accessible as a combined PDF. Short textual records have been made available as JPEGs, with any documents longer than five pages being available as PDFs that have been run through Optical Character Recognition software. All JPEG images include a title, alt-tags, and, where possible, information about the context of the image is included in the file-level record. Decisions about which format materials appear in was largely informed by the technical limitations of the SRSC Drupal website and by a desire to create searchable documents when placing textual records online.

A comment feature was built into the SRSC website during its re-launch in 2011, with the goal of encouraging users to identify individuals in photographs and submit contextual information about records online. Despite the inclusion of a comment feature, online engagement through the website via this feature has remained relatively low – with the SRSC having much more success using social media as an engagement tool.

Photo Identification and Social Media

Social media has created new ways in which people can connect with each other across the world. Many Survivors did not return to their home community or First Nation when they left Residential School, and so many Indigenous peoples are as they always were: spread throughout Turtle Island. Physically, the SRSC is situated on Robinson-Huron Treaty territory, which is comprised of a diverse Indigenous population. The SRSC has done a lot of regional outreach with Indigenous communities,

---

18. Data based on SRSC archival material is hosted on http://archives.algomau.ca, as of November 11, 2018.

but outreach to more distant communities has been challenging and limited by grant funding. Use of the SRSC's digitized photographic holdings presents the opportunity to connect with a wider range of Indigenous communities via social media.

The SRSC's social media strategy is guided by the principle of "sharing, healing, and learning" with material being shared to further education and connection to the history of Residential Schools. Additionally, the SRSC is advised by the CSAA, which has established guidelines for archival content being shared online. A number of the photographs and documents held by the SRSC are in the public domain; however—out of respect for Indigenous ownership, privacy, and Intellectual rights—not all of this public domain material is available online.[19] Staff avoid sharing archival records that document student death, medical statuses, and other very personal details. Likewise, photographs that document students in compromising ways are not shared online. These personal materials are accessible to Survivors and their families through direct contact with the SRSC.

Through use of the *Algoma University Archives* Facebook account, the SRSC has been able to share online collections to generate interest in research use of the collections, interest in site history, and general online engagement. For example, the SRSC Artifact Collection, which includes the Beadwork series comprised of beadwork from the 1800s and early 1900s, has been shared on social media to find regional and stylistic information. The Beadwork collection was donated to the SRSC with little contextual information about who made the pieces or the communities of origin. Upon examination of the beadwork, it is clear that the collection includes a range of styles and represents the work of multiple artists and cultures. By sharing photographs of this beadwork online, the SRSC has been able to identify approximate geographic regions of origin and link the beadwork to specific Indigenous styles of beading. The SRSC also continues to share photographs of this beadwork in

---

19. Allison Mills, "Learning to Listen: Archival Sound Recordings and Indigenous Cultural and Intellectual Property," *Archivaria* 83 (Spring 2017): 109-24.

hopes that descendants of the original makers will recognize the work, offering an opportunity for reconnection and possible repatriation.

When some of the student photographs from different Residential Schools were shared via social media, it was hoped that more names could be added to the notes. However, what transpired was both names and comments, which provided new context to archival images. This is a space where Survivors, intergenerational Survivors, families, and the community can come together to remember. Social media spaces can be places where Indigenous peoples find each other and share information with other communities or share strength. For example, on October 23, 2018, the SRSC posted a set of photographs on the *Algoma University Archives* Facebook page that highlighted a judo club at the Moose Factory Residential School around the year 1965. The post featured photographs donated by the judo teacher Arthur Bear Chief and included a request from the SRSC for help identifying the students in the photos. It began by one person identifying a family member and then snowballed with others doing the same.

Comments on the photograph seen in **Figure 1** include Survivors identifying themselves, friends, and relatives. One Survivor noted, "Wow that is a long time ago. Don't know the guy behind me, I'm with the glasses 2nd to the left…Bert Chilton is to my left. I forget the guy holding Allen."[20] Intergenerational Survivors also commented on the post and learned more about their parents though image and comment storytelling. The final image in the set brought on a full conversation by Survivors who were trying to recall that moment. A community conversation began to develop in virtual space—a sharing of stories, kids reminiscing about throwing each other to the ground during judo. It was surprising that the responses came from all genders, a stark contrast to the widely held belief that female-identified persons did not participate in contact sports while at Residential School. One female Survivor recalled holding her own against a boy who was much shorter than her

---

20. Shingwauk Residential Schools Centre, "Judo Photographs," *Algoma University Archives* Facebook page, October 23, 2018, https://www.facebook.com/AUarchives/photos/pcb.2672021046145146/2672020642811853/.

Figure 1. Bert Chilton (far left), Brian Davey (second from left, with glasses), Ernie Sutherland (middle, holding Allen), Allen Sailors (middle), John Turner (back to camera). Girls on right of image include Flossy Georgekish (also known as Florence Peace). Photo from SRSC archives, reference number: 2011-001/001(005).

and pinning him to the ground. By the end of the second day that the images were online, the Survivor community had identified nearly all the people in the photograph, where before none were known. They begin to recall details, each remembering something unique about the moment captured on film. Other Survivors who could not put names to faces began to remember more information as details were talked out in the comments. And, on December 12, 2018, the SRSC shared four photographs of students at St. John's Indian Residential School (Chapleau, Ontario) circa 1940. These photographs sparked a number of intergenerational conversations, with some individuals seeing a photograph of their grandmother for the first time. Likewise, there were conversations about the interconnectedness of community with one individual remarking, "Didn't know Mary was your grandmother knew her ver [sic] well she used to babysit my brothers and I and when we got married she embroider [sic] us a nice set of pillow cases."[21] In this instance, the photographs sparked a realization of family connections and brought people together through shared stories. The photograph comment section also saw people sharing names of family members who attended St. John's Indian Residential School and descendants expressing an interest in knowing if there were archival records about their relatives. Sharing these images on Facebook allowed the SRSC to extend community outreach and connect with individuals who may have otherwise not contacted the archives.

This instance of sharing of stories via Facebook was overwhelmingly positive, with a sense of community building up around the photographs. Likewise, other photographs digitally shared by the SRSC for naming purposes have also met with positive comments. Many intergenerational Survivors viewing these photographs have seen photographs of their parents or grandparents as children for the first time. This is not to detract from the overwhelmingly negative feelings associated with Residential Schools. Rather, it complicates Residential School history and highlights that we cannot simply consider Indigenous peoples victims of colonization. Survivors often made the best of horrific situations, and adding personal experiences to archival photographs helps restore the recognition of Survivor agency and provides space for community-driven narratives. Residential Schools were sites of forced assimilation and trauma, but they were also sites of strength and resilience. Stories of friendship, special activities, and sports provide examples of how some students survived Residential School.[22]

Given the wide reach of social media, it is possible that these images will not always generate positive memories or conversation. The SRSC

---

21. Shingwauk Residential Schools Centre, "Photo of Senior Girls at Chapleau," *Algoma University Archives* Facebook page, December 12, 2018, https://www.facebook.com/AUarchives/photos/pcb.2779322552081661/2779321942081722/.

22. Paul Seesequasis, "Turning the Lens: Indigenous Archival Photo Project," *Shekon Neechie*, June 21, 2018, https://shekonneechie.ca/2018/06/21/turning-the-lens/.

has on-site health support resources available through partnerships that provide support to Survivors and their families, but social media presents health support challenges. For some members of both the Survivors' and intergenerational Survivors' communities, the very mention of Residential Schools or images of them can trigger states of emotion that become hard to resolve over social media. Currently, at the end of any social media posts that include images of Residential School students or discussion of the impacts of Residential Schools, the *Algoma University Archives* social media accounts link to the twenty-four hour national crisis line staffed by the Indian Residential School Resolution Health Support Program.[23] In all of its outreach practices, the SRSC strives to create safe spaces for community dialogue and input. The social media outreach and Facebook conversations illustrate one way of creating digital spaces for dialogue. The SRSC staff members readily acknowledge that simply linking to a crisis line isn't ideal, but at this stage the SRSC is still exploring what other forms of virtual mental health and cultural support could be provided alongside digital outreach initiatives.

Decolonizing Archival Description

One of the core ways that decolonized archival practice at the SRSC has intersected with digital technology is through the use of technology to describe, arrange, and incorporate community knowledge within the archival records. The SRSC describes its archival holdings at the file level. For the SRSC, there are numerous advantages to this level of description: it allows for community knowledge to be directly connected to individual files and photographs, digital arrangement can reflect community needs, and access restrictions based on Survivor feedback can be implemented on a case-by-case basis. Names and context contributed to photographs

---

23. Under the Indian Residential Schools Settlement Agreement (2007), the Indian Residential Schools Resolution Health Support Program was established to provide mental health and emotional and cultural support to Survivors and their families. Details on the program can be found at: https://www.canada.ca/en/indigenous-services-canada/services/first-nations-inuit-health/health-care-services/indian-residential-schools-health-supports/indian-residential-schools-resolution-health-support-program.html.

via social media are added into online archival descriptions to ensure that records are described with as much community input as possible. In the case of photographs or records labeled by creators in languages now viewed as outdated, the SRSC has actively worked to re-describe these photographs online. Original titles are moved to notes fields and new culturally appropriate titles are added to the files. This renaming of records and photographs not only re-contextualizes the material, it also allows for the records to be accessed using a range of search terms. During the re-description process, the SRSC staff prioritized the inclusion of individual names, place names, Indigenous language words, and culturally appropriate descriptions of activities. For example, the SRSC has a collection of images that include photographs from the Residential Schools in Spanish, Ontario depicting students dressed in pan-Indigenous costumes for an ice-skating carnival. These photographs were incorrectly labeled as students "dressed in traditional regalia." This description is incorrect and misleading in that it suggests that students had the ability to practice traditional Indigenous cultural activities while at school—which is not what is being represented in these photographs. The SRSC staff have re-titled these images as "Photographs of an ice carnival" with an entry in the notes field about the clothing being worn.[24] Re-describing thousands of photographs takes a substantial amount of staff time and effort. It is also representative of a type of cultural shift advocated for by DeEtta Jones, who argued that, "you must let go of the idea that the way you've learned to see the world is 'the right way' and become open to the idea that the same event, story, or problem can be viewed in multiple, valid ways."[25] Archival description must be flexible, adaptable, and responsive to the needs of Indigenous communities. It must recognize the cultural identity of those who created the material and an understanding of the colonial implications of archival

---

24. Unknown author, Photographs of an ice carnival, 1955, 2011-044, Box 5, Folder 16, Spanish Indian Residential School series, Rev. Father William Maurice fonds, Shingwauk Residential Schools Centre, Algoma University, Sault Ste. Marie, Canada.

25. DeEtta Jones, "Cultural Competency: Why it Matters," August 15, 2018, http://www.deettajones.com/cultural-competency-why-it-matters/.

practices. Description is always retrospective and has the potential to impact how records will be used and interpreted.[26] The language used to describe Residential School records can change their meaning and have a tremendous impact on how the material is received by Survivors and their families. This ongoing work of decolonizing description is part of a larger effort to ensure that the SRSC archival holdings are as accessible and searchable as possible.

In addition to examining archival descriptions, the SRSC is considering how technology can be used to facilitate new arrangements of archival information that are based on community, kinship, and Survivor knowledge. For example, many of the photographs in the SRSC archives have been donated by former Residential School staff. Standard archival practice and the archival principle of provenance would see these fonds named after the donor and creator of the records – the staff member. Tom Nesmith argues that provenance is not a single person or institution, but rather that "records are a product of a variety of factors acting across their entire history."[27] Framing provenance as extending beyond an individual donor or creator is an integral part of decolonizing the SRSC archives and has the potential to provide greater historical context to Residential School records. Many of the records in the SRSC have multiple provenance, i.e., they have more than one history attached to them. Though a record might have been physically created by a Residential School staff member, the government and church organizations would have been involved in the preservation and use of many Residential School records.[28] Likewise, taking into consideration societal provenance and the acknowledgment of the colonial context, how Residential School records were created can greatly change how a record

---

26. K.J. Rawson, "The Rhetorical Power of Archival Description: Classifying Images of Gender Transgression," *Rhetoric Society Quarterly* 48, no. 4 (2018): 327-51.

27. Tom Nesmith, "The Concept of Societal Provenance and Records of Nineteenth-Century Aboriginal-European Relations in Western Canada: Implications for Archival Theory and Practice," *Archival Science* 6, no. 3-4 (2006): 352.

28. Lessha M. Cowan, "Decolonizing Provenance: An Examination of Types of Provenance and Their Role in Archiving Indigenous Records in Canada," (Master's thesis, University of Manitoba, 2018), 41, http://hdl.handle.net/1993/33429.

is shared, used, and described. So, what does this mean in practice? It means acknowledging that creating archival fonds and collections named after Residential School principals and staff is problematic and, indeed, that naming—particularly if the individual mentioned was a perpetrator of abuse—could be triggering to Residential School Survivors or descendant communities. Likewise, presenting detailed autobiographical information about school principals who collected Residential School photographs while providing little information about the students in the images reinforces colonial relationships and concepts of paternalism. In order to provide different arrangement and access pathways to archival materials, the SRSC has created PDF "photo albums," which are organized by school, time period, and theme. For example, the photographs from the Residential Schools in Spanish, Ontario have been organized into eight thematic photo albums including such topics as boys, sports, confirmation, girls, and early years. These digital albums allow users to explore photographs thematically.[29] The albums also place more of an emphasis on the experience of the students, instead of highlighting the role of staff members in collecting the images. The SRSC is currently exploring other forms of digital arrangement and hopes to further challenge colonial archival principles through providing new arrangements, access, and use options for the Residential School records in its holdings.

Conclusion

The SRSC is a unique example of a grassroots Indigenous community archive that has actively worked to meet the needs and desires of Residential School Survivors and intergenerational Survivors. The use of technology has allowed the SRSC to find new ways to connect with geographically diverse users, transform archival descriptive processes, and build spaces for community discussions. The SRSC regularly updates collections with contextualized information from the Survivor

---

29. Shingwauk Residential Schools Centre, Residential School Photo Album Series, 2011, 2011-019/001, Shingwauk Project Collection, Shingwauk Residential Schools Centre, Algoma University, Sault Ste. Marie, Canada, http://archives.algomau.ca/main/?q=node/21413.

community, with names added to photographs as Survivors look back and remember. In continuing to work with the community, these records tell the Survivor story of the Shingwauk Indian Residential School. The work of the SRSC pre-dates the TRC and the current era of reconciliation dialogue. However, the TRC's Calls to Action have reaffirmed the SRSC's commitment to access and to working with Survivors. The use of technologies by the SRSC has furthered these calls in digital space for Survivors to remember, connect, and talk about their photographs on their own terms. The use of social media as a tool for gathering context and naming photographs has brought Survivors together in a way that breaks down geographic barriers.

This engagement goes beyond simply providing access to records and photographs; it provides a space for healing and reconciliation for the Survivor community while providing all communities with a deeper understanding of life at Residential Schools and their continued impacts on contemporary Canadian life. The SRSC's commitment to the Survivor and intergenerational Survivor communities has led to unique uses and adapted uses of archival technologies. The SRSC believes in working with these colonial mediums in new ways that go beyond serving researchers. By working with the communities that these documents represent, the SRSC has found new ways to alter Western archival tradition to make Indigenous voices the key focus.

Bibliography

Brown, Jennifer S.H., and Elizabeth Vibert, eds. *Reading Beyond Words: Contexts for Native History*. 2nd ed. Peterborough: Broadview Press, 2003.

Caswell, Michelle, Joyce Gabiola, Jimmy Zavala, Gracen Brilmyer, and Marika Cifor. "Imagining Transformative Spaces: The Personal-Political Sites of Community Archives." *Archival Science* 18, no. 1 (2018): 78-93.

Cowan, Lessha M. "Decolonizing Provenance: An Examination of Types of Provenance and Their Role in Archiving Indigenous Records in

Canada." Master's thesis, University of Manitoba, 2018. http://hdl. handle.net/1993/33429.

Fraser, Crystal, and Zoe Todd. "Decolonial Sensibilities: Indigenous Research and Engaging with Archives in Contemporary Colonial Canada." *L'internationale.* February 15, 2016.

Jones, DeEtta. "Cultural Competency: Why it Matters." August 15, 2018. http://www.deettajones.com/cultural-competency-why-it-matters/.

Lawson, Kimberly L. "Precious Fragments: First Nations Materials in Archives, Libraries, and Museums." Master's thesis, University of Victoria, 2004. https://open.library.ubc.ca/cIRcle/collections/ubctheses/831/items/1.0091657.

Logan McCallum, Mary Jane. "Indigenous People, Archives and History." *Shekon Neechie.* June 21, 2018. https://shekonneechie. ca/2018/06/21/indigenous-people-archives-and-history/.

McCracken, Krista. "Archival Photographs in Perspective: Indian Residential School Images of Health." *British Journal of Canadian Studies* 30, no. 2 (2017): 163-82.

McCracken, Krista. "Community Archival Practice: Indigenous Grassroots Collaboration at the Shingwauk Residential Schools Centre." *American Archivist* 78, no. 1 (2015): 181-91.

Mills, Allison. "Learning to Listen: Archival Sound Recordings and Indigenous Cultural and Intellectual Property." *Archivaria* 83 (Spring 2017): 109-24.

Nesmith, Tom. "The Concept of Societal Provenance and Records of Nineteenth-Century Aboriginal-European Relations in Western Canada: Implications for Archival Theory and Practice." *Archival Science* 6, no. 3-4 (2006): 351-60.

Rawson, K.J. "The Rhetorical Power of Archival Description: Classifying Images of Gender Transgression." *Rhetoric Society Quarterly* 48, no. 4 (2018): 327-51.

Seesequasis, Paul. "Turning the Lens: Indigenous Archival Photo Project." *Shekon Neechie.* June 21, 2018. https://shekonneechie. ca/2018/06/21/turning-the-lens/.

Shingwauk Project. "Talking Circle Forum—INDEX," *Internet Archive.* December 14, 2002. https://web.archive.org/web/*/http://www. shingwauk.auc.ca/.

Shingwauk Residential Schools Centre. "Judo Photographs." *Algoma University Archives* Facebook page. October 23, 2018. https://www. facebook.com/AUarchives/photos/pcb.2672021046145146/2672 020642811853/.

Shingwauk Residential Schools Centre. "Photo of Senior Girls at Chapleau." *Algoma University Archives* Facebook page. December 12, 2018. https://www.facebook.com/AUarchives/photos/pcb.2779322552 081661/2779321942081722/.

Shingwauk Residential Schools Centre. Residential School Photo Album Series. 2011. 2011-019/001. Shingwauk Project Collection. Shingwauk Residential Schools Centre, Algoma University, Sault Ste. Marie, Canada. http://archives.algomau.ca/main/?q=node/21413.

Terrance, L.L. "Resisting Colonial Education: Zitkala-Sa and Native Feminist Archival Refusal." *International Journal of Qualitative Studies in Education* 24, no. 6 (2011): 621-26.

Truth and Reconciliation Commission of Canada. *The Final Report of the Truth and Reconciliation Commission of Canada.* Vol. 6, *Canada's Residential Schools: Reconciliation.* Montreal & Kingston: McGill-Queen's University Press, 2015.

Truth and Reconciliation Commission of Canada. *The Truth and Reconciliation Commission of Canada: Calls to Action.* Montreal & Kingston: McGill-Queen's University Press, 2015.

Tuck, Eve. "Suspending Damage: A Letter to Communities." *Harvard Educational Review* 79, no. 3 (2009): 412-15.

Tuck, Eve, and Wayne K. Yang, "Decolonization Is Not a Metaphor." *Decolonization: Indigeneity, Education & Society* 1, no. 1 (2012): 1-40.

Unknown author. Photographs of an ice carnival. 1955. 2011-044, Box 5, Folder 16. Spanish Indian Residential School series, Rev. Father William Maurice fonds. Shingwauk Residential Schools Centre, Algoma University, Sault Ste. Marie, Canada.

Younging, Gregory. *Elements of Indigenous Style: A Guide for Writing By and About Indigenous Peoples.* Toronto: Brush Education Inc., 2018.

Chapter 13

"Certain Moral Reflections": Digital Exhibits and Critical Scholarship—The Case of the Kipling Scrapbooks Digital Exhibit

Jessica Ruzek, Roger Gillis, and Diana Doublet

Dalhousie Libraries' Kipling Collection is noted for its reputation as one of the most comprehensive collections of Rudyard Kipling's publications. Kipling was one of Britain's most celebrated authors, best known for *The Jungle Book* (1894-1895) and *Captains Courageous* (1897). In 2017, the Kipling Collection became a site of contestation during a project to digitize nineteenth-century scrapbooks devoted to Kipling's life and letters. These scrapbooks represent a wide range of responses to Kipling and his writings at the height of his career; as well, they contain several of his early works, including the "Letters of Marque" (hereinafter referred to as "Letters"), which document Kipling's travels through India in the 1880s. Digitizing and creating an exhibit around these scrapbooks resulted in the Kipling Scrapbooks Digital Exhibit: an interactive, open-access website that includes the digitized scrapbooks; an interactive map and timeline; and scholarship on the British Empire and travel writing, the Indian State of Rajputana, and the history and practice of scrapbooking.

Due to the cloistered nature of the Kipling Collection, the digital exhibit was initially designed to simply widen the point-of-entry to Dalhousie's Kipling Collection without compromising the physical archive, and to garner greater recognition of Dalhousie's special collections as a whole. The scrapbooks were intended to be digitized without any critical engagement, despite the library's request for contextualization of the scrapbooks' contents. However, as Kipling is himself a contested figure due to his colonial attitudes—"The White Man's Burden" is only one of many examples—it became rapidly apparent in reading "Letters" that a neutral contextualization of the scrapbooks would be impossible. Kipling's often negative and damaging representations of and attitudes about India and its people indicated that even a basic framing of the Kipling Scrapbooks would result in the unequal representation of colonizer and colonized, and would fundamentally support—even celebrate—the British imperial project on the Indian subcontinent.

The issue in creating the exhibit, consequently, became one of providing a context for "Letters" that not only situated Kipling's travelogues in a historical framework, but also outlined the ways in which colonial attitudes became embedded within cultural productions, including travel writing. The framing of the scrapbooks and "Letters" within the milieu of British imperialism demanded a critical awareness during the construction of the exhibit. Because the popularity of Kipling's works continues to the present day, and as his works contain a useful model for understanding and scrutinizing British colonialism, the Kipling Scrapbooks Digital Exhibit offers several reference points to understand the development of British rule in India, and how these ideas were invested within the seemingly innocuous popular culture of Britain. The Kipling Collection—which, as a physical collection, is largely inaccessible to the public—functions as a space that maintains the cultural hegemony of the British colonial project. Kipling's works and ideas—archaic now, but always problematic—appear supported and, moreover, protected by the institution in which the collection is held. Conversely, the Kipling Scrapbooks Digital Exhibit contests the privileged position of the colonial subject over the colonized object, and exists in a virtual space where access is opened and a critical discourse of Kipling's works and ideas is invited. In this chapter, we provide the context around Dalhousie's Kipling Collection and the mechanics of undertaking a digital humanities/digital exhibit project of this nature. We also examine how such projects can help to draw attention to controversial special collections by not only digitizing and providing access, but by allowing for critical engagement and scholarship to build around them. In questioning the role of libraries in supporting special collections that communicate a biased worldview, we demonstrate in this chapter the social and cultural importance of such collections by utilizing them as tools for social justice and discourse.

Around 1920, Nova Scotian lawyer James McGregor Stewart, fueled by a passion for the works of Rudyard Kipling, began to actively collect various editions and publications—legitimate and otherwise—by the author. Resulting from what could only be described as a hodge-podge of publications with varying degrees of credibility and value, Stewart undertook what Dalhousie special collections librarian Karen Smith calls, "the challenge of untangling [Kipling's] complicated publishing history."[1] He eventually compiled an exhaustive bibliography of Kipling's works, which is still considered the singularly definitive bibliography of the author's publications.[2] Stewart's collection contains many first and rare editions of Kipling's works, original manuscripts and illustrations, letters, and various ephemera held in the library's special collections closed stacks. Kipling scholar A.W. Yeats speculates on Stewart's motivations behind the collection, commenting that, as a collector, "Mr. Stewart…appears not to have been motivated so much by fondness for specific Kipling titles as by an effort to build a collection of great academic value."[3]

Befitting a highly respected barrister in Halifax, Nova Scotia, Canada, and one so dedicated to the academy, Stewart donated a portion of his collection to his alma mater, Dalhousie University, in 1954, and the university then acquired the manuscript portion of Stewart's collection

---

1. Karen Smith, *Vessels of Light: A Guide to Special Collections in the Killam Library, Dalhousie University Libraries* (Halifax, NS: Dalhousie University Libraries, 1996), 19.

2. Smith, *Vessels of Light*, 19.

3. A.W. Yeats, "The Stewart Kipling Collection and Some Notes on Its Significance," *Dalhousie Review* 36, no. 2 (1956): 113.

some thirty years later. The consequence of Stewart's collecting labor and donation was that Dalhousie designed a room with archival specifications to preserve these works of literary and archival value, to house what is now known as Dalhousie's Kipling Collection (see **Figure 1**).

Figure 1. The entrance to the Kipling room on the Dalhousie University campus. Photo by Roger Gillis.

Largely inaccessible to the public (would-be patrons must request access), the door to the Kipling Collection is alluring with its small brass plate indicating its presence, but is easy to miss while wandering through Dalhousie's campus grounds. Indeed, it is not commonly known that Dalhousie University owns this impressive collection. This alone foregrounds the problem not only of the Kipling Collection, but also of special collections as institutional praxes: while the priority of such collections is the preservation of rare books, media, and ephemera, the communication of these collections' value remains obscured when access is limited. Access limitations tend to indicate that permission to enter such spaces is, at most, gauged by institutional affiliation, field/level of study or class demarcation, and not least by a baseline curiosity or personal interest. The central questions surrounding such spaces, therefore, do not depend solely on the definition of access, though that remains crucial, but on the following concerns: What are the interests of the institution safeguarding these works? For whom, and to what end, are they preserving these works? The answers to these questions lie in defining access and determining whether special collections are fulfilling their duty to researchers and scholars alike.

Barbara M. Jones, head of the Rare Book and Special Collections Library at University of Illinois at Urbana-Champaign, defines access thus:

> The term "access"…refers to a means of discovery—through such surrogates as descriptive metadata, word of mouth, and references in the literature—that a particular body of information exists. This is coupled with the means of looking at the materials either directly or virtually. Access encompasses the processes followed to make materials of all formats available to users; the tools used to publicize materials to potential users; and the openness with which we allow our collections to be used by the public.[4]

Relying on Jones's first axiom—that access may be a means of discovery—exposes problems with special collections more generally, but with the Kipling Collection uniquely. While it is no secret that the Kipling Collection exists, it is a fact more commonly known among already established Kipling scholars.[5] It is difficult to assess how well known

---

4. Barbara Jones, "Hidden Collections, Scholarly Barriers: Creating Access to Unprocessed Special Collections in America's Research Libraries," *RBM: A Journal of Rare Books, Manuscripts, and Cultural Heritage* 5, no. 2 (2004): 90, https://doi.org/10.5860/rbm.5.2.230.

5. Smith, *Vessels of Light*, 18.

this collection is overall, but even any recent information about it from Dalhousie itself is buried in the university's blog archives or in now outdated publications, such as *Vessels of Light: A Guide to Special Collections in the Killam Library, Dalhousie University Libraries*, published in 1996. As a traditional brick and mortar collection, the Kipling Collection by and large fails to make itself known unless, after glimpsing the collection door's brass plate, one is compelled to request a visit.

The Kipling Collection also fails in Jones's second and third points. As her second point states, some means of looking at the material, directly or virtually, must exist. Unless one receives special permission from the library to enter the Kipling Collection or requests the retrieval of materials, it remains largely inaccessible and, consequently, unusable by scholars or enthusiasts wishing to engage with the materials directly. Jones's final point, that access must include materials made available through multiple formats, in which the platforms and means of access are themselves made available to a general and public audience, also forecloses the Kipling Collection from her definition of access. While the Kipling Collection points to the unique special collections Dalhousie has to offer as a whole and has been successful in preserving works and ephemera by Rudyard Kipling, the Kipling Collection overall fails to provide access to patrons and scholars wishing to use these works.[6] Special collections, and especially literary collections such as the Kipling Collection, are often the result of "agents" such as Stewart, who actively seek to "create or acquire objects for the collection,"[7] as well as by those who assembled the scrapbooks. However, collections, such as the Kipling Collection may not be entirely comprehensive, insofar as the rationales for including specific material are unclear, and the collectors may have been selective in determining which material to include. Similarly, libraries also act as "agents" in vetting to whom and how collections are preserved, catalogued, and accessed, and to what extent this access is

---

6. Other Dalhousie Libraries literary special collections include the Sir Francis Bacon, Oscar Wilde, and Thomas Raddall collections.

7. Geoffrey Yeo, "The Conceptual Fonds and the Physical Collection," *Archivaria* 73 (Spring 2012): 45.

provided. As Chris Bourg notes, "libraries are not now nor have they ever been merely neutral repositories of information." She goes on:

> But what I mean when I say libraries are not neutral is not just that libraries absorb and reflect the inequalities, biases, ethnocentrism, and power imbalances that exist throughout our host societies and (for those of us who work in academic libraries) within higher education…we live in a society that still suffers from racism, sexism, ableism, transphobia and other forms of bias and inequity; but libraries also fail to achieve any mythical state of neutrality because we contribute to bias and inequality in scholarship, and publishing, and information access.[8]

In response to the cloistered nature of the Kipling Collection, which resists the mythical state of neutrality to which Bourg refers, and Dalhousie Libraries' growing digitization and digital humanities initiatives, Dalhousie Libraries launched a digital humanities project in 2017 to digitize and display certain fragile materials from the Kipling Collection, to both avoid compromising the physical archive and to garner greater recognition of Dalhousie's special collections as a whole. This digital preservation project made for a ripe opportunity to present the works of Kipling uniquely and creatively.

Delicate scrapbooks filled with published information about the author's life and letters were chosen for digitization. These eleven scrapbooks, known as the Kipling Scrapbooks, are a subset of the broader Kipling Collection created by notable nineteenth- and twentieth-century Kipling enthusiasts from England and the United States who admired the author and his work so extensively that they dedicated entire books to compiling writing by and about him. Five of these scrapbookers are known: Sir William Garth, Ellis Ames Ballard, G.D. Wells, and James Todman Goodwin, while the remaining three collectors remain unidentified. The Kipling Scrapbooks are informal compilations that include many of Kipling's early journalistic works: newspaper prints of various versions and editions of poems, short stories, and serials, many of which

---

8. Chris Bourg, "The Library is Never Neutral," in *Disrupting the Digital Humanities*, eds. Jessie Stommell and Dorothy Kim (Santa Barbara, CA: Punctum Books, 2018), 456-57.

no longer survive in their original form.[9] While some scrapbooks in the collection are dedicated to Kipling's fame and personal life, others reveal a wider corpus of literary and popular criticism regarding his work. One scrapbook is devoted almost entirely to parodies of Kipling's now infamous poem, "The White Man's Burden" (1899), which advocates for America's imperial control of the Philippines, and includes such parodic titles as, "The Black Man's Burden," "The Red Man's Burden," and "The Dear Wife's Burden," demonstrating the wide circulation and popularity of his work, as well as the equally wide criticism contemporaneous to Kipling's literary outputs. While this scrapbook would have been the more socially relevant of the Kipling Scrapbooks around which to center a digital exhibit, it was perhaps for that very reason that it was not chosen as the central work for the digital Kipling exhibit. Instead, a scrapbook by Sir William Garth—which includes the original newspaper printings of Kipling's early travelogues, "Letters" and "From Sea to Sea"—was chosen for the exhibit, and the significance of this scrapbook is self-evident, as Kipling scholar A.W. Yeats confirms:

> No library possesses anything like complete files of the four Indian newspapers to which he contributed—*The Civil and Military Gazette, The Pioneer, The Pioneer News,* and *The Week's News.*[10]

These two works, "Letters of Marque" and "From Sea to Sea," were written on assignment for *The Pioneer Mail* between 1887 and 1890 while Kipling was based in Lahore, India. Commissioned to travel widely for *The Pioneer,* Kipling wrote about his experiences in India, Hong Kong, Singapore, Japan, America, and Canada, and became a spokesperson for the British Empire by using his mastery of the short story form and attracting a significant following that inspired collectors like Stewart to collect his works in various forms. As the initial intention behind the digital exhibit was to simply widen the point-of-entry to Dalhousie's

---

9. The full scrapbooks are available in Dalspace. http://dalspace.library.dal.ca/handle/10222/73241.

10. Yeats, "The Stewart Kipling Collection and Some Notes on Its Significance," 114.

Kipling Collection, the digitized scrapbooks were to be included in the exhibit without any critical engagement, despite the request for a contextualization of the scrapbooks and their contents. However, as became clear when working with the scrapbooks, the works of Kipling never did, nor do they now, exist in a vacuum—quite the opposite. As the title of his poem, "The White Man's Burden" indicates, the works of Kipling expose the problematic nature of colonial attitudes that is impossible to ignore, especially given contemporary social justice movements that are laboring against the lingering impacts of colonial oppression: Global Climate Strike, Black Lives Matter, #MeToo, Idle No More, and DREAMers movements, to name a few. As the strength of the imperial gaze served as the overarching theme in his many of his works, Kipling's works fundamentally resist a neutral positionality. "White Englishmen," Erik Mueggler writes, "were able to use the power of the colonial stage to disrupt the traditional class relations of their country and enjoy new forms of direct power of subject peoples."[11] Because many of the English travel narratives of the eighteenth and nineteenth century—Kipling's works included—relied on "cartographies of difference,"[12] in which seeing becomes an act of possession and control, such works demonstrate that they were not simply products of a specific time, but were political works central to the project of oppressing lands and peoples to expand the British Empire and exercise vast control. Thus, contextualizing scrapbooks about Kipling in a digital exhibit without including any social or political commentary to frame the production of his works seemed to function as both an evasion and endorsement of his views and the motivations of the British Empire more broadly.

Returning to the notion that the physical sites of special collections resist access and critical commentary, the Kipling Collection, and by extension the initially desired digital exhibit, would continue to

---

11. Erik Mueggler, *The Paper Road: Archive and Experience in the Botanical Exploration of West China and Tibet* (Berkeley, CA: University of California Press, 2011), 48.

12. Mueggler, *The Paper Road*, 48.

serve as a space that maintains the cultural hegemony of the British colonial project and would appear to be supported and protected by the institution in which the collection is held. As such, a neutral contextualization of the scrapbooks would have resulted in the unequal representation of colonizer and colonized, and would have fundamentally supported—even celebrated—the British imperial project on the Indian subcontinent and the oppression of its people. Thus, early on in the project, the impossibility of maintaining neutrality in contextualizing Kipling was revealed, and, in opposition to the institution's initial request, the Kipling Scrapbooks Digital Exhibit (as it came to be titled) contests the privileged position of the colonial subject over the colonized object by existing in a virtual space in which access is open and where a critical discourse of Kipling's works is invited. By treating the Kipling exhibit in the context of social and political commentary, the project consequently dovetails with postcolonial digital humanities which, according to digital humanities scholar Roopika Risam, is "an approach to uncovering and intervening in the disruptions within the digital cultural record produced by colonialism and neocolonialism."[13] As the initial focus was to digitize the Kipling Scrapbooks without critical commentary, it became evident that the digital humanities and the creation of digital scholarship have the potential to reproduce the same colonial themes demonstrated throughout Kipling's works and the physical Kipling Collection. Not solely a technical feat, but one that also relies on postcolonial criticism and the history of imperial travel writing, the Kipling Scrapbooks Digital Exhibit involves considerations for digital humanities resources that serve to "actively resist reinscriptions of colonialism and neocolonialism,"[14] while providing the digital resources necessary to advance scholarly work in literary and colonial histories.

Kipling's writings are not without controversy, due to his being a spokesperson for the British Empire. He was employed by Anglo-Indian

---

13. Roopika Risam, *New Digital Worlds: Postcolonial Digital Humanities in Theory, Praxis, and Pedagogy* (Evanston, IL: Northwestern University Press, 2018), 3.

14. Risam, *New Digital Worlds*, 4.

newspapers in India in the late 1880s and, as a result, was on the journalistic front-line of colonial life on the Indian subcontinent. Commissioned to write travel reports for *The Civil and Military Gazette* in Lahore and then *The Pioneer Mail* in Allahabad, Kipling rapidly developed a keen understanding, not only of Indian customs and traditions, but of international politics and military efforts in India and abroad as well.[15] As an Anglo-Indian, a term that identifies the English in an acquired land as naturalized, Kipling described the British presence in India, the so-called jewel in the crown of the British Empire, as a necessary civilizing force that would transform India, making the nation Britain's greatest colonial acquisition.

Speaking to the British Empire's interests, Kipling became a popular name throughout British India during his appointment at *The Civil and Military Gazette* in 1887. After moving to Allahabad in 1887, Kipling took up his position at *The Pioneer Mail*, a publication with a reputation for "fearless reporting...for covering news on a national rather than parochial basis."[16] Commissioned in 1887 to travel throughout the north Indian state of Rajputana (present day Rajasthan), Kipling documented his experiences in the Princely (Native) State. These writings on his escapades in the north were published as the series "Letters," the title of a naval reference to ships decreed under government ordinance to function as privateers and condemn other ships, taking them and their bounty as prizes. It is a reference that one critic, Jan Montefiore, calls a "joke."[17] Biographer Harry Ricketts, on the other hand, observes that the reference identifies Kipling himself as "a kind of journalistic privateer, licensed to raid foreign lands for newspaper booty," which is an apt criticism, since Kipling, notoriously tongue-in-cheek, fulfills his journalistic-cum-privateering mission with imperial fervor as he collects

---

15. Lord Birkenhead, *Rudyard Kipling: The Long-Suppressed Biography* (New York: Random House, 1978), 56, 69.

16. Birkenhead, *Rudyard Kipling*, 58.

17. Jan Montefiore, "Vagabondage in Rajasthan: Kipling's North Indian Travels," in *In Time's Eye: Essays on Rudyard Kipling*, ed. Jan Montefiore (Manchester, UK: Manchester University Press, 2013), 159.

experiences in Rajputana, a state that had not yet been absorbed into British India, but that had accepted the British paramountcy in the region.[18]

Using the mode of travel writing, which relies on a colonial planetary consciousness that situates the author as an expert, or one in possession of a particular territory, Kipling engages in a complex dialogue with the powers of imperialism and those subordinate to it, as the "Letters" contain glimpses of condemnations of a land that is so unlike his own. Though he would identify himself as Anglo-Indian, Kipling's anxiety regarding the subcontinent is visible throughout the "Letters" as he toggles between disgust and bafflement at its people, and fascination and dread regarding its ancient history and India's transition into modernity, with nineteenth-century British values. "Kipling's attitude to India," Martin Seymour-Smith writes, "was torn in two: reverence for the ancient, mysterious and wise…and contempt for its political childishness,"[19] particularly demonstrated in the second and third chapters of the "Letters," in which Kipling describes the Indian land as ancient, empty, and exotic, and, ultimately, unbefitting of contemporary Indian subjects:

> A somewhat extensive experience of palace-seeing had taught him [Kipling] that it is best to see palaces alone, for the Oriental as a guide is undiscriminating and sets too great a store on corrugated iron roofs and glazed drainpipes.…The modern side of Jaipur must not be mixed with the ancient.[20]

Kipling was unable to participate in any wars himself due to his poor eyesight. His "Letters," with their vision of India as a prize to be raided, is his compensation as a "man of action" in the midst of imperial strategy. His journalistic privateering authorizes him as an ideologue of the British imperial project, enabling him to "give back" to his nation's

18. Harry Ricketts, *The Unforgiving Minute: A Life of Rudyard Kipling* (London: Chatto & Windus, 1999), 104.

19. Martin Seymour-Smith, *Rudyard Kipling* (London: Queen Anne Press, 1989), 76.

20. Kipling, Rudyard, "Letters of Marque – III," *Dalhousie Libraries Digital Exhibits*, accessed December 27, 2018, https://digitalexhibits.library.dal.ca/items/show/376.

mission of expansion by witnessing India's transformation under colonial rule. Kipling found a hungry audience in his Anglo-Indian readers, since few works at the time represented, according to Lord Birkenhead, India's "exotic surroundings to kindle the imagination."[21] But Kipling's representations of India and social propriety aided in the production of a new middle-class sensibility that, dependent on myths of racial purity, sexual virtue, and masculinity, were instrumental to the broad support of imperial rule in the colonies.[22] Kipling's descriptions in the "Letters" recount his experiences of and attitudes about India, tourism, and the British national identity. Charged with the task of defining the spectacle of India's colonization, Kipling became uniquely positioned to hold the British national imagination by firmly grasping and defining the imperial project and its self-proclaimed responsibilities in India.[23] Such visions of India and Britain's imperial dominance are contained within Kipling's "Letters" and the Garth Scrapbook, in which the original newsprints are carefully preserved.

Collections such as the Kipling Scrapbooks, which are preserved as a part of library special collections, are unique, not only for the content of the collections themselves, but also for the practices that surround such collections. Special collections occupy a peculiar position between memory institutions[24]; while they are usually housed by libraries, they do not provide the individual, unmediated experience that most library visits offer. Consequently, they cannot be treated the same as archival collections that originate organically from records produced in the course of a person's or organization's life, as they result from the active collection efforts of agents.[25] Because of this, special collections are more similar to museum collections: curated, highly mediated, and requiring

21. Birkenhead, *Rudyard Kipling*, 96.

22. Mueggler, *The Paper Road*, 48.

23. Birkenhead, *Rudyard Kipling*, 93.

24. Libraries, archives, and museums. Also referred to as GLAMs when galleries are included.

25. Yeo, "The Conceptual Fonds," 45.

contextualization to clarify the elements behind their creation. As a result, their placement within libraries and management by library professionals can prove troublesome. Offers Jennifer Trant: "Very different assumptions about patrons' needs and their preferred methods of interaction are embedded in the practices of libraries, archives, and museums and the systems that support them."[26] Treating special collections which contain contested material—such as the Kipling Collection—in the same way as other library resources that are provided without context for users to engage with and interpret individually, too closely resembles a celebration and approval of that collection's content. Libraries that wish to present such material respectfully and accurately need more than what is typically provided by standard library collections: basic bibliographic description, placement in library catalogues, and unlimited access, either in a physical location or digital collection—or, more than the simple point-of-entry the Kipling Scrapbooks Digital Exhibit was initially envisioned to be. They must also employ practices from other memory institutions, including justification for the selection of particular materials from the collection, and contextualization and critical engagement on a larger scale than is usually employed by libraries and archives.

The need to contextualize, mediate, and curate special collections comes to the foreground in the creation of digital exhibits. Users have ever-increasing expectations for digital collections and exhibits: "Providing access is no longer enough—libraries, archives, and museums are expected to enable the discovery, collation, use, and representation of the content they hold."[27] Representation is especially crucial for special collections' digital exhibits like the Kipling Scrapbooks Digital Exhibit, as presentation without opinion has the potential to be received as acceptance or even celebration of problematic materials from the hosting institution, even if it is not intended as such. Memory institutions have been grappling with these issues for some time, both within

26. Jennifer Trant, "Emerging Convergence? Thoughts on Museums, Archives, Libraries, and Professional Training," *Museum Management and Curatorship* 24, no. 4 (2009): 372, https://doi.org/10.1080/09647770903314738.

27. Trant, "Emerging Convergence," 375.

and beyond digital spaces. In 2004, Canada went so far as to merge its national library and archives into a single institution, Library and Archives Canada, which includes both library and archives and provides many of the functions of a museum.[28] This "arose from the vision of a new kind of knowledge organization, fully integrated between two disciplines, and equipped to respond to the information demands of the 21st century."[29] Part of these information demands include addressing the contestation of Kipling in relation to today's political and social justice climate and allowing for discussion from multiple voices and viewpoints. As such, it is appropriate that the Kipling Scrapbooks Digital Exhibit project was undertaken by an interdisciplinary team, with specialties in digital humanities, digitization, archives, and literary and critical analysis, using a digital platform at a Canadian university. In moving beyond solely providing access, like a library or archives, and by providing engagement, interaction, and scholarship around the Kipling Collection, the Kipling Scrapbooks Digital Exhibit aims to provide engagement, interaction, and scholarship around the collections through the framing and manifestation of the digital exhibit as a digital humanities project: digital and open access, collaborative and cross-disciplinary, and inviting discussion and debate.

Part of this invitation prompted the decision to include a disclaimer on the exhibit, alerting users to Kipling's often problematic assessments of India and Indian peoples. Because the very nature of the scrapbooks themselves makes them products of the curatorial approaches of those who compiled them, understanding the scrapbooks' collectors was another necessary component of the project. It is clear that the collectors of the scrapbooks held Kipling's works in high esteem; however, a more contemporary approach to Kipling's works reveals a need to

28. Lisa Given and Lianne McTavish, "What's Old Is New Again: The Reconvergence of Libraries, Archives, and Museums in the Digital Age," *Library Quarterly* 80, no. 1 (January 2010): 7.

29. Guy Berthiaume, "Rethinking the Role of Libraries and Archives and Museums in the Age of Google," Library and Archives Canada, last modified January 30, 2018, https://www.canada.ca/en/library-archives/news/2017/07/rethinking_the_roleoflibrariesandarchivesandmuseumsintheageofgoo.html.

frame these estimations more appropriately, especially with respect to Kipling's views on race and his depictions of the people who were often the subject of his writings. In developing the digital exhibit, the team took into consideration that the exhibit should not be seen as venerating Kipling and his works, but rather providing context around them. The disclaimer reads:

> The "Letters of Marque" by Rudyard Kipling are products of their time and contain representations of racial and ethnic prejudices that were conventional during Kipling's life, although no less harmful and inaccurate than they are today. The views that Kipling depicts in his "Letters" are presented as originally published in *The Pioneer Mail*.[30]

Including this disclaimer addresses the contestation of Kipling's writings, drawing attention to the exhibit's purpose of critically framing his writings in the context of postcolonial and decolonial critiques.

Projects like the Kipling Scrapbooks Digital Exhibit exemplify the key strengths that libraries bring to digital humanities projects: digitization facilities and expertise, project management, technical infrastructure support, preservation assistance, as well as various forms of other technical support and information management expertise.[31] It was through already mature digitization facilities and established digitization procedures that Dalhousie Libraries was able to pursue this project.[32] The Dalhousie Libraries had already undertaken considerable digitization as a part of its archives' efforts, although less had been done to digitize special collections. Project management and technical expertise, alongside server

---

30. Dalhousie University Libraries, "Disclaimer," https://digitalexhibits.library.dal.ca/exhibits/show/kipling-scrapbooks/about/disclaimer.

31. Shun Han and Rebekah Wong, "Digital Humanities: What Can Libraries Offer?" *Portal: Libraries & the Academy* 16, no. 4 (2016): 684, https://doi.org/10.1353/pla.2016.0046.

32. The Dalhousie Libraries digitization workflows are made available as a part of its Digital Collections Handbook: https://dallibraries.atlassian.net/wiki/spaces/DCH/overview.

infrastructure able to run and maintain an open source platform like Omeka, were also key elements that made this project possible.[33]

The combined expertise of the project staff was another important element that demonstrates the value of reaching beyond the professional practices and knowledge of a singular memory institution for projects. Research backgrounds and expertise in literature, combined with staff experienced in digitization, information management, and digital humanities projects, played a vital role in realizing the project. The detailed knowledge and expertise of Dalhousie's special collections librarian further complemented the project team. Indeed, projects of this nature are highly collaborative, borrowing from a wide array of skill-sets and expertise. As Trant states:

> Whatever their subject matter, professionals in libraries, archives, and museums will increasingly need to work together to meet challenges of digital collections creation, management, use and preservation because the underlying problems of digital collections management and integrated network use are shared and the public policy view of their roles is unified.[34]

Digital humanities have intersected with the use of digitized special collections in particular. As noted in *A New Companion to Digital Humanities*, "The use of digital content, tools, and methods is transforming humanities research through greater access to materials and new modes of collaboration and communication."[35] Libraries have long been keen to digitize and provide access to archival and special collections material, which is unquestionably crucial work. However, inviting conversation and scholarship around said digitized material is just as important. Positioning digital special collections material in such a way that it can be interacted with (and contested and debated) allows for greater engagement and learning. Librarian and Archivist of Canada,

33. The Kipling Scrapbooks Digital Exhibit was developed on the Omeka platform—a web publishing platform commonly used for the development of digital exhibits. More information on Omeka can be found at https://omeka.org.

34. Trant, "Emerging Convergence," 383.

35. Lorna Hughes, Panos Constantopoulus, and Costis Dallas, "Digital Methods in the Humanities: Understanding and Describing their Use across the Disciplines," in *A New Companion to Digital Humanities*, eds. Susan Schreibman, Raymond George Siemens, and John Unsworth (Malden, MA : Chichester, Wiley/Blackwell, 2016), 153.

Guy Berthiaume, calls memory institutions "places where connections can be made, where collaboration can take place, where history can be understood, and where the future can be imagined."[36] The online environment particularly allows for many of these opportunities by inviting a broader range of users than the physical space of a single memory institution, and by providing a platform for contextualization and discussion.

One key advantage of digital exhibits (as opposed to print scholarship) is their ability to be expanded over time. The Kipling Scrapbooks Digital Exhibit focused on just one small aspect of the Kipling Collection—the scrapbooks, specifically, the original "Letters" newsprint featured in the Garth Scrapbook. The "Letters" were chosen as the focus of the exhibit for several reasons. First, they were a self-contained subset of the scrapbook content that was succinct enough to be digitized and integrated into the exhibit within the limited timeframe for the project. Second, their physical condition was good enough to enable easy digitization and Optical Character Recognition (OCR), allowing for full text searching. Finally, the travel narrative and chronological layout of the "Letters" provided multiple visualization opportunities for the exhibit that allowed users to interact with the materials in multiple ways. This was necessary for several reasons: first, even within the Kipling Scrapbooks, there was such a wide range of material that it was necessary for the team to focus its efforts on a singular aspect. The Garth Scrapbook provided the greatest opportunity for a succinct, complete, and interactive digital exhibit, one that yet offers possibilities of eventual expansion. By digitizing the scrapbooks and carrying out steps that facilitated access to the text contained therein, there is the possibility for expansion to other materials contained within the scrapbooks or creation of future digital exhibits. Although there are no immediate plans to expand the exhibit, the project lays the groundwork for further engagement with the scrapbooks as source material for further analysis and scholarship.

---

36. Berthiaume, "Rethinking the Role of Libraries and Archives and Museums in the Age of Google."

This fits well with the potential of the open-ended nature of digital scholarship (and thus digital humanities), allowing for the incorporation of new findings and documents.[37]

In constructing the Kipling Scrapbooks Digital Exhibit, the team—comprised of this chapter's authors—wanted to not only present the digitized scrapbooks and the context surrounding them, but to do so with some measure of visual interest and innovation. Working within the limitations and features offered by the Omeka platform through which the digital exhibit was created, we considered the visual and interactive elements that would necessarily shape an exhibit that supported a critical contextualization of Kipling's writings, while also demonstrating the influence and scope of his works. This took the shape of a timeline and map of Kipling's "Letters," done through Neatline, "an interactive tool for telling stories using maps, timelines."[38] Digital mapping is a key method within digital humanities to visualize and present information using, as Lorna Hughes, Panos Constantopoulus, and Costis Dallas note: "historical mapping of 'time-layers' to memory maps, linguistic and cultural mapping, conceptual mapping, community-based mapping, and forms of counter-mapping that attempt to de-ontologize cartography and imagine new worlds."[39] With critical theory on imperial cartographies in mind during the initial construction of the exhibit, the significance of relying on maps as a visual interface for the exhibit became evident. The Neatline map in the Kipling Scrapbooks Digital Exhibit provides an interactive display of Kipling's "Letters" using spatial and chronological elements to highlight his movement through India's interior from 1887 to 1888. It likewise displays a visual cue to the research component of the exhibit dedicated to the historical development of tourism and travel

37. Jennifer Edmond, "Collaboration and Infrastructure," in *A New Companion to Digital Humanities*, eds. Susan Schreibman, Raymond George Siemens, and John Unsworth (Malden, MA: Chichester, Wiley/Blackwell, 2016), 61.

38. Neatline is a suite of plugins for the Omeka platform that allow for spatial and temporal interpretation. For more information on Neatline, see https://neatline.org.

39. Todd Presner and David Sheperd, "Mapping the Geospatial Turn," in *A New Companion to Digital Humanities*, eds. Susan Schreibman, Raymond George Siemens, and John Unsworth (Malden, MA: Chichester, Wiley/Blackwell, 2016), 202.

writing. The exhibit's map, therefore, contained a crucial dual function: to visually represent the reach of Britain's colonization in India and Kipling's travels within that nation, and to signal the role that mapping plays in colonizing – as well as decolonizing – already bordered spaces.

The painstaking drawing of borders in Neatline, however, revealed yet another limitation in Omeka: drawing even a relatively accurate overlay onto the Neatline map was a consuming endeavor, and due to the limited time afforded the project as a whole, it was impossible to visually represent the extent of British India's power in the subcontinent. Even so, the map provides two visual overlays: the state through which Kipling traveled for his commission, Rajputana, now Rajasthan, and the westernmost portion of India, West Bengal (see **Figure 2**). For this reason, a small disclaimer is featured in the dialogue box for this latter region of the map—"Note: While British India did indeed colonize much of India, for the purpose of this exhibit, British India is visually constrained to the region of West Bengal, in which the British Raj, and the East India Company before it, held its headquarters in Calcutta (present-day Kolkata)"—as a recognition that British India's control was not geographically limited to West Bengal. As Mary Louise Pratt writes in *Imperial Eyes*, "the systematic surface mapping of the globe correlates with an expanding search for commercially exploitable resources, markets, and lands to colonize,"[40] demonstrated through the consistent revision of eighteenth- and nineteenth-century maps of India. Redeploying this cartographic habit to contest Kipling's perspective of India and the alleged supremacy of the lettered white British male, the Neatline map and visual overlays resist a neutral envisioning of Kipling. The visual and textual dialogue contained within the exhibit points to the layered conceptions of bordered spaces and the historical narratives embedded within and surrounding them, while also signaling the spread of the British Empire's knowledge formation in the nineteenth century. The hybridity of the exhibit's paratextual content—historical maps and

---

40. Mary Louise Pratt, *Imperial Eyes: Travel Writing and Transculturation*, 2nd ed. (London: New York: Routledge, 2008), 30.

an overview of India and the British Empire, and images of the sites Kipling visited—additionally interrupts an impartial framing of Kipling's travels through India during the time of Britain's dominance and indicates that any neutral contextualization of contested colonial figures like Kipling are, indeed, highly political and fundamentally non-neutral choices. Repositioning Kipling, thus, within the context of postcolonial and decolonial frameworks using a contemporary map of India, a nation that is still encumbered by the lingering impacts of colonial rule, dialogically blends digital mapping with critical contextualization, hence inviting greater reflection regarding the works of Kipling.

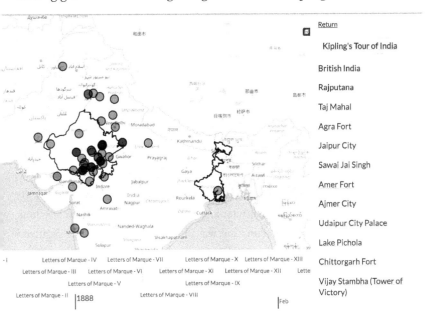

Figure 2. A screenshot of the map from the Kipling Scrapbooks Digital Exhibit.[41]

Metadata standards and systems for digital library projects have elements in common with both the traditional library catalogue record and archival finding aids. Most assume that digital items will be described at

41. The map and timeline can be viewed at https://digitalexhibits.library.dal.ca/exhibits/show/kipling-scrapbooks/map-and-timeline.

the item level. They do, however, include structural and relational metadata that provides for the description of complex digital objects and for
the definition of relationships between objects. Creating metadata for
digital library purposes is a time-consuming and expensive process, as
more traditional forms of metadata can require extensive reworking and
enhancing to meet the needs of the online environment and its users.
Metadata for projects like the Kipling Scrapbooks Digital Exhibit and
the material it contains is especially tricky, as it must attempt to accurately represent the material and make it accessible to the widest possible
audience without providing any biases about its problematic contents.

Metadata for both the fully digitized scrapbooks uploaded to Dalhousie's institutional repository and the items included in the digital exhibit
was kept clear and simple for maximum searchability. Only neutral
subject headings were used in the digital repository to avoid making
any statements in the metadata: "Rudyard Kipling," "Travelogues," and
"British Travel Writing" were used for the Garth Scrapbook containing the "Letters," and "Rudyard Kipling" and "Scrapbooks" were used
for the other scrapbooks. This allowed for maximum searchability, and
confined any interpretation of the material to the exhibit itself, which
would not bar access to any potential users. The most intensive portion of the digital exhibit metadata, and perhaps the most rewarding,
was providing full text searching for all of the "Letters." The digitized
Letters were run through ABBYY Finereader for initial OCR, and then
were edited manually for cleanliness and accuracy. The process was as
time-consuming as one would expect, and would likely not be feasible
for larger-scale projects. For the scope of the Kipling Scrapbooks Digital
Exhibit, however, it provided a richness of searching not possible with
subject headings and keywords alone. Users can search a line of text
from a "Letter" and be directed to the exhibit (it appears in the first
page of Google results), which provides access to another level of users
who may not understand how to search with subject headings or even
know the author of the piece they are searching.

The metadata includes a Creative Commons Attribution 4.0 International License, indicating to users how the material in the exhibit

and digitized scrapbooks can be used. Jones notes the "openness with which we allow our collections to be used by the public,"[42] which is just as important in the physical realm as it is in the digital realm. There are limitations for the physical materials in special collections in terms of the degree to which they can be examined by users, often due to their fragile and unique nature and the requirement for specialized care and handling. These same limitations, however, are usually not the case for digital surrogates of the physical items, as digital files can be used without running the risk of damaging the material. In a similar vein, and related to Jones's point, the openness with which we allow our collections to be used by the public must also be considered. As special collections and archives are involved in digitizing their collections, the question of how special collections/archives enable use by the public and the uses they permit users to engage in with their digital collections must be asked. This determines how well (and accurately) libraries clarify the copyright status of such material, how they license it, and how they communicate this to users. Making it clear to users that they may reuse digital objects in their own research—i.e., giving explicit permission to do so—is important, as users may wish to use the digital objects in a variety of ways, some of which are not anticipated by the creators of the digital collection. Clearly stating the copyright status of digital objects and noting that reuse of digital objects is allowed offers users much more than just being able to view the items; it enables users to take them and reuse them for their own purposes.

For opening up special collections, "[t]he proper use and application of open licenses provides a fundamental bedrock to an open approach."[43] Further, Gill Hamilton and Fred Saunderson write that using open licenses "is particularly relevant for public organisations and those dealing in faithful reproductions of works that are themselves intellectually

---

42. Jones, "Hidden Collections, Scholarly Barriers," 91.

43. Gill Hamilton and Fred Saunderson, *Open Licensing for Cultural Heritage* (London, UK: Facet Publishing 2017), 69.

in the public domain (out-of-copyright and related rights.)"[44] This was certainly the case with the Kipling Scrapbooks, as the age of the material put the material in the public domain. When putting the fully digitized scrapbooks online in the institutions' digital repository (Dalspace), it was ensured that the items' public domain status was noted in the rights metadata field, with a public domain dedication mark.[45]

Applying public domain labels and open licensing, such as Creative Commons, to digital collections is still a growing area, but there are a large number of cultural heritage organizations pursuing open licensing policies with their digital collections.[46] It was important for the purposes of the Kipling Collection that digitized material that was in the public domain remain in the public domain.[47] There is still debate in many jurisdictions as to whether the digitizing of public domain works constitutes the creation of a new work and thus a new copyright, but employing open licensing that is true to the nature of the copyright status of the items being digitized is an approach being employed by many cultural heritage organizations. For the purposes of this project, it was crucial that the resulting digitized works be made available as open access resources, as well as available in the public domain for any and all who wish to reuse them.

This project was made possible through funds provided through an endowment fund geared specifically towards activities associated with the Kipling Collection. Like many digitization projects, there is a flurry of short-term effort and then the project is completed and set aside to make room for other projects. This project had to be completed in the span of approximately five months, limiting what could be accomplished.

---

44. Hamilton and Saunderson, *Open Licensing for Cultural Heritage*, 70.

45. The Creative Commons Public Domain Dedication for items in the public domain can be viewed at https://creativecommons.org/publicdomain/zero/1.0/.

46. The Open GLAM survey documents open licensing policies in place in various cultural heritage organizations: https://t.co/vqKmXWvSzq.

47. Jane Park, "For Faithful Digital Reproductions of Public Domain Works Use CC0." *Creative Commons* (blog), January 23, 2015. https://creativecommons.org/2015/01/23/for-faithful-digital-reproductions-of-public-domain-works-use-cc0/.

Staffing for projects of this nature tends to be short-term and based on using contract staff with funds not devoted to employing staff on an ongoing basis for doing digital humanities projects. The precarity of staffing is quite typical of digital humanities projects being carried out in libraries, given the nature of librarians who often have roles that extend beyond digital humanities, and the nature of staffing in digital humanities projects, i.e., people who are usually on contract and grant-funded.[48] For this particular project, the project team focused on carrying out the digitization of the scrapbooks (and the necessary work entailed in that, i.e., digitization, metadata, and OCR) and the contextualization of the "Letters" specifically because it could be exhibited within the digital exhibit and completed within the limited timespan of the project. This speaks to the larger issues around digital humanities projects of this nature: they tend to ebb and flow depending on available funding, and those with skill-sets in digital humanities are not always available to carry out this work.

One additional limitation of this project was the availability of a Kipling scholar who shared the same vision for the project as the team. Ideally, the project team would have included a faculty member with an interest both in digital humanities and Kipling or nineteenth-century British literature. Given the short-term nature of the project, this was not achievable and became a constraint for the project, limiting the critical scope of its contextualization endeavor. The time limits imposed by having short-term contract staff also meant that the project required clear focus on a single aspect of the collection, even though the material in the Kipling Collection lends itself to a wide range of exhibition possibilities. The nature of this project demonstrates that short-term and funding-dependent digital humanities projects are limited in their abilities to be expanded over time to include more scholarship relevant to special collections.

---

48. Miriam Posner, "No Half Measures: Overcoming Common Challenges to Doing Digital Humanities in the library," *Journal of Library Administration* 53, no. 1 (2013): 44.

It is possible that future projects for Dalhousie Libraries' Kipling Collection may be explored, since this project has laid the ground-work for future digital humanities work using the Kipling Scrapbooks. Facilitating the readability of scrapbooks' text using OCR can serve as a basis for future projects, such as textual analysis of Kipling's writings. Such work would be suited to collaborations that might occur between faculty members or researchers with appropriate research backgrounds and interest in doing such analyses, and the Dalhousie Libraries.[49] While typically digitization projects carried out by the Dalhousie Libraries do not extend beyond the creation of digital images of the materials, providing critical context, in addition to digitization, was a key part of this project. Making the text of the Kipling Scrapbooks searchable and, consequently, better suited to textual analysis, was a shift in the approach taken by many digitization projects, demonstrating the additional schol-arly possibilities afforded by digital humanities exhibition projects.[50]

However, an issue associated with digital humanities projects of this nature is their open-endedness and the challenge of maintaining them past the libraries' or other sponsoring institutions' lifetimes. Many digital humanities projects fall into disrepair over the years, as legacy systems maintained by libraries or other sponsoring bodies may no longer be operational, or the web technology on which the project was based becomes outdated. This is a growing area of concern for libraries and the digital humanities community.[51] Dalhousie Libraries has recognized this to some degree, as it works to develop its own digital preservation program that will help preserve sites such as the Kipling Scrapbooks

---

49. Faculty-library collaborations are key ways that libraries are engaged in digital humanities projects. Chris Alen Sula, "Digital Humanities and Libraries: A Conceptual Model," *Journal of Library Administration* 53, no. 1 (2013): 10-26.

50. Digitizing collections and making them suited to textual analysis or other forms of digital humanities projects involves taking a "Collections as Data" approach, whereby libraries strive to not only provide access to digitized images, but also encour-age the reuse of collections in order to support computational-driven research and teaching in areas including but not limited to the digital humanities. The "Collections as Data" project can be found here: https://collectionsasdata.github.io/.

51. Projects like "The Endings Project" examine issues around sustainability in digi-tal humanities projects: https://projectendings.github.io/.

Digital Exhibit. Moreover, the items digitized (i.e., the Kipling Scrapbooks) are stored in Dalhousie Libraries' digital repository, Dalspace, and will undergo digital preservation workflows, which may help the longevity of the digital objects created in the course of the project. The fate of some of the other outputs of the project, especially the more interactive aspects of the site, such as the Neatline map and the timeline, are less certain as they hinge on the ongoing functionality of the Omeka platform, as well as Dalhousie Libraries' desire and commitment to support digital humanities projects over the long term.

While such preservation efforts are in development across the digital humanities, the work of questioning the role of libraries in supporting troubling special collections must continue as access to these collections is opened. Without providing both access to and context surrounding such collections, the societal and cultural value previously afforded these works may experience a redundancy, making them no longer relevant for contemporary study. The digital humanities offer special collections a departure from many library and archival practices, and it is this departure, as demonstrated by the Kipling Scrapbooks Digital Exhibit that equips digital exhibit projects with the ability to engage in social justice discourse and provide new critical opportunities for literary, cultural, and library scholars. It was important to the project team that Kipling's colonial opinions not be reinstated through the digital exhibit, but be offered instead using a critical framework and carefully chosen digital exhibit interfaces and interactions to challenge those colonial attitudes, while continuing to present works belonging to the Kipling Collection as they truly are. In this way, the Kipling Scrapbooks Digital Exhibit meets the definition of access, while also offering the collection as a valuable resource for social justice discourse and contemporary critical engagement.

Bibliography

Berthiaume, Guy. "Rethinking the Role of Libraries and Archives and Museums in the Age of Google." Library and Archives Canada. Last modified January 30, 2018. https://www.canada.ca/en/library-archives/news/2017/07/rethinking_the_roleoflibrariesandarchives-andmuseumsintheageofgoo.html.

Bourg, Chris. "The Library is Never Neutral." In *Disrupting the Digital Humanities*, edited by Jessie Stommel and Dorothy Kim, 455-71. Santa Barbara, CA: Punctum Books, 2018.

Edmond, Jennifer. "Collaboration and Infrastructure." In *A New Companion to Digital Humanities*, edited by Susan Schreibman, Raymond George Siemens, and John Unsworth, 54-66. Malden, MA: Wiley/Blackwell, 2016.

Given, Lisa, and Lianne McTavish. "What's Old Is New Again: The Reconvergence of Libraries, Archives, and Museums in the Digital Age." *Library Quarterly* 80, no. 1 (January, 2010): 7-32. https://doi.org/10.1086/648461.

Hamilton, Gill, and Fred Saunderson. *Open Licensing for Cultural Heritage*. London, UK: Facet Publishing, 2017.

Han, Shun, and Rebekah Wong. "Digital Humanities: What Can Libraries Offer?" *Portal: Libraries & the Academy* 16, no. 4 (2016): 669-90. https://doi.org/10.1353/pla.2016.0046.

Hughes, Lorna, Panos Constantopoulos, and Costis Dallas. "Digital Methods in the Humanities: Understanding and Describing their Use across the Disciplines." In *A New Companion to Digital Humanities*, edited by Susan Schreibman, Raymond George Siemens, and John Unsworth, 150-70. Malden, MA: Wiley/Blackwell, 2016.

Jones, Barbara. "Hidden Collections, Scholarly Barriers: Creating Access to Unprocessed Special Collections in America's Research Libraries." *RBM: A Journal of Rare Books, Manuscripts, and Cultural Heritage* 5, no. 2 (2004): 88-105. https://doi.org/10.5860/rbm.5.2.230.

Kipling, Rudyard. "Letters of Marque—III." In Dalhousie Libraries Digital Exhibits, accessed December 27, 2018, https://digitalexhibits. library.dal.ca/items/show/376.

Lord Birkenhead, Frederick Winston Furneaux Smith. *Rudyard Kipling: The Long-Suppressed Biography.* New York: Random House, 1978.

Montefiore, Jan. "Vagabondage in Rajasthan: Kipling's North Indian Travels." In *In Time's Eye: Essays on Rudyard Kipling,* edited by Jan Montefiore, 159-76. Manchester, England: Manchester University Press, 2013.

Mueggler, Erik. *The Paper Road: Archive and Experience in the Botanical Exploration of West China and Tibet.* Berkeley, CA: University of California Press, 2011.

Park, Jane. "For Faithful Digital Reproductions of Public Domain Works Use CC0." *Creative Commons* (blog), Last modified January 23, 2015. https://creativecommons.org/2015/01/23/for-faithful-digital-reproductions-of-public-domain-works-use-cc0/.

Posner, Miriam. "No Half Measures: Overcoming Common Challenges to Doing Digital Humanities in the library." *Journal of Library Administration* 53, no. 1 (2013): 42-52.

Pratt, Mary Louise. *Imperial Eyes: Travel Writing and Transculturation.* 2nd ed. London: New York: Routledge, 2008.

Presner, Todd, and David Shepard. "Mapping the Geospatial Turn." In *A New Companion to Digital Humanities,* edited by Susan Schreibman, Raymond George Siemens, and John Unsworth, 201-12. Malden, MA: Wiley/Blackwell, 2016.

Ricketts, Harry. *The Unforgiving Minute: A Life of Rudyard Kipling.* London: Chatto & Windus, 1999.

Risam, Roopika. *New Digital Worlds: Postcolonial Digital Humanities in Theory, Praxis, and Pedagogy.* Evanston, IL: Northwestern University Press, 2018.

Seymour-Smith, Martin. *Rudyard Kipling*. London: Queen Anne Press, 1989.

Smith, Karen. *Vessels of Light: A Guide to Special Collections in the Killam Library, Dalhousie University Libraries*. Halifax, NS: Dalhousie University Libraries, 1996.

Trant, Jennifer. "Emerging Convergence? Thoughts on Museums, Archives, Libraries, and Professional Training." *Museum Management and Curatorship* 24, no. 4 (2009): 369-87. https://doi.org/10.1080/09647770903314738.

Yeats, A.W. "The Stewart Kipling Collection and Some Notes on Its Significance." *Dalhousie Review* 36, no. 2, (1956): 112-15.

Yeo, Geoffrey. "The Conceptual Fonds and the Physical Collection." *Archivaria* 73 (Spring 2012): 43-80.

Chapter 14

CONTROVERSY AND CAMPUS LEGACIES: A UNIVERSITY ARCHIVES CAUGHT IN THE CROSSFIRE

Anne S.K. Turkos and Jason G. Speck

The last several years have seen a number of pitched battles on college and university campuses over buildings named for historical figures who engaged in causes or behaviors that modern society abhors. In February 2017, Yale University changed the name of a dormitory that previously honored pro-slavery politician John C. Calhoun to that of alumna Grace Murray Hopper, a pioneering computer scientist and rear admiral in the U.S. Navy.[1] Later that same year, officials at Georgetown University in Washington, D.C. announced that two campus buildings named for former presidents who sold slaves to pay school debt would be renamed.[2] At the University of Michigan, two buildings were renamed in early 2018, removing the names of a former university president who championed eugenics, as well as a professor whose theories are championed by white

---

1. "Yale to Change Calhoun College's Name to Honor Grace Murray Hopper," *YaleNews*, February 11, 2017, accessed May 20, 2019, https://news.yale.edu/2017/02/11/yale-change-calhoun-college-s-name-honor-grace-murray-hopper.

2. Ian Simpson, "Georgetown University Renames Buildings to Atone for Slavery Ties," Reuters, April 18, 2017, accessed May 20, 2019, https://www.reuters.com/article/us-washingtondc-georgetown-slavery/georgetown-university-renames-buildings-to-atone-for-slavery-ties-idUSKBN17K2AR.

supremacists.[3] The University of Scranton changed the names of three buildings, removing references to Catholic priests linked to sex abuse cases in Pennsylvania that filled the news in late summer 2018.[4]

Not all of these battles have resulted in successful renaming. At Clemson University and Winthrop University, name change groups have been unsuccessful in removing the name of white supremacist, lynching advocate, and former Governor Benjamin Ryan Tillman from their respective campuses, in no small part due to a South Carolina state law that makes doing so nearly impossible.[5] Clemson officials did agree to erect historical signs describing the role of African American prison labor in the construction of campus buildings; these signs, however, make very little mention of slavery and its interconnections with Clemson's origins.[6] At Winthrop, they removed the image of Tillman Hall from the university's logo.[7] The University of North Carolina imposed a sixteen-year moratorium on renaming buildings after changing Saunders Hall, named for alleged Ku Klux Klan leader William Saunders, to Carolina Hall, in 2015, leaving the name of noted white supremacist and former Governor Charles Aycock in place.[8]

3. Lauren Love, "U-M to Remove Little, Winchell Names from Campus Facilities," *The University Record*, March 29, 2018, accessed May 20, 2019, https://record.umich.edu/articles/u-m-remove-little-winchell-names-campus-facilities.

4. Bobby Allyn, "Names of Accused Bishops to Be Removed rom Buildings at 2 Catholic Pa. Colleges," National Public Radio, August 22, 2018, accessed May 20, 2019, https://www.npr.org/2018/08/22/640904769/names-of-accused-bishops-to-come-down-at-university-of-scranton.

5. Nathaniel Cary, "Clemson Not Alone in Debate over Renaming Tillman Hall," *USA Today*, March 10, 2015, accessed May 20, 2019, https://www.usatoday.com/story/news/education/2015/03/09/clemson-alone-debate-renaming-tillman-hall/24666467/.

6. Cathy Sams, "New Signs Installed as Part of Board's 'Clemson History' Plan," *The Newsstand*, January 10, 2018, accessed May 20, 2019, http://newsstand.clemson.edu/mediarelations/new-signs-installed-as-part-of-boards-clemson-history-plan/; Georgie Silvarole, "Here's How New Signs Share Clemson University's 'Complete' History," The State, January 14, 2018, accessed May 20, 2019. https://www.thestate.com/news/local/article194640944.html.

7. Tea Franco, "New Logo: A Different Perspective," *MY TJ Now*, March 20, 2018, accessed May 20, 2019, http://mytjnow.com/2018/03/01/new-logo-different-perspective/.

8. "Trustees Rename Saunders Hall, Freeze Renamings for 16 Years," *Carolina*

In some cases, efforts of varying kinds are being made to accede to demands for change by naming more areas or structures for people of color, most often African Americans. Washington and Lee University renamed two buildings for notable African Americans connected to the university and committed itself to a holistic review of Robert E. Lee's presence on campus, in order to more accurately reflect his role as a former president, rather than celebrating him as a Confederate general.[9] In 2018, Duke University began discussions to rename a building, currently dedicated to a racist donor, for the first African American history professor on the campus.[10] Two years earlier, Vanderbilt University formally changed the name of Confederate Memorial Hall to simply "Memorial Hall," after being forced by the state of Tennessee to return a $50,000 donation the Daughters of the Confederacy made in 1933, which, after appreciation, ended up costing the university $1.2 million.[11]

In looking for literature on this topic, one is as likely to come across it in law or sociology journals as within archival journals. To understand how we have arrived at this moment in history, we must examine the following: the purpose and validity of archives in discussions of contestation and memory; how contentious debates regarding memory are/are not resolved; and the general origin of the monuments and memorializations that have led to many of the current campus debates involving race. This provides a platform to understand the issues at

---

Alumni Review, May 28, 2015, accessed May 20, 2019, https://alumni.unc.edu/news/trustees-vote-to-rename-saunders-hall-put-16-year-freeze-on-renamings/.

9. Washington and Lee University, "Report of The Commission on Institutional History and Community," May 2, 2018, accessed May 20, 2019, https://www.wlu.edu/presidents-office/issues-and-initiatives/commission-on-institutional-history-and-community/report-of-the-commission-on-institutional-history-and-community.

10. Delaney Dryfoos, "The History Department Wants to Rename the Carr Building for Him, So Who Was Raymond Gavins?" *The Chronicle*, October 25, 2018, accessed May 20, 2019, https://www.dukechronicle.com/article/2018/10/raymond-gavins-legacy-a-look-at-the-man-behind-the-proposed-new-name-for-the-carr-building.

11. Marina Koren, "The College Dorm and the Confederacy," *The Atlantic*, August 16, 2016, accessed May 20, 2019, https://www.theatlantic.com/news/archive/2016/08/vanderbilt-confederate-hall/495941/.

play and, hopefully, place archivists in a better position to engage in the dialogue taking place on their respective campuses.

"The origin of archives as written acts of remembrance," argues Barbara L. Craig, "is the reason for their immediate usefulness and later, for their timelessness as cultural sources." The role of the archivist, concludes Craig, is to "ensure that archives remain true to the realities of their witness so these can be used in the courts of history and public memory."[12] One circumstance informing Craig's writing at the time was the growth in the movement of Holocaust deniers and their impact on the interpretation of the historical record. Moving forward in time, Craig's insights are also useful in the current issues of contesting the past as a way to redress past injustices.

Contentious issues of collective memory and proposals to expunge its more negative aspects or representations are not new, though they are fairly new to college campuses. In "To Remember and Forget: Archives, Memory, and Culture," Professor Kenneth Foote reminds us that "society's need to remember is balanced against its desire to forget," particularly when the memory is deemed negative or uncomfortable.[13] Acts of revision, correction, or forgetting can happen passively or actively, and some of the most intense debates center around acts of memorialization. According to Foote, these debates lead to one of four outcomes: sanctification, designation, rectification, or effacement.[14] Sanctification and/or designation involve the remembrance, formal or informal, of a particular event, with or without a physical memorial. Rectification involves re-purposing a negative public space to "put right" past injustices, and effacement is the act of forgetting through passive

---

12. Barbara Craig, "Selected Themes in the Literature on Memory and Their Pertinence to Archives," *American Archivist* 65, no. 2 (2002): 289, accessed May 20, 2019, https://americanarchivist.org/doi/abs/10.17723/aarc.65.2.362773030n128265.

13. Kenneth E. Foote, "To Remember and Forget: Archives, Memory, and Culture," *American Archivist* 53, no. 3 (1990): 385, accessed May 20, 2019, https://americanarchivist.org/doi/abs/10.17723/aarc.53.3.d87u013444j3g6r2.

14. Foote, 387-91.

neglect or direct action, such as Germany actively demolishing buildings and other structures used by the Nazis.

Debates about the remembrance or memorialization of problematic figures on college campuses revolve around all of the potential outcomes above. Efforts to remove problematic individuals by those in favor represent acts of rectification, often accompanied by the proposed memorialization of an individual who, it is argued, was unjustly neglected, often those who have been historically underrepresented in archives, such as women and people of color. Those who disagree argue that this represents effacement, often echoed in the words "you can't change the past," or accusations of political correctness. In a college or university setting, it is imperative that the archives is consulted by those making decisions in these matters, and it falls to the archives staff to ensure that the decision makers have as much historical and contextual information as possible prior to making decisions.

As seen above, in some cases, state law can play a role in determining whether renaming can take place, and whether there are other legal considerations, such as remuneration to a donor. Legal scholar Alfred L. Brophy, in his article "The Law and Morality of Building Renaming," admits, however, "building renamings are fraught with more moral than legal questions."[15] In discussing the Vanderbilt case, Brophy makes several important points about issues of race and memory on college and university campuses. Both the South and the North had a vested interest in healing the wounds caused by the Civil War, he writes, and "in that process of reconciliation, African Americans were left with little protection, as the meaning of the anti-slavery struggle and the war was forgotten."[16] An additional complication was the "belief that monuments to the Confederacy had no relationship to slavery or to the era of Jim

---

15. Alfred L. Brophy, "The Law and Morality of Building Renaming," *South Texas Law Review* 52, no. 1 (2010): 46.

16. Brophy, 50. In discussing the Vanderbilt case, Brophy notes that the Tennessee Court of Appeals made several "interesting" arguments in ruling for the United Daughters of the Confederacy, upholding a contract that was never signed and including a clause ruling it null and void should federal funding not accompany the initial donation, which it never did.

Crow segregation that followed."[17] Each of these factors, when combined with a lack of diversity and inclusion on campus, led to both the creation of these memorializations, as well as their passive acceptance by the majority of campus members for an extended period. A key issue in most campus debates regarding name changes and race is a general lack of awareness of the pain and distress inflicted on African American students, faculty, and staff when they are continually confronted by the memorialization of those who fought the Civil War to protect the right to own slaves, or those who openly practiced racist beliefs.

As campuses continue to become more diverse and inclusive, issues surrounding slavery, segregation, and white supremacy have and will continue to arise. Unsurprisingly, a movement started at the University of Maryland, College Park (UMD) in 2015 to remove the name of Harry Clifton Byrd, former university president, alumnus, and proponent of segregation, from the football stadium. What was surprising, however, was how the university chose to involve the University Archives staff, some of the individuals most knowledgeable about the campus' history, in the research and decision-making process. Further, once decisions had been made, the University Archives was required to assist campus administration in the attempt to satisfy groups on both sides of the issue.

The unrest and discontent among members of the UMD community over Byrd's racial views had been building for many years. The university, founded in 1856 by planter and slave-owner Charles Benedict Calvert as the Maryland Agricultural College, had long viewed itself as a southern institution, much like many citizens of Maryland considered themselves as residents of a southern state. The segregationist hold on the institution began to break down with a court decision forcing the integration of the university's law school in 1935, yet the undergraduate and graduate student bodies did not begin to integrate until the late 1940s/early 1950s, and then only at a painfully slow pace. The first African American students at the graduate level, Myrtle Holmes Wake, Rose Shockley Wiseman, and John Francis Davis, took all of their classes

17. Brophy, 51.

outside UMD beginning in 1948 and only set foot on the College Park campus on commencement day in 1951. In 1952, Parren J. Mitchell, who later represented the state of Maryland for eight terms in the U.S. Congress, became the first African American graduate student to take all of his classes on campus and receive a degree, an M.A. in Sociology. Hiram Whittle, the university's first African American undergraduate, enrolled in January 1951 but never completed his degree. Both Mitchell and Whittle sued the university, with the support of the NAACP, to gain their admission. The number of African American students climbed slowly thereafter, reaching 586 in 1968 and 4,143 thirty years later. In recent years, these numbers have seen a steady decline, due in part to alleged hate bias incidents, including a noose found in a fraternity house and the killing of a visiting African American student.[18] In fall 2018, African American students made up only 11.6% of the total undergraduate population, and only 7.3% of freshmen, down from 12.9% and 12.2% in 2016.[19]

The earliest African American students matriculated during the tenure of Byrd, who served as UMD president from 1935 to 1954. Byrd was a 1908 graduate of the university, during its days as the Maryland Agricultural College. After a brief stint as a graduate student, semi-professional athlete, and newspaper reporter, he returned to his alma mater in 1912 as an instructor in English and football coach. Byrd rose through the administrative ranks, serving as athletic director, assistant to the president, vice president and, ultimately, president of the university for eighteen years.[20]

18. Jillian Atelsek, "UMD's Black Freshman Enrollment Is at Its Lowest Level in Decades," *The Diamondback*, October 31, 2018, accessed May 20, 2019, https://dbknews.com/2018/11/01/umd-enrollment-data-black-students-freshman-class-diversity-hate-bias/. U.S. Army Lieutenant Richard Collins III, a visiting student from Bowie State University, was stabbed and killed by white UMD student Sean Urbanski on May 20, 2017, while waiting at a campus bus stop. Urbanski went on trial for first-degree murder and hate crime charges in fall of 2019.

19. "University of Maryland Campus Counts." Institutional Research, Planning and Assessment, accessed May 20, 2019, https://irpa.umd.edu/CampusCounts/index.html. See figures in the "Enrollments" section.

20. For further biographical information on Byrd, see the summary created as part

As a proponent of separate but equal education, which was the policy of the state of Maryland at the time, Byrd stated publicly that he did not want African American students on campus. He seemed to realize, however, that integration was coming, no matter his personal feelings. In 1947, he told the state legislature:

> Gentlemen, the decision as to what you wish the University to do is yours to make, but please remember that the question is one that goes deep into the lives of our people, has broad implications, and has narrow, fine lines for its legal borders. We, therefore, ask that your decision be not based on temporary expedience, but that it be conclusive and settle the question, insofar as it can be settled. Such makeshift provisions as we have had so far neither give the Negro what he is entitled to, nor prevent him entering the University of Maryland.[21]

The mounting lawsuits, which began in the early 1930s when Byrd was still vice president, and were now multiplying, ultimately led the Board of Regents, the governing body for the entire University System of Maryland (USM), in consultation with Byrd, to the conclusion that African American students must be admitted to all branches of the university, including UMD.

A sense of exclusion remained and simmered below the surface for decades, as the university was painfully slow to admit African American students or hire faculty and staff of color. There were major confrontations between African American students and the administration in the 1960s and 1970s, with students highly critical of the university's efforts to increase the racial diversity of the entire campus community. In the 1990s, the university argued in court for the maintenance of a scholarship specifically for African American students, stating that it was an

---

of the renaming debate, https://president.umd.edu/sites/president.umd.edu/files/documents/President-Byrd-Biographical-Notes.pdf, and the biographical information from Byrd's personal papers, https://archives.lib.umd.edu/repositories/2/resources/1029, accessed May 23, 2019.

21. University of Maryland Libraries, Special Collections and University Archives, Papers of Harry Clifton Byrd, Series I, Box 8, Folder 6, "Negro Education, 1947-1949," "The University of Maryland and Higher Education for Negroes," July 6, 1947. Digitized document accessed May 23, 2019, https://hdl.handle.net/1903.1/38527.

attempt to deal constructively with the lingering effects of racism at the institution.[22] Thus, a student-led protest movement over the name of the football stadium was a continuation of challenging the university to live up to its stated beliefs regarding diversity and inclusion. The university transferred Byrd's name from the original stadium, dedicated in 1923 to honor his contributions to the university's athletic program, to the current structure when it opened in 1950, and the students wanted his name removed. To them, and to their supporters, Byrd's name on such a highly visible campus landmark created a "hostile and unwelcoming climate" and was a reminder of his segregationist views.[23] The students, who delivered a petition calling for the name change to UMD President Wallace Loh in March 2015, began a series of protests and wrote editorials for the student newspaper, *The Diamondback*, calling for action.[24] The Student Government Association, which represents undergraduates, passed a resolution supporting the name change at the end of the spring semester, and a close examination of the situation resumed in earnest in the fall.[25]

To address the growing concerns on campus, Loh formed a special working group to examine the name change issue. Chaired by the Dean of the College of Arts and Humanities, the group consisted of nineteen members, including the president of the Alumni Association Board of Governors, the chair of the University Senate, staff from University Relations, Athletics, and Student Affairs, the university's Chief Diversity

22. University of Maryland, Office of the President, Decision and Report of the University of Maryland at College Park Regarding the Benjamin Banneker Scholarship Program, College Park, MD: The University, 1993. University Archives University Publications Collection, UPUB P24.002.

23. University of Maryland, Byrd Stadium Naming Work Group, "Arguments For and Against Changing the Stadium Name and Alternative Considerations," December 4, 2015, accessed May 20, 2019, https://president.umd.edu/sites/president.umd.edu/files/documents/Arguments-for-&-against-stadium-name-change.pdf.

24. DBK Admin, "Wallace Loh Forms a Work Group to Help Consider Renaming Byrd Stadium," *The Diamondback*, September 24, 2015, accessed May 20, 2019, https://dbknews.com/2015/09/24/article_385d78d0-62e1-11e5-bcf7-e32ca19dd581-html/.

25. DBK Admin, "Wallace Loh Forms a Work Group to Help Consider Renaming Byrd Stadium."

Officer, a member of the University of Maryland College Park Foundation (UMCPF) Board of Trustees, seven faculty members, one graduate student, and two undergraduate students.

Despite the fact that the working group was dealing with an issue with a strong university history orientation, Loh did not request any representation from the UMD Archives staff, the individuals with the most intimate knowledge of the resources documenting Byrd's views and accomplishments, nor was it immediately clear what role the Archives staff would be allowed to have in the process. They only learned secondhand about plans for a working group from a researcher who visited the reading room to do some preliminary examination of Byrd's correspondence and public statements on race; this researcher was later named a member of the committee. When the University Archivist questioned the UMD Libraries' administration about whether it was worth the political capital necessary to be named to the working group, she was told that it was not. Oddly enough, there was also no representation from the campus chapter of the NAACP on the working group.[26]

The body began its labors on September 28, 2015, and was required to submit its final report by December 4, so the time to complete the examination of this highly charged issue was relatively short. Although meetings of the group were open to all members of the campus community, this fact was not well publicized, and the University Archivist learned about the opportunity to observe the working group in action only several weeks into its operations, and then only really by chance. One of the assistant vice presidents for University Relations, who was serving on the committee, had several questions about building naming practices in place at the time of the naming of the current stadium in 1950 and asked the University Archivist to attend a meeting of the sub-group on naming practices that she was chairing. It came to light at that session that observers could attend the meetings of the entire

---

26. Anne S.K. Turkos served as University Archivist from 1993 to 2017; DBK Admin, "UMD's NAACP Chapter Objects to Exclusion from Byrd Renaming Group," *The Diamondback*, October 20, 2015, accessed May 20, 2019, https://dbknews.com/2015/10/20/article_f877ded6-7776-11e5-bff5-77cadb3b3c69-html/.

group. The University Archivist also met individually with the chair of the Sociology Department, who was heading the sub-group charged with examining Byrd's career and racial views. This was the researcher who had first alerted the University Archives that a working group was being constituted.

It made perfect sense for the University Archivist to meet with individuals on the working group (or sub-units of it), but the University Archives staff was also concerned about the accuracy of the presentation of Byrd's entire story, so the University Archivist decided to attend the remaining meetings of the whole group as an observer. At different points, she was called upon to provide factual information in these meetings, and she had the opportunity to comment at the end of each session if there were points she wanted to raise or factual corrections that needed to be made at that day's discussion. At one of the meetings, she also suggested that, if the name of the stadium was to be changed, historical information about Byrd and the reason for the stadium's new name could be included on a plaque inside the main entrance to the facility, so that this significant part of the University of Maryland's history would not go unrecognized and would be placed in an appropriate historical context. This proposal was rejected, since there appeared to be a desire to obliterate as many references to Byrd on campus as possible.

Because the working group had such a short time to complete its research and report its findings, it was immediately apparent that no member of this body was going to have the time, nor did anyone have the desire, to examine the entire archival record of Byrd's career and accomplishments. His personal papers and presidential records housed in the UMD Archives are quite extensive, over 225 linear feet, so it was not unexpected that the primary focus of the research conducted would be on files labeled "Negro Education," or "University of Maryland and Higher Education for Negroes," or other headings in a similar vein. Upon reviewing the documents, it was immediately obvious that Byrd held racial views that are considered abhorrent in the twenty-first century, and that he fought long and hard to keep African American students from enrolling at UMD.[27] The lack of examination of other aspects of Byrd's career, however, was very discouraging for the Archives staff.[28]

Beginning in 1948, six years before *Brown v. Board of Education*, however, Byrd allowed African American students to enroll in and receive degrees from the university, though, as previously noted, they were not initially allowed to take classes on the UMD campus. The Archives staff was able to determine, through conversations with faculty and students on campus during this period and examination of the student newspaper and other administrative sources, that there were no overt protests at that time, nor any angry editorials in the student newspaper. It was much more likely due to pragmatism than a change of heart, but it was evident that Byrd's position had begun to change.

Byrd's other significant accomplishments on behalf of the university, such as transforming it from a "cow college" to the beginnings of the internationally known university it is today, as well as the negative impacts of some of his other actions, also received minimal attention in the working group's discussions and its final report. Byrd worked tirelessly and mostly successfully to make UMD the preeminent university in the state, and the growth he fostered is demonstrably responsible for the university's current status. Nonetheless, the growth he engendered was rooted in segregation and controlled almost entirely by Byrd himself, which led the university to find itself not only in severe academic straits in the early 1950s, but at odds with the governor of Maryland and with its accreditation at risk.[29] By failing to acknowledge *all* aspects of Byrd's career, his supporters—and there were indeed some—questioned whether working group members had entered the process with

27. University of Maryland, Byrd Stadium Naming Work Group, "Arguments for and Against Changing the Stadium Name and Alternative Considerations."

28. Finding aids for Byrd's presidential and personal papers may be accessed at https://archives.lib.umd.edu/repositories/2/archival_objects/348157 (presidential) and https://archives.lib.umd.edu/repositories/2/resources/1029 (personal).

29. George H. Callcott, "Chapter 13: The Age of Curley Byrd," in *A History of the University of Maryland* (Baltimore, MD: Maryland Historical Society, 1966), 313-65.

open minds and whether the outcome had been predetermined.[30] Byrd's legacy is incredibly complex, and it did not appear that the committee was either willing or prepared to engage with it in detail, though, to be fair, it was hardly allowed the time to make more than a cursory review.[31]

On December 7, 2015, three days after the working group submitted its arguments for and against changing the stadium name and alternative considerations, Loh announced his recommendation to change the name to "Maryland Stadium" in a memo to USM Chancellor Robert Caret and the USM Board of Regents, an action that the board ratified at its meeting four days later.

A parade of witnesses, most of whom were in favor of the name change, testified in front of the Regents prior to the vote. The University Archivist took the opportunity to note that the institution can neither change its history, nor make it more palatable, by sweeping past events under the carpet or attempting to erase that history, just because it is painful to the UMD community today. She told the board that the university needed to be honest about its past, learn from it, admit its failings, and work to overcome mistakes, rather than ignoring or obliterating them and hoping they will disappear.

When Loh submitted his recommendation for the name change, he announced three follow-up actions that would be taken upon approval by the Regents.[32]

- Memorialize President Byrd in the library: UMCP [University of Maryland, College Park] will identify a suitable and visible location inside one of our main University libraries and install a permanent exhibit recognizing the enormous contributions of Harry Clifton

---

30. Conversations with University Archivist, September 2015.

31. The Byrd Stadium Naming Work Group received its charge on September 28, 2015, with a deadline to complete its work by December 11, 2015. The group issued its report on December 4, 2015.

32. "Recommendation for Board Action," President of University of Maryland, Wallace D. Loh, to USM Chancellor Robert Caret, December 7, 2015, accessed May 20, 2019, https://president.umd.edu/sites/president.umd.edu/files/documents/Byrd-Stadium-recommendation-to-BOR-12-7-15.pdf.

"Curley" Byrd during his presidency (1936-1954) and in the 25 preceding years as teacher, football coach, and university administrator. As an institution of learning, we are duty-bound to memorialize his complete legacy.

- Announce a moratorium on any other honorific renaming: There will be a five-year moratorium on any honorific renaming of other buildings that recognize historical figures.

- Move from symbolic change to institutional improvements: True change is not realized by name change alone. This controversy is symptomatic of deeper divides on campus and in the nation at large. Early next semester, UMCP will launch a campus-wide "Maryland Dialogues on Diversity and Community" to help bridge the differences and to align better our practices and policies with our 21st century moral and academic vision.

The first directive specifically affected the University Archives. Since neither the UMD Libraries' administration nor the Archives were aware that such a project—charged with a great deal of emotion on both sides of the stadium naming question—was about to be added to the workload, this announcement caused a good deal of consternation. The Libraries—in particular, the University Archives—were now in the awkward position of seeming to defend Byrd while trying to show both positive and negative aspects of his presidency. If having his name on the football stadium created a "hostile and unwelcoming climate," would the Libraries be seen in the same light? Certainly, that was not a desired outcome.

There were numerous discussions with top-level university administrators about where such an exhibit should be located. Although Loh had specified that the display should be in one of the main campus libraries, would the Main Administration building, site of Byrd's office, or the former basketball arena, about to be converted into an indoor practice facility for the football team (that Byrd had coached for many years), be more visible locations? What kind of security could be provided for the exhibit, particularly if it was to include original materials and not just facsimiles? Due to the strong feelings of Byrd's opponents and proponents, was there any potential for vandalism?

The ultimate choice for the exhibit's location was the reading room for Special Collections and University Archives (SCUA) in Hornbake Library, the research facility in which Byrd's personal papers and presidential records are consulted. While this space is less heavily trafficked than some of the others that were considered, it does provide a higher level of security for the materials and dramatically reduces the chances of damage from individuals unhappy with this representation of Byrd's legacy. The University Archives staff are also more readily available to answer visitors' questions and can more easily maintain the exhibit in this space.

The analog exhibit, as currently constituted, consists of two display cases, an enlargement of a photographic portrait of Byrd, which was taken in the President's Office, and a poster providing the title of the exhibit and relevant contact information. Content is drawn from a more extensive analog display about Byrd that was featured in SCUA's exhibit gallery in 2002 and rotates approximately every six months. Even four years after the UMD Libraries were tasked with this memorialization, there remains discussion about the appropriate size for the installation or whether it should be moved to a different location. While locating the exhibit in the secure reading room protects it and its original content, the fact that the reading room is secure acts as a *de facto* limitation on its visibility. There is no outside advertisement that such an exhibit exists, so, while the university may be honoring Loh's charge to the letter, whether the display is in the spirit of furthering the understanding of such a complex figure and his legacy is debatable.

The Archives staff also felt strongly that a digital exhibit about Byrd's personal and professional life was an appropriate supplement/complement to the analog version in the reading room. This piece would be available at any time and in any place in the world with an internet connection, and would be an excellent vehicle for providing more in-depth coverage of all aspects, positive and negative, of his legacy. Drawing again on the resources of the previous analog exhibit about Byrd,

University Archives staff collaborated with staff in the Instruction and Outreach unit in SCUA to create a web exhibit, *From Vision to Reality: The Life and Career of Harry Clifton Byrd.*[33] It is important to note that, as of late 2019, the university has not made any effort to publicize the site's presence and has been unwilling to let the Libraries do so. There are important donors on both sides of the name change issue, leaving the university in the difficult position of trying to acknowledge Byrd while not seeming to celebrate him. In addition to the aforementioned hate bias incidents, the recent scandal over the death of an African American football player due to medical negligence has increased the already substantial criticism of the university regarding its treatment of African American students on campus, making issues surrounding Byrd's legacy essentially radioactive for the foreseeable future.

What, then, are the lessons the University Archives learned from this controversy?

- Continue to strive to make the University Archives program better known on campus, so that when current issues that touch on campus history arise, the Archives staff and collections are considered to be essential resources to be consulted.
- Be ready to insert Archives staff into issues where their perspectives are needed and valued.
- Make certain the Archives has a stake in the damage control resulting from such contentious situations that is recognized by university and Libraries' administration. Know when and how to speak up.
- Remain neutral on the issue at hand, and remove emotion from the discussion, regardless of one's personal feelings. Let the documents entrusted to your care tell the story.
- Identify important materials that may have an impact on the matter at hand and encourage their review. Archivists can provide valuable

33. University of Maryland Libraries, Special Collections and University Archives, "From Vision to Reality: The Life and Career of Harry Clifton Byrd," accessed May 20, 2019, https://lib.umd.edu/byrd.

historical and contextual information that can have a positive impact on these issues, endeavoring to ensure a more holistic understanding of what has transpired. However, there is only so much that they can do to force examination of documents they consider to be critical to the conversation.

- Be prepared to suggest appropriate actions to avoid elimination of recognition and discussion of controversial topics or individuals, with great sensitivity to the concerns of those on both sides of any question. Determine the most suitable methods and outlets that could be used to allow the campus to approach and address complex historical issues.

As the University of Maryland and its archives move forward from this controversy, it will be intriguing to see where this story leads. Will the UMD Archives and the Libraries encounter a lot of flak for fulfilling Loh's commitment? Will Byrd's name ever again grace a major space on campus? Will the donors who remain angry about the decision to rename the stadium have a visible impact on the ways in which Byrd's contributions are recognized? As the years go by, it is absolutely clear that these kinds of naming issues will continue to occur, and that institutions will struggle to balance complicated legacies with contemporary social mores. Issues such as race may seem to be clear cut, but it is not unreasonable to imagine an era where other social or political matters cause choices for memorialization to be re-examined. While it is appropriate that we make room for diversity in the creation of the historical record, we must also find better ways to grapple with the imperfection of human beings. We may decide that naming is simply too fraught an act and abandon it altogether, but each proposed naming also represents an opportunity to engage in difficult topics that have direct connections to where we are now. Only time will tell how Byrd's legacy will ultimately be addressed. This story, and others like it, is far from over.

Bibliography

Admin, DBK. "UMD's NAACP Chapter Objects to Exclusion from Byrd Renaming Group." *The Diamondback*. October 20, 2015. Accessed May 20, 2019. https://dbknews.com/2015/10/20/article_f877d-ed6-7776-11e5-bff5-77cadb3b3c69-html/.

Admin, DBK. "Wallace Loh Forms a Work Group to Help Consider Renaming Byrd Stadium." *The Diamondback*. September 24, 2015. Accessed May 20, 2019. https://dbknews.com/2015/09/24/article_385d78d0-62e1-11e5-bcf7-e32ca19dd581-html/.

Allyn, Bobby. "Names of Accused Bishops to Be Removed from Buildings at 2 Catholic Pa. Colleges." National Public Radio. August 22, 2018. Accessed May 20, 2019. https://www.npr.org/2018/08/22/640904769/names-of-accused-bishops-to-come-down-at-university-of-scranton.

Atelsek, Jillian. "UMD's Black Freshman Enrollment Is at Its Lowest Level in Decades." *The Diamondback*. October 31, 2018. Accessed May 20, 2019. https://dbknews.com/2018/11/01/umd-enrollment-data-black-students-freshman-class-diversity-hate-bias/.

Brophy, Alfred L. "The Law and Morality of Building Renaming." *South Texas Law Review* 52, no. 1 (2010): 37-67.

Callcott, George, H. "Chapter 13: The Age of Curley Byrd." In *A History of the University of Maryland*, 313-65. Baltimore, MD: Maryland Historical Society, 1966.

Cary, Nathaniel. "Clemson Not Alone in Debate over Renaming Tillman Hall." *USA Today*. March 10, 2015. Accessed May 20, 2019. https://www.usatoday.com/story/news/education/2015/03/09/clemson-alone-debate-renaming-tillman-hall/24666467/.

Craig, Barbara. "Selected Themes in the Literature on Memory and Their Pertinence to Archives." *American Archivist* 65, no. 2 (2002): 276-89. Accessed May 20, 2019. https://americanarchivist.org/doi/abs/10.17723/aarc.65.2.362773030n128265.

Dryfoos, Delaney. "The History Department Wants to Rename the Carr Building for Him, So Who Was Raymond Gavins?" *The Chronicle*. October 25, 2018. Accessed May 20, 2019. https://www.dukechronicle.com/article/2018/10/raymond-gavins-legacy-a-look-at-the-man-behind-the-proposed-new-name-for-the-carr-building.

Foote, Kenneth, E. "To Remember and Forget: Archives, Memory, and Culture." *American Archivist* 53, no. 3 (1990): 378-92. Accessed May 20, 2019. https://americanarchivist.org/doi/abs/10.17723/aarc.53.3.d87u013444j3g6r2.

Franco, Tea. "New Logo: A Different Perspective." *MY TJ Now.* March 20, 2018. Accessed May 20, 2019. http://mytjnow.com/2018/03/01/new-logo-different-perspective/.

Koren, Marina. "The College Dorm and the Confederacy." *The Atlantic.* August 16, 2016. Accessed May 20, 2019. https://www.theatlantic.com/news/archive/2016/08/vanderbilt-confederate-hall/495941/.

Love, Lauren. "U-M to Remove Little, Winchell Names from Campus Facilities." *The University Record.* March 29, 2018. Accessed May 20, 2019. https://record.umich.edu/articles/u-m-remove-little-winchell-names-campus-facilities.

"Recommendation for Board Action." President of University of Maryland, Wallace D. Loh, to USM Chancellor Robert Caret, December 7, 2015. Accessed May 20, 2019. https://president.umd.edu/sites/president.umd.edu/files/documents/Byrd-Stadium-recommendation-to-BOR-12-7-15.pdf.

Sams, Cathy. "New Signs Installed as Part of Board's 'Clemson History' Plan." *The Newsstand.* January 10, 2018. Accessed May 20, 2019. http://newsstand.clemson.edu/mediarelations/new-signs-installed-as-part-of-boards-clemson-history-plan/.

Silvarole, Georgie. "Here's How New Signs Share Clemson University's 'Complete' History." *The State.* January 14, 2018. Accessed May 20, 2019. https://www.thestate.com/news/local/article194640944.html.

Simpson, Ian. "Georgetown University Renames Buildings to Atone for Slavery Ties." Reuters. April 18, 2017. Accessed May 20, 2019. https://www.reuters.com/article/us-washingtondc-georgetown-slavery/georgetown-university-renames-buildings-to-atone-for-slavery-ties-idUSKBN17K2AR.

"Trustees Rename Saunders Hall, Freeze Renamings for 16 Years." *Carolina Alumni Review*. May 28, 2015. Accessed May 20, 2019. https://alumni.unc.edu/news/trustees-vote-to-rename-saunders-hall-put-16-year-freeze-on-renamings/.

University of Maryland, Byrd Stadium Naming Work Group. "Arguments For and Against Changing the Stadium Name and Alternative Considerations." December 4, 2015. Accessed May 20, 2019. https://president.umd.edu/sites/president.umd.edu/files/documents/Arguments-for-&-against-stadium-name-change.pdf.

University of Maryland, Byrd Stadium Naming Work Group. "President Harry Clifton 'Curley' Byrd: Biographical Notes." December 4, 2015. Accessed May 20. 2019. https://president.umd.edu/sites/president.umd.edu/files/documents/President-Byrd-Biographical-Notes.pdf.

"University of Maryland Campus Counts," Institutional Research, Planning, and Assessment. Accessed May 20, 2019. https://irpa.umd.edu/CampusCounts/index.html.

University of Maryland Libraries, Special Collections and University Archives. Finding Aid. Papers of Harry Clifton Byrd. Accessed May 20, 2019. https://archives.lib.umd.edu/repositories/2/resources/1029.

University of Maryland Libraries, Special Collections and University Archives. Finding Aid. Records of the Office of the President, University of Maryland. Accessed May 20, 2019. https://archives.lib.umd.edu/repositories/2/archival_objects/348157.

University of Maryland Libraries, Special Collections and University Archives. "From Vision to Reality: The Life and Career of Harry Clifton Byrd." Accessed May 20, 2019. https://lib.umd.edu/byrd.

University of Maryland Libraries, Special Collections and University Archives. Papers of Harry Clifton Byrd, Series I, Box 8, Folder 6, "Negro Education, 1947-1949," "The University of Maryland and Higher Education for Negroes," July 6, 1947. Digitized document accessed May 23, 2019, https://hdl.handle.net/1903.1/38527.

University of Maryland, Office of the President. *Decision and Report of the University of Maryland at College Park Regarding the Benjamin Banneker Scholarship Program*. College Park, MD: The University, 1993.

Washington and Lee University. "Report of The Commission on Institutional History and Community." May 2, 2018. Accessed May 20, 2019. https://www.wlu.edu/presidents-office/issues-and-initiatives/commission-on-institutional-history-and-community/report-of-the-commission-on-institutional-history-and-community.

"Yale to Change Calhoun College's Name to Honor Grace Murray Hopper." *YaleNews*. February 9, 2017. Accessed May 20, 2019. https://news.yale.edu/2017/02/11/yale-change-calhoun-college-s-name-honor-grace-murray-hopper.

Suggestions for Further Reading

Beckert, Sven, Katherine Stevens, and the Students of the Harvard and Slavery Research Seminar. *Harvard and Slavery: Seeking a Forgotten History*. Cambridge, MA: Harvard University, 2011. Accessed May 14, 2019. http://www.harvardandslavery.com/wp-content/uploads/2011/11/Harvard-Slavery-Book-111110.pdf.

Brown University. *Report of the Brown University Steering Committee on Slavery and Justice*. Providence, RI: The University, 2006. Accessed May 14, 2019. https://www.brown.edu/Research/Slavery_Justice/documents/SlaveryAndJustice.pdf.

Clarke, Max, and Gary Alan Fine. "'A' for Apology: Slavery and the Collegiate Discourses of Remembrance – the Cases of Brown University and the University of Alabama." *History and Memory* 22, no. 1 (2010): 81-112.

College of William and Mary. "The Lemon Project: A Journey of Reconciliation, Report of the First Eight Years." Williamsburg, VA: The College, February 2019. Accessed May 13, 2019. https://www.wm.edu/sites/lemonproject/_documents/the-lemon-project-report.pdf.

Duke University. "Report: Commission on Memory and History." Durham, NC: The University, 2017. Accessed May 14, 2019. https://memoryhistory.duke.edu/report/.

Duke University. "Report of the Committee on the Carr Building." Durham, NC: The University, November 20, 2018. Accessed May 14, 2019. https://memoryhistory.duke.edu/carr-building/.

Foote, Kenneth E., and Maoz Azaryahu. "Toward a Geography of Memory: Geographical Dimensions of Public Memory and Commemoration." *Journal of Political and Military Sociology* 5, no. 1 (Summer 2007): 125-44. Accessed May 13, 2019. https://www.researchgate.net/publication/276325758_Toward_a_geography_of_memory_Geographical_dimensions_of_public_memory_and_commemoration.

Georgetown University. "Report of the Working Group on Slavery, Memory, and Reconciliation to the President of Georgetown University." Washington, DC: The University, Summer 2016. Accessed May 14, 2019. http://slavery.georgetown.edu/report/.

Gordon-Reed, Annette, and Annie Rittgers. "A Different View." Cambridge, MA: Harvard Law School, 2016. Accessed May 13, 2019. https://today.law.harvard.edu/wp-content/uploads/2016/03/Shield_Committee-Different_View.pdf.

Harvard Law School. "Recommendation to the President and Fellows of Harvard College on the Shield Approved for the Law School." Cambridge, MA: The Law School, March 3, 2016. Accessed May 13, 2019. https://hls.harvard.edu/content/uploads/2016/03/Shield-Committee-Report.pdf.

Johnson, David Alan, Quintard Taylor, and Marsha Weisiger. "Report on the History of Matthew P. Deady and Frederick S. Dunn." Portland, OR: The University, September 5, 2017. Accessed May 14, 2019. https://president.uoregon.edu/sites/president2.uoregon.edu/files/deady_dunn_final_report_08-05-16.pdf.

Levinson, Sanford. *Written in Stone: Public Monuments in Changing Societies.* Durham, NC: Duke University Press, 1998.

Loh, Wallace. "Letter to the University Community on Byrd Stadium Renaming." College Park, MD: University of Maryland, December 7, 2015. Accessed May 14, 2019. https://president.umd.edu/communications/statements/president-loh-recommendation-byrd-stadium-naming.

Mulhere, Kaitlin. "Racist Enshrined." *Inside Higher Ed*, February 13, 2015. Accessed May 13, 2019. https://www.insidehighered.com/news/2015/02/13/clemson-debates-whether-rename-building.

Princeton University. "Report of the Trustee Committee on Woodrow Wilson's Legacy at Princeton." Princeton, NJ: The University, April 2, 2016. Accessed May 14, 2019. https://www.princeton.edu/sites/default/files/documents/2017/08/Wilson-Committee-Report-Final.pdf.

Princeton University, Executive Committee of the Trustees. "Policy on Naming of Programs, Positions, and Spaces." Princeton, NJ: The University, July 8, 2016. Accessed May 14, 2019. https://namingcommittee.princeton.edu/sites/namingcommittee/files/naming_policy.pdf.

Stanford University. "Report of the Advisory Committee on Renaming Junipero Serra Features." Stanford, CA: The University, August 18, 2018. Accessed May 14, 2019. https://campusnames.stanford.edu/pdf/Serra-Report.pdf.

Wilder, Craig Steven. *Ebony and Ivory: Race, Slavery, and the Troubled History of America's Universities.* New York: Bloomsbury Press, 2013.

Yale University. "Report of the Committee to Establish Principles on Renaming." New Haven, CT: The University, November 21, 2016. Accessed May 14, 2019. http://president.yale.edu/sites/default/files/files/CEPR_FINAL_12-2-16.pdf.

Yale University, Committee to Establish Principles on Renaming. "Bibliography of Committee Materials." New Haven, CT: The University, November 2016. Accessed May 14, 2018. https://president.yale.edu/advisory-groups/presidents-committees/committee-establish-principles-renaming/appendix-documents/bibliography-committee-materials.

Chapter 15

CONTESTING COLONIAL LIBRARY PRACTICES OF ACCESSIBILITY AND REPRESENTATION

Margarita Vargas-Betancourt, Jessica L. English, Melissa Jerome, and Angelibel Soto

Introduction

The purpose of this chapter is to discuss how Library and Information Science (LIS) specialists at the University of Florida (UF) navigate the challenges of the colonialist and hegemonic nature of archives and the aspiration of special collections to be sites of contestation. We will describe the development of UF's Latin American and Caribbean Collection within the framework of US colonialism and hegemony in the twentieth century. As a response, UF and the partners of the Digital Library of the Caribbean (dLOC) developed a consortium based on shared governance and open access content. However, dLOC's metadata is predominantly in English, which again restricts access to non-English-speaking patrons.

We will analyze three cases to illustrate the initial steps taken in the creation of bilingual points of access to Latin American collections. The Florida and Puerto Rico Digital Newspaper Project constitutes an attempt to bridge UF's gap of Puerto Rican material while, at the same time expanding access to Spanish language newspapers at the Library of

Congress' portal, Chronicling America, and dLOC.[1] Given the historical, political, economic, and demographic connections between Florida
and Cuba, UF has established a collaborative international agreement
with the Biblioteca Nacional de Cuba José Martí (José Martí National
Library of Cuba). This collaboration has brought to the forefront the
need to create bilingual metadata for dLOC content. However, the
resources needed to do so go beyond those available at UF. The Cuban
American Dream was the pilot project for the creation of bilingual
English-Spanish metadata at UF. The analysis of the implementation
of such a prototype illustrates the challenges that LIS specialists faced
and the strategies they developed to overcome them.

Imperialism

The Latin American and Caribbean Collection at the George A. Smathers
Libraries at UF is one of the most renowned collections of Latin Americana and Caribbeana in the United States.[2] Like other repositories, one
of the most serious dilemmas that UF faces is to challenge the colonialist and hegemonic nature of its special collections. To do so, LIS
specialists are working first to provide better access to cultural heritage
content to people in Latin America and the Caribbean, and second to
develop collections and materials that represent the Latinx communities
that live in the US.

Uncoincidentally, the history and content of the Latin American and
Caribbean archival collections at UF parallels US history. Most of the
Caribbean archival collections at UF correspond to the nineteenth and
twentieth century and document the economic and political interests
of US corporations in the Caribbean.[3] In fact, most of these collections

---

1. Library of Congress, Chronicling America, Historic American Newspapers, last
accessed November 7, 2018, https://chroniclingamerica.loc.gov; Digital Library of
the Caribbean, last accessed November 8, 2018, http://www.dloc.com/.

2. In fact, it is one of three US libraries that have a separate space. The others are the
Nettie Lee Benson Latin American Collection at the University of Texas Austin and
the Latin American Library at Tulane University.

3. George A. Smathers Libraries, "Latin American and Caribbean Collections,"
Finding Aids, last accessed November 7, 2018, http://www.uflib.ufl.edu/spec/brow-
seu_lacc.htm.

represent the voices and perspective of individuals and US corporations who traveled to the Caribbean to invest. For instance, the Braga Brothers Collection, the largest and most renowned archival collection at UF, documents the development of a major US sugar corporation, which was located in Cuba from 1860 to 1961.[4] A similar collection, the Taco Bay Commercial Company Records, includes a letter in which the US Department of State promises that it will assist the US company in its quest against Cuban individuals who are "encroaching" the company's land in Cuba.[5] The Frank R. Crumbie Papers document the life of a US customs inspector in Haiti during the US occupation of the island (1915-1934).[6] The voices represented in these collections are, not surprisingly, those of white US men.

Historically, the origin of archives is connected to colonialist empires. Imperial metropolises controlled their colonies through extensive record-keeping. Archives allowed the construction of classificatory systems, for instance, of racial difference or origin. Colonial states used such classifications to ensure the hegemony of a small group of European colonists over masses of Indigenous, African, and Asian people. The ideology that legitimized colonization was that of the "white Man" who brought "humanity and civilization to the lesser races."[7] The US used this white nationalism to usher in a policy of US domination in the Americas. In 1823, President James Monroe stated that the US would attack European countries that attempted to colonize any country in

---

4. George A. Smathers Libraries, "A Guide to the Braga Brothers Collection," Finding Aids, last accessed November, 2018, http://www.library.ufl.edu/spec/manuscript/Braga/braga.htm.

5. George A. Smathers Libraries, "Letter to Senator Henry Cabot Lodge from Acting Secretary of State Alvey A. Adee," Digital Library of the Caribbeam, last accessed November, 2018, http://ufdc.ufl.edu/AA00055812/00001.

6. George A. Smathers Libraries, "A Guide to the Frank R. Crumbie Papers," Finding Aids, last accessed November, 2018, http://web.uflib.ufl.edu/spec/manuscript/guides/crumbie.htm.

7. Caroline Elkins, "Looking beyond Mau Mau: Archiving Violence in the Era of Decolonization," *American Historical Review* 120:3 (June 2015): 853, last accessed December 17, 2018, https://doi.org/10.1093/ahr/120.3.852.

the American continent.[8] However, the Monroe Doctrine transformed into economic, political, and military hegemony of the US over Latin America and the Caribbean. The Spanish American War (1898) is one example of US interference in the region. The US used racial differentiation to justify its war against Spain and its expansion over Puerto Rico, Cuba, and the Philippines, whose inhabitants were considered inferior to the Anglo-Saxon people.[9]

In the nineteenth and twentieth centuries, US intellectuals followed US policy and sought to position the US as a hegemonic intellectual power in the Americas and the world. The result was that US scholars and collectors removed a great part of Latin America's and the Caribbean's cultural heritage from the countries of origin. This activity went against the 1815 Convention of Vienna, whose main principle was that each nation held rights over their cultural heritage. Although the doctrine became popular in the mid-nineteenth century, collectors in the US continued to acquire archival and cultural items from Latin America and to deposit them in US private and public institutions.[10] They showed special interest in the acquisition of materials that documented the colonial history of the Caribbean and Latin America. The development of Latin American collections followed this direction not only to increase institutional prestige, but also because the nineteenth and early twentieth centuries witnessed the expansion of US interests and hegemony over the continent. US scholars not only sought to understand the region's history, but also to compare and contrast European colonialism with US informal imperialism. Interest in Latin American and Caribbean

---

8. *Dictionary of World History* (Oxford, UK: Oxford University Press, 2015), s.v. "Monroe Doctrine."

9. David W. Blight, *Race and Reunion: The Civil War in American Memory* (Cambridge, MA: Belknap Press, 2003), 347; Ussama Makdisi, "Diminished Sovereignty and the Impossibility of 'Civil War' in the Modern Middle East," *American Historical Review* 120, no. 5 (2015): 1750, last accessed December 17, 2018, https://doi.org/10.1093/ahr/120.5.1739.

10. Bruce Montgomery, "Reconciling the Inalienability Doctrine with the Conventions of War," *American Archivist* 78:2 (Fall/Winter 2015): 297, https://doi.org/10.17723/0360-9081.78.2.288.

content increased after WWI, when the closing of European markets to Latin America gave way to the expansion of US markets in the region.[11]

At UF, there are important examples of colonial Caribbean and Latin American collections, including the Jérémie Papers, a collection of seventeenth to nineteenth-century notarial records from the jurisdiction of Jérémie in Saint-Domingue (present-day Haiti). UF purchased the collection from Austrian archaeologist Kurt Fisher in 1959.[12] The Luis García Pimentel Collection is another example of a preeminent cultural heritage collection. It includes documents from the sixteenth to the twentieth centuries that chronicle the development, management, and activities of several sugar plantations in Mexico; UF purchased it in 2007.[13] As a consequence of such acquisition policies, Latin American and Caribbean scholars must travel to the US in order to study their cultural heritage and history; needless to say, access is extremely restricted.

The Latin American and Caribbean Collection and the Digital Library of the Caribbean

In the 1930s, UF president John J. Tigert established the School for Inter-American Affairs. He believed that UF had a special role in the Americas because of Florida's proximity to the Caribbean.[14] Consequently, George A. Smathers Libraries began to acquire Latin American and Caribbean content. After WWII, US librarians recognized that, in

---

11. Ricardo D. Salvatore, "Library Accumulation and the Emergence of Latin American Studies," *Comparative American Studies: An International Journal* 3, no. 4 (2005): 423-27, https://doi.org/10.1177/1477570005058958.

12. George A. Smathers Libraries, "A Guide to the Jérémie Papers," Finding Aids, last accessed November 8, 2018, http://web.uflib.ufl.edu/spec/manuscript/guides/jeremie.htm. Another part of the collection was acquired by the New York Public Library and is now known as the Kurt Fisher Haitian Collection. The New York Public Library, "Kurt Fisher Haitian Collection 1727-1958," Archives & Manuscripts, last accessed November 8, 2018, http://archives.nypl.org/scm/20798.

13. George A. Smathers Libraries, "A Guide to the Luis García Pimentel Collection," Finding Aids, last accessed November 8, 2018, http://www.library.ufl.edu/spec/manuscript/guides/pimentel.htm.

14. Center for Latin American Studies at the University of Florida, "History," last accessed December 3, 2018, http://www.latam.ufl.edu/about/history/.

order for the US to become the world's leader, it had to collect national resources from all regions. Since a single library could not succeed in such a Herculean task, in 1948 librarians developed a collaborative effort known as the Farmington Plan, outlining which libraries would specialize in which region.[15] Based on the strength of its Caribbean holdings, the Farmington Plan assigned UF as the repository for the Caribbean in 1951. Two years later, the Farmington Plan recognized that US librarians should emphasize the acquisition of Latin American material in general.[16]

In 1961, acknowledging the limits of the School for Inter-American Affairs, the Graduate School at UF proposed the creation of the Center for Latin American Studies with the purpose of serving Latin American students and preparing US students for careers related to Latin America. The establishment of the Center coincided with the Cuban Revolution, and the subsequent efforts of the US to curtail the expansion of Communist ideas to other Latin American and Caribbean nations.[17] Due to the importance of the region as a Cold War battlefield, US repositories continued to acquire manuscripts, rare books, and artifacts from Latin America and the Caribbean. Such interest, however, did not factor into the restitution of cultural property.

During the 1950s and 1960s, a UF librarian traveled by boat throughout the Caribbean to microfilm historical newspapers and documents located in local repositories. The result was the creation of one of the most complete collections of Caribbean newspapers and, equally important, the establishment of strong partnerships with Caribbean institutions.[18] Such relationships laid the groundwork for dLOC and,

15. Ralph D. Wagner, *A History of the Farmington Plan* (Lanham, MD: Scarecrow Press, 2002), 86.

16. Wagner, 209-10.

17. The Graduate School, University of Florida, Proposal for an Inter-American Cultural and Scientific Center (Gainesville, FL: 1961), 1-3, last accessed December 3, 2018, http://ufdc.ufl.edu/AA00002847/00001.

18. Laurie Taylor, "Librarian on a Boat or Digital Scholarship, Caribbean Studies, and the Digital Library of the Caribbean (dLOC): Alternative Sabbatical Proposal for 2016-2017," University of Florida Digital Collections (UFDC), last accessed December 3, 2018, http://ufdc.ufl.edu/AA00037232/00001.

in 2004, it was officially established by nine founding partners.[19] Under the leadership of Florida International University (FIU), the University of the Virgin Islands, and UF, the founding institutions—along with a growing number of partners—have contributed digital content from their holdings to the open access repository. dLOC is now "the largest open access collection of Caribbean materials with over 2 million pages of content, 39 institutional partners, and over 1 million views each month."[20] The administrators of the consortium are FIU and UF; the former provides administrative support, while the latter provides technical infrastructure.[21]

dLOC is a digital repository for resources from and about the Caribbean and circum-Caribbean (mainland regions that share Caribbean culture) from archives, museums, libraries, academic institutions, and private collections. It is a platform that provides a scholarly cyberinfrastructure for Caribbean studies. As a research foundation, dLOC includes technical, social, governmental, and procedural support, including open source tools, executive and scholarly advisory boards, a permission-based rights model to support intellectual property, as well as cultural and moral rights, and a core support team. As a scholarly resource, dLOC also provides context by placing Caribbean materials within academic discourse through curation.[22]

To provide equitable access to materials, dLOC uses an open access platform. This helps in resolving the potential lack of trust from Latin

---

19. Archives Nationale d'Haïti; Caribbean Community Secretariat (CARICOM); National Library of Jamaica; La Fundación Global Democracia y Desarrollo (FUNGLODE); Universidad de Oriente, Venezuela; University of the Virgin Islands; Florida International University; University of Central Florida; University of Florida. Digital Library of the Caribbean, "About dLOC," last accessed December 3, 2018, http://dloc.com/dloc1/about.

20. Taylor, "'Librarian on a Boat' or Digital Scholarship, Caribbean Studies, and the Digital Library of the Caribbean (dLOC)."

21. "About dLOC."

22. Laurie Taylor, Margarita Vargas-Betancourt, and Brooke Wooldridge, "The Digital Library of the Caribbean (dLOC): Creating a Shared Research Foundation," *Scholarly and Research Communication. Simon Fraser University* 4, no. 3 (2013), last accessed December 17, 2018, https://doi.org/10.22230/src.2013v4n3a114.

American and Caribbean partners, which is the result of a historic, uneven, and for many years unregulated flow of Latin American and Caribbean cultural material to the US. Such an unequal relationship has prevented institutions in such regions from feeling that they are partners of US institutions. To overcome this perspective, dLOC is based on shared governance. Latin American and Caribbean partners participate in dLOC's governance through the executive board and scholarly advisory board. In addition, they retain copyright for the material they contribute. Finally, the funding model is geared towards equity. Members from the US and other higher-income countries contribute funding, while partners from Latin America and the Caribbean contribute content. The participation of members and partners in dLOC's governance is equal.

The Florida and Puerto Rico Digital Newspaper Project

The history and structure of the Latin American and Caribbean Collection and of dLOC have given way to a growing number of digital projects, such as the Florida and Puerto Rico Digital Newspaper Project.[23] This project is significant, because cultural institutions tend to marginalize Puerto Rican content due to its ambiguous position as a Latin American nation and a US territory. For instance, Title VI funding from UF's Center for Latin American Studies cannot be used to acquire Puerto Rican content or to travel to the island, resulting in a void within the collection.

To counteract such omissions, UF partnered with the University of Puerto Rico-Río Piedras (UPR-RP) to participate in the National Digital Newspaper Program (NDNP). Since 2013, UF has worked with UPR-RP through a National Endowment for the Humanities grant to digitize historic newspapers from Florida and Puerto Rico published between 1690 and 1963.[24] The content is freely available online on sev-

---

23. George A. Smathers Libraries, "Florida and Puerto Rico Digital Newspaper Project," University of Florida Digital Collections, last accessed November 7, 2018, http://ufdc.ufl.edu/ndnp.

24. George A. Smathers Libraries, "Florida and Puerto Rico Digital Newspaper Project: National Digital Newspaper Program (NDNP) Grant Proposal,"

eral platforms, including Chronicling America, a website created and managed by the Library of Congress where all newspapers digitized for the NDNP can be accessed.[25] The Florida and Puerto Rico Digital Newspaper Project, therefore, provides access to newspaper content that is published in English (Florida material) and Spanish (Puerto Rico material). Following the Library of Congress's technical specifications, issue and reel level metadata for all selected newspaper titles must be submitted in English. Per the technical guidelines for this program, issue level metadata includes elements such as title, Library of Congress Control Number, issue date, issue present indicator (denotes if issue is missing), and page present indicator (denotes if page is missing). Reel level metadata includes elements such as titles found on the reel, start and end dates for present titles, and microfilm quality information such as resolution and density readings. In addition to the required metadata, participants must submit essays for each selected newspaper title. These essays provide an overview of the history and significance of the publication and are accessible on Chronicling America.[26]

Scholars of Puerto Rican history originally wrote the essays for the Puerto Rican selected titles in Spanish. However, to meet NDNP requirements, LIS specialists translated the essays into English. The essays provide information about the papers, offering insights about their content so users can easily navigate the materials, given that this newspaper collection offers varying perspectives. For example, the Spanish government published one of the Puerto Rican papers, while Luis Muñoz Rivera, one of the founders of the *Partido Autonomista*

Digital Library of the Caribbean, last accessed December 8, 2018, http://ufdc.ufl. edu/AA00019344/00001;George A. Smathers Libraries, "Florida and Puerto Rico Newspaper Digitization Project–Phase II," Digital Library of the Caribbean, last accessed December 8, 2018, http://ufdc.ufl.edu/AA00028169/00001; George A. Smathers Libraries, "Florida and Puerto Rico Digital Newspaper–Phase III," Digital Library of the Caribbean, last accessed December 8, 2018, http://ufdc.ufl.edu/ IR00009659/00001.

25. Library of Congress, Chronicling America, Historic American Newspapers.

26. Library of Congress, "Guidelines & Resources. Technical Guidelines & Specifications," National Digital Newspaper Program, 12-14, 19-36, last accessed December 8, 2018, https://www.loc.gov/ndnp/guidelines/.

(Autonomist Party), whose main tenet was the island's independence, published another one. This information is not readily available in the limited metadata of the bibliographic records. Without the essays, these facts remain hidden from those who are unaware of the historical context. Although the English translations provide context, they are not of much use to Spanish speakers, not only because the essay is only available in English, but also because there is a loss of context in translation. Spanish-speaking users need essays in Spanish to find information of interest.

In response to this, the project coordinator worked with other LIS specialists to develop a study that would examine the way biases in North American cataloging standards influence research practices and how inclusion of cataloging descriptors (such as essays and subject headings) in the native language of the materials could more accurately reflect their meaning. The study involved interviewing scholars external to the libraries, as well as LIS specialists at UF, to identify how current cataloging and metadata standards affect research practices. The scholars were asked about their research methods, specifically whether bilingual metadata affected how their newspaper research was conducted. LIS specialists were interviewed in a group setting and were asked to address how enhancing metadata records with bilingual metadata would affect research and workflows within the library.

Although most of the scholars interviewed for this study did not use metadata when researching, they all recognized that metadata is important for facilitating access to materials. One scholar specifically noted the importance of newspapers as primary sources for research and the value of the historical context provided in the essays. LIS specialists at UF also agreed that metadata is important, especially to those for whom English is a second language and who are therefore at a disadvantage when using large digital collections comprised of non-English languages that are only described in English. The library group suggested that the language of the metadata should, at the very least, match the language of the original source in order to make the content more accessible for Spanish speakers. In addition to including bilingual metadata, interviewees suggested that the Spanish essays be submitted for inclusion in Chronicling America.

The Spanish-speaking community in the US continues to steadily grow, and not providing information in Spanish adds to their difficulty in finding and accessing information. This is especially important in Florida, where the population of Puerto Ricans increased dramatically after Hurricane Maria devastated the island in September 2017. Libraries, especially those serving non-native English speakers, must recognize that current Anglo-American cataloging and metadata standards are limited, biased, and impede access to information. The foundation of libraries rests on principles of access, service, and diversity; to ensure that these values drive their work, LIS specialists must assess user needs and implement standards that will challenge the problem of English-language dominance in cataloging and ensure ease of access to information for all users.

To address these issues, a goal of the Florida and Puerto Rico Digital Newspaper Project is to enhance the bibliographic records for Puerto Rican newspapers by providing metadata in both English and Spanish. Because Chronicling America does not allow for non-English language essays, the bilingual metadata specialist added the Spanish language essays written by Puerto Rican scholars to a Machine-Readable Cataloging (MARC) note field in the catalog records for the Puerto Rican titles. This allows users to access both essay versions at once in Chronicling America, given that it displays the English essay and the bibliographic record on the same page. The project team is also working with other LIS specialists to identify an authority file for Spanish language subject headings to augment metadata for these newspaper records.

Celebrating Cuba! Collaborative Digital Collections of Cuban Patrimony

Cuban scholars based in the United States, Cuba, and other parts of the world are eager for complete access to the island's rich historical record. As with many other Latin American countries, Cuba's history embodies an interplay of colonialism, Catholicism, slavery, race and ethnic relations, monoculture, immigration and emigration, economic dependency, and authoritarian governments. In Cuba's case, proximity to the United States has both particularly shaped these dynamics and broadened the community of interested students and scholars. Persistent population movements between the two countries and an unpredictable political relationship are among the elements of added depth and complexity. Cuba's 1959 Revolution and the country's subsequent course similarly reflect its multi-layered past. The thawing of relations in 2015 followed by a tightening in 2017 illustrates the volatility of the US-Cuba political situation.[27]

In this context, librarians in Cuba and the US have long been organizing efforts to digitize and provide access to source materials for research in Cuban studies. The ever-changing political relationship between Cuba and the US affects trends in scholarship, yet scholarship has flourished since the 1960s and has remained fairly steady in the 2010s.[28] Political and technical challenges in coordinating such work are complicated, but not insurmountable. Managing digitization and access to source materials for Cuban studies provides opportunities to reduce costs and redundancy, and to aggregate valuable collections that would otherwise be unavailable in both countries. While technical challenges exist in Cuba, and exchange of digitization equipment is difficult, coordinating digital file transfer between cultural heritage institutions increases access to unique source material in both countries. LIS specialists in the US have focused work on monographs, serials, legal materials, and maps; they envision further expanding the project's scope to include special collections, which is of interest to researchers in Cuba and the US. The experience gained through previous digital projects, such as those in dLOC, can be used to facilitate this complicated endeavor.

UF's initiative to coordinate the digitization of Cuban material in the US and Cuba began in 2016 when UF and the Biblioteca Nacional

27. George A. Smathers Libraries, "Charge," Guides@UF, Collaborative Digital Collections of Cuban Patrimony, last accessed December 12, 2018, http://guides.uflib.ufl.edu/c.php?g=706545&p=5017398.

28. Jessica L. English, "Preservation is Political: International Collaboration for Preserving Cuban Bibliographic Heritage," (paper presented at the Latin American Studies Association, Barcelona, Spain, 23-26 May, 2018).

de Cuba José Martí formalized their existing partnership with an official collaborative agreement. The initial project was to digitize nineteenth-century monographs published in Cuba. Representatives from institutions with strong Cuban holdings came together for an informational and planning meeting at the George A. Smathers Libraries in September 2017, where they formalized UF's leadership. This meeting set the foundations for the Collaborative Cuban Digital Collections Steering Committee, which defined its mission in 2018. The Steering Committee coordinates activities for preservation and global access to Cuban digital collections. It has advisory and operational responsibilities, such as advising on the scope of and the strategy for developing collaborative Cuban digital collections and contributing institutional content to collaborative collections.[29]

The first challenge is to establish a shared bibliography of Cuban publications to determine the authoritative known universe of publications to digitize. UF is leading the development of such a checklist, identifying holding locations for imprints and systematically assigning digitization responsibilities to institutions, in addition to transferring files and metadata among institutions and platforms. The nine volumes of the *Bibliografía cubana* (Cuban Bibliography) by Carlos M. Trelles serve as the foundation of the Cuban authoritative bibliography.[30] However, the large amount of content to digitize makes the task daunting.

LIS specialists used the *Catálogo Colectivo de Impresos Latinoamericanos* (*CCILA*), a bibliographic database that the University of California Riverside (UCR) developed from the bibliographies by Trelles and José

---

29. Steering committee partners 2017-2019 include Harvard University, New York Public Library, University of North Carolina at Chapel Hill, Duke University, University of Florida, University of Miami, Florida International University, and the University of California Los Angeles. George A. Smathers Libraries, "Collaborative Digital Collections of Cuban Patrimony: Digital Cuban Collections," Guides@UF, last accessed December 3, 2018, https://guides.uflib.ufl.edu/cuba.

30. Carlos M.Trelles, *Bibliografía cubana de los siglos XVII y XVIII* (Havana: Impr. del Ejército, 1965); Carlos M. Trelles, Francisco Llaca y Argudín, and Manuel Pérez Beato, *Bibliografía cubana del siglo XIX* (Matanzas: Kraus Reprint, 1965); José Toribio Medina, *La imprenta en La Habana, 1707-1810* (Amsterdam: Israel, 1964).

Toribio Medina, as foundational data.[31] UCR provided UF with a MARC file of the full *CCILA* database, and LIS specialists tried to parse the file into project-specific data. However, the MARC records for the *CCILA* database were so rich that UF decided that generating a list of actual library holdings and eventually comparing it the *CCILA* bibliographic database would be a better strategy for identifying materials for digitization.

In order to produce replicable and universal data standards, LIS specialists shifted the focus for developing library holdings database to Online Computer Library Center (OCLC). "OCLC is a global library cooperative that provides shared technology services, original research and community programs for its membership and the library community at large," and provides library management, discovery, cataloging, digital libraries, virtual reference, and resource sharing services.[32] The coordinator of the project generated datasets of unique holdings from OCLC and supplied them to IT to populate the database. Currently, UF is only adding unique holdings from partner institutions as possibly eligible items for digitization, but is expanding the list to include rarer (four or fewer libraries holdings) materials and has instituted a tracking mechanism so that holding libraries can "flag" items for digitization. Using OCLC has been useful; first, because it supplies an accession number that functions as a unique, although imperfect, identifier, and second, because of its consistent cataloging data.

Furthermore, UF is coordinating with the Biblioteca Nacional de Cuba José Martí to include their catalog records into OCLC. The purpose is twofold: to increase knowledge of works available in Cuba and to include the records of Cuba's National Library in the bibliographic

---

31. The scope of *CCILA* includes "Spanish/Portuguese holdings in Latin America, Caribbean United States and Philippines from the first printing in Latin America (about 1539) through the end of 1850," spanning twenty-four modern day countries. Center for Bibliographic Studies and Research, University of California Riverside, "Scope of the Project," *Catálogo Colectivo de Impresos Latinoamericanos bibliography*, last accessed December 3, 2018, http://ccila2.ucr.edu/scope.html.

32. OCLC, "Advancing our shared mission," OCLC.org, last accessed December 3, 2018, https://www.oclc.org/en/home.html.

database of Cuban holdings. In turn, this strategy will reduce duplication of labor in the digitization process. However, when the Biblioteca Nacional de Cuba José Martí first appeared in WorldCat, the bibliographic records showed "University of Florida GASL" as the holding institution. Since the acronym "GASL" stood for the George A. Smathers Libraries, the name of the library system at UF, one of the unintended results was the perception of the project as a colonialist approach, for UF seemed to appropriate Cuba's holdings. Thus, UF and OCLC discussed a way to indicate Cuba's ownership; today the records show "University of Florida BNCJM" Biblioteca Nacional de Cuba José Martí as the holding institution (**Figure 1**). Although UF still appears in the records, such compromise helps to overcome the fact that Cuba's National Library is not an OCLC member (**Figure 2**). Yet, to challenge colonialism, it is important to acknowledge that such a solution needs improvement to indicate Cuba's sole ownership.

In addition to problems of accessibility, sustainability is one of the greatest challenges that LIS specialists in Florida and Cuba face. Given the lack of current technology and unreliable access to internet on the island, a standalone project like this cannot alleviate true problems for preservation and access in Cuba. In the works is a long-term sustainable plan based, not only in the improvement of technology and infrastructure, but also in a formal and effective exchange of resources and communication, with sustainable planning and funding.

Challenges of Bilingual Metadata

The Florida and Puerto Rico Digital Newspaper Project and the Cuba initiative suggest that one of the greatest challenges in providing access to digital collections for Latin American and Caribbean people is using their native language in bilingual metadata. Although dLOC's interface is multilingual, prior to 2017 the metadata has only been in English. With the continual expansion of Latin American partnerships like the Biblioteca Nacional de Cuba José Martí, LIS specialists proposed to add Spanish language subject headings to records.

Figure 1. Sample OCLC record of a holding belonging to the Biblioteca Nacional de Cuba José Martí displaying the holding location as "University of Florida BNCJM." OCLC WorldCat, last accessed December 17, 2018, http://www.worldcat.org/title/israelia/oclc/1011457615&referer=brief_results.

Prior to this, catalogers at the George A. Smathers Libraries had never included Spanish language subject headings. The Cuban American Dream, an online exhibit, was the first project in which LIS specialists implemented bilingual metadata.[33] The timeline used the immigration of Cubans to Florida in the twentieth century as a case study to discuss matters related to immigration in general, such as the pressure brought to local and state governments, the reactions of Floridian communities to Cuban immigrants, the ways in which Cuban immigrants adapted to their new reality, and the contribution of Cuban immigration to the state of Florida. The purpose of the project was to democratize the historical record: first, by providing digital open access to records that

---

33. George A. Smathers Libraries, "The Cuban American Dream: A Timeline," Latin American and Caribbean Collection Home, last accessed December 10, 2018, http://exhibits.uflib.ufl.edu/cubanamericandream/.

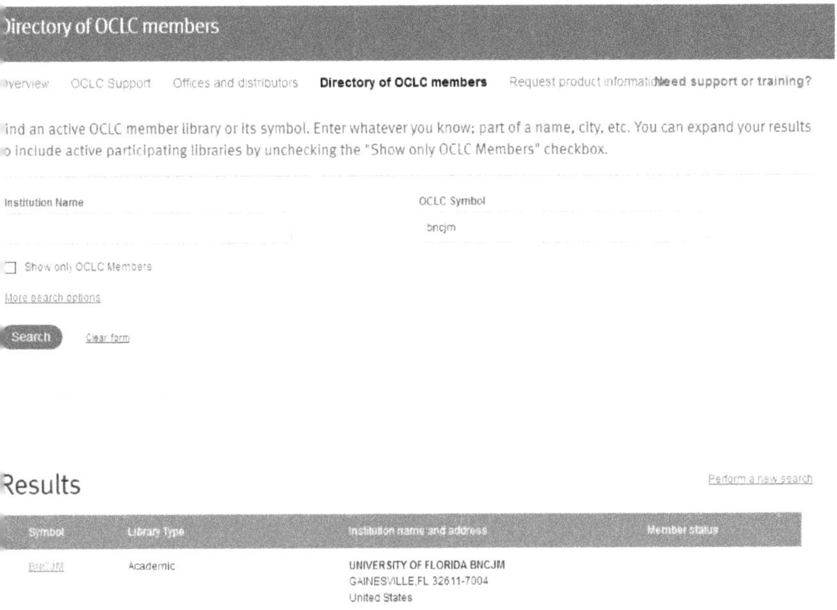

Figure 2. Directory information for the OCLC symbol "BNCJM," showing the institution as UF, rather than the Biblioteca Nacional de Cuba José Martí. OCLC, "Directory of OCLC members," OCLC.org, last accessed December 17, 2018, https://www.oclc.org/en/contacts/libraries.html.

document Cuban immigration to Florida; and second, by providing bilingual metadata to ensure access for a Spanish-speaking audience.

The first challenge for this new initiative was to find reputable authority files of Spanish language subject headings. Since the ideal was to utilize authority files recognized by the Library of Congress, UF's bilingual metadata specialist first consulted a Library of Congress source list.[34] Fortunately, the creators of lcsh-es.org, "a prototype for a new kind of shared bilingual file," compiled some of these authorities in a convenient database in which users insert a Library of Congress Subject Heading (LCSH), and the database provides results from various Spanish

---

34. Library of Congress, Network Development & MARC Standards Office, "Subject Heading and Term Source Codes," Source Codes for Vocabularies, Rules, and Schemes, last accessed December 3, 2018, https://www.loc.gov/standards/sourcelist/subject.html.

language authority files.[35] Six were aggregated to lcsh-es.org: Biblioteca Nacional de España, Bilindex, Consejo Superior de Investigaciones Científicas (Spain), LCSH, Queens Library Spanish language subject headings (QLSP), and San Francisco Public Library.[36] Since lcsh-es. org provides greater accessibility and ease of use, it was preferred over searching multiple Spanish language authorities on the Library of Congress source code list.

A centralized database of Spanish language authorities was the most realistic approach to assigning Spanish language headings, mainly because of the limited labor force assigned to create bilingual metadata. For this reason, only one collection was selected to receive bilingual metadata. Thus, the George A. Smathers Libraries tasked the bilingual metadata specialist with creating English and Spanish metadata only for Cuban Collections in University of Florida Digital Collections (UFDC).[37] UFDC Cuban Collections contain manuscripts, maps, books, serials, ephemera, photographs, theses and dissertations, born digital records, and government documents.[38] UFDC contains over 300 collections, with dLOC having the most extensive Spanish language content. UFDC and dLOC allow George A. Smathers Libraries to better serve global patrons whose locations do not allow for accessibility to UF's preeminent physical collections. In continuing with this pursuit of gapping the divide, bilingual metadata was the next logical step to ensure accessibility for a multilingual patron population.

However, the sources utilized in lcsh-es.org assume that Spanish is monolithic. For example, most authorities used in lcsh-es.org come from either European (Spain) or North American institutions; thus,

35. Kreyche, Mike, "About lcsh-es.org," lcsh-es.org, last accessed December 3, 2018, http://lcsh-es.org/about.html.

36. "Sources of Headings," lcsh-es.org, last accessed December 3, 2018, http://lcsh-es.org/sources.html.

37. George A. Smathers Libraries, UFDC University of Florida Digital Collections, last accessed November 8, 2108, http://ufdc.ufl.edu/.

38. George A. Smathers Libraries, "Celebrating Cuba! Collaborative Digital Collections of Cuban Patrimony," Digital Library of the Caribbean, last accessed December 3, 2018, http://ufdc.ufl.edu/cuba.

the process fails to represent national and regional variations in Spanish terminology.[39] Furthermore, Latin American institutions created only three out of the twenty-one listed in the Library of Congress source code list; the rest come from European and North American institutions. The only authority file of Latin American heritage in lcsh-es.org is Bilindex (sometimes abbreviated as BIDEX), which was derived from Lista de encabezamientos de materia para bibliotecas (LEMB), a Colombian based authority list. ARMARC (Lista ARMARC de encabezamientos de materia para bibliotecas mayores), which is only available through Rojas Eberhard, a Colombian publisher, has supplanted LEMB.[40] The other Latin American authority files recognized by the Library of Congress are from Chile (RENIB: base de datos de autoridad) and Puerto Rico (EBFEM: Encabezamientos bilingües de la Fundación Educativa Ana G. Mendez).[41] In assigning Spanish language subject headings to Cuban collections, the bilingual metadata specialist observed that very few OCLC records contained Spanish language subject headings, and those that did were from RENIB. Utilizing Spanish language databases such as ARMARC, RENIB, and the Universidad Nacional Autónoma de México, which the Library of Congress does not recognize, is not as easy as utilizing lcsh-es.org. First, it is arduous to find these databases. Second, some are not free (such as ARMARC), and some are unavailable for use (as was the case with Universidad Nacional Autónoma de México at the time of writing this article). However, while lcsh-es.org contains the most available Latin American subject authority files, "the data is not current and much of it has not been checked thoroughly."[42] The aggregation of Spanish language authority files into lcsh-es.org was completed over a decade ago and few, if any, updates have occurred. There have been many changes in cataloging since then, like the addition

39. Michael Kreyche, "Subject Headings in Spanish: The lcsh-es.org Bilingual Database," *Cataloging & Classification Quarterly* 51, no. 4 (2013): 392, last accessed December 17, 2018, https://doi.org/10.1080/01639374.2012.740610.

40. Kreyche, 392.

41. Library of Congress, "Subject Heading and Term Source Codes."

42. Kreyche, "About lcsh-es.org."

of many more subject headings to the LCSH authority file. Perhaps the most impactful for subject authority control has been the wide use of FAST (Faceted Application of Subject Terminology), "a faceted-navigation-friendly subject schema derived from LCSH."[43]

FAST is widely used when creating metadata, because it is more compatible with the semantic web and utilizes simplified syntax instead of subject heading strings. It is more compatible because the narrow results selection (on the left pane of Online Public Access Catalog's and digital library platforms, such as UFDC and dLOC) allows users to construct their own search result set without the limitation of catalogers' judgments. Not only does FAST benefit users; it is also simpler for catalogers to use. Simplified syntax is much needed in bilingual metadata because there is "an absence of clear linkage between headings and their subdivisions in most of the Spanish language systems."[44] For instance, when searching for a LCSH string in lcsh-es.org, a user must search each term within the subject string. While creating bilingual metadata for Cuban Collections, it was observed that QLSP provided the most complete subject strings.[45] For example, the bilingual metadata specialist would start off using Bilindex (the only authority derived from Latin America), but when one of the terms within the subject string did not have a Bilindex equivalent, QLSP often had to be used because only one authority file can be used per string, as per MARC standards (**Figure 3**).[46]

43. OCLC, "FAST (Faceted Application of Subject Terminology)," last accessed December 3, 2018, https://www.oclc.org/research/themes/data-science/fast.html.

44. Álvaro Quijano-Solís, Pilar María Moreno-Jiménex, and Reynaldo Figueroa-Servín, "Automated Authority Files of Spanish-Language Subject Headings," *Cataloging & Classification Quarterly* 29, no. 1-2 (2000): 209-23, last accessed December 17, 2018, https://doi.org/10.1300/J104v29n01_15.

45. Library of Congress, "Queens Library Spanish language subject headings," Linked Data Service, last accessed December 3, 2018, http://id.loc.gov/vocabulary/subjectSchemes/qlsp.html.

46. Bilindex, last accessed December 3, 2018, http://www.bilindex.com/.

650	0	Buccaneers ǂv Early works to 1800.
650	0	Pirates ǂv Early works to 1800.
650	0	Adventure and adventurers ǂv Early works to 1800.
650	0	Blacks ǂz West Indies ǂv Early works to 1800.
651	0	Spanish Main ǂv Early works to 1800.
651	0	West Indies ǂx History ǂy 17th century ǂv Early works to 1800.
651	0	Africa, West ǂx Discovery and exploration ǂv Early works to 1800.
650	7	Adventure and adventurers. ǂ2 fast ǂ0 (OCoLC)fst00797447
650	7	Blacks. ǂ2 fast ǂ0 (OCoLC)fst00833880
650	7	Buccaneers. ǂ2 fast ǂ0 (OCoLC)fst00839967
650	7	Discoveries in geography. ǂ2 fast ǂ0 (OCoLC)fst00894950
650	7	Pirates. ǂ2 fast ǂ0 (OCoLC)fst01064776
651	7	Africa, West. ǂ2 fast ǂ0 (OCoLC)fst01239521
651	7	South America ǂz Spanish Main. ǂ2 fast ǂ0 (OCoLC)fst01244688
651	7	West Indies. ǂ2 fast ǂ0 (OCoLC)fst01243265
648	7	1600-1699 ǂ2 fast
655	4	Electronic books.
655	7	History ǂ2 fast ǂ0 (OCoLC)fst01411628
655	7	Early works. ǂ2 fast ǂ0 (OCoLC)fst01411636

Figure 3. Example of multiple Library of Congress subject headings without a Bilindex equivalent in lcsh-es.org: "Early works to 1800," "Spanish Main," "Discoveries in geography," "17th century," and "Buccaneers." Subject keywords for *The History of the Bucaniers of America*, 1771. A.O. (Alexandre Olivier) Exquemelin, OCLC# 123428503. George A. Smathers Libraries catalog, *The History of the Bucaniers of America: Exhibiting a particular account and description of Porto Bello, Chagre, Panama, Cuba, Havanna, and most of the Spanish possessions on the coasts of the West Indies, and also all along the coasts of the South Sea: with the manner in which they have been invaded, attempted, or taken by these adventurers the whole written in several languages by persons present at the transactions*, last accessed December 20, 2018, http://uf.catalog.fcla.edu/permalink.jsp?20UF036503552.

As of yet, however, no Spanish language subject authority file found in MARC records lists FAST in its linking entries (750 fields); only LCSH equivalents and corresponding identifiers are listed. Also, while FAST contains virtually the same subject headings as LCSH, there have been some changes; for example, LCSH "Description and travel" is now "Travel" in FAST. These factors might deter the adaptation of FAST to Spanish language authority control, but LCSH strings are too time consuming to ignore this option. While adding Spanish headings to maps in the Cuban Collections, it became laborious and unrealistic for the sole person creating bilingual metadata to input the Spanish equivalents of LCSH strings when every topical term would have to be repeated for every geographical subdivision used. So, if there were four topical terms, each term would have to be repeated based on the number of geographical subdivisions and any other subdivision of relevance (such as form and chronological subdivisions) (**Figure 4**). After searching a few records this way, it became clear that finding Spanish language subjects for FAST headings was the way to go.

Subjects

Subjects / Keywords:	Maps -- West Indies (lcsh)
	Maps -- Caribbean Area (lcsh)
	Maps -- Havana (Cuba) (lcsh)
	Caribbean Area (fast)
	Cuba -- Havana (fast)
	West Indies (fast)
	Mapas -- Antillas (bidex)
	Mapas -- Región Caribe (qlsp)
	Mapas -- La Habana (Cuba) (qlsp)
Genre:	Mapas (bidex)
	Maps (fast)

Figure 4. Subject keywords for the map *West Indien und Mittel America.* Carl Christian Franz Radefeld, *West Indien und Mittel America,* 1863-1867, George A. Smathers Libraries, "West Indien und Mittel America," Digital Library of the Caribbean, last accessed December 17, 2018, http://ufdc.ufl.edu/AA00059310/00001/citation.

While the linked data movement has encouraged commitment among libraries to share data, this has not quite been the case for Latin American institutions, whose datasets are unavailable or inaccessible without a fee. The George A. Smathers Libraries do not currently have the Spanish-speaking labor force to provide bilingual metadata for the full scope of its Spanish language collections. Diversity in librarianship has been a continual challenge due to "the difficulty of recruiting and keeping catalogers with a good grasp of Spanish."[47] Therefore, some of the ways that libraries can combat this challenge is through collaboration and centralization. As mentioned previously, a centralized database like lcsh.es-org is the most realistic option, given libraries' limited labor force and funds, and collaboration between institutions is essential to bringing about centralization. For this reason, George A. Smathers Libraries have begun collaborating with the Hispanic American Periodicals Index (HAPI) from the University of California, Los Angeles.[48] HAPI has created a locally controlled vocabulary list that includes subject headings more suitable for Latin American terminology. Since HAPI also understands the disparity between Latin American subject authority files and those of North American and European subject authority files, this collaboration might bring about the enhancement of lcsh-es.org by including more Latin American authority files and adding missing LCSH, or by creating a new database modeled more after FAST. To date, public libraries, especially the Queens Borough Public Library and San Francisco Public Library, have led the way for Spanish language authority control in North America; it's time for academic libraries to pick up the baton of providing equal accessibility for their multilingual patrons.[49]

Conclusion

In addition to the development of Latin American collections, a significant result of the expansion of US business in the world was the development of "the rational organization of corporate industry."[50]

---

47. Laurence S. Creider, "What Are Academic Libraries Doing with Spanish Languages Subject Headings?" *Journal of Academic Librarianship* 29, no. 2 (March 2003): 90.

48. HAPI, "About HAPI," Hispanic American Periodicals Index (HAPI) from the Latin American Institute, University of California, Los Angeles (UCLA), last accessed December 17, 2018, http://hapi.ucla.edu/about.

49. Creider, "What Are Academic Libraries Doing with Spanish Languages Subject Headings?"

50. Salvatore, "Library Accumulation and the Emergence of Latin American Studies," 420-22.

Mass production relies on a large number of workers who specialize in a standardized system. The principles adopted by the American Library Association at its foundation in 1876 suggest that libraries were always intended to follow the business model. The axioms were "democratic access, rational order, and mass production." The ultimate goal was to develop a system that would enable patrons to find and locate material rapidly. In order to achieve this, librarians developed a system of uniform classification rules and "an orderly arrangement of collections." In this way, libraries became like "mass-producing factories."[51]

In relation to Latin American collections, a result of this paradigm was that access in the form of subject headings and library catalogs was English only. This fact conflicts with dLOC's mission to democratize access to Caribbean content, which can only be achieved through bilingual or multilingual metadata. The cases analyzed here highlight the challenges that LIS specialists have faced in doing so. The Florida and Puerto Rico Digital Newspaper Project Coordinator developed a study with the object of evaluating the significance of bilingual metadata for research. One of the main takeaways of this analysis is the need to raise awareness of such significance. The UF initiative, "Celebrating Cuba! Collaborative Digital Collections of Cuban Patrimony," illustrates the complexity of designing a sustainable program of international collaboration between Cuba and the US. Finally, the study of the creation of bilingual metadata for The Cuban American Dream timeline has revealed a major obstacle: the heterogeneity of Spanish subject heading systems, which reflects the diversity of nations and regions where Spanish is spoken.

In order to overcome these challenges, UF must implement a program of bilingual Spanish-English metadata that includes the hiring of more personnel with second language skills, the creation of efficient workflows, and adequate planning to provide time for employees to do retrospective cataloging and description.

---

51. Salvatore, 420-22.

Some of the solutions that we suggest are first, the design of well-defined, contained, and sustainable projects that can function as pilots, and second, centralization and collaboration with other institutions, such as HAPI, in order to develop Spanish language datasets. Above all, the creation of bilingual ports of access requires a mindset that departs from the conception of libraries as factories, whose goal is mass production, and acknowledges that the creation of bilingual metadata is more artisanal than industrial, for it requires intensive and specialized labor.

Bibliography

Bilindex. Accessed December 3, 2018. http://www.bilindex.com/.

Blight, David W. *Race and Reunion: The Civil War in American Memory.* Cambridge, MA: Belknap Press, 2003.

Center for Bibliographic Studies and Research, University of California Riverside. "Scope of the Project." *Catálogo Colectivo de Impresos Latinoamericanos bibliography.* Accessed December 3, 2018. http://ccila2.ucr.edu/scope.html.

Center for Latin American Studies at the University of Florida. "History." Accessed December 3, 2018. http://www.latam.ufl.edu/about/history/.

Creider, Laurence S. "What Are Academic Libraries Doing with Spanish Languages Subject Headings?" *Journal of Academic Librarianship* 29, no. 2 (March 2003): 88-94.

Digital Library of the Caribbean. Accessed November 8, 2018. http://www.dloc.com/.

Digital Library of the Caribbean. "About dLOC." Accessed December 3, 2018. http://dloc.com/dloc1/about.

Elkins, Caroline. "Looking beyond Mau Mau: Archiving Violence in the Era of Decolonization." *American Historical Review* 120, no. 3 (June 2015): 852-68. https://doi.org/10.1093/ahr/120.3.852.

English, Jessica L. "Preservation is Political: International Collaboration for Preserving Cuban Bibliographic Heritage." Paper presented at the

Latin American Studies Association. Barcelona, Spain, 23-26 May, 2018.

George A. Smathers Libraries. "A Guide to the Braga Brothers Collection." Finding Aids. Accessed November 8, 2018. http://www.library.ufl. edu/spec/manuscript/Braga/braga.htm.

George A. Smathers Libraries. "A Guide to the Frank R. Crumbie Papers." Finding Aids. Accessed November 8, 2018. http://web.uflib.ufl. edu/spec/manuscript/guides/crumbie.htm.

George A. Smathers Libraries. "A Guide to the Jérémie Papers." Finding Aids. Accessed November 8, 2018. http://web.uflib.ufl.edu/spec/ manuscript/guides/jeremie.htm.

George A. Smathers Libraries. "A Guide to the Luis García Pimentel Collection." Finding Aids. Accessed November 8, 2018. http://www. library.ufl.edu/spec/manuscript/guides/pimentel.htm.

George A. Smathers Libraries. "Celebrating Cuba! Collaborative Digital Collections of Cuban Patrimony." Digital Library of the Caribbean. Accessed December 3, 2108. http://ufdc.ufl.edu/cuba.

George A. Smathers Libraries. "Charge." Guides@UF, Collaborative Digital Collections of Cuban Patrimony. Accessed December 12, 2018. http://guides.uflib.ufl.edu/c.php?g=706545&p=5017398.

George A. Smathers Libraries. "Collaborative Digital Collections of Cuban Patrimony: Digital Cuban Collections." Guides@UF. Accessed December 3, 2018. https://guides.uflib.ufl.edu/cuba.

George A. Smathers Libraries. The Cuban American Dream: A Timeline, Latin American and Caribbean Collection Home. Accessed December 10, 2018. http://exhibits.uflib.ufl.edu/cubanamerican-dream/.

George A. Smathers Libraries. "Florida and Puerto Rico Digital Newspaper Project." University of Florida Digital Collections. Accessed November 7, 2018. http://ufdc.ufl.edu/ndnp.

George A. Smathers Libraries. "Florida and Puerto Rico Digital Newspaper Project: National Digital Newspaper Program (NDNP) Grant Proposal." Digital Library of the Caribbean. Accessed December 3, 2018. http://ufdc.ufl.edu/AA00019344/00001.

George A. Smathers Libraries. "Florida and Puerto Rico Newspaper
Digitization Project—Phase II." Digital Library of the Ca-
ribbean. Accessed December 3, 2018. http://ufdc.ufl.edu/
AA00028169/00001.

George A. Smathers Libraries. "Florida and Puerto Rico Digital Newspaper—Phase III." Digital Library of the Caribbean. Accessed
December 3, 2018. http://ufdc.ufl.edu/IR00009659/00001.

George A. Smathers Libraries. "Latin American and Caribbean Collections."
Finding Aids. Accessed November 7, 2018. http://www.uflib.ufl.
edu/spec/browseu_lacc.htm.

George A. Smathers Libraries. "Letter to Senator Henry Cabot Lodge from
Acting Secretary of State Alvey A. Adee." Digital Library of the
Caribbean. Accessed November 8, 2018. http://ufdc.ufl.edu/
AA00055812/00001.

George A. Smathers Libraries. UFDC University of Florida Digital Collections. Accessed November 8, 2108. http://ufdc.ufl.edu/.

George A. Smathers Libraries. "West Indien und Mittel America." Digital
Library of the Caribbean. Accessed December 17, 2018. http://
ufdc.ufl.edu/AA00059310/00001/citation.

The Graduate School, University of Florida. *Proposal for an Inter-American Cultural and Scientific Center.* Gainesville, FL: 1961. Accessed December
3, 2018. http://ufdc.ufl.edu/AA00002847/00001.

HAPI. "About HAPI," Hispanic American Periodicals Index (HAPI) from
the Latin American Institute. University of California, Los Angeles
(UCLA). Accessed December 17, 2018. http://hapi.ucla.edu/
about.

Kreyche, Mike. "About lcsh-es.org." lcsh-es.org. Accessed December 3,
2018. http://lcsh-es.org/about.html.

Kreyche, Michael. "Subject Headings in Spanish: The lcsh-es.org Bilingual
Database," *Cataloging & Classification Quarterly* 51, no. 4 (2013): 389-
403. http://doi.org/10.1080/01639374.2012.740610.

Library of Congress. Chronicling America. Historic American Newspapers.
Accessed November 7, 2018. https://chroniclingamerica.loc.gov/.

Library of Congress. "Guidelines & Resources. Technical Guidelines & Specifications." National Digital Newspaper Program. Accessed December 3, 2018. https://www.loc.gov/ndnp/guidelines/.

Library of Congress. "Queens Library Spanish language subject headings." Linked Data Service. Accessed December 3, 2018. http://id.loc.gov/vocabulary/subjectSchemes/qlsp.html.

Library of Congress. Network Development & MARC Standards Office. "Subject Heading and Term Source Codes." Source Codes for Vocabularies, Rules, and Schemes. Accessed December 3, 2018. https://www.loc.gov/standards/sourcelist/subject.html.

Makdisi, Ussama. "Diminished Sovereignty and the Impossibility of 'Civil War' in the Modern Middle East." *American Historical Review* 120, no. 5 (2015): 1739-1752. https://doi.org/10.1093/ahr/120.5.1739.

"Monroe Doctrine." In *Dictionary of World History*. Oxford, UK: Oxford University Press, 2015.

Montgomery, Bruce. "Reconciling the Inalienability Doctrine with the Conventions of War." *American Archivist* 78:2 (Fall/Winter 2015): 288-316. https://doi.org/10.17723/0360-9081.78.2.288.

Medina, José Toribio. *La imprenta en La Habana, 1707-1810*. Amsterdam: Israel, 1964.

New York Public Library. "Kurt Fisher Haitian Collection 1727-1958." Archives & Manuscripts. Accessed November 8, 2018. http://archives.nypl.org/scm/20798.

OCLC. "Advancing our shared mission." OCLC.org. Accessed December 3, 2018. https://www.oclc.org/en/home.html.

OCLC. "Directory of OCLC members." OCLC.org. Accessed December 17, 2018. https://www.oclc.org/en/contacts/libraries.html.

OCLC. "FAST (Faceted Application of Subject Terminology)." OCLC.org. Accessed December 3, 2018. https://www.oclc.org/research/themes/data-science/fast.html.

OCLC. "Sample OCLC record of a holding belonging to the Biblioteca Nacional de Cuba José Martí displaying the holding location as University of Florida BNCJM." OCLC WorldCat. Accessed

December 17, 2018. http://www.worldcat.org/title/israelia/
oclc/1011457615&referer=brief_results.

Quijano-Solís, Álvaro, Pilar María Moreno-Jiménex, and Reynaldo Figueroa-
Servín. "Automated Authority Files of Spanish-Language Subject
Headings." *Cataloging & Classification Quarterly* 29, no. 1-2 (2000):
209-23. https://doi.org/10.1300/J104v29n01_15.

Salvatore, Ricardo D. "Library Accumulation and the Emergence
of Latin American Studies." *Comparative American Studies.
An International Journal* 3, no. 4 (2005): 415-36. https://doi.
org/10.1177/1477570005058958.

"Sources of Headings." lcsh-es.org. Accessed December 3, 2018. http://
lcsh-es.org/sources.html.

Taylor, Laurie. "'Librarian on a Boat' or Digital Scholarship, Caribbean Studies, and the Digital Library of the Caribbean (dLOC): Alternative
Sabbatical Proposal for 2016-2017." University of Florida Digital
Collections (UFDC). Accessed December 3, 2018. http://ufdc.ufl.
edu/AA00037232/00001.

Taylor, Laurie, Margarita Vargas-Betancourt, and Brooke Wooldridge.
"The Digital Library of the Caribbean (dLOC): Creating a Shared
Research Foundation." *Scholarly and Research Communication.* Simon
Fraser University 4, No. 3 (2013). Accessed December 3, 2018.
https://doi.org/10.22230/src.2013v4n3a114.

Toribio Medina, José. *La imprenta en La Habana, 1707-1810.* Amsterdam:
Israel, 1964.

Trelles, Carlos M. *Bibliografía cubana de los siglos XVII y XVIII.* Havana: Impr.
del Ejército, 1965.

Trelles, Carlos M., Francisco Llaca y Argudín, and Manuel Pérez Beato.
Bibliografía cubana del siglo XIX. Matanzas: Kraus Reprint, 1965.

University of Florida Libraries Catalog. *The History of the Bucaniers of America:
Exhibiting a particular account and description of Porto Bello, Chagre, Panama, Cuba, Havanna, and most of the Spanish possessions on the coasts of the
West Indies, and also all along the coasts of the South Sea: With the manner
in which they have been invaded, attempted, or taken by these adventurers the
whole written in several languages by persons present at the transactions.* Ac-

cessed December 20, 2018. http://uf.catalog.fcla.edu/permalink. jsp?20UF036503552.

Wagner, Ralph D. *A History of the Farmington Plan.* Lanham, MD: Scarecrow Press, 2002.

Chapter 16

THE IMPORTANCE OF COLLECTING, ACCESSING, AND CONTEXTUALIZING JAPANESE-AMERCAN HISTORICAL MATERIALS: A CALIFORNIA STATE UNIVERSITY COLLABORATIVE

Gregory L. Williams and Maureen Burns

Introduction

We're supposed to try to emphasize the <u>home</u>, but it's rather an idealistic thing to talk about here in Manzanar where we have to live in a little 2 x 4 with a desperate attempt of a living room, kitchenette, bedroom, and what have you. I think I shall attempt to make a model doll house so the poor kiddies will at least get the picture of what a home is supposed to look like.[1]
—Letter from Miriko Nagahama, Manzanar kindergarten teacher, to her friend in Glendale California, Betty Salzman, January 20, 1943

---

1. Miriko Nagahama to Betty (Salzman), letter, January 20, 1943, Manzanar Collection, Special Collections and Archives, Robert E. Kennedy Library, California Polytechnic State University San Luis Obispo, via CSUJAD, http://digitalcollections. archives.csudh.edu/digital/collection/p16855coll4/id/290/rec/129. The epigraphs in this chapter have all been obtained through the California State University Japanese American Digitization Project cited in footnote 2. When archival items from this project are cited, it will be indicated by the addition of "via CSUJAD" to the footnote to clearly designate this source.

The traditional archival response to historical events has rarely been proactive. This is both because of the lifecycle of records and because records are often donated to an archive decades after events happen. With the advent of the twenty-four-hour news cycle and social media that never stops churning out the latest meme, it is now incumbent upon archivists to dive into preserving the recent past (especially given the ephemeral nature of media and internet resources), but it is also essential to prevent older historical events from sinking into oblivion. Thus, the materials related to the incarceration of Japanese Americans in World War II (WWII) are ripe for the archival profession to continue to collect, digitize, make accessible, and preserve. Their importance lies in the fact that they document one of the prime assaults on civil liberties in the United States in the last 100 years, and that their connections to other racist outrages, both current and throughout U.S. history, are evident in other attempts at restricting immigration and snuffing out the rights of immigrants.

The infringement of the rights of Japanese Americans began easily enough. Early twentieth-century laws that prohibited Japanese Americans from owning property came about in response to older anti-Chinese laws. The bombing of Pearl Harbor on December 7, 1941 led to the incarceration of approximately 120,000 Japanese Americans in purposely isolated and often environmentally extreme camps. While there was some murmur of unease among the majority population, the panic that war brought easily morphed into the fear of an immigrant group that was indirectly associated with the war. Japanese Americans were swept up from the West Coast in a manner both efficient and illogical.

Documenting the history of the people of Japanese descent in the U.S. before, during, and after the WWII era has been the central goal of the California State University Japanese American Digitization (CSUJAD) project.[2] Once important Japanese-American archival materials within California State University (CSU) and other archival collections have

---

2. "California State University Japanese American Digitization Project," Collaborative Digital History Project of the California State University Libraries, updated May 9, 2018, http://www.csujad.com/index.html.

been identified, it is essential to digitize and describe them at the item level. This makes them searchable, accessible, and discoverable from a centralized website that is readily available to a global community of scholars, students, and interested citizens. These project goals, in turn, have attracted an expanding group of partner institutions, stimulated a number of additional donations of pertinent materials, and highlighted the urgency of procuring the passing WWII generation's documentation and remembrances, before they are lost.

In this chapter, we will explore the issues associated with the critical practice necessary to shape the development of such a collaborative archival project around a topic loaded with racism, political and social strife, and controversy. From collection development, curation, cataloging, and stewardship to outreach and contextualization, this project has provided the CSUJAD project partners with many interesting challenges and opportunities.

Collecting Information about the WWII Incarceration

> As we understand it, there are two main reasons back of this evacuation order: to forestall any possible subversive activities, and as a matter of protection to the Japanese themselves in case of uncontrollable anti-Japanese hysteria. To the best of our knowledge however, neither of these reasons has any sound basis in fact....For the most part, these Japanese-Americans are as good or better citizens than most of us, and to say that they are potentially more dangerous than some other group is fascist in the extreme, unless well backed up by facts.[3]
> —Anonymous letter to President Franklin D. Roosevelt, 1942

Even before the Pearl Harbor bombing, the government began keeping records on people of Japanese ancestry. California State officials (to their later shame) listened to the fears of their majority constituents, and Executive Order 9066, which was intended to eliminate the

---

3. Anonymous to President Franklin D. Roosevelt, letter, 1942, Japanese American Relocation Collection, University Archives and Special Collections, California State University, Fullerton, via CSUJAD, http://digitalcollections.archives.csudh.edu/digital/collection/p16855coll4/id/15246/rec/115.

Japanese-American presence from the West Coast, was drafted for President Roosevelt's signature. More records were created as citizens were taken to temporary assembly centers. Newspapers generated copy in favor of eliminating Japanese Americans from the West Coast. The military and an early government bureaucracy created announcements for citizens to gather for what was then called "evacuation." Later, 120,000 people were sent to ten War Relocation Authority (WRA) camps, most of whom were American citizens. This, in turn, generated thousands of forms, including questionnaires that forced Japanese Americans to answer poorly worded questions that caused confusion, consternation, anger, and even potential deportation. Photographers Dorothea Lange, Ansel Adams, and Toyo Miyatake documented the forced diaspora and life in the camps.[4] Journalists such as Carey McWilliams wrote about the camps.[5] Sociologists from the University of California and elsewhere interviewed and observed prisoners in an attempt to help the government, but also to analyze them for a variety of social science purposes, which often resulted in "ethical lapses" by field workers and resentment by the prisoners, who felt they were exploited.[6] After the war, only a limited number of historical works were generated, such as *The Politics of Prejudice: The Anti-Japanese Movement in California and the Struggle for Japanese Exclusion* by Roger Daniels.[7] Throughout the 1940s, 1950s, and 1960s, there was a general silence about the WWII incarceration among those who were imprisoned, but there certainly were some exceptions to that, especially in historical monographs and artistic works. The Japanese-American community's willingness to discuss the many controversies associated with the WWII incarceration and its aftermath has evolved

---

4. Jasmine Alinder, *Moving Images: Photography and the Japanese American Incarceration* (Urbana, IL: University of Illinois Press, 2009).

5. Carey McWilliams, *Prejudice: Japanese Americans, Symbol of Racial Intolerance* (Boston: Little, Brown and Company, 1944).

6. "Japanese American Evacuation and Resettlement Study," Densho Encyclopedia, accessed May 26, 2019, http://encyclopedia.densho.org/Japanese_American_Evacuation_and_Resettlement_Study/.

7. Roger Daniels, *The Politics of Prejudice: The Anti-Japanese Movement in California and the Struggle for Japanese Exclusion* (Berkeley, CA: University of California Press, 1962).

over time. Inspired by the civil rights movement in the 1960s, many Japanese Americans began to question their WWII incarceration, and a movement to address the physical, spiritual, and monetary damages caused by the incarceration experience began. This process, often called "redress," eventually resulted in a governmental apology and some meager financial compensation.

The records of the government's views of and work on incarceration were scattered throughout the U.S. National Archives and various military and institutional archives. By the late 1970s and throughout the 1980s, Japanese Americans began to generate their own response to incarceration. For example, Jeanne Wakatsuki Houston and James D. Houston wrote the book *Farewell to Manzanar*.[8] Michi Weglyn wrote her memoir, *Years of Infamy: The Untold Story of America's Concentration Camps*, which was followed by a whole host of histories.[9] The redress movement led to an almost universal demand that citizens receive an apology and some kind of recompense for their travails, thus generating investigations, testimony, and an extensive attempt by Japanese Americans to research, in the National Archives, the reasons behind incarceration.

Archivists at CSU campuses take a keen interest in the people and history of the communities across the state of California in which they are situated; as a result, the collections that have been accumulated in the Libraries' Archives and Special Collections have a distinctly localized flavor. For the past fifty years, an important area of focus has been the history and progress of people of Japanese descent. Archivists at San Jose State University preserved the records of Japanese Americans, especially those who insisted on answers while their relatives at Tule Lake Segregation Center were imprisoned inside the infamous stockade. A program at CSU Sacramento encouraged Japanese Americans who lived in the local Florin community and were sent to WRA camps to

---

8. Jeanne Wakatsuki Houston and James D. Houston, *Farewell to Manzanar: A True Story of Japanese American Experience During and After the WWII Internment* (New York: Bantam Books, 1973).

9. Michi Weglyn, *Years of Infamy: The Untold Story of America's Concentration Camps* (New York: Morrow, 1976).

donate their materials. By the 1970s, the Oral History program at CSU-Fullerton had begun interviewing a wide range of citizens who had either been in the camps, running the camps, or had some association with the WWII incarceration. Citizens often think first about giving their memorabilia or stories to local history repositories, which often are the CSU archives mentioned above, as well as CSU campuses at Dominguez Hills (CSUDH), Fresno, Northridge, Sonoma State, and others.

In the last two decades of the twentieth century, the Japanese American National Museum (JANM) in Los Angeles collected such an extensive collection that at times they couldn't accept new materials due to capacity issues.[10] The Go For Broke National Education Center was founded to pay tribute to the Japanese Americans who served in the U.S. armed forces during WWII and they have also collected associated archival materials and oral histories.[11] Other museums and several Japanese-American or other local historical societies throughout California, as well as the California State Archives and the California Historical Society, also have interesting collections of Japanese-American archival material.[12] West Coast repositories in Oregon, Washington, Idaho, Arizona, and Arkansas, often near where the WRA camps were located, collected this material, as did individual historians and social scientists doing oral and video histories on the topic. The University of California at Berkeley as well as the Los Angeles and Santa Barbara campuses also gathered large collections. In the late 1990s, archival digitization projects began. One of the earliest was the Japanese American Relocation Digital Archive, which was sponsored by the Online Archive of California (OAC) as it merged into the California Digital Library (CDL).[13]

---

10. Japanese American National Museum, 2019, www.janm.org.

11. Go For Broke National Education Center, 2019, http://www.goforbroke.org/index.php.

12. "California State Archives," California Secretary of State, accessed May 26, 2019, https://www.sos.ca.gov/archives/; California Historical Society, 2019, https://www.californiahistoricalsociety.org/.

13. "Japanese American Relocation Digital Archive," Calisphere, accessed May 26, 2019, https://calisphere.org/exhibitions/t11/jarda/; "Resources," CSUJAD, updated May 9, 2018, http://www.csujad.com/links.html.

In 1996, the Densho Digital Repository was established as a grassroots community organization operating out of Seattle that made it a priority to gather oral histories from Japanese Americans who were incarcerated during WWII.[14] Densho has over 2,000 oral histories online, making the name—a Japanese term meaning "to pass on to the next generation" or "to leave a legacy"—quite appropriate. As a model twenty-first-century historical society, Densho has expanded its mission to educate, preserve, collaborate, and inspire action for equity. With no physical collections other than computer servers, Densho staff digitize archival materials and encourage the collecting of historic materials. Through public support and with the help of grants from various organizations and governmental entities such as the National Park Service (NPS) (Japanese American Confinement Sites Program), the National Historical Publications and Records Commission (NHPRC), and the National Endowment for the Humanities (NEH), Densho has generated important resources for research, including the Densho Encyclopedia (a vibrant source for almost any topic on the subject of Japanese-American history), a digital repository, a blog, a Facebook page, and more.

CSUJAD and Collaboration between Partner Archives

> Since I was arrested and put in the stockade thirty-four days have passed. Why I was arrested I do not know; it has never been made clear to me. I have never entertained radical ideas....Needless to say, life in the stockade is meaningless to me. It does not make sense besides being unpleasant.[15]
> —Letter from William J. Fujimoto from the stockade at Tule Lake Segregation Center to Tule Lake Project Director, Raymond R. Best, February 23, 1944

In 2014, the CSUJAD project commenced, bringing together a unique, functional, and growing collaboration of, at first five, and now over

---

14. Densho, accessed May 26, 2019, https://densho.org.

15. William J. Fujimoto to Raymond R. Best, letter, February 23, 1944, Schmidt Papers, Department of Special Collections and Archives, San Jose State University, via CSUJAD, http://digitalcollections.archives.csudh.edu/digital/collection/p16855coll4/id/6134/rec/3.

twenty institutions whose goal it is to expand, make accessible, contextualize, and preserve Japanese-American archival materials through digitization. The resulting web portal provides researchers with an opportunity to study primary sources and to explore civil liberties issues, with a special emphasis on the Japanese-American incarceration during WWII (mentioned above, footnote 2). As of 2020, the CSUJAD project consists of a database with over 36,000 entries (it is expected to grow to 45,000 by the end of 2020). It is neither the first nor the largest Japanese-American history digitization project, but it has focused its growth on what historian Lane Ryo Hirabayashi calls the "vernacular" to discuss unique data sets that speak directly to the experiences of Japanese Americans and their travails during WWII.[16] Therefore, database searches often turn up archival materials that tell stories of the incarceration from the perspectives of those who experienced it. While there are certainly governmental records scattered amongst the CSUJAD material, the primary focus of the project has been to collect this type of local materials. The CSUJAD primary sources provide ample opportunities to examine the WWII incarceration from every angle. These vernacular materials—letters, diaries, photos, artwork, oral histories, and other expressions of daily personal experience in camp—reveal the personal struggles and the hoops that both citizens and immigrants had to jump through to maintain residency in the U.S. Digital technology brings these geographically disparate archival collections together in one online location and provides researchers with rich opportunities to find and interpret new information. Additional contextual information, extended resources, and associated activities combine to deepen the experience as users explore the website or participate in the exhibits, symposia, film screenings, teacher workshops, or scanning days intended to involve the community and publicize the project. CSU archivists not only want to improve access to humanities

---

16. Lane Ryo Hirabayashi, "Everyday Sources about Life in the Camps: The Value of the Vernacular," essay written for California State University Japanese American Digitization Project, April 2015, http://www.csujad.com/images/HolisticRepresentations_Hirabayashi.pdf.

collections focused on Japanese-American history, but also to develop a sustainable model for collaboration amongst various archival and library communities.

To better understand how the CSUJAD project began, some background information is helpful. The CSU system (once called the "1,000 mile campus") is the largest university system in the U.S.[17] The CSU system has an enrollment of close to 437,000 students at twenty-three university campuses throughout the state of California. Therefore, CSU archival collections scattered throughout California are too disparate to offer scholars a complete story or easy access. All of these campuses are defined by their communities and therefore take an abiding interest in the people and history of those communities. Over the last fifty years, CSU Libraries and Archives have followed the history and progress of Japanese Americans in their communities, which has resulted in archival collections of remarkable depth. For this reason, the collections that have been accumulated at CSU Libraries and Archives have a highly localized flavor. For example, in 1942, an estimated 250 Japanese-American students were forced to leave the CSU campuses and relocate to WRA camps. Many other students were removed from other West Coast colleges as well. In September 2009, the CSU Board of Trustees unanimously voted to honor the academic intentions of these students by awarding each of them a Special Honorary Bachelor of Humane Letters degree.[18]

The CSUJAD project grew out of discussions between CSU archivists at the Society of American Archivists Annual Meeting in 2012 and at the Society of California Archivists Annual Meeting in 2013.[19] The talks centered not only on the digitization of collections, but also

17. "About the CSU," California State University, accessed May 26, 2019, https://www2.calstate.edu/csu-system/about-the-csu.

18. "CSU Nisei Diploma Project," YouTube, updated December 20, 2011, https://www.youtube.com/playlist?list=PLC6AA4FF74AA6937C.

19. Society of American Archivists, accessed May 26, 2019, https://www2.archivists.org/; Society of California Archivists, accessed May 26, 2019, https://www.calarchivists.org/.

on the desire to create an all-encompassing portal for the materials that each CSU archive possesses. CSU archivists realized how important it was to digitize their archival materials and tell "local" stories about Japanese-American history (as opposed to governmental records or interpretations). The physical collections have always been accessible on the various CSU campuses and have collection-level digital finding aids in the OAC, but most were not digitized or cataloged at the item level.[20] Even if some of the archival items had been digitized, the objects tended to be isolated and lacked standardized metadata or consistent terminology. The archivists realized that researchers increasingly expect that documents and photographs be available digitally to expanded groups of humanities scholars, and they decided they needed to make each archival object more readily available. CSU archivists are the primary players and collaborators behind this CSUJAD project. Greg Williams (Director of Archives and Special Collections at CSUDH and co-author of this chapter), took the lead by writing the grants, assuming the role of project director/principal investigator, and taking on the responsibility of being the central hub for the CSUJAD grant projects. The archivists who took the lead on their campuses at the various CSU partner institutions include: Julie Thomas at Sacramento; Natalie Navar and Stephanie George at Fullerton; Danelle Moon at San Jose State University and now the University of California Santa Barbara; Tammy Lau at Fresno; Stephen Kutay and Ellen Jerosz at Northridge; Lynn Prime and Julie Dinkins at Sonoma; Yoko Okunishi, Rachel Mandell, Stella Castillo, Christina Pappous, Alexandra Cauley, Jennifer Hill, Lindsay Anderson, and staff at CSUDH; and many others at a variety of different institutions.[21] The project was inspired by the activism of CSUDH faculty emeritus Donald Hata, Ph.D., and encouraged by CSUDH Library Dean, Stephanie Brasley, Ed.D.

---

20. "Online Archive of California," California Digital Library, accessed May 26, 2019, https://oac.cdlib.org/.

21. "Participants," CSUJAD, updated May 9, 2018, http://www.csujad.com/participants.html.

In 2013, the CSUDH Archives and Special Collections applied for
NEH funding to begin a concerted effort to digitize CSU's extensive
holdings of Japanese-American historical materials and to develop a web
portal to deliver the content. A Humanities Collections and Reference
Resources (HCRR) planning grant was provided the following year to
help with the formative stages of this initiative. The archives that were
most eager to participate included the six CSU campuses with the most
extensive holdings of historical materials related to Japanese-American
history and the WWII incarceration.[22] Before this initial grant ended
a year later, nine additional CSU campuses took an interest and contributed digitized archival materials, even though they were not part
of the original grant proposal.[23] After the pilot project was completed,
NEH encouraged CSU to apply for a full HCRR implementation grant.
The NEH proposal was funded in 2016. Meanwhile, this demonstration of collaboration and follow-through led to a second grant from
the NPS's Japanese American Confinement Sites Program to digitize
more Japanese-American materials, including another 10,000 archival
items (textual documents, images, etc.) and 100 oral histories. The NEH
implementation and the NPS grant projects commenced in 2015-2016
and continued through 2018. Funding for a variant from this standard
CSUJAD grant came through in 2017 from the Haynes Foundation and
the California Civil Liberties Public Education Program (CCLPEP) with
the accessioning of the Ninomiya Photo Studio Collection at CSUDH.[24]

The Ninomiya Collection was separated by social media and then
brought back together by social media. That is, after years of trying to

---

22. The following CSU campuses participated in the initial NEH grant: Dominguez
Hills, Fresno, Fullerton, Northridge, Sacramento, and San Jose.

23. The second wave of CSU campuses included Bakersfield, Channel Islands, East
Bay, Long Beach, San Bernardino, San Diego, San Francisco, San Luis Obispo, and
Sonoma.

24. Alexandra Arai Cauley and Christina Pappous, "The Ninomiya Photo Studio
Collection," Los Angeles Archivists Collective (blog), accessed May 26, 2019, http://
www.laacollective.org/work/ninomiya-photo-studio/; "Inventory of the Ninomiya
Photography Studio Collection, 1949-1970," Online Archive of California, accessed
May 26, 2019, https://oac.cdlib.org/findaid/ark:/13030/c84t6q6p/entire_text/.

figure out what to do with the work product of a portrait and community photo studio located in Los Angeles' Little Tokyo neighborhood, family members were unable to find an institution willing to accept this collection of over 100,000 prints and negatives. The images from over forty years of photography were saved by a contractor who was remodeling the building where the images were stored. Rather than dumping the whole lot, he placed an ad on Craig's List offering the photographs. At least three separate groups took various parts of the collection. One new owner wanted to digitize the images and create a website; another wanted the images for her daughter, who was interested in photography; and the third considered selling the images or scraping off the silver

Figure 1. Nisei Week Queen being driven down Los Angeles' First Street in Little Tokyo. The Ninomiya Photo Studio is in the background, 1959.[25]

---

25. "Nisei Week, 1959," photograph, 1959, Ninomiya Studio Collection, Gerth Archives and Special Collections, California State University, Dominguez Hills, via CSUJAD, http://digitalcollections.archives.csudh.edu/digital/collection/p16855coll4/id/29984.

each image may have contained. After five years of trying, the archivist was able to locate the Ninomiya materials from these three different parties and acquired the photographs for CSUDH. The collection contains two generations of family and event photos from Little Tokyo and throughout Los Angeles. There are over 100,000 negatives and prints in the Ninomiya Collection within 15,000 packets (one packet per job). Over 7,000 of these items have been digitized and are cataloged within the CSUJAD project.

Combining both the incarceration era materials and the Ninomiya photos, the CSUJAD project received a grant from the NHPRC in 2018, which will go through 2020. Additionally, the CSUJAD project reached out to a number of non-CSU archives of various types.[26] This aggressive and opportunistic approach to project funding has resulted in over 36,000 items being digitized and fully cataloged in five years.

To date, the CSUJAD project has been funded by four federal grants, two state grants, two private grants, and one in-house university grant. Both the NEH and NPS grants reached their goals, as did the next set of grants (Haynes and CCLPEP). The project has been rejected by one state granting agency (a second attempt from an agency that had funded the project the year before). In 2020, while the NHPRC is in progress, CSUJAD has received three additional grants, including a second NPS grant. Unlike science and education grants, which are funded in the millions of dollars, the CSUJAD humanities grants generally range from $40,000 to $320,000. The collaborative grant project is both an exercise in intellectual access and discovery as well as a project fraught with learning curves, deadlines (met and missed), and challenges with standards. This repeated need to apply to several different agencies is both exhausting and well worth pursuing.

With each grant, CSUJAD funds were divided up between CSUDH, the host institution, and several other partner archives. CSUDH received funds for salaries for a project archivist to oversee the cataloging of

---

26. These non-CSU archives include: the Claremont College Libraries, the University of California at Santa Barbara, the Go For Broke Foundation, the Palos Verdes Public Library, the Historical Society of Long Beach, and the Eastern California Museum.

partner records and a part-time employee to scan materials. Partner archives received anywhere from $1,000 to $30,000 for digitization and cataloging. The project archivist then had the job of leading training workshops for the partners, cataloging CSUDH materials, reviewing partner records, incorporating those records into the CSUJAD database, quality checking digital files, and cajoling partners who were lagging behind. The project director and several consultants were responsible for administering the project (finding new partners, hiring staff, gathering new collections, writing new grants, generating exhibitions, and adding context to the website).

Generally, the partners with more funding were able to catalog more records. Initially, in order to include as many CSU archives as possible, it didn't matter how much material the archive had to add to the project, so one partner added one record, another partner added twenty records, while other partners generated thousands of records. It was clear during the early grants that each new partner needed an overview of the CSUJAD technical and metadata standards as well as to be made aware of the deadlines.[27] Each grant had a set number of records for the project that needed to be completed from specific collections, both in total and for individual partners. All partners, to varying degrees, were able to meet their goals and stick to the original collections they intended to catalog. Partners were found at archival conferences and through regular CSU archives communications. The first NPS grant required the CSUJAD project to catalog 10,000 records. The NEH grant required 7,000 records. The administration of the CSUJAD project became a race to complete a certain number of records for each grant. Both the NEH and NPS grants reached their goals, as did the next set of grants (Haynes and CCLPEP; the NHPRC is still in progress). The new collections for the latter grants were the result of community outreach and invitations to new partners that extended beyond the CSU archives. Granting agencies appear to be attracted to collaborative grants, as well

---

27. "CSUJAD Best Practices," CSUJAD, updated May 9, 2018, http://www.csujad.com/practices.html.

as to the topic of Japanese-American history (especially the WWII incarceration). It's also possible that some agencies are favorable to projects that are similar to others that have received funding. This type of aggressive grant writing is reliant on consistent project staffing, the need to jump when a grant opportunity is announced, an understanding of the grant outlook for archives, and the ability to customize proposals to the values of granting agencies.

CSU faculty and students are the primary users of the archival and digital materials collected and produced for the CSUJAD project. These collections are among the most used materials in each CSU campus archive, not only for faculty research and instruction, but also by students in their research and learning experiences. Both the actual archival objects and the digitized surrogates are used for undergraduate and graduate CSU courses to provide an introduction to the WWII incarceration and life in the WRA camps, as well as for teaching Japanese-American and other areas of history. All of the archives in this project make these materials part of their introduction to archives presentations. They also make them available for research in undergraduate or graduate courses. In addition, they serve as tools for instruction about primary sources, demonstrating how to use these types of archival materials to discover new information. The collections are used by teaching faculty and are embraced by students because the material is personal, local, relates to seminal events in U.S. history, and focuses on the struggles of a diverse population (CSU has one of the most diverse student populations in the U.S.). The CSUJAD project allows a new generation of scholars to re-analyze what has already been discovered, attend to what may have been missed, and access hidden collections that have never been accessible before.

Several distinguished scholars, who are specialists in Japanese-American history, have been involved in the CSUJAD project.[28] Among them,

---

28. The CSUJAD advisory group of scholars includes: Roger Daniels, emeritus history professor from the University of Cincinnati; Donald Hata, emeritus professor of history at CSU Dominguez Hills; Rita Takahashi, professor of social work at San Francisco State University; Art Hansen, emeritus professor of history at CSU Fullerton;

the late Aiko Herzig-Yoshinaga, an independent researcher who was instrumental in the redress movement, stated, "Making this collection available online is a good step toward informing more people about what happened." Recounting her own experience, she noted, "I was only a senior in high school when I was taken away…it was just so arbitrary." She was held for three and a half years in several camps, including Manzanar, before she and her family were released. Herzig-Yoshinaga said that, in the years following WWII, she did not think too much about the "traumatic experience" that had befallen her until she was well into her fifties. "My family and I were raised to respect authority, but eventually I started to feel that my rights had been deprived by having been picked up simply because of my ancestry," she said. "It has bothered me a lot.…It didn't dawn on me until later that the government had really done us wrong."[29] This group of faculty and community activists believed it was essential that future researchers have digital access to CSU archival materials in order to weave a more nuanced record of the incarceration and how it challenged the constitutional rights of all Americans. Roger Daniels, an expert on immigration and the plight of Japanese Americans during WWII, suggested "Uniting these unique archives that illuminate the wartime incarceration is long overdue."[30]

The CSU Japanese-American archival collections represent approximately 400 linear feet of archival materials that focus on some of the most striking events related to the treatment of minorities in U.S. history. The topics cover an enormous range of subjects central to Japanese-American life before, during, and after WWII, including immigration, the California Alien Land Acts of 1913 and 1920, the WRA, redress,

---

Cherstin Lyon, professor of history at CSU San Bernardino; Tom Ikeda, executive director of Densho; Martha Nakagawa, journalist and researcher; and the late Aiko Herzig-Yoshinaga.

29. Aiko Herzig-Yoshinaga to Gregory Williams, letter, October 7, 2014, in the author's possession. These quotes were retrieved from unpublished letters written in support of the CSUJAD project.

30. Roger Daniels to Gregory Williams, letter, July 10, 2015, in the author's possession. This quote was retrieved from unpublished letters written in support of the CSUJAD project.

Japanese Peruvians, hostage exchanges on the *S.S. Gripsholm*, and the U.S. Army's 442nd Regimental Combat Team. Camps represented include Jerome, Gila River, Rohwer, Manzanar, Tanforan, Poston, Amache/ Granada, Heart Mountain, Crystal City, and more. The archival materials digitized for the CSUJAD project are primary historical sources that include letters, photographs, oral histories (audio and video), transcriptions of those oral histories, camp publications, papers of camp administrators and counselors, poetry, artwork, leases, birth certificates and other documents used to prove citizenship, school yearbooks, applications, bulletins, checks, forms, guidebooks, leases, letters, maps, paintings, pamphlets, postcards, etc.

It is not by serendipity that these CSU archives have a great deal of material focused on this issue. Immigration patterns that determined where Japanese Americans (Nikkei) settled also relate to where CSU campuses are located. Sacramento, San Jose, and Fresno had early Japanese-American agricultural populations. The Nikkei populations of Little Tokyo, Terminal Island, Gardena, and Palos Verdes in Los Angeles County are directly connected to the materials that CSUDH, Fullerton, and Northridge have collected. Collections at Sacramento have mostly come from citizens of the Florin neighborhood and others throughout northern California. CSU Fullerton's Japanese-American oral histories were generated by residents of Orange County and other areas of southern California. San Jose's Flaherty Collection consists of materials from Colonel Hugh T. Fullerton of the Western Defense Command. Materials from CSU Fresno and elsewhere document Japanese Americans in the agricultural areas of the San Joaquin Valley. Highlights from other collections include Sonoma's focus on life north of the San Francisco Bay Area and their partnership with the local Japanese American Citizens League; Long Beach's oral histories dealing with life on Terminal Island and in the South Bay Area of Los Angeles; yearbook excerpts from San Diego State University and San Francisco State University documenting the lives of students prior to incarceration; and San Luis Obispo's important Manzanar letters.

The collections at CSUDH originate mostly from the South Bay Area of Los Angeles County, where some of the largest concentrations of Japanese Americans reside. Anti-Japanese land laws prevented Japanese Americans from owning land and therefore they had to lease farm lands. Large agricultural landowners, such as those who owned the Rancho Dominguez, were required to keep extensive records, including birth certificates, passports, and proof of residency for their Japanese-American tenants. Close to 2,000 of those tenant records are part of the CSUJAD project. The records contain scores of leases and letters, both business-like and heartbreaking, that document everything from a tenant farmer's removal by the federal government to the pleas of a tenant to his former landlord to vouch for a relative's loyalty to the U.S. The attempts of businesses to work within the policies of the Alien Land Acts of the early twentieth century are integral to understanding how immigration clashed with prejudice and commercial interests, leading to the WWII incarceration. Strikingly, a 1930s Gardena High School yearbook includes a photograph of a group of Japanese-American students who were the majority of the students in the Spanish Club, which focuses in on a time when integration into the mainstream was assumed.

At CSUDH, headquarters for CSUJAD, the principal investigator is the only permanent employee. The project staff fluctuates depending on the extent of the grant, but the combination of an aggressive collection development policy and an opportunistic grants program ensures several more years of collecting and cataloging. This multi-year seat-of-the-pants project approach also results in a wide variety of projects that bring about work beyond the basic scanning and metadata creation. They include public programing, classroom work, exhibitions, lesson plans, art workshops, and instruction on how to use the CSUJAD database. This contextual work is often a result of instructions from the granting agencies and adds to the workload.

It is the experience of the CSUJAD team that online access and word of mouth can lead to new collections. Community organizations (gardener's associations, photo studios, prefecture organizations, and social groups) have not only donated their materials, but also assisted

Lease #9
....

THIS INDENTURE, made this....1st....day of....July...., in the
year Nineteen Hundred and....forty...., between....CARSON ESTATE COMPANY....
a corporation organized and existing under the laws of the State of California, and hereinafter designated as the Lessor,
which expression shall include its successors or assigns, where the context so requires or admits and....
MOMOO MOCHIZUKI ....of the County of Los Angeles, State of California, hereinafter
designated as the Lessee, which expression shall include his heirs, executors, administrators and assigns, where the context
so requires or admits:
WITNESSETH, That the Lessor for and in consideration of the rents, covenants and agreements hereinafter mentioned,
reserved and contained, on the part and behalf of the Lessee, to be paid, kept and performed, has demised and farm let, and
by these presents does demise and farm let unto the said Lessee all those certain lands situated in and being a part of the
lands of....Carson Estate Company....
located in the County of Los Angeles, State of California, and particularly described as follows, to-wit:
(Description)

Nine (9) acres, more or less, being a portion of the 349 acre tract of
the Rancho San Pedro, situated in the County of Los Angeles, as per map
on file in the office of the Secretary of Carson Estate Company, and known
as Lease #9.

Cancelled 4-6-42; Tenant Evacuated by U.S. Govt

Figure 2. Land lease between the Carson Estate Company and Momoo
Mochizuki with the post-Pearl Harbor cancelation and tenant "evacuation"
mentioned, April 6, 1942.[31]

CSUJAD with locating additional materials destined for the dump. While
the generation that survived the camps as teenagers and young adults
is largely deceased, there is the occasional nonagenarian who donates
materials. Collections these folks have contributed include photographs
and documents from the Jerome Camp, Manzanar, Tule Lake, Heart
Mountain, Terminal Island, and elsewhere. While it should be noted that
large collections of Japanese-American materials are located at other
institutions, as mentioned above, the focus for CSUJAD has been to
collect community materials that will connect people and documents.
That is, those incarcerated in specific camps did not always return to
the home towns they came from, which meant that materials became

---

31. Carson Estate Company and Momoo Mochizuki, land lease, canceled in 1942,
Rancho San Pedro Collection, Gerth Archives and Special Collections, California State
University, Dominguez Hills, via CSUJAD, http://digitalcollections.archives.csudh.
edu/digital/collection/p16855coll4/id/4331/rec/45.

scattered among many CSUJAD partners. After the WRA camps were closed and time passed, those who were incarcerated started to return to these sites—for reunions and then for pilgrimages (pilgrimages are organized annual visits to the WRA camp sites by Japanese Americans, starting in the late 1960s, which have expanded to include participation by many communities confronting civil rights violations). Some donated materials to nearby museums, like the Eastern California Museum near Manzanar. The creation of the Heart Mountain Foundation allowed Heart Mountain materials to mostly end up at the incarceration site. Now that the majority of the WRA camps are National Historic Landmarks, Monuments, or Sites run by the NPS, archival materials can be donated to them directly.

Yet, the experience of the CSUJAD project is that community contacts sometimes bring in long-lost materials that are one step away from the dumpster. A photo album full of Heart Mountain documentation was given to a CSUJAD donor just after the album's original owner had died. This donor, the head of a dwindling professional organization who donated his own materials, is an active community contact who will now be able to tell others about CSUJAD so similar materials won't be lost. Photo albums from Manzanar, Amache, Poston, and Minidoka have found their way to CSUJAD in a similar word-of-mouth manner. The purpose of this active collection development is to build physical collections and add new and diverse digital materials for CSUJAD. The results are rich new collections, as well as content for the next grant. The success of this collection development work has come about less from planning and more from community contact: archival staff in the community; publicity in local newspapers; scanning days; exhibitions; archival open houses; and the evidence of past work that has resulted in the CSUJAD portal. CSUJAD staff, in most instances, are able to connect with potential donors, either in Japanese, with traditional formality, or in English, with twenty-first-century informality. Another tactic, most often used with the children of those incarcerated, is to offer them a home for the physical materials and/or offer to scan the materials if they want to keep them in the family. Some donors recognize that CSUJAD will preserve the digitized materials and that the physical items will be readily accessible to family members if donated. For donors who do not want to donate the physical materials, the archives will scan and return the items. This extra work, of course, leads to a backlog and sometimes a rush to get materials scanned and back to their owners, but generally CSUJAD's backlogs are much smaller than those at larger institutions. This is also a selling point.

The story of Japanese Americans in the twentieth century—their migration to the U.S.; the Alien Land Acts, under which they lived; their incarceration during WWII; and the redress movement—is a complex

Figure 3. Ishibashi family party the day before the Pearl Harbor attack, December 6, 1941.[32]

32. "Ishibashi family party the day before the Pearl Harbor attack," photograph, December 6, 1941, Ishibashi Collection, Gerth Archives and Special Collections, California State University, Dominguez Hills, via CSUJAD, http://digitalcollections. archives.csudh.edu/digital/collection/p16855coll4/id/3134/rec/2.

Figure 4. Ishibashi family and friends in front of the Buddhist Hall
in the Poston WRA Camp, circa 1942.[33]

local, state, and national one, as well as being of great historical importance for students, scholars, and wider international audiences. It is a
subject ripe for further exploration and scholarly interpretation by a
new generation of students, scholars, and others, with the hope that a
more nuanced record of the incarceration and how it challenged the
civil liberties of all Americans can be written.

Temporal Change in Perspectives

I am writing to you from "Fresno Assembly Center." The life out here is
pretty fair, at least, better than I expected. In camp we have no tree nor
green grass around; so it is very hot here, beside that we have to be in a
line waiting for a mess hall in the hot heat. Here in camp there is no work
to do just eat and sleep; but I lose [an obscured number of] pounds since I

---

33. "Ishibashi family and friends in front of the Buddhist Hall in the Poston WRA
Camp," photograph, circa 1942, Ishibashi Collection, Gerth of Archives and Special
Collections, California State University, Dominguez Hills, via CSUJAD, http://digi-
talcollections.archives.csudh.edu/digital/collection/p16855coll4/id/3137/rec/2.

came here. I rock my baby morning until night because it is so noisy here.[34]
—Letter from Minnie Umeda at the Fresno Assembly Center to Mrs.
Waegell, June 8, 1942

The first wave of Japanese immigration to the U.S. was in the late 1800s
and the early 1900s. Most arrived on the West Coast, and they were
greeted with the same hostility with which other ethnic groups have
been greeted, as well as with restrictive laws dealing with property rights
and attempts to limit citizenship. For a while, Japanese-American property owners could deed their property to their underage, but American
citizen, children.

Japanese Americans initially landed in agricultural areas and then
moved to the cities. While hostility toward them in the 1920s and 1930s
did not lessen, they established community through churches, language
schools, and a variety of commercial establishments. Even as they paid
taxes and sent their children to public schools, they were required to
submit additional government identification when they signed leases
and other bureaucratic forms. Pictures of Japanese-American children
in school yearbooks indicate how prevalent these students were in urban
areas and that they were largely an accepted part of school culture.
For example, the 1935 Gardena, California high school yearbook used
Japanese art and graphics throughout to inspire "the Spirit of World
Friendship," and there appear to be about fifty-seven students in the
Japanese Club.[35] In the 1930s, as Japan continued its aggression in China,
the racism and hostility in the U.S. against Japanese Americans escalated.
Throughout the late 1930s and early 1940s, law enforcement agencies
mimicked this hostility by collecting information on Japanese-American
community leaders. The bombing of Pearl Harbor on December 7, 1941

---

34. Minnie Umeda to Mrs. Waegell, letter, June 8, 1942, Japanese American Archival Collection, Department of Special Collections and University Archives, California
State University, Sacramento, via CSUJAD, http://digitalcollections.archives.csudh.
edu/digital/collection/p16855coll4/id/7358/rec/1.

35. *El Arador*, Gardena High School yearbook, 1935, Greaton Gardena Collection,
Gerth Special Collections and Archives, California State University, Dominguez Hills,
6.

led to the immediate arrest of those community leaders, along with a wide variety of other life-changing events.

In the months that followed the attack on Pearl Harbor, a wave of hysteria merged with anti-Asian xenophobia enveloped the West Coast. The ensuing fear opened the door for an attack on the civil and political rights of Japanese Americans, not only by local, state, and national politicians, but also by the military brass and commercial interests. President Roosevelt signed Executive Order 9066 on February 19, 1942, which resulted in the incarceration of 120,000 Japanese Americans, who were banned from coastal regions, sent to assembly centers, and then sent to inland incarceration camps operated by the WRA.

During WWII there were a variety of reactions and philosophical perspectives within the Japanese community—full compliance with the government, military service to prove loyalty, dissidence, draft resistance, nationalism, and renunciation—that create much complexity when studying this period. There were also generational differences that are best summarized using the Japanese terminology outlined in the **Table 1**.

By October 1942, the WRA developed leave clearance procedures to enable about 17,000 Japanese-American citizens (the majority of whom were between eighteen and thirty years of age) to re-enter civilian life as students and workers (about 7% of the total number of Japanese-American incarcerees).[36] The WRA reviewed their loyalty, prospects for self-support, and the reception of the community where they intended to move; the majority went to Chicago, Denver, Salt Lake City, and New York—places far removed from their West Coast birthplaces. There were a myriad of ways to get out of the WRA camps, from volunteering for military service to even more extreme responses. For example, those incarcerated at the Tule Lake camp were caught in a situation where Japanese nationalism offered an alternative, further dividing the camp's population. Many immigrants and citizens determined that it was possibly safer to be "repatriated" to Japan rather than to stay in the U.S.

---

36. Roger Daniels, *Concentration Camps North America: Japanese in the United States and Canada in World War II* (Malabar, FL: R.E. Krieger, 1981), 110.

TERMINOLOGY	DEFINITION
Nikkei	Overall term to describe Japanese emigrants and their descendants who reside in foreign countries.
Issei	The first generation of Japanese immigrants to the U.S., most of whom were prohibited from obtaining citizenship due to naturalization laws.
Nisei	The generation of people of Japanese descent born outside of Japan to at least one Issei or one non-immigrant Japanese parent.
Kibei	The second generation of Japanese Americans and American-born children of Issei educated in Japan (often stigmatized as "un-American" because of this).
Sansei	The third generation, American-born children of Nisei.
Renunciants	Nikkei who gave up their U.S. citizenship and were described as "enemy aliens."

Table 1. Terminology differentiating people of Japanese ancestry and citizenship status.[37]

The concept of giving up U.S. citizenship, though shocking to some, was a viable option, though it had serious implications.[38] Many feared

---

37. This table was informed by the definitions in the Densho Encyclopedia, accessed June 10, 2018, https://encyclopedia.densho.org/.

38. Barbara Takei and Judy M. Tachibana, *Tule Lake Revisited: A Brief History and Guide to the Tule Lake Concentration Camp Site*, 2nd ed. (San Francisco: Tule Lake Committee, 2012), 14-15.

for their safety in hostile white communities if they were released from the camps before the war was over and thought Japan would be safer than the U.S. Others were outraged by their imprisonment, and were disillusioned. Renunciation was made easier by an Act of Congress, the so-called Denaturalization Act of 1944. Initially, fewer than two dozen Tule Lake incarcerees applied to renounce their citizenship, but when the WRA announced that the camp would close in a year, the resulting panic and confusion caused 7,222 (one-third of Tule Lake's incarcerees) Nisei and Kibei to renounce, 65% of whom were American-born.[39] In contrast, only 128 people from the other nine WRA camps renounced their American citizenship. Ultimately, many were repatriated to Japan, while others who signed up to go to Japan realized it was a mistake. Wayne Mortimer Collins, a civil liberties attorney, prevented the Department of Justice from deporting people of Japanese descent who renounced their U.S. citizenship en masse. The effort to restore citizenship took twenty-two years—eventually nearly all, except for about forty to fifty people, had their citizenship restored.[40]

The WWII generation rarely discussed their camp experiences with their children and were initially reluctant to talk about the incarceration; yet, at the same time, there were activists who did not want the incarceration to be forgotten. As Japanese Americans moved through the 1950s and established a renewed sense of community, there was also a sense of isolation and distrust. That sense of community is evident in the CSUJAD Ninomiya photographs of weddings, funerals, graduations, births, and other events. With the exception of a few activists, the silence of the WWII incarcerees was not broken until the late 1960s, largely as a result of inspiration from the anti-war and civil rights movements. At that point, much of the community still believed the government's rationale of "military necessity" for their incarceration during the war. The archival recovery of government documents in the National Archives by two former incarcerees, Michi Weglyn and Aiko

---

39. Daniels, *Concentration Camps North America*, 116-17.
40. Takei and Tachibana, *Tule Lake Revisited*, 16.

Herzig-Yoshinaga, dramatically affected political events.[41] The former
is known as the "mother of redress" for her 1976 book, *Years of Infamy*,
in which she used an array of government documents to prove that
the rhetoric about "military necessity" was a lie.[42] Herzig-Yoshinaga
followed by finding proof that the government had actively sought to
cover up the fact that it knew the "military necessity" rationale was a
lie; she found the original draft (with editorial deletions suggested) of
what would eventually become the government's final report on the mass
incarceration, along with instructions to destroy the original documents.
As Mira Shimabukuro stated, "This proof would be instrumental in
more than one redress case that would soon be reargued in front of the
US Supreme Court. But no one would have known the significance of
the marked-up copy of the final report sitting on the archivist's table
without the elaborate web of documents Herzig-Yoshinaga had not
only reCollected, but had organized, and cross-referenced, rhetorically
attending the National Archives to help set right what she could now
prove the government knew was wrong."[43]

Throughout the 1970s and 1980s, the redress movement was dedicated to getting the U.S. government to acknowledge the damage of
the incarceration experience. This movement eventually led to a governmental apology and some financial compensation. As Shimabukuro
pointed out, "The community's effort to garner an official apology, as
well as a token monetary payment for rights violated and injuries sustained, from the federal government resulted in a new climate where

---

41. Mira Shimabukuro, *Relocating Authority: Japanese Americans Writing to Redress Mass
Incarceration* (Boulder: University Press of Colorado, 2015), 40-47.

42. Weglyn, *Years of Infamy*, 1976.

43. Shimabukuro, Relocating Authority, 46-47. The author coins the phrase "rhetorically attended" and develops this idea in the book stating (the emphases are hers),
"Given the 'strict attention' such a time-consuming process entails, I would argue that
Herzig-Yoshinaga rhetorically attended the National Archives, first becoming present
at, then taking charge of, and then applying herself to the archives as she stretched
her mind toward what was not readily obvious, all with the intent of helping facilitate
social change." She is pointing out that Herzig-Yoshinaga had the right combination
of clerical experience to create a "massive intertextual web of information" and political savvy from her activism, to allow her to develop "a sensitivity to implicit meanings."

ordinary people could openly testify about what had happened to them and their families, neighbors, and ethnic communities, many of which were broken economically and demographically by mass removal and postwar dispersal."[44]

The earliest scholarly research and institutional projects focused on the WWII incarceration used official sources, like the WRA's own records, since the government collected, analyzed, and published copious amounts of demographic and statistical information. This served a useful purpose, but provides the "official" perspective of the people who ran the WRA camps rather than the "vernacular" of the people incarcerated in them, where new kinds of critical cultural analysis could have taken place. Shimabukuro looks at how Japanese Americans used writing, during and after the war, to resist and redress the WWII mass incarceration by mining diverse texts and examining literary practices through the use of community archives. She suggests that official accounts must be questioned and that the vernacular—produced during times of stress and travail—should be consulted to see that the "writing-to-redress" was occurring in the WRA camps. "That is, much writing from camp can be seen as the codification of a desire to set right what is wrong or to relieve one's suffering from the psychological and physical imposition of forced 'relocation' and incarceration."[45] In this way, we can obtain a more balanced understanding of the WWII incarceration events and a variety of perspectives. Shimabukuro's research benefited from the democratization of the available information through the mass digitization of a wide variety of archival materials and ready access through the internet. The vernacular is at the heart of the CSUJAD project, although official documents are also being digitized to capture every viewpoint. CSUJAD is among the resources mentioned in Shimabukuro's book, along with Densho and the archival work of the JANM.[46]

---

44. Shimabukuro, *Relocating Authority*, viii.

45. Shimabukuro, *Relocating Authority*, 26.

46. Shimabukuro, *Relocating Authority*, ix, 31-32.

Terminology Issues

> But, when you come into camp and you see all the military there,
> the fences, barbwire now [laughs] you know you're coming into—
> they call it a relocation camp. That's a bunch of baloney to me. How
> can anybody mention it that way? It's a concentration camp. You're
> detained until they make their decision. It wasn't right, all along. You
> know, eventually you start seeing things. Before you're just a kid play-
> ing and trying to survive. Now, this is becoming emotional. We're
> getting thrown in camp, and I did not feel hurt too much for myself
> because I didn't lose anything. But these other people, when I hear
> they lost their whole house, all their goodies and everything, you
> know, personal belongings, kimonos, and all kinds of stuff. You know?
> You can't buy that every day. So, I know they must have been really
> hurt, and I felt for them, more than myself. I had nothing to lose.[47]
> —Oral history with Takeshi Isozaki, resident of the Children's Village
> for orphans at Manzanar, March 13, 1993

The terminology and controlled vocabulary used by libraries and archives
for subjects relating to Native Americans, African Americans, and
LGBTQIA2+ people are often evolving and open to debate. Describing wartime Japanese-American history is controversial and evolving in
a similar manner. Often, before delving deeply into the history of the
treatment of Japanese Americans during WWII, the public tends to
associate the term "internment" or "internees" with the WRA camps and
the people living in them. This is so ingrained in contemporary society
that some scholars continue to use this terminology for its immediacy.
It is intriguing how the old terminology maintains its power in the current political landscape. Activists have maintained that "evacuation,"
"internment," and "relocation center" should be replaced with "mass
removal," "incarceration," and "concentration camp." Historical documents provide evidence that President Franklin D. Roosevelt referred to
the camps as "concentration camps." Some would go as far as referring
to the network of WRA camps as a "gulag." When the Trump administration began separating immigrant and refugee children from their

---

47. Takeshi Isozaki, oral history, March 13, 1993, Center for Oral and Public History,
California State University, Fullerton, via CSUJAD, http://digitalcollections.archives.
csudh.edu/digital/collection/p16855coll4/id/7974/rec/1.

parents and imprisoning them in 2018, the political opposition to this practice used the term "Japanese-American internment" to equate the situations and bring an immediate response as well as an understanding of the associated civil and human rights issues. In this case, the use of the older euphemistic terminology allowed the public to understand that the term "tender-age shelters," in reality, referred to child prison camps. Though child separation policies were in the headlines for a month in the middle of 2018, the Trump administration has continued to "incarcerate," "jail," or "house" several thousand children in tents, temporary shelters, and homes operated by contractors through the end of 2018. The debate over the use of the term "concentration camp" was highlighted again when a congresswoman was accused of overreach by referring to the prisons for migrants on the Texas border as "concentration camps" in the summer of 2019.[48] These terminology debates are not new to those interested in WWII Japanese-American incarceration.

During WWII, government officials, politicians, and journalists used euphemistic language to refer to the incarceration of Japanese-American citizens – mild expressions for harsh realities. While two generations of social justice activists have maintained that government euphemisms attempt to lessen the impact of the WWII incarceration, questions continue to be raised. Densho explains the issue as follows: "Should euphemistic language from an earlier era be used today? This is an important question for students, teachers, and all people concerned with historical accuracy. Many Japanese Americans, some scholars, and other credible sources use the terminology of the past, which they believe is true to that era and unlikely to invite controversy. In contrast, many Japanese Americans, historians, educators, and others use terminology that they feel more accurately represents the historical events."[49]

---

48. John McWhorter, "AOC's Critics Are Pretending Not to Know How Language Works: A great deal of communication is based on metaphor," The Atlantic (June 20, 2019), https://www.theatlantic.com/ideas/archive/2019/06/defense-ocasio-cortez-concentration-camp-comment/592180/.

49. "Terminology," Densho, https://densho.org/terminology/.

The work of Aiko Herzig-Yoshinaga described in "Words Can Lie
or Clarify" and Roger Daniels' "Words Do Matter" provides a legal and
historical perspective on the use of these terms.[50] In the former, Herzig-
Yoshinaga tells the story of her 1980s work as a research staff member
employed by the Commission on Wartime Relocation and Internment of
Civilians (CWRIC) and how she drew this group's attention to terminology issues by compiling a list of problematic terms from primary sources
in the National Archives and other repositories. "During the course of
my work as a CWRIC researcher I learned that 'relocation center,' 'non-
aliens,' and 'evacuation' were only a few of many euphemisms that were
deliberately used to obscure and conceal what was done to American
citizens under the fraudulent rationale of 'military necessity.' In fact, it
was not lost on me that the extremely problematic word 'internment' was
in the very title of the Commission on Wartime Relocation and Internment of Civilians."[51] Herzig-Yoshinaga also mentions other euphemistic
words, such as "relocation," "relocation centers," "assembly centers," and
"internment." She then suggests preferred terminology, such as "forced
removal," "expulsion," "uprooting," "American concentration camps,"
"incarceration," "imprisonment," "prisoner," "inmates," "incarcerees,"
"temporary concentration camps," and "confinement."

Both Daniels and Herzig-Yoshinaga persuasively argue that "incarceration," and by extension "incarceree" are the appropriate terms to use
for the 80,000 American citizens of Japanese ancestry, and the 40,000
Japanese nationals barred from naturalization by race and imprisoned
in WRA camps under the authority of Executive Order 9066. There
were approximately 11,000 people who were actually interned following

---

50. Aiko Herzig-Yoshinaga, "Words Can Lie or Clarify: Terminology of the World
War II Incarceration of Japanese Americans," Discover Nikkei, February 2, 2010,
http://www.discovernikkei.org/en/journal/2010/02/02/terminology-incarceration-
japanese-americans/; Roger Daniels, "Words Do Matter: A Note on Inappropriate
Terminology and the Incarceration of the Japanese Americans," in *Nikkei in the Pacific
Northwest: Japanese Americans and Japanese Canadians in the Twentieth Century*, eds. Louis
Fiset and Gail Nomura (Seattle: University of Washington Press, 2005), 183-207,
https://www.nps.gov/tule/learn/education/upload/RDaniels_euphemisms.pdf.
51. Herzig-Yoshinaga, "Words Can Lie or Clarify," 2.

a recognized legal procedure. They were Japanese citizens, the nation with which the U.S. was at war, seized for reasons supposedly based on their behavior, and entitled to individual hearings before a board, whereas the 120,000 Japanese-American men, women, and children in the WRA camps had no due process of law; the violation of their civil and human rights was justified on the grounds of military necessity.[52] The CWRIC concluded that Executive Order 9066 and the policy decisions that followed were not driven by an analysis of military conditions: "The broad historical causes which shaped these decisions were race prejudice, war hysteria and a failure of political leadership....A grave injustice was done to American citizens and resident nationals of Japanese ancestry who, without individual review or any probative evidence against them, were excluded, removed and detained by the United States during World War II."[53] This legal differentiation was the basis for the redress movement, which led to the Civil Liberties Act of 1988, involving an apology and $20,000 payment to more than 80,000 camp survivors.

Connie Chiang starts her book, *Nature Behind Barbed Wire*, with a note clarifying her terminology choices. She points out that all of the choices have problems, but she uses "incarceration," "confinement," and "detention," rather than "internment." Similarly, "forced removal," "mass removal," and "expulsion" are used, rather than the milder government terms of "evacuation" and "relocation."[54] Scholars writing on the subject continue to need to clarify their use of terminology. The Tule Lake unit of the NPS provides links to the key readings related to the terminology controversy.[55] As previously mentioned, Densho has an extensive discussion of the terminology issue as well as a thorough glossary of terms and a comprehensive online encyclopedia. These resources outline the many different types of camps used for

---

52. Daniels, "Words Do Matter," 11.

53. Daniels, "Words Do Matter," 5.

54. Connie Y. Chiang, *Nature Behind Barbed Wire: An Environmental History of the Japanese American Incarceration* (Oxford, UK: Oxford University Press, 2018), xiii-xv.

55. "Suggested Reading," Tule Lake Unit National Park Service, March 1, 2015, https://www.nps.gov/tule/learn/education/suggestedreading.htm.

incarceration during WWII; they are summarized in the table below to clarify the categories of people who were detained in them. It is easy to see why "internment" is appropriate when referring to Department of Justice and U.S. Army camps, where detainees experienced the due process of law. They lived a different experience than did those confined in the WRA and other camps.

For the CSUJAD project, archivists, scholars, and technical experts gathered for two days at its commencement in 2014 to work their way through historical, philosophical, and practical issues. One of the first orders of business was to discuss the controversial topic of terminology as it applies to the Japanese-American experience during WWII. The CSUJAD scholarly advisory group was in attendance, with a range of expertise—from people who were in WRA camps during WWII to distinguished scholars and community activists—which led to some lively debate. In the end, the consensus was on "incarceration" over "internment"—not surprising, given that Herzig-Yoshinaga and Daniels were at the table. By extension, the people in the WRA camps should therefore be referred to as "incarcerees" and the camps themselves as "incarceration camps." The use of "incarceration" was a relatively easy initial determination, although there were some who preferred the term "concentration camp" for the WRA camps. Donald Hata still uses "gulag," having been in the WWII camps with his family, and Densho uses "concentration camp," but these terms have inextricable associations with Soviet forced-labor camps and Nazi death camps respectively, so the consensus was to not use them for the CSUJAD project. It is worth noting, though, that the use of terms such as "gulag" and "concentration camp" dramatically broadens the meaning of the wartime imprisonment of civilians in the U.S. and reflects on the problems and the impotence of the word "internment."

In addition to assistance with the terminology, the CSUJAD scholars shared information about their specific research interests and general trends in the scholarship on Japanese-American history, especially as it relates to the WWII era and incarceration events. They provided guidance on gaps in the available documentation and valuable feedback on

Temporary Assembly Center (Santa Anita, Fresno, etc.)	People of Japanese ancestry born in Japan, immigrants to the U.S., and Japanese-American citizens
WRA (Manzanar, Rohwer, Granada, etc.)	People of Japanese ancestry born in Japan, immigrants to the U.S., and Japanese-American citizens
Segregation Center (Tule Lake)	People of Japanese ancestry born in Japan, immigrants to the U.S., and Japanese-American citizens – especially those considered to be disloyal or troublemakers
Immigration Detention Facility (Honolulu, Seattle, San Francisco, etc.)	Japanese nationals arrested by the FBI
Department of Justice Internment Camp (Crystal City, etc.)	German and Italian nationals, Japanese Latin Americans, and enemy aliens
U.S. Army Internment Camp (Camp Lordsburg, etc.)	Prisoners of war
U.S. Federal Prison	Draft resisters

Table 2. Different types of camps and the categories of people detained in them.

how the CSU collections might fill those lacunae. An inclusive approach was suggested that has led to many more CSU archival collections being added, as well as those from other institutions with Japanese-American collections, from small rural museums, historical societies, public libraries, and other research institutions. Scholars continue to support the CSUJAD project in an advisory capacity by providing letters for grant applications, constructive feedback about the project, and participation in educational programing and outreach.

Rather than starting from scratch, the planners and catalogers for the CSUJAD project relied heavily on the Densho glossary and encyclopedia, as well as Densho's "Digitization and Preservation Manual" for the terminology employed. Tom Ikeda, Densho's executive director, is a member of the scholarly advisory group. He and all the Densho project staff have generously provided technical support, have shared their extensive experience and work on terminology, and have included the CSUJAD team members in their expanded thesaurus work. Densho was open to sharing the most current version and allowing CSU to build upon it. Yoko Okunishi, a University of California Los Angeles librarian who later became the CSUJAD digital archivist at CSUDH, was hired to synthesize this information and determine the project's initial terminology choices. She enhanced the Densho list of controlled terms with Library of Congress subject terms. Other metadata consultants and project catalogers used this information as the starting point for the development of a CSUJAD project-specific data dictionary with an associated Excel template, extended cataloging guidelines, and a list of controlled vocabulary with subject terms that the CSUJAD project can use.[56] Okunishi continues to update these guiding documents.

Realizing the power of language, the CSUJAD partners carefully developed a controlled vocabulary for the subject fields associated with the archival objects. Although this effort commenced with Densho's terminology, the advice of the advisory scholars and the iterative work of multiple catalogers have differentiated the CSUJAD controlled vocabulary and influenced its growth. These guiding documents have been updated, discussed, and disseminated to all of the participating CSUJAD partners. The goal is to have each archive use this information to develop its cataloging records more extensively at the campus level, while a central CSUDH cataloger provides quality control and any final enhancements for the records. Because of the different nature of each archive and the varying amount of materials coming into the

---

56. "CSUJAD Best Practices," CSUJAD, May 9, 2018, http://www.csujad.com/practices.html.

project, an extended group of catalogers was hired at the participating CSUJAD partner institutions to strive for the consistent handling of the project documentation. Catalogers continue to expand the controlled vocabulary, enhance the metadata guidelines based on the iterative process of the actual cataloging, provide necessary descriptive metadata, and manage the materials in the collection management system. The CSUJAD resolution of terminology issues has been summarized and posted to the project website to explain to users the reasoning behind these decisions. The example below shows how descriptive metadata can objectify even the most startling images.

However, these practical and educational efforts to standardize terminology are not without challenges. The CSUJAD team had to consider

Figure 5. Sample of CSUJAD archival object and descriptive metadata, including controlled subject terms.[57] Title: G.S. Hantf, a barber in Kent, Washington. Description: G.S. Hantf, a barber in Kent, Washington, who opposed the return of the incarcerees to their homes after the war, March 2, 1944. Photo shows him pointing to a sign "We don't want any Japs back here –ever!" Subjects: Race and racism – Discrimination; WWII – Pearl Harbor and aftermath – Responses of non-Japanese.

57. "G.S. Hantf, a barber in Kent, Washington," photograph, March 2, 1944, Japanese Americans in World War II Collection, California State University, Fresno, via CSUJAD, http://digitalcollections.archives.csudh.edu/digital/collection/p16855coll4/id/11493/rec/5.

that a complete avoidance of the term "internment" in the database would be inaccurate in the case of the Department of Justice and U.S. Army camps and could cause search and discovery problems that might make it more difficult for researchers to find the content they need. A technological solution was suggested that could allow for a search term to link to multiple terms, but the current system doesn't support this feature. The possibilities are still being explored to make it so that when a user types in "internment," it will also turn up items tagged with "incarceration." CSUJAD started with six institutional partners and now has twenty-five; ensuring that this extended network of catalogers attends to the project's current metadata standards is a challenge. Terminology determinations are sometimes overlooked by CSUJAD partners, and it is not always possible to delete this information from titles once they have been centralized. Therefore, "internment" has not been completely eliminated from the CSUJAD database, but regular updates and ongoing communication about the project standards generally has worked to focus on the use of "incarceration" over "internment."

In this way, the CSUJAD project has taken controversial terminology into consideration, consulted with the experts, and found a functional solution based on current scholarship to allow an extended group of partners to aggregate archival collections of Japanese-American history and consistently describe them while also raising awareness about the terminology issues. The scholarly terminology debate continues, of course, and a mix of terms can be found in the actual CSUJAD archival objects which, for historical accuracy, are not altered in any way. This CSUJAD terminology determination can be a contested point. Newspaper style guides still use "internment." The attempt to eliminate sexist, euphemistic, or racist language that would have been commonplace a hundred, or even twenty-five, years ago is an appropriate goal for cataloging. Rewriting history, however, is not. History, warts and all, should be quoted as its contemporaries described it. Indeed, imperialist euphemisms can be instructive, if only to alert students to a worn out worldview. The CSUJAD project balances controlled vocabulary for online discoverability with respect for history and individual choice.

Contextualizing Archival Materials

> There sprung a rumor that all aliens will be deported and with it, there occurred a possibility our family being separated. I was utterly confused as to what I should do. But my bitterness towards my country for depriving us of our Constitutional rights made my citizenship seem unimportant compared to separating from our parents. Then and there I renounced my citizenship. That was my great mistake but the pressure we were living under at that time was tremendous. I guess my father's bitterness towards this country in losing all his life's work had a great deal of influence on me too.[58]
> —Masaru Teshiba, Fort Lincoln Internment Camp, Bismarck, North Dakota to his former high school teacher, Virginia Lowers, requesting a character reference to help avoid deportation to Japan, January 24, 1946

The CSUJAD primary sources provide ample opportunities to examine the WWII incarceration from every angle. Vernacular materials—letters, diaries, photos, artwork, oral histories, and other expressions of daily personal experience in camps—reveal personal struggles and the hoops both citizens and immigrants had to jump through to maintain their residency in the U.S. In an article written specifically to illuminate the value of the project, Lane Ryo Hirabayashi explains through multiple examples the importance of making vernacular materials more widely accessible online.[59] The examples he provides vividly demonstrate how artwork, personal letters, and diaries have already been used to effectively generate first-hand, personal, and historical accounts of the Japanese-American incarceration experience. Hirabayashi posits that a new generation of scholarship, one that bases its work on sources distinct from the previous WRA-generated and -influenced work, will result. He suggests that this newfound access to primary, vernacular materials donated by

58. Masaru Teshiba to Virginia B. Lowers, letter, January 24, 1946, Virginia B. Lowers Collection, Gerth Archives and Special Collections, California State University, Dominguez Hills, via CSUJAD, http://digitalcollections.archives.csudh.edu/digital/collection/p16855coll4/id/7042/rec/1.

59. Hirabayashi, "Everyday Sources about Life in the Camps," http://www.csujad.com/images/HolisticRepresentations_Hirabayashi.pdf.

"ordinary" men and women to their local university libraries will greatly expand our knowledge of what happened to Japanese Americans in the 1940s and how it felt to go through this painful experience. The scholars involved in the project provided links to important aspects of their work, helped build a select bibliography for the CSUJAD project, and provided critical feedback for improvements.

Although it is primarily up to the users of the CSUJAD database—students, educators, researchers, and the interested public—to interpret the archival objects, the scholar advisory group and archivists agreed that some curation and ongoing contextualization is important. A web portal—where access to the centralized database is combined with contextual information that can be compiled in an ongoing fashion and made available to a global audience—was the vision from the start. The web designer, Sean Smith, a historian teaching at CSU Long Beach, developed an aesthetically pleasing, user-friendly look and feel for the project's website, which is the face of the CSUJAD project. Every page has a button that links users to the project-generated search page that contains the primary sources, while providing project information and topically associated resources. It is visually compelling, with scrolling images of the archival materials and rotating featured collections. The director and consultants wrote and developed the text and provided all the necessary information for a substantive web presence, while the designer organized and linked everything.

The website includes the following additional information: acknowledgment of the grant funding received to date as well as CSU and other institutional partner support; statements about the CSUJAD mission and goals; CSU archival collection information with links to finding aids (in case researchers want to know where they can access the primary analog materials); an interactive map; educational guides; scholarly contributions and bibliographies; resource links; exhibitions; and additional information about project best practices, citations, the participants, collections, and contacts. The Google map offers researchers access to content relating specifically to pertinent geographical sites; clicking on the flags provides immediate access to the archival materials in the project that can be associated with a given location—especially useful for the WRA and other types of WWII camps.[60] The educational guides included to date are a user's guide to help with database searches, an extensive lesson plan, and a statement about the CSUJAD project's terminology decisions.[61] Links to key digital resources focused on the Japanese-American experience are provided along with information about the WRA sites, for those who might want to visit or obtain more information.[62] An online exhibition is available through the last tab (discussed more below), providing a place to document current and past physical exhibits. Links to current versions of the project's data dictionary, cataloging guidelines, and controlled vocabulary are provided for information professionals.[63] Citation recommendations for the archival materials, using the most popular style guides for this area of study, are also provided for students and researchers.[64]

To expand the reach of the CSUJAD project and bring it to key audiences, CSU archivists are collaborating with the CDL to have the CSUJAD digital objects added or ingested into the CDL's archival service and delivery projects. All of the CSUJAD archive partners have created, or are in the process of creating, finding aids for each of the Japanese-American collections in the OAC to help researchers locate the physical archival items (mentioned above, footnote 20). These guides provide collection-level descriptions of the archival materials and also link to the item-level digitized material on the CSUJAD project website. In addition, the digital objects are being harvested into Calisphere, CDL's

60. "Site Distribution Map," CSUJAD, updated May 9, 2018, http://www.csujad.com/distribution.html.

61. "Education Guides and Resources," CSUJAD, updated May 9, 2018, http://www.csujad.com/edguides.html.

62. "Japanese American Resources," CSUJAD, updated May 9, 2018, http://www.csujad.com/links.html.

63. "CSUJAD Best Practices," CSUJAD, updated May 9, 2018, http://www.csujad.com/practices.html.

64. "How to Cite Our Sources," CSUJAD, updated May 9, 2018, http://www.csujad.com/cite.html.

gateway to primary sources.[65] This additional level of item-level access expands the reach of the project to all Calisphere users, who are already familiar with the existing Japanese American Relocation Digital Archive available there (mentioned above, footnote 13). Themed collections that support the California History-Social Science Framework for K-12 schools provide another search entry point to these materials, making these primary sources easier for teachers, students, and the public to find in relation to the other content featured in Calisphere.[66] Since the CDL is a content hub for the Digital Public Library of America, the CSUJAD collection is exposed through that project too.[67] Preservation quality digital objects and metadata are also sent to Densho, where they will be sustained into the future.[68] With a combination of in-kind contributions and project support, Densho is ingesting the CSUJAD materials to reach wider audiences. In this way, the CSU content is made accessible to more people in the primary target audiences of higher education students, scholars, and researchers of Japanese-American history, as well as K-12 education and the Japanese-American community.

Often, the granting agencies that have provided aid for the CSUJAD project require educational components or request community outreach. Therefore, the CSUJAD team has planned, developed, and implemented a variety of physical and online exhibits, a lesson plan, professional development, and educational workshops using the archival materials acquired and digitized for this project. Community events, such as scanning days and presentations to historical societies, have involved the local community in project activities to allow for contributions to the archival descriptive information and encourage additional donations. These activities are intended to contextualize, interpret, and publicize the CSUJAD project and to enhance the CSUJAD user experience.

65. "Calisphere," California Digital Library, accessed May 26, 2019, https://calisphere.org/.

66. "History-Social Science Framework," California Department of Education, accessed June 23, 2019, https://www.cde.ca.gov/ci/hs/cf/hssframework.asp.

67. Digital Public Library of America, accessed June 19, 2019, https://dp.la/.

68. "Densho Digital Repository," Densho, https://ddr.densho.org/.

To prepare for the development of these resources and activities, site visits were made to most of the CSUJAD partners to assist with curating the archival collections, to learn more about the specific materials that would be added to the CSUJAD project, and to answer any project questions. Similarly, site visits to the two California WRA camps, Manzanar and Tule Lake, were made to touch base with the NPS staff about potential collaborations. A stop at the Eastern California Museum in Independence (a few miles from Manzanar) led to their active participation in the project.

The seventy-fifth anniversary of Executive Order 9066 authorizing the mass incarceration of Japanese-American citizens during WWII was commemorated in February 2017, and the CSUJAD project had progressed enough for this occasion to be a great opportunity to showcase it. CSUDH had a major exhibition of the primary sources, photographs, artwork, and other artifacts related to Japanese-American history entitled "And Then They Came For Us…."[69] Associated with the exhibit were a full-day symposium, film screenings, and panel discussions. A historical timeline and associated posters were created to provide historical information to contextualize the archival objects. These posters were made available to the other CSUJAD partners who developed ten CSU and five community college campus exhibitions. They are now downloadable for anyone to use.

To extend the efforts made on the physical exhibitions to an online environment, Stephen Kutay, the Digital Services librarian at CSU Northridge, who has provided technical support for the CSUJAD project from its inception, developed an online exhibition using the Scalar tools.[70] It presents a documentary narrative of Japanese-American history—from before WWII through the incarceration experience to resettlement and

69. Mary-Michelle Moore, "And Then They Came For Us….," CSUDH University Library, February 23, 2017, https://torolink.csudh.edu/news/107759.

70. "About Scalar," The Alliance for Networking Visual Culture, accessed June 19, 2019, https://scalar.me/anvc/scalar/; "California State University Japanese American Digitization Project: An Exhibit," accessed June 19, 2019, http://scalar.usc.edu/works/csujad-exhibit/index.

redress—using the posters mentioned above and a variety of textual and visual archival materials from the CSUJAD project to tell the story as an engaging visual experience.

Since the California state standards for teaching history recommend teaching the WWII incarceration in the eleventh grade, and since it is a topic that is also frequently taught in higher education, a teaching guide with suggested lesson plans was developed to assist secondary- and college-level teachers in using the CSUJAD primary sources in the classroom. The guide focuses on the consternation caused by the questionnaire that was used to determine the loyalty of the Japanese and Japanese Americans incarcerated in the WRA camps and the subsequent removal of "disloyals" to the Tule Lake Segregation Center. Exploring the question of what loyalty meant to the people of Japanese ancestry incarcerated during WWII, the lesson provides activities and guiding questions to encourage students to search for and analyze archival documents that might shed light on the issues and controversies that arose during WWII. For an example of the ways that archival objects are being used in the lesson plan and online exhibit, the following is one suggested activity:

Activity 6[71]

Look at the three photographs below showing life at Tule Lake. Notice the dates that the pictures were taken and look at the timeline. Consider the transition of Tule Lake from a WRA camp to a segregation center.

Guiding Questions
What did the photographer want you to see in these images?
What can you learn about daily life at Tule Lake from these photographs?
What do they tell us about the changes to the camp over time?

---

71. "Educational Guides and Resources," CSUJAD, updated May 9, 2018, http://www.csujad.com/edguides.html.

Figure 6. "A fashion show was one of the many exhibits held at this relocation center on Labor Day. Great skill was shown in dressmaking and tailoring,
and was thoroughly appreciated by the large audience which witnessed this
display." Francis Stewart, WRA photographer, 1942.[72]

Figure 7. Two soldiers holding guns "standing by for possible difficulty" at
Tule Lake. Owen M. Sylvester, photographer, circa 1943.[73]

---

72. Francis Stewart, "Tule Lake fashion show," photograph, September 7, 1942, John
M. Flaherty Collection of Japanese Internment Records, Department of Special Collections and Archives, San Jose State University, via CSUJAD, http://digitalcollections.
archives.csudh.edu/digital/collection/p16855coll4/id/8887/rec/1.

73. "Soldiers and Incarcerees," photograph, circa 1943, Owen Sylvester Tule Lake
Photo Collection, Gerth Archives and Special Collections, California State University,
Dominguez Hills, via CSUJAD, http://digitalcollections.archives.csudh.edu/digital/

Figure 8. Photograph of the policemen at Tule Lake Segregation Center,
August 30, 1943.[74]

A user's guide was also developed to provide information about
the CSUJAD collection management software and tips for the search
and discovery of the digitized archival materials.[75] To spread the word
about these educational resources, two professional development workshops for elementary and high school teachers took place at CSUDH
in 2018. Members of the scholar advisory group who were children
in the WRA camps shared their WWII experiences, and the teachers were introduced to the CSUJAD project and the various teaching
resources associated with it, which are linked from both the project
website and the online exhibit. A new type of creative workshop took
place in the spring of 2019 targeting high school and college students.
Alan Nakagawa, an interdisciplinary artist consultant, spent four days
at CSUDH teaching different groups of students about art making and

collection/p16855coll4/id/7054/rec/93.

74. "Policemen at Tule Lake Segregation Center," photograph, August 30, 1943, John
M. Flaherty Collection of Japanese Internment Records, Department of Special Collections and Archives, San Jose State University, via CSUJAD, http://digitalcollections.
archives.csudh.edu/digital/collection/p16855coll4/id/12108/rec/1.

75. "Educational Guides and Resources," CSUJAD, updated May 9, 2018, http://
www.csujad.com/edguides.html.

the Japanese-American WWII incarceration. These students also visited the CSUDH Library Archives and Special Collections Department to experience handling the archival materials and to learn more from the archivists about the CSUJAD online project, which provided the resources for the art project. These workshops are part of the CSUDH Praxis Studio, which brings students together to explore their history, social conditions, neighborhoods, and storylines through art.[76] Using methodologies from the CSUDH arts curriculum and those developed by Praxis, students created drawings, watercolor paintings, and collages based on the collected stories that emerged from the CSUJAD archival materials and brought them together in an art zine publication and campus exhibition.[77] Students' reactions to the WWII incarceration of people of Japanese ancestry are being shared with the community in this way, and the zines are being distributed to local and national archives, Japanese-American organizations, schools, and arts organizations in both hard copy and electronic versions. These activities extended the reach of the CSUJAD project through the workshop products and associated activities.

Other historical, cultural, and professional organizations are being informed about this project through community events, publicity, conference presentations, and publications. For example, in fall 2018, a CSUDH scanning day was held at the Gardena Valley Japanese Cultural Institute; attendees brought in applicable archival materials for scanning, learned about the CSUJAD collection from archivists, viewed and discussed these archival objects, and toured the website and online exhibit. The CSUDH scanning day was successful because of publicity in the local Japanese-American press. New images were acquired for the CSUJAD project and new family collections were donated to the archives at CSUDH. As the WWII generation passes, it is not only those who were in the WRA camps who donate materials, but also

76. "Mission," Praxis, accessed June 20, 2019, http://www.csudhpraxis.org/about/.

77. "Unfinished Proof Ninomiya," CSUDH University Art Gallery, May 8 through September 18, 2019, https://gallery.csudh.edu/.

their children and grandchildren. Throughout 2017 and 2018, CSUDH received close to twenty-five new accessions of family materials relating to the Japanese-American incarceration. This was partially because of the existence of the CSUJAD project and its outreach to the community (through news outlets), and partially because of community contacts. Williams also presented the project to the Little Tokyo Historical Society in Los Angeles and is planning a follow-up scanning day activity with this group. Having acquired the Ninomiya Photo Studio Collection, the next event will have an added crowd-sourcing component to help build the descriptive information for this remarkable collection of portraiture as well as community events documenting post-war resettlement and daily life in Los Angeles. The plan is to leverage the knowledge and family interest of online volunteers and encourage them to search the CSUJAD project. They will be asked to enhance the descriptive metadata and add value by tagging and commenting on the digitized photographs directly in the online system.

This chapter grew out of a 2016 presentation we gave at the Art Libraries of North America and Visual Resources Association Conference in Seattle, where the CSUJAD project was presented in a session entitled "Connecting the Past to the Present: Promoting Cultural Understanding through Collections and Exhibitions." Numerous similar presentations at local and national archival (such as the Society of American Archivists and the Society of California Archivists) and library professional organizations have taken place and are planned for the future, where the CSUJAD project is publicized and project experiences are shared. Press releases, blog postings, and other social media outlets are being used to further the reach to regional, national, and global audiences.

The above is not a comprehensive list of activities, but it is representative of the efforts that are being made to contextualize the CSUJAD project, encourage usage, and enhance the experience of the community of users and interpreters connected to this subject. The CSUJAD archival materials deepen the user experience when searching the database, exploring the website, or experiencing exhibits, symposia, film screenings, teacher workshops, or scanning days, which involve the community and publicize the project. The compounding connections between digitization, accurate description, contextualization, and expanding collecting opportunities allows for not only a broader historical interpretation, but also for a focus on the building blocks of community-based collection development. This is important for new scholarship, public interpretation, and for allowing the Japanese-American community to delve deeply into its history.

Currency Today

> As you might know, since the war ended some kind of presure came to us Japanese. The immigration officers are investigating every issei's past records. It goes back to 1929. In January of that year I had a pass from the Calexico port, Imperial Valley, California, to cross the boarder to Mexico to visit a Mexican school and came back the same afternoon. The pass is usable for one year or over without any visa. The immigration office did not [stamp the] visa as it was not required. But, today, the government says I came in illegally.[78]
> —Letter from Toske Hoshimiya from Ann Arbor, Michigan to Ralph McFarling, November 1, 1945

Japanese Americans who were in camps or in the military during WWII have found a variety of ways to commemorate their wartime experiences. After the 1960s, there were reunions at the incarceration camps, and in major cities when the camps were too far away to visit. Later, activists in the Japanese-American community used what they learned about incarceration to memorialize its role in U.S. history. This resulted in the establishment of the WRA camps as National Parks (Manzanar and Tule Lake) or sites of historical importance (Heart Mountain and Amache). Generations of Japanese Americans continue to have annual "days of remembrance." Each year, Manzanar, Tule Lake, and other sites hold annual pilgrimages. Hundreds of Japanese Americans are joined

---

78. Toske Hoshimiya to Ralph McFarling, letter, November 1, 1945, J. Ralph McFarling Collection, Gerth Archives and Special Collections, California State University, Dominguez Hills, via CSUJAD, http://digitalcollections.archives.csudh.edu/digital/collection/p16855coll4/id/316/rec/9.

by supporters to commemorate their relatives who endured the WWII incarceration. These events have also resulted in archival documentation that is of historical importance. The CSUJAD project has digitized many reunion and other commemorative booklets.

Figure 9. 23rd Annual Manzanar Pilgrimage program, April 25, 1992.[79]

---

79. "23rd Annual Manzanar Pilgrimage," program, April 25, 1992, Japanese American Relocation Collection, University Archives and Special Collections, California State University, Fullerton, via CSUJAD, http://digitalcollections.archives.csudh.edu/

The community of Japanese-American activists has long been involved in a variety of causes relating to redress, the commemoration of sites, and civil liberties issues. After the attacks of September 11, 2001, a good number of Japanese Americans supported Muslim Americans who faced discrimination because of the attacks. The connection between December 7, 1941 and September 11, 2001 was evident not only to the public, but also to Japanese-American activists who understood how a momentous event can lead to the harsh, violent, and prejudicial treatment of innocent people just because of race or religion. Today, Muslim Americans attend events such as the annual Manzanar Pilgrimage to support civil liberties, and Japanese Americans continue to support Muslim Americans facing discrimination in a variety of ways.

In his 1993 book, *Prisoners Without Trial*, Roger Daniels asks whether something like the incarceration of Japanese Americans during WWII could happen again. He cites a number of post-WWII events that have come close, such as the Cold War's Emergency Detention Act of 1950. He notes that, despite great improvement in American race relations, these incidents demonstrate "an American propensity to react against 'foreigners' in the United States during times of external crisis."[80] Sadly, he anticipated current events. In a foreword to a book focused on Karl Bendetsen and Perry Saito, Daniels discusses a government response that occurred after the terrorist attacks of September 11, 2001, which triggered a reaction from the Japanese-American community. Those in the Muslim community with foreign roots came under suspicion and 762 immigrants were arrested by the FBI and held for many months. Many were deprived of the right to counsel, verbally and physically abused, tried, and in some cases deported, all in secret.[81] He indicates that many were discovered to be in the country illegally (visa overstayers) and were deported, but not one of them was charged with anything in connection

---

digital/collection/p16855coll4/id/15093/rec/3.

80. Roger Daniels, *Prisoners Without Trial: Japanese Americans in World War II* (New York: Hill and Wang, 1993), 113.

81. Klancy Clark de Nevers, *The Colonel and the Pacifist: Karl Bendetsen, Perry Saito, and the Incarceration of Japanese Americans During World War II* (Salt Lake City: University of Utah Press, 2004), x-xi.

to the events of September 11, 2001 or any other terrorist activity. "It was a shocking revelation of the Department of Justice's violations of its own rules." And, it "indicates just how thin a shield our Bill of Rights can be in times of crisis."[82] The similarity of the government's response to the Pearl Harbor bombing was not lost on the Japanese-American community, especially since it received the overwhelming support of the vast majority of Americans. One major difference that Daniels points out is that, in the case of WWII, this happened to American citizens of Japanese descent, rather than un-naturalized Muslim foreigners. "But in each instance, the spirit if not the letter of the Constitution has been violated."[83]

Through its blog, Densho provides historical information, clarifies parallels, and denounces many current U.S. government actions that affect the Muslim community.[84] For example, they decried Donald Trump's Executive Order suspending or blocking entry of Muslims into the U.S. (January 28, 2017); they denounced using the Japanese-American incarceration as a precedent for a Muslim registry (November 23, 2016); they publicized the problems with conflating internment camps with concentration camps when discussing incarcerating Muslims after the European terrorist attacks (June 8, 2017); and they condemned the racial profiling associated with the Muslim travel ban (September 22, 2017). The blog writers have also spoken out about the "troubling similarities" between the Japanese-American and Latino experiences in family detention (August 9, 2016) and have drawn parallels with early Issei immigrants (December 15, 2017) and Japanese-American repatriation and deportation during and after WWII (October 27, 2016). These same activists noted with alarm the arrest and separation of children near the U.S. border in 2018.

In 2018, a *National Geographic* article, "I AM AN AMERICAN: Scenes from the Japanese Internment Resonate Today," juxtaposes photographs

---

82. Clark de Nevers, *The Colonel and the Pacifist*, xi.

83. Clark de Nevers, *The Colonel and the Pacifist*, xi.

84. "Densho Blog," Densho, accessed June 20, 2019, https://densho.org/blog/.

of Japanese Americans taken during WWII with images of the same people photographed recently by Paul Kitagaki, Jr. to document their resilience and courage.[85] It provides some historical information and discusses the issues surrounding the WWII incarceration. The author, Ann Curry, suggests that the answer to the questions of how American citizens were locked up without due process during the war "lies not just in fear and prejudice but in the power of politics to exacerbate both." Curry points out that "The incarceration is cited in today's immigration debates, including over the detention of migrant children and families crossing the southern border in June and the current ban on people from several Muslim-majority countries entering the United States."[86] Curry also points out that many Japanese Americans who were incarcerated during WWII and their children are now speaking up and taking a stand against the Trump administration's policies. Kitagaki's photographs, which are the focus of Curry's article, are currently on display in an exhibition entitled, "Gambatte! Legacy of an Enduring Spirit" at the JANM in Los Angeles.[87] Compounded by the 2001 and subsequent global terrorist attacks and the difficulties along the border with refugee children, the topic of Japanese-American incarceration continues to resonate.

Conclusion

> I had been living in Compton, California with my sister and was attending school when the war broke out....In Poston I wanted to apply for relocation and some of my friends were going to leave to relocate but my father and whole family objected to my leaving as they were very fearful that I might be harmed by Caucasians who hated us because of our race....It was either relocate to some hostile area where we would have a difficult time and risk being harmed and never seeing our parents

---

85. Ann Curry, "I AM AN AMERICAN: Scenes from the Japanese Internment Resonate Today," *National Geographic* (October 2018): 124-38.

86. Curry, "I AM AN AMERICAN," 126.

87. "Gambatte! Legacy of an Enduring Spirit," Japanese American National Museum, accessed June 20, 2019, http://www.janm.org/exhibits/gambatte/.

again or requesting repatriation to stay with them and be sent to Japan.[88]
—Tsugitada Kanamori, affidavit regarding his life in camps and deportation to Japan, which lasted until 1956

The archival materials in the CSUJAD project relating to the lives of Atsushi (Art) Ishida and George Naohara document personal and community history, but also the extent to which the WWII government-imposed imprisonment led to personal hardship and a tireless resilience in the face of an intense violation of civil rights. The physical papers of Ishida's and Naohara's families are housed at the CSUDH Archives and consist of the contents of four photo albums and scrapbooks. Within the CSUJAD project, this covers close to 1,000 items never before accessible.

Naohara and Ishida, friends in their early twenties, were first generation Japanese Americans from the Los Angeles area. They spent the summer of 1941 farming near Long Beach, California, until the Japanese government attacked Pearl Harbor on December 7th, and the lives of 120,000 Japanese Americans were irrevocably changed. Ishida ended up in horse stalls at the Santa Anita Race Track, which served as a temporary assembly center. Ishida kept his meal tickets at Santa Anita and his timesheet for work done at a Santa Anita dining hall as mementos. Naohara went out to Manzanar to help build the incarceration camp. After that, he found agricultural work in Utah and Idaho.

Eventually, both Ishida and Naohara landed in the Jerome Camp in Denson, Arkansas, where Ishida initially worked as a lumberjack in and around the camp area. It was here that Ishida took photographs using a camera he had bought through the Sears catalog while in camp. The CSUJAD project now has several hundred of Ishida's images from the Arkansas camp. The papers that both Naohara and Ishida retained document their lives in Jerome, including their responses to the WRA survey that asked whether they forswore loyalty to the Japanese Emperor

---

88. "Attached Answers to Affidavit Questions," official document, circa 1945, Tsugitada Kanamori Collection, Gerth Archives and Special Collections, California State University, Dominguez Hills, via CSUJAD, http://digitalcollections.archives.csudh.edu/digital/collection/p16855coll4/id/7060/rec/3.

and whether they would serve in the U.S. military. Some first generation Japanese Americans didn't care much about the Emperor, but they did wonder why they should fight in the U.S. military, given that their families were imprisoned. By answering "no" to each of the questions in the survey, they became known as "no-no boys." Ishida answered "no-yes" and Naohara answered "no-no." Ishida and then later Naohara were transferred to Tule Lake Segregation Center, where the no-no boys and their families were sent for eventual deportation to Japan—American-born citizens deported to a country in which they had never resided.

In late 1944, at Tule Lake, Ishida was interviewed by camp officials; he told them that he wanted out. They let him out, suggesting either the unequal treatment of some prisoners or selective bureaucratic rules gone haywire. Ishida then visited a friend at the Minidoka Camp in Hunt, Idaho. Eventually, he arrived in Chicago. Naohara ended up in Chicago, too, followed by his fiancé Mitzi Masukawa (after she spent four years in the Poston, Arizona camp as a pre-school teacher). When the war ended, Naohara volunteered for and Ishida was drafted into the U.S. military. When the Korean War broke out, both Naohara and Ishida were assigned to Japan. They both had relatives in Hiroshima. Eventually both Naohara and Ishida settled in Gardena, California. Naohara and Masukawa became local barbers and Ishida went into landscaping. In 2017, ninety-seven-year-old Ishida donated his photographs and papers to the CSUJAD project. Also in 2017, Naohara's widow and their daughter, Eileen Yoshimura, donated their family's papers to the CSUJAD project.

Ishida's and Naohara's stories are only a fraction of what is now available in the CSUJAD project. The myriad of stories scattered throughout the CSUJAD website are rich with examples of human strength in the face of adversity, bureaucratic befuddlement, and administrative irritation, and they provide an in-depth look at the violations of civil liberties in the U.S. They are told through primary sources—official documents, personal letters, photographs, ephemera, oral histories, etc.—focused on thousands of people. These stories, borne of racism and war, are now available on the CSUJAD website.

Figure 10. Photograph of Atsushi Ishida (center), George Naohara (right), and an unidentified man posing at the entrance to a mess hall in Jerome, Arkansas, 1944.[89]

The purpose of a collaborative project such as the CSUJAD is to bring together once hidden and dispersed archival materials, to connect the experience of these individuals, and to bring their stories to light. Additionally, the building of a database on the topic of Japanese-American incarceration, on the face of it, is to create evidence and documentation for students, scholars, and the interested public to interpret and create a more nuanced history of the period. This includes materials

---

89. "Atsushi Ishida, George Naohara, and Man," photograph, 1944, Atsushi Ishida Collection, Gerth Archives and Special Collections, California State University, Dominguez Hills, via CSUJAD, http://digitalcollections.archives.csudh.edu/digital/collection/p16855coll4/id/27346/rec/11.

not only from the WWII years, but also from both the pre- and post-war periods, in order to create a more holistic picture of events in the twentieth century. The database was also created to provide evidence and documentation that backs up facts and sheds light on outdated interpretations. The project has stimulated a number of additional dona-tions of pertinent materials and hopes to continue to do so, especially considering the urgency of procuring the passing WWII generation's remembrances before they are lost.

The compounding connections between digitization, accurate descrip-tion, contextualization, and expanding collecting opportunities allows for not only a broader historical interpretation, but also for a focus on the building blocks of community-based collection development. The careful consideration of terminology to increase public awareness of misleading language is an important step towards eliminating govern-mental and institutional bias in archival description. Our ability to readily find and examine personal documents online democratizes the histori-cal record, humanizes past experiences, and transforms interpretation. The CSUJAD project is important for enriching new scholarship and encouraging those interested in Japanese-American history to delve more deeply into the WWII incarceration, as well as the events that led up to and followed it. Ironically, current immigration controversies and other threats to civil rights increase the value of such archival projects by allowing for community-based or activist viewpoints and, thus, deepen our understanding of recent history.

Bibliography

Alinder, Jasmine. *Moving Images: Photography and the Japanese American Incarcera-tion*. Urbana, IL: University of Illinois Press, 2009.

California State University. "California State University Japanese American Digitization Project." Collaborative Digital History Project of the California State University Libraries. Updated May 9, 2018. http://www.csujad.com/index.html.

Cauley, Alexandra Arai, and Christina Pappous. "The Ninomiya Photo Studio Collection." *Los Angeles Archivists Collective* (blog), 2017. http://www.laacollective.org/work/ninomiya-photo-studio/.

Chiang, Connie Y. *Nature Behind Barbed Wire: An Environmental History of the Japanese American Incarceration.* Oxford, UK: Oxford University Press, 2018.

Clark de Nevers, Klancy. *The Colonel and the Pacifist: Karl Bendetsen, Perry Saito, and the Incarceration of Japanese Americans During World War II.* Salt Lake City, UT: University of Utah Press, 2004.

Curry, Ann. 2018. "I AM AN AMERICAN: Scenes from the Japanese Internment Resonate Today." *National Geographic* (October): 124-38.

Daniels, Roger. *The Politics of Prejudice: The Anti-Japanese Movement in California and the Struggle for Japanese Exclusion.* Berkeley, CA: University of California Press, 1962.

Daniels, Roger. *Concentration Camps North America: Japanese in the United States and Canada in World War II.* Malabar, FL: R.E. Krieger, 1981.

Daniels, Roger. *Prisoners Without Trial: Japanese Americans in World War II.* New York: Hill and Wang, 1993.

Daniels, Roger. "Words Do Matter: A Note on Inappropriate Terminology and the Incarceration of the Japanese Americans." In *Nikei in the Pacific Northwest: Japanese Americans and Japanese Canadians in the Twentieth Century,* edited by Louis Fiset and Gail Nomura, 183-207. Seattle, WA: University of Washington Press, 2005.

Greaton Gardena Collection. Gerth Special Collections and Archives, California State University, Dominguez Hills.

Herzig-Yoshinaga, Aiko. "Words Can Lie or Clarify: Terminology of the World War II Incarceration of Japanese Americans." *Discover Nikkei.* February 2, 2010. http://www.discovernikkei.org/en/journal/2010/02/02/terminology-incarceration-japanese-americans/.

Hirabayashi, Lane Ryo. "Everyday Sources about Life in the Camps: The Value of the Vernacular." Essay written for California State University Japanese American Digitization Project. April 2015. http://www.csujad.com/images/HolisticRepresentations_Hirabayashi.pdf.

McWhorter, John. "AOC's Critics Are Pretending Not to Know How Language Works: A great deal of communication is based on metaphor." *The Atlantic,* June 20, 2019. https://www.theatlantic.com/ideas/archive/2019/06/defense-ocasio-cortez-concentration-camp-comment/592180/.

McWilliams, Carey. *Prejudice: Japanese Americans, Symbol of Racial Intolerance.* Boston: Little, Brown and Company, 1944.

Moore, Mary-Michelle. "And Then They Came For Us….." CSUDH University Library, February 23, 2017, https://torolink.csudh.edu/news/107759.

Shimabukuro, Mira. *Relocating Authority: Japanese Americans Writing to Redress Mass Incarceration.* Boulder: University Press of Colorado, 2015.

Takei, Barbara, and Judy M. Tachibana. *Tule Lake Revisited: A Brief History and Guide to the Tule Lake Concentration Camp Site.* 2nd ed. San Francisco, CA: Tule Lake Committee, 2012.

Wakatsuki Houston, Jeanne, and James D. Houston. *Farewell to Manzanar: A True Story of Japanese American Experience During and After the WWII Internment.* New York: Bantam Books, 1973.

Weglyn, Michi. *Years of Infamy: The Untold Story of America's Concentration Camps.* New York: Morrow, 1976.

Chapter 17

SIGNED, SEALED, DELIVERED (WITH CLARITY, CONTEXT, AND PATIENCE): ETHICAL CONSIDERATIONS FOR DEEDS OF GIFT AND TRANSFER AGREEMENTS

Katrina Windon and Lori Birrell

Regularly, in the course of the archival enterprise, archivists execute contracts bearing legal and financial consequences. We, as archivists, may treat these documents as such, or we may consider them *pro forma* paperwork, but how should we present them to donors and potential donors? These contracts may include deeds of gift and other donation instruments, which are increasingly mandatory, but often unfamiliar— and intimidating—to new donors. A standard deed of gift instrument involves intersections of multiple professional areas of knowledge: archives; copyright law; rights management; appraisal; information security; public records laws; contract law; property law; and intellectual property law. Particularly when archivists work with those in vulnerable populations or those whose native language is not the same as the form's language, a critical approach is needed to ensure mutual understanding and agreement, rather than simply contiguous signatures. Historical instances of early research studies of Native Americans and token consent forms in medical research cases serve as cautionary tales about what can occur when research missions overwhelm respect for individual rights and privacy.

This chapter explores the concept of information literacy and donor education within the context of informed consent and rights negotiation as part of the archival donation process, as well as the ways institutions may be able to assist users during that process, which privileges those with greater legal consciousness (and, perhaps even more so, those with lawyers and accountants on retainer). We explore three facets out of the many considerations for deed of gift development and application: how archivists can guide the creation or revision of the initial documents; what should be points of flexibility and *in*flexibility for archivists in negotiating individual deeds of gift; and how archivists can present deeds of gift with supplementary context in order to educate donors and mitigate inequities. There exists a careful balance, which without conscious efforts may become *im*balanced, between ensuring the rights and protections of donors, and safeguarding the interests of the institution and its researchers. Donors unfamiliar with archives may be unaware of the implications of their donations—of how academic criticism, artistic endeavors, and creative use and reuse may occur; of how their words may be taken out of context; and of how their images may be commercialized. Supporting open access, an information commons, and a democratized historical record are all decisions that involve calculated risks in the name of the public good. However, if donors are unaware of the risks and rewards, signatures may be, at best, meaningless gestures, and, at worst, uninformed relinquishing of personal rights. Information literacy is developed, not innate, and part of its development depends on continually gaining new information to compare to the old.[1] Archivists may mitigate these concerns by developing an awareness of potential inequities that can then inform careful creation and presentation of transfer documents, particularly through donor education and transparency.

---

1. American Library Association, "Presidential Committee on Information Literacy: Final Report," July 24, 2006, http://www.ala.org/acrl/publications/whitepapers/presidential, accessed June 1, 2018, doi: 106e5565-9ab9-ad94-8d9f-64962ebcde46.

How Can Archivists Guide the Creation or Revision of Deeds of Gift?

An archivist may arrive at an institution that already has an established deed of gift that has been cleared by legal counsel, used for decades, and challenged by no one. Or an archivist may arrive at an institution that has no formalized donation documentation procedures whatsoever. The former is no basis for complacency; the latter is no reason for panic (probably). Regardless of where one starts, there is probably room for improvement; even fixed documents likely have room for flexible context—e.g., the way the donation form is introduced and explained to donors, the media through which it is presented, and the level of urgency the archivist brings to those conversations to initiate an agreement. Archivists bring professional expertise, but donation form development must be done in collaboration with others, such as administrators and legal counsel, or, in some cases, and most delicately, members of vulnerable or previously mistreated donor populations.

At its core, the deed of gift serves as "the written agreement...[and] formal expression of the terms of the gift and its acceptance and transfer of ownership of records and copyright to the archives."[2] Archivist Menzi L. Behrnd-Klodt argues in her 2008 book, *Navigating Legal Issues in Archives,* that archivists play multiple roles during the acquisition process. Archivists balance three interests: a "duty to donors [that] involves dealing fairly in all aspects yet facilitating the donor's wishes as much as possible," "an obligation to uphold the standards and ethics of the archival profession," and, no less important, "a duty to themselves, their careers, and their personal ethics and moral standards."[3] These interests, although often complementary, are sometimes competing, and the balancing between them is both a skill that archivists must hone throughout their careers and, occasionally, an ethical quandary.

---

2. Menzi L. Behrnd-Klodt, *Navigating Legal Issues in Archives* (Chicago: Society of American Archivists, 2008), 42.

3. Behrnd-Klodt, *Navigating Legal Issues in Archives,* 42.

Archival ethics should remain consistent, but approaches toward the latter two categories will vary substantially depending on region and institution. For instance, a publicly funded institution may/should err more on the side of access than a privately funded institution, whose funders and/or governing board may support more stringent restrictions. Public institutions in states with strong public records laws are even more constrained in terms of what restriction options may be responsibly granted to donors. In a case where a contract violates state or federal law, the contract does not govern.

A typical deed of gift has signatories from two parties, the donor and the donee; depending on organizational complexity, there may be multiple signatories on either side. Those signatories, however, are not the only parties invested in the agreement, nor are they, typically, the only parties involved in drafting that agreement. From the donee's perspective, there are three primary ethical and legal components to consider, each encompassing immense and prismatic complexities:

- Archival ethics (for which archivists are best able to advocate);
- International, federal, state, and local laws (upon which an institution's legal counsel is best able to offer guidance, but which archivists nonetheless have standing to comment upon[4]); and
- Institutional policies and mission (for which administrators may be best able to advocate—but, again, which archivists should have a say in, as members and representatives of the institution).

Depending on the institutional context, archivists may have very little say in the text of a deed of gift instrument, but will likely have a great deal of say in the execution and use of it. Archivists should establish how flexible their deeds of gift are, i.e., what can and cannot be changed.

---

4. Behrnd-Klodt notes, "as the lawyer's client, the archivist also plays a significant professional role in directing the overall course and outcome of the legal matter and managing the flow of financial, human, and other resources. Foremost among the archivist's tasks, as a legal services' consumer, is educating the attorney about archives." Behrnd-Klodt, *Navigating Legal Issues in Archives*, 8.

Considerable time and headaches can be saved by determining, at the outset, what types of changes require approval, and from whom. Ideally, each deed of gift has at least some sections that can be considered to be blank slates, with archivists encouraging donors to review and consider how each component impacts them—but that offer a framework to guide the discussion of a deed of gift including common considerations for each party. Flexibility may offer donors opportunities to advocate for their concerns and unique circumstances; this is particularly critical when working with donors who may have, historically, been asked or required to sign away their rights.[5] If sufficient flexibility does not exist, the form may be in need of revision. Depending on the organization, revision of any deed may require several layers of approval, including review from a possibly overworked legal team. Archivists who are dissatisfied with their institutions' existing deeds of gift may consider whether the problems they are seeing (upset donors, demands for return of materials, etc.) justify revising the deeds. New laws or institutional policies, as well as a significant change in collection development policy or scale, are two other opportunities to review existing deeds of gift.

When drafting or revising a deed of gift, it is worth considering not just what boxes must be checked (title transfer, copyright transfer, attribution requirements, restrictions, etc.), but also *how* those boxes are being checked. Be cautious about fields that, if left blank, signify a transfer of some right. When possible, forms that require positive consent (checking or initialing a box, or writing "N/A," for instance) are preferable, if marginally more onerous for in-a-hurry donors and staff members, and are more likely to reflect donors' informed decision-making. If using a digital form, certain fields may be programmed as "required," but paper forms—still the norm across archives—require personal oversight to ensure they are properly completed.

---

5. For instance, Native American groups whose cultural heritage was appropriated by unauthorized anthropologists, or groups misled during medical trials. See: Cara S. Bertram, "Avenues of Mutual Respect: Opening Communication and Understanding between Native Americans and Archivists" (master's thesis, Western Washington University, 2012), 58, https://cedar.wwu.edu/wwuet/240.

A good deed of gift instrument, poorly filled out, is not a good deed of gift record. Consider whether all the information requested is, in fact, required, and whether your institution has, and is, applying the necessary staff time to follow through until all information has been acquired. Are anonymous donations allowed? What effect would this allowance have on provenance and diplomatics? If deeds of gift are documents that are subject to the Freedom of Information Act, are there cases where, if donors have valid concerns for privacy, those concerns may supersede the archival ideal of transparency and of providing the greatest context for records? Donor contact information is essential for maintaining lines of communication between repositories and donors, but contact information can be for intermediaries, such as friends or family members, if donors do not have fixed addresses, and this option can be treated as standard, rather than as something unusual.

Archivists who work with donors should consistently document deed of gift exceptions for their repositories. Furthermore, archivists must consider which exceptions they can make, given archival ethics and their institutional context, and go no further, as tempting as it may be to make exceptions for collections that are particularly historically rich or for particularly significant donors. Exceptions, once made, set precedent, even if not necessarily *legal* precedent—and potentially not only for a single archivist, but also for archivists' colleagues and successors; as such, these decisions should be documented, explained, and, as appropriate, extended to all equivalent situations.

A repository should also consider its collection development policy when considering its deed of gift. If the repository's scope includes Native American materials, does the deed of gift offer the flexibility to carve out the kinds of exceptions the *Protocols for Native American Archival Materials* recommends?[6] If the repository's scope includes materials of immigrant communities, is the deed of gift available in the native languages of those communities? If the repository's scope includes

---

6. Cara S. Bertram, "Avenues of Mutual Respect: Opening Communication and Understanding between Native Americans and Archivists," 58.

materials of communities that have previously been (or are currently) victims of systemic racism or prejudice, does the deed of gift in any way perpetuate those inequities?

Ideally, archivists treat all donors with the same level of respect and appreciation. Such practice requires intentionality and being mindful of power imbalances, language barriers, mental and physical health conditions, and educational and socioeconomic backgrounds. However, the shift away from best practices in favor of responding to stakeholder demands can be all too easy—whether those stakeholders are donors, university development officers, or administrators. Therefore, defined approaches are necessary to actively, rather than reactively, drive conversations with donors in a productive direction.

Archival teams must have a strong understanding of and experience in implementing best practices for appraisal, arrangement, and description. The Society of American Archivists' Code of Ethics identifies as one of the profession's core values to "promote and provide the widest possible accessibility of materials, consistent with any mandatory access restrictions, such as public statute, donor contract, business/institutional privacy, or personal privacy," noting that, apart from those required access restrictions, "archivists seek to promote open access and use when possible."[7] Both the Code of Ethics and subsequent statement of values provide critical foundations for archival practice, necessary as part of archivists' efforts to construct deeds of gift and develop relationships with donors. Some archivists have advocated that we have ethical responsibilities beyond those stated in professional organizations' codes of ethics.[8] For deeds of gift, specifically, Antoinette E. Baker declares it to be the responsibility of archivists to advocate in negotiations not just for the donor's own concerns, but also for protections of

---

7. Society of American Archivists, "Code of Ethics for Archivists," last modified January 2012, https://www2.archivists.org/statements/saa-core-values-statement-and-code-of-ethics.

8. Richard Cox, in particular, has explored the ways in which codes of ethics fall short, particularly in terms of enforcement and application. See: Richard J. Cox, "Rethinking Archival Ethics," *Journal of Information Ethics* 22, no. 2 (2013): 13; *Ethics, Accountability, and Record Keeping in a Dangerous World* (London: Facet Publishing, 2006).

third-party ("blind donor") interests, and even to "be prepared to turn down donated archives if the donor is not willing to address fundamental privacy concerns."[9] If, due to archival ethics, archivists are faced with turning down a collection, they should work in consultation and in full transparency with stakeholders such as university administrators, civic leaders, and development officers.

When writing model deeds of gift, archivists often use words like "simplicity and ease of use,"[10] and "clear, unambiguous."[11] In this regard, as on other issues, archivists may find a difference of opinion with legal counsel. Ultimately, however, documents created and exchanged in order to protect the interests and limit the liability of an archival repository should not alienate donors or unnecessarily impede upon their agency. There are certain points that may be worthy hills on which to stake one's ground (preferred sites of contestation, if you will), and several are outlined in the next section.

What Can and Should Be Negotiable?

Donor relations work is a form of management and, similar to other kinds of management, it requires clear, frequent, and transparent communication. Something as simple as learning what modes of communication your donors prefer can save tremendous time and can help to ensure that they feel valued. University development files often include such preferences. Having strong working relationships with development officers is immensely helpful as archivists establish connections with donors (the balance being, of course, ensuring that collection donors do not feel that their relationship with the archives is being monetized). Understanding from colleagues how the donor has worked

---

9. Antoinette E. Baker, "Ethical Considerations in Web 2.0 Archives," *School of Information Student Research Journal* 1 no. 1 (July 2011): 9, http://scholarworks.sjsu.edu/slissrj/vol1/iss1/4.

10. Society of American Archivists, and Association of Records Managers and Administrators, *Sample Forms for Archival and Records Management Programs* (Lenexa, KS: ARMA International, 2002), xv.

11. Trudy Huskamp Peterson, "The Gift and the Deed," *American Archivist* 42, no. 1 (January 1979): 61-66.

with the department or institution in the past is another time saver. The donor may have strong ties to the institution, but not to the archives; the donor may even have a contentious relationship with the larger institution. Archivists must build trust with all donors, regardless of previous dealings.

Restrictions and Representations

Discussions of restricting content take place at various points in collection development and in the process of establishing relationships with donors. Restrictions have the potential to impact not only future researchers, but also archival staff; as Behrnd-Klodt notes, "all potential restrictions, limitations, or exceptions that will affect the archives' ability to effectively and efficiently manage its holdings should be discussed fully with the donor in advance and recorded on the donor agreement."[12] For those archivists who work collaboratively on collection development and donor relations, it is important to clearly articulate with all partners what restrictions the institution will accept, in keeping with archival best practices.

Archivists must decide what, if any, deal-breakers there are with regard to establishing restrictions at the point of filling out the deed of gift. Will the restrictions require extensive staff time to implement, communicate, and, when the time comes, lift? Could the restrictions create public relations problems?

When dealing with donors with long-standing ties to the institution, university development and administrators often become involved in the negotiation of the deed of gift. While archivists may not feel comfortable asserting themselves into these power dynamics, they must, whether directly or through their department's head. These more high-profile donors may also be more likely than typical donors might be to consult with lawyers when determining what, if any, restrictions to place on their collections. Although no direct equivalent of a public defender exists for contract law, there are resources to which archivists may direct

---

12. Behrnd-Klodt, *Navigating Legal Issues in Archives*, 49.

potential donors in order to better educate them about their rights, as well as, depending on institutional context, varying degrees of advice that archivists may offer directly to donors. Unlike organizational or political donors, donors with family or personal papers may not have that experience negotiating terms. Archivists can share relevant best practices and (anonymized) examples from other, similar collections, to guide the decision-making process.

In addition to being cognizant of donors' differing levels of legal literacy and resource access, archivists should also consider the physical and mental capacity of donors to advocate for themselves. When working with donors in ill health, archivists may wish to suggest that they involve friends or family members to assist them in evaluating their collection for potential privacy concerns; these designees may be there for support only, or they may be designated as proxies. Depending on the circumstances, archivists may want to document these conversations, as well as the decisions made, to ensure that donors' wishes are honored and can be explained to family members should donors no longer be able to make decisions.

For those organizations working with or representing at-risk or underrepresented communities, archivists should consider privacy-based restrictions for both their organizations' documents and any materials gathered from their stakeholders to ensure there are no negative consequences for donors. Citizenship status, as well as federal or state benefits, could all be impacted. Will these restrictions be for the lifetime of the donor? How will personally identifiable information be included in the collection? Initiating these conversations falls to archivists, utilizing translators to ensure all donors associated with the organization are aware of archival practices and the meaning of restrictions and access to archival materials once donated. In some cases, archivists may have ethical responsibilities to serve as advocates (or to recommend advocates) for those lacking social and political capital to advocate for themselves in negotiations.

Sensitivity to the concerns discussed above must be balanced with the capacity of archival staff to address those concerns. Donors specifying

designees to act in their absence, for instance, may leave archival staff
with obligations to follow up with subsequent generations of family
members or estate executors, rendering archivists private detectives working through out-of-date contact information and no-longer-applicable
maiden names. Archivists and their broader institutions should decide
when such conditions are acceptable and what burden of responsibility rests with archival staff—in other words, what constitutes "due
diligence." Defined documentation, systems, and workflows to ensure
commitments can be met—during an archivist's tenure and that of an
archivist's successors—are keys to avoid simply passing on unfunded
mandates to future archivists.

Copyright and Use

An archive's deed of gift (or accompanying information) should explain
the impact that transferring copyright—or not—has on the research
and publishing process. As archivist Elizabeth Druga has noted, it is
important "that donors know the value of the rights they are handing
over."[13] If an archivist understands why a donor is interested in donating
a collection in the first place, that knowledge may provide a basis for discussion on how decisions about copyright and reproduction restrictions
may impede those goals. However, artists' and authors' livelihoods may
depend on the retention of their copyright, and being prepared to offer
compromises, such as posthumous copyright transfers, can ease negotiations. Not all donors will agree to transfer copyright to institutions.
Revisiting the question of copyright as archivists continue to develop
their relationships with donors may be beneficial. For heavily used collections, donors may eventually see the value in transferring copyright
to the archives to best ensure the use of the materials. In these cases,
writing an addendum to be signed by both the donor and the donee can
remove an administrative barrier for archivists when providing guidance
to researchers about publishing materials from the collection.

---

13. Elizabeth Druga, "Raising Money Raises Questions: The Ethics of Generating
Revenue from Archival Materials," *Journal of Information Ethics* 19, no. 1 (Spring 2010):
145, doi: 10.3172.

Big Asks

In some cases, donors may have a clear picture for how they want their collections processed, and that picture may not align with the policies and resources of the donee institution. These expectations may include things like a desire for items to be on permanent display, a desire for immediate processing of a large collection, an expectation of complete editorial privileges over finding aids (descriptive records for archival collections) and other research products, or—very commonly—an expectation of wholesale collection digitization. In negotiating deeds of gift, it is important to consider that those following classic negotiation strategies may intentionally be asking for more than they really expect to get. Also, for donors with a very personal connection to the records they are donating, what seems like an unreasonably big ask to archivists may, to those donors, feel like extreme concessions on their part. Different forms of argument may work better for different donors—researcher impact assessments may hold more sway with donors who have themselves been researchers, while cost-benefit analyses and hard budget numbers may be more effective in convincing those well-versed in business negotiations. When explaining the costs of arranging and describing collections, archivists should state that they must work with vendors, conservators, and digitization units, and they should have clear cost models to share with donors should the topic arise. Often discussions about digitization offer archivists the opportunity to educate donors and advocate for archival work as they explain the differences between different access models. If the archives have a duplication service or proxy research service, explaining those programs to donors can also help to clarify archival work. Regardless of an institution's workflow, archivists must clearly understand organizational priorities in order to avoid making untenable commitments documented in the deed of gift.

Processing Considerations

A common question most donors ask during discussions about their collections is: *when will the collection be processed?* They may not use that phrase, but most do want to know when researchers will be able to use the materials. Some donors will want to add specific processing time-lines into the deed of gift. In addition, a donor with significant ties to the university or community may be asked by a member of university development, or may offer, to make a monetary gift to pay for the costs associated with arranging and describing the collection. Writing about the problems of donor demands for special accommodations, New York Public Library General Counsel Robert Vanni wryly concedes that "[o]ne balm that can often soothe such pains is, of course, money. If special processing or accessing requirements are sought by the donor, then once they are educated to the realities of maintaining an entire division, a request that the donation include a cash fund or endowment to cover, for example, the cost of hiring a freelance cataloger or a portion of a new staff member's salary, may well be met with success."[14] A success in terms of institutional financial health and processing statistics, however, may be a failure in collection development, donor relations, and, potentially, archival ethics. Receiving money to process a collection inherently makes the value of that collection more important to the institution. Archivists must honor the terms of the gift, which can result in a change in processing priorities to accommodate this new acquisition. Having safeguards in place to ensure that donor funding does not become a primary driver of processing prioritization—thus potentially delaying the inclusion of other voices into the archival record—is important. Clear processing priorities and criteria through which to evaluate new collections are one such safeguard. Archivists should work with their university development officers, administrators, and donors to establish clear expectations when it comes to processing any collection—regardless of whether there is a monetary gift set aside for this work. Given the costs associated with processing manuscript and archival collections, archivists should actively work with their development officers to manage the expectations of all stakeholders and to infuse details about the costs of collection stewardship into conversations with all donors.

---

14. Robert J. Vanni, "Deeds of Gift: Caressing the Hand that Feeds," in *Libraries, Museums, and Archives: Legal Issues and Ethical Challenges in the New Information Era*, ed. Tomas A. Lipinski (Lanham, MD: Scarecrow Press, 2002), 11.

How Can an Archivist Best Present a Deed of Gift in Order to Mitigate Concerns and Inequities?

Once an archivist has advocated for a deed of gift that is in line with professional best practices, respectful of institutional requirements, adherent to all governing laws and ethical codes, and has shepherded said document through whatever regulatory channels are required, then it is to be implemented. It is at this point that the most complex ethical considerations arise; this is when the considerations are no longer generalized and abstract but, instead, are individual and personal. Perhaps a donor is a friend of the dean, or on the state senate's Appropriations Committee; perhaps the donor is a particularly gifted storyteller and the archivist is a particularly soft touch for stories involving veterans, orphans, puppies, or any combination thereof.

It is interesting but perhaps not surprising that, as archives have attempted to become more democratic, they have also become more bureaucratic and, in becoming so, have introduced new forms of barriers to the new communities they wish to represent and serve. Vanni notes that, in the early twentieth century, when deeds of gift were less *de rigeur*, "[d]onors made their wishes known through simple letters or relatively uncomplicated deeds of gift or bequests to nascent institutions overseen by the local elite, with whom they shared their friends, their mores and their clubs—secure in the knowledge that their will be done!"—while "[b]y contrast, today the business of charity has become a bit more complicated. Not only has the donor base become much broader, but with it has come a more varied range of donor concerns and agendas."[15] Embedded in this history is the privileging of whose history belonged in an archives—the validity of a "gentleman's agreement" was implicitly dependent on all parties being "gentlemen."

Consistency and documentation are, in many cases, the easiest ways to ensure fair treatment to all donors—but easiest, in this case, does not necessarily equate to *most effective* or *most equitable*. A deed of gift is a written, legal document. As such, it is most easily understood by those

---

15. Vanni, "Deeds of Gift," 3.

who have strong literacy skills in the document's language, and at least a
moderate degree of legal literacy. A deed of gift is even *more* easily navi-
gated by those who have legal counsel and tax accountants on retainer
to provide them with advice and guidance tailored to their particular
situations and who have their individual interests at heart. Is the language
of the deed of gift straightforward, and as free of legalese as possible?
Is the deed of gift available in all the primary languages of the institution's constituencies? Archivists cannot and should not provide financial
or legal counsel for donors; but they should be aware that, in making
concessions to those who have financial or legal counsel that are not
equally accessible to others without those resources, they are perpetuating
systemic inequities. As archivist Lisa Browar has noted, "knowledgeable
donors tend to ask more questions."[16] There is no easy solution to this
conundrum. If your city or county offers free legal services, contact
information for those services may be something to include in your deed
of gift explanatory documents. If legally astute donors have frequently
questioned certain aspects of a deed of gift, it may be beneficial for
archivists to create and make available an FAQ document. Conducting
deed of gift negotiations like a reference interview—narrowing in on
concerns and suggesting avenues for further research—may be another
useful approach. Part of an archivist's responsibility when working on a
collection donation is to explain to the donor some of the core aspects
of archival practice and the lifecycle of the donor's collection; even if
the donor is not particularly interested in what happens to their donation, a certain level of donor education must occur in order to ensure
informed consent. Regardless of whether donors ask the "right questions," archivists should take a proactive approach when documents that
fall within privacy or confidentiality principles apply. Archivist Timothy
Pyatt's advice regarding family papers is equally applicable to archivists
working with all types of collections: "be honest with potential donors

---

16. Lisa Browar, "An Oral Contract Isn't Worth the Paper It's Printed On," *Rare
Books and Manuscripts Librarianship* 6, no. 2 (September 1991): 104, doi: https://doi.
org/10.5860/rbml.6.2.70.

and explain access intentions as well as offer some thoughts on how the papers might be used."[17]

Deed of gift execution typically takes place on a donor's timeline, and may stretch across months or even years, with a back-and-forth of correspondence and suggested edits. Best practice prescribes acquiring transfer documentation at or before the point of transfer, but discussions should, ideally, begin long before this point.[18] This approach is standard for a variety of reasons: to prevent surprises, to allow time for productive dialogue, and, most importantly, to ensure that donors do not feel rushed to make commitments, particularly if they are in a state of instability, transition, or mourning. Out-of-state donors on leave from work to execute the estates of deceased parents may want to donate materials physically as soon as possible so that they can return home; but, they may be reluctant to sign over rights as quickly. Compromises—like preliminary agreements to transfer title that are later amended by both parties to transfer copyright—may be possible, but for many repositories, the likelihood of getting paperwork from a donor diminishes with time and distance. Negotiating with grieving donors is particularly fraught territory, as archivist Megan Garbett-Styger has explored.[19] Reasonable delays should be accommodated, but the archivist must be careful that reasonable accommodation does not become a *de facto* deposit agreement, rather than an outright donation.

Deed of gift negotiation is an opportunity for donor education about the archival process, not only so donors can make better-informed decisions, but also so they may become more aware of how their gifts will be used and why their donations are important. This education may simply arise through informal conversations, or an archive may

---

17. Timothy Pyatt, "Southern Family Honor Tarnished? Issues of Privacy in the Walker Percy and Shelby Foote Papers," in *Privacy and Confidentiality Perspectives*, eds. Menzi L. Behrnd-Klodt and Peter J. Wosh (Chicago: Society of American Archivists, 2005), 158.

18. For more on this point, see Behrnd-Klodt, *Navigating Legal Issues in Archives*, 42-43.

19. Megan Garbett-Styger, "Death, Dying and Archives: Learning to Work with Grieving and Dying Donors" (master's thesis, Western Washington University, 2014), https://cedar.wwu.edu/wwuet/395.

offer more formalized resources. Documentation may take the form of written explanatory documents, resource lists, or an FAQ page on a website. The University of Arkansas Special Collections Department, for instance, has developed for its "long form" (more legally complex) deed of gift an annotated version that attempts to translate, for the layperson, the legal and archival terminology (Appendix A).[20] When creating explanatory documents or developing boilerplate emails, archivists should consider the ways in which certain common examples may default to a historically dominant culture, and should be open to revising texts and examples as needed. Archivists may partner with those in the organization or on campus who can provide translation support and bridge any cultural gaps that may arise.

It is not the responsibility of an archivist to advocate against the best interests of an archival repository; however, it may be appropriate to refer donors to outside resources that may be able to inform them of additional considerations. Here, the archival *profession* may step in to create resources that provide context that an individual archivist, constrained by institutional responsibilities, cannot. Guides like the Society of American Archivists' "A Guide to Deeds of Gift" can offer an introduction to donors who may be skeptical of an institutional archive's potential vested interests.[21] Guides like the *Artist'* [sic] *Studio Archives: Managing Personal Collections & Creative Legacies*[22] go even further, alerting potential donors to options and considerations of which they may be unaware, that may not be in a repository's best interests to preemptively disclose. Archivist Colin Post proposes an artist's archives donation framework in which "[t]he primary tenets…are to maintain the artists'

---

20. For examples of other institutions' deed of gift forms, see the Society of American Archivists Museum Archives Section's Appraisal and Acquisition/Accession resource guide at https://www2.archivists.org/groups/museum-archives-section/2-appraisal-and-acquisitionaccession.

21. Society of American Archivists, "A Guide to Deeds of Gift," https://www2.archivists.org/publications/brochures/deeds-of-gift, last modified 2013.

22. Heather Gendron, Eumie Imm Stroukoff, Joan E. Beaudoin, and Neal Ambrose-Smith, "Artist' Studio Archives: Managing Personal Collections & Creative Legacies," *Library Staff Publications* (2016): 2, http://elischolar.library.yale.edu/yul_staff/2.

agency over their materials, to utilize collaborative methods for appraisal and description, and to develop flexible donor agreements that give artists continued access to and control of their materials and the ability to add to their archival collections easily throughout their careers."[23] There is a substantive difference between transparency (honestly answering donor questions and concerns) and public self-flagellation (announcing to donors about that one time your predecessor promised a donor their 1,000 box collection would be digitized, free of charge). Writing of appraisal policies, but also more broadly in terms of the profession, archivist Chris Hurley notes: "in order to be trusted with autonomy, archival judgment must first be professionally constrained."[24] Even the lone arranger is not, as an archival ethicist, alone, but bulwarked by a professional code of ethics and shared ideals.

Conclusion

Taking the time to step back from current donor relations and deeds of gift practices and policies to consider questions of inequities and literacies helps to ensure that archivists continue the work to democratize collecting processes. This work requires clear communication, documentation, and building strong relationships with donors, as well as with internal and external stakeholders. Though this work is sometimes difficult, archivists must lean into potential discomfort as they strive to balance the needs of donors with their institutional policies. In her 2001 article, archivist and records manager Cynthia Sauer reflects on the results of her survey of collection development policy processes, which "suggests a certain resignation to elements beyond the archivist's control, which no policy written or unwritten, can combat."[25]

23. Colin Post, "Ensuring the Legacy of Self-Taught and Local Artists: A Collaborative Framework for Preserving Artists' Archives" *Art Documentation: Journal of the Art Libraries Society of North America* 36, no. 1 (Spring 2017): 75.

24. Chris Hurley, "The Role of the Archives in Protecting the Record from Political Pressure," in *Political Pressure and the Archival Record*, eds. Margaret Procter, Michael Cook, and Caroline Williams (Chicago: Society of American Archivists, 2005), 170.

25. Cynthia K. Sauer, "Doing the Best We Can? The Use of Collection Development Policies and Cooperative Collecting Activities at Manuscript Repositories," *Archival Outlook* 64, no. 2 (Fall/Winter 2001): 320.

Throughout donor relations activities, and particularly in the processes involved with developing deed of gift agreements, archivists may find themselves in a position where sometimes "no," or "yes, but" is the only tenable response to a stakeholder's wishes. As Sauer identifies, in this service-oriented profession, archivists find themselves prey to "archival altruism,"[26] where saying "no" is fraught with political and financial concerns and a possibly negative impact on the archives. However, clear policies, precedents, and industry best practices mitigate these challenges. As long as an archive and its archivists continue to work with donors, archivists will continue to navigate the balancing act described in this chapter. Professional recordkeeping may reduce deed of gift negotiation to a series of discrete events (*Agreement Sent, Agreement Signed, Agreement Received*), but the underlying reality can be a slow, fraught process that challenges the empathy, patience, and legal acuity of the professional archivist. We offer this chapter as an acknowledgment that yes, always, "it depends," but also that there are approaches that may be broadly applied to help mitigate the inherent power imbalances in archival acquisition work, and to help ensure, whenever possible, the highest degree of informed—and uncoerced—consent.

---

26. Sauer, "Doing the Best We Can?," 324.

Appendix A
Annotated version of University of Arkansas Special Collections' "Long form" deed of gift

TEMPLATE

DEED OF GIFT
(PAPERS AND OTHER MATERIALS)
(Donor Name)

1. I, (Name) (hereinafter referred to as the "Donor"), have collected professional records (in hard copy and digital and/or electronic format), including, but not limited to correspondence, notebooks, photographs, newspaper clippings, audiovisual, and other materials documenting the career or personal life of donor, of which I currently desire to donate as hereinafter set forth and some of which I may hereafter designate to be donated (hereinafter collectively referred to as the "Materials").

2. Donor _____ hereby gives, donates, and conveys to the University of Arkansas Libraries, an agency of the University of Arkansas, Fayetteville (hereinafter collectively referred to as the "Donee"). Title to the Materials shall pass to the Donee upon the execution of this Deed of Gift; provided, however, that Donor shall retain copyright to the Materials as set forth in this Deed of Gift.

(or if donor wishes to relinquish copyright)

2a. Donor _____ does hereby assign and transfer to the University of Arkansas, its successors and assigns, the entire right, title and interest in and to the copyright in the Materials and any registrations and Copyright applications relating thereto and any renewals and extensions thereof, and in and to all works based upon, derived from, or incorporating the Materials, and in and to all income, royalties, damages, claims and payments now or hereafter due or payable with respect thereto, and in and to all cause of action, either in law or in equity for past, present, or infringement based on the copyrights, and in and to all rights corresponding to forgoing throughout the world.

3. This Deed of Gift supersedes and replaces any and all previously signed versions of this agreement related to the Materials between the Donor and the Donee. _____

4. The collection shall be known and referred to as the "_____."

5. Notwithstanding the transfer of title from the Donor to the Donee, Donor shall maintain and exercise all rights of ownership and control of the copyright rights in the Materials throughout (his/her) entire life to the extent that Donor possesses such right. Upon the death of the Donor

---

Commented [KDW1]: This section describes the materials you're donating, in general terms, and provides some information about your relationship to the materials. This helps to provide context about that collection, and your relation to it. For instance, if you're donating on behalf of an organization, this is the place to note that.

Commented [KDW2]: This section indicates that you're conveying title—physical ownership—over the materials to Special Collections, but you're still retaining copyright (intellectual ownership). We understand that in many cases, our donors make their livelihood from their created works, and we respect their desire to maintain intellectual control. This means that researchers whose desired usage doesn't fall within fair use guidelines will need to get your permission first before reproducing collection materials

Commented [KDW3]: On the other hand, if you're willing to transfer copyright (or at least, any copyright you hold to the collection materials), you can opt for this section instead. This allows Special Collections staff and researchers the greatest flexibility in citation and use of your materials, and it means we won't need to let you know about each relevant case when a researcher wants to reproduce collection materials.

Commented [KDW4]: A deed of gift is a legal tool, and it can be a complicated one, so we might go through several drafts before we get the language to a point where it meets both the donor's needs and the Libraries'. This sentence means that the last deed of gift that both parties sign will be the authoritative deed of gift.

Commented [KDW5]: This assigns a preliminary title to the collection materials. It's possible that, during processing, there may be alterations to the title to better reflect the collection's creator or contents, but this preliminary title is a way for us to learn how you, as the donor, think about the materials—are they primarily family

(or if donor wishes to relinquish copyright)

5a. Donor _____ does hereby assign and transfer to the University of Arkansas , its successors and assigns, the entire right, title and interest in and to the copyright in the Materials and any registrations and Copyright applications relating thereto and any renewals and extensions thereof, and in and to all works based upon, derived from, or incorporating the Materials, and in and to all income, royalties, damages, claims and payments now or hereafter due or payable with respect thereto, and in and to all cause of action, either in law or in equity for past, present, or infringement based on the copyrights, and in and to all rights corresponding to forgoing throughout the world.)

6. In consideration for the Donee's efforts to preserve, catalog and make the Materials available for scholarly research, Donor hereby grants to the Donee an irrevocable and perpetual, royalty-free, and world-wide nonexclusive license to copy, distribute, display, adapt, and otherwise use, and hereby authorizes the use of, the Materials for non-commercial research and non-commercial educational purposes effective immediately upon the execution of this Deed of Gift. |

7. The Materials shall not be used for commercial purposes without the prior written approval of the Donor or the Donor's designated representative and Donee. |

8. Individuals desiring to publish any portion of the Materials will be required to complete the "Intent to Publish" form, which is attached hereto as Exhibit A and incorporated herein by reference, and obtain written prior permission and copyright clearance from the Donor or the Donor's designated representative. |

9. Following delivery, the Materials shall be organized, maintained and administered by the Donee through Donee's Special Collections Department or its successor. The Donor and the Donor's designated agent may utilize any of the Materials for any use, commercial or otherwise, as long as the Materials are credited to the Special Collections Department, University of Arkansas Libraries, according to the then current procedures. |

10. Donor desires for the Materials to be made publicly available for scholarly research following their transfer to Donee. However, the Donor recognizes that the Materials, as a whole, might include individual materials that are of a sensitive or personal nature. Specifically, to the extent permitted by Arkansas law and in recognition of Donor's constitutional rights of privacy in certain items contained in the Materials, Donee agrees to restrict access to certain Materials for a period of twenty (20) years (beginning upon the execution of this agreement) to those Materials, identified by the Donor, in consultation with the Donee (hereinafter referred to as the "Restricted Materials"). The Donor does not intend for this restriction to apply to all of the records comprising the Materials, and the Donor agrees that the Materials that are not so

Commented [KDW6]: Even if you choose to retain copyright, there are a number of things that the Libraries need to do in order to process, preserve, and promote your materials that might go beyond fair use. This statement gives us the right to go ahead and do our job to make sure your materials get the care they need.

Commented [KDW7]: This section is optional. If you're very concerned about commercial (for-profit) use of your materials, you can elect to restrict that use. Our reading room staff would then pass on information about all desired commercial usage to you for your approval.

Commented [KDW8]: This just lets you know about our Department policy of having researchers file forms with us when they intend to publish materials from our collections. This lets us keep statistics about publication based on our holdings. If you've chosen to transfer copyright to the Libraries, we'll remove the last part of this section, but if you are retaining copyright, it means that you'll be asked to approve or reject each publication request.

Commented [KDW9]: This states our commitment to processing your donation. It also means that you (and/or another person you designate) can use your own collection, even if it's unprocessed or restricted to others.

designated as Restricted may be opened immediately for scholarly research and all other purposes authorized under this Deed of Gift. Donee and its employees shall be entitled to access all Materials at all times for the purpose of organizing and preserving the Materials.

11. In the event that Donee receives a request to release any of the Restricted Materials, Donee will notify Donor or Donor's designee of the request, and Donee will advise Donor whether Donee must comply with the request to open the Restricted Materials for inspection and review; provided, however, that Donee will not release any of the Restricted Materials if Donor seeks an opinion from a court or other appropriate tribunal to determine whether the request must be honored as a matter of law.

> **Commented [KDW10]:** This recognizes that there may be sensitive materials within the collection. If you know of any, please make a note of the specifics at the end of the section. If they need restricted for a specific time frame, the default language regarding 20 years can be adjusted to reflect your desired time frame, provided that it's a reasonable request. We try to balance two competing demands—respecting the privacy and confidentiality of our donors, and respecting our mission of making materials available for use. You can help us do that by letting us know what the potential issues are, so that we can work together to determine what restrictions might be appropriate.

> **Commented [KDW11]:** If materials were restricted, this section means that we'll let you know if anyone asks to access them (whether through a FOIA request or otherwise), and we'll let you know if we think we might be legally obligated to allow access to the materials to the requester.

12. As part of the process of organizing and preserving the Materials and after consulting with Donor, the Donee may dispose of any or all of the Materials that the Donee determines to have no permanent value or historical interest. If, in the opinion of the Donee, the Materials should be preserved in a different physical format, such as microfilm, digital format, or other format, the Donee may perform the necessary processing to convert and preserve the Materials, and thereafter the Donee will consult with the Donor and/or Donor's designee to determine whether the original Materials may be destroyed. Prior to disposing of any of the Materials, such Materials shall first be made available for transfer to the Donor, or if the Donor is unavailable, to the Donor's immediate family or heirs, as the case may be, by written notification (hereinafter referred to as the "Notice"). In the event the Donor, or the Donor's immediate family or heirs, desires to take possession of the Materials at issue, a written response stating their intent to receive the Materials identified for destruction, together with the names and addresses of the parties desiring the Materials (hereinafter referred to as the "Successor Owners") within sixty (60) days following the receipt of the Notice, will be sent to the Donee. The Donee shall, then, transfer such Materials to the Successor Owners within a reasonable time after the Donee receives the Response. If the Donee does not receive the Response within said sixty (60) day period, then the Donee will be free to dispose of such Materials then at issue. The process set forth in this Paragraph 8 shall also apply to the Restricted Materials.

> **Commented [KDW12]:** Many collections we receive include materials that, for one reason or another, aren't a good fit for permanent retention in the collection. Maybe they're old cigar boxes that used to hold some of the collection, but after rehousing they don't serve a purpose, maybe it's 1000 sheets of blank stationery, maybe it's three copies of the same report, maybe it's someone's personal materials that they accidentally included in their work materials, maybe it's just something that's better suited to another institution's collections. In those cases, we might want to transfer or discard items. This section allows you to specify if you'd like to be notified in the event of any deaccessioning, and given a chance to have the materials in question returned to you, if you'd like.

13. The Donor acknowledges that the Library acquires born-digital materials with the intent of making them available for an ongoing or indefinite period of time. In order to accomplish this, the Library may need to transfer some or all of these materials from the original media as supplied by the donor to new forms of media to ensure their ongoing availability and preservation. The Donor grants the library the rights to make preservation and access copies of materials in the collection and to make those copies available for use. The Library may contract with university staff or outside contractors to store, evaluate, manage, and / or analyze born-digital materials in the collection. Any such arrangements must abide by the terms of such agreement.

> **Commented [KDW13]:** This is very similar to the section above regarding what the Libraries can do in the course of our preservation and processing work, but this section is specific to born-digital materials, which come with a host of their own issues!

14. In the case of born-digital records, the Donor agrees that the Library or contractor has permission to crack passwords or encryption systems, if any, to gain access to electronic data received as part of the materials; to discard deleted files or file fragments and that the Library has

permission to preserve and provide access to log files, system files, and other similar data that document use of computers or systems, if any are received with the materials. In the case of media carriers for born-digital content, the Library will either return them to the Donor or physically destroy them after the content has been migrated to new media or a digital preservation system and verified through check sums.

Commented [KDW14]: Another issue that may come up with born-digital files is that some of them may be password-protected or encrypted. This language grants us the right to break encryptions to access and evaluate that material, if needed

15. In the event that the Donor may from time to time hereafter, give, donate, and convey to the Donee, additional papers and other historical documentation, title to such items shall pass to the Donee upon their delivery from Donor and acceptance by Donee. This Deed of Gift shall be applicable to all such additional items which shall be part of the Materials or reproductions of these Materials and maintained as part of the collection.

Commented [KDW15]: Many of our donors don't give us everything at once—they (or their organization) may still be creating records, and donate them incrementally, or they might find another few boxes up in an attic years down the road. This section just means that when that happens, as long as those materials are going to be part of the same collection, we won't need to execute a new deed of gift form—this one can still apply to the new donation.

16. This Deed of Gift shall be governed by the laws of the State of Arkansas without regard to its choice of law principles.

17. This Deed of Gift is executed on this xxx day of (month), (year).

Commented [LAB16]: Please edit this text to indicate the day the donor completed editing the information in the above sections of the form.

_____

Chancellor   Date

_____

Dean of University Libraries   Date

_____

Head of Special Collections   Date

_____

(donor name)   Date

Commented [KDW17]: This is where you'll sign and date, once the form reflects your desires and conditions for the donation. The form will then be passed on to several administrators at UA, and once everyone has signed it, a copy will be returned to you for your records.

Bibliography

American Library Association. "Presidential Committee on Information Literacy: Final Report, July 24, 2006." http://www.ala.org/acrl/publications/whitepapers/presidential. Accessed June 1, 2018. Document ID: 106e5565-9ab9-ad94-8d9f-64962ebcde46.

Baker, Antoinette E. "Ethical Considerations in Web 2.0 Archives." *Student Research Journal* 1, no. 1 (2011): 1-14. http://scholarworks.sjsu.edu/slissrj/vol1/iss1/4.

Behrnd-Klodt, Menzi L. *Navigating Legal Issues in Archives*. Chicago: Society of American Archivists, 2008.

Bertram, Cara S. "Avenues of Mutual Respect: Opening Communication and Understanding between Native Americans and Archivists." Master's thesis. (2012). Western Washington University. WWU Graduate School Collection. https://cedar.wwu.edu/wwuet/240.

Browar, Lisa. "An Oral Contract Isn't Worth the Paper It's Printed On." *Rare Books and Manuscripts Librarianship* 6, no. 2 (September 1991): 100-07.

Cox, Richard J. *Ethics, Accountability, and Record Keeping in a Dangerous World*. London: Facet Publishing, 2006.

Cox, Richard J. "Rethinking Archival Ethics." *Journal of Information Ethics* 22, no. 2 (2013): 13-20.

Druga, Elizabeth, "Raising Money Raises Questions: The Ethics of Generating Revenue from Archival Materials," *Journal of Information Ethics* 19, no. 1 (Spring 2010): 141-56, doi: 10.3172.

Garbett-Styger, Megan. "Death, Dying and Archives: Learning to Work with Grieving and Dying Donors." Master's thesis. (2014). Western Washington University. WWU Graduate School Collection. https://cedar.wwu.edu/wwuet/395.

Gendron, Heather, Eumie Imm Stroukoff, Joan E. Beaudoin, and Neal Ambrose-Smith, "Artist' Studio Archives: Managing Personal Collections & Creative Legacies." *Library Staff Publications* (2016): 2. http://elischolar.library.yale.edu/yul_staff/2.

Hurley, Chris. "The Role of the Archives in Protecting the Record from
    Political Pressure." In *Political Pressure and the Archival Record*, edited
    by Margaret Procter, Michael Cook, and Caroline Williams, 151-72.
    Chicago: Society of American Archivists, 2005.

Peterson, Trudy Huskamp. "The Gift and the Deed." *American Archivist* 42,
    no. 1 (January 1979): 61-66.

Post, Colin. "Ensuring the Legacy of Self-Taught and Local Artists: A
    Collaborative Framework for Preserving Artists' Archives." *Art
    Documentation: Journal of the Art Libraries Society of North America* 36,
    no. 1 (Spring 2017): 73-90.

Pyatt, Timothy. "Southern Family Honor Tarnished? Issues of Privacy in the
    Walker Percy and Shelby Foote Papers." In *Privacy and Confidential-
    ity Perspectives,* edited by Menzi L. Behrnd-Klodt and Peter J. Wosh,
    149-58. Chicago: Society of American Archivists, 2005.

Sauer, Cynthia K. "Doing the Best We Can? The Use of Collection Devel-
    opment Policies and Cooperative Collecting Activities at Manu-
    script Repositories." *Archival Outlook* 64, no. 2 (Fall/Winter 2001):
    308-49.

Society of American Archivists. "Code of Ethics for Archivists." Last modi-
    fied January 2012. https://www2.archivists.org/statements/saa-
    core-values-statement-and-code-of-ethics.

Society of American Archivists. "A Guide to Deeds of Gift." https://
    www2.archivists.org/publications/brochures/deeds-of-gift. Last
    modified 2013.

Society of American Archivists, and Association of Records Managers and
    Administrators. *Sample Forms for Archival and Records Management
    Programs.* Lenexa, KS: ARMA International, 2002.

Society of American Archivists Museum Archives Section. "Appraisal and
    Acquisition/Accession." https://www2.archivists.org/groups/
    museum-archives-section/2-appraisal-and-acquisitionaccession.

Vanni, Robert J. "Deeds of Gift: Caressing the Hand that Feeds." In *Librar-
    ies, Museums, and Archives: Legal Issues and Ethical Challenges in the New
    Information Era*, edited by Tomas A. Lipinski, 1-29. Lanham, MD:
    Scarecrow Press, 2002.

About the Authors

Lara K. Aase is a Youth Services Librarian at Farmington Public Library in New Mexico. From 2016 to 2019, she worked as the Special Collections Librarian at a Native American-serving, non-tribal liberal arts college in the Southwestern United States. During her MLIS at the University of Washington, she focused on special collections, multilingual metadata, and non-majority user populations, and she worked as a library technician and associate librarian for many years prior to obtaining her degree. Aase is an active member of the Seminar on the Acquisition of Latin American Library Materials, as well as the American Indian Library Association. She has an MA in Comparative Literature and has published several articles on decolonizing special collections.

Kimberley Bell is Coordinator of public services at W.D. Jordan Rare Books and Special Collections at Queen's University in Kingston, Ontario. She is completing a thesis on Canadian publishers' bindings and late nineteenth-century culture. Other areas of research include outreach to prisoners and other marginalized groups. She also runs the Instagram and Twitter accounts for W.D. Jordan Rare Books and Special Collections (@jordan_library).

Lori Birrell is the Head of the Special Collections Department at the University of Arkansas. She holds an EdD in Higher Education Administration from the University of Rochester, where she served as manuscripts curator for six years. Birrell also holds an MLIS from Simmons College, and a Master's in History from the University of Massachusetts, Amherst.

Jennifer Bowers, Professor, is the Social Sciences Librarian at the University of Denver. She is the co-editor of *Rethinking Reference for Academic Libraries: Innovative Developments and Future Trends*, and the co-author of the article "'If You Want the History of a White Man, You Go to the Library': Critiquing Our Legacy, Addressing Our Library Collections Gaps" published in *Collection Management*. Bowers' research focuses on critical approaches to teaching with archival materials in the social sciences, collaborative research consultations, and popular press reception of the pioneering archaeologist, Harriet Boyd Hawes.

Maureen Burns, EdD, works on a consulting basis through IMAGinED after thirty years of curating photographic archives at the University of California at Irvine, the Getty Villa, and California State University, Long Beach. Most of her professional activities have been associated with the Visual Resources Association, an international association focused on image management, serving on a variety of committees and as President from 2009-2012. She received a doctorate in Educational Administration from the Joint Leadership Program at the University of California, Irvine and Los Angeles, in 2002, with her dissertation research concentrating on the development of artistic creativity through service learning.

Elizabeth Call is the University Archivist at the Rochester Institute of Technology in Rochester, New York. Prior to this role, Call held positions at the University of Rochester, Columbia University, and the Brooklyn Historical Society. Her professional and research interests include connecting individuals and communities to information, the ethics of institutions' collecting and collection development, and special collections pedagogy.

Katherine Crowe, Associate Professor, is Curator of Special Collections and Archives at the University of Denver, where she oversees the acquisition and curation of collections, as well as all instruction, reference, and outreach for the department. Crowe's research interests include gaps and silences in the historical record, exhibitions as archival outreach, and critical pedagogy utilizing primary sources.

François Dansereau is the Archivist at the McGill University Health Centre, in Montreal, Quebec. He holds a Master's degree in History from Université de Montreal and an MLIS with a concentration in archives from McGill University. His research interests include gender and the archives, photography, outreach, and archival literacy.

Diana Doublet is the Orchestra Librarian for Symphony Nova Scotia in Halifax, where she is responsible for all aspects of music preparation and maintaining the performance library. She has worked with a variety of archives and special collections, including the Canadian Architectural Archives at the University of Calgary, the Howard Cable Collection held by the symphony, and the Kipling Scrapbooks Digital Exhibit at Dalhousie University. Her experience includes music librarianship, archives and special collections, digitization, and reference and instruction.

Jessica L. English received her MLIS from the University of Illinois, where she completed her thesis field research at the Museo de la Campaña de Alfabetización in Havana, Cuba, on the digital preservation of the community memory of the Cuban National Literacy Campaign. Formerly the Cuban Heritage Coordinator at the University of Florida Libraries, she has served in leadership roles in REFORMA and Seminar on the Acquisition of Latin American Library Materials (SALALM).

Jesse Ryan Erickson, PhD, MLIS, is the Coordinator of Special Collections and Digital Humanities, Assistant Professor in the Department of English in the College of Arts and Sciences, and Associate Director of the Interdisciplinary Humanities Research Center at the University of Delaware. His research specializations are in ethnobibliography, alternative printing and non-canonical textuality, African American print culture, and the transnational printing history of the works of Ouida.

Daniel German joined Canada's national archives (now, Library and Archives Canada) in 1992 and quickly became involved with issues surrounding access to sensitive material. He is the Senior Archivist responsible for the records of Canada's federal security and intelligence agencies.

Roger Gillis is the Copyright and Digital Humanities Librarian at Dalhousie University in Halifax, Nova Scotia. He served as the Project Director for the Kipling Scrapbooks Digital Exhibit (https://digitalexhibits.library.dal.ca/exhibits/show/kipling-scrapbooks). His interests relate to copyright and publishing, as well as to project management and sustainability in digital humanities/scholarship projects.

Melanie Hardbattle is the Archivist for Simon Fraser University Library's Special Collections and Rare Books division, and has served as project coordinator for several of the Library's digitization and community engagement projects, including the *Multicultural Canada* and *Komagata Maru: Continuing the Journey* websites, and related events. Her research interests include the preservation and accessibility of the documentary record of groups not traditionally represented in the archival record.

Elizabeth Hobart is the Special Collections Cataloging Librarian at Pennsylvania State University. She holds an MLS from Indiana University, and has previously held cataloging positions at Indiana University's Lilly Library and the Louis Round Wilson Special Collections Library at the University of North Carolina at Chapel Hill. Her research interests include user-center descriptive practices, catalog assessment, and implicit bias in cataloging.

Skylee-Storm Hogan is a Historical Research Associate with Know History Inc. in Ottawa, Ontario. They hold an MA in Public History from the University of Western Ontario. From the Mohawk Nation of Kahnawá:ke, Hogan's work has primarily focused on North American Indigenous intersections with Archives, Digital History, Residential Schools, and Canadian/Crown Policy. Hogan has worked extensively with the Shingwauk Residential Schools Centre in Sault Ste. Marie, Ontario.

Heidi L.M. Jacobs, PhD, is a librarian at the University of Windsor's Leddy Library and the Co-Director of their Centre for Digital Scholarship. She has published in the areas of information literacy and critical librarianship. She is part of the project teams for the award-winning "Breaking the Colour Barrier: Wilfred 'Boomer' Harding and the Chatham Coloured All-Stars" and for "The North Was Our Canaan," a project documenting the rich Underground Railroad history of Sandwich, Ontario in image, text, and film.

Melissa Jerome is the Project Coordinator for the Florida & Puerto Rico Digital Newspaper Project, housed at the George A. Smathers Libraries at the University of Florida. She is pursuing her MS in Information from Florida State University and her research interests include digital libraries and multilingual metadata.

Mary Kandiuk, MA, MLS, is the Visual Arts, Design & Theatre librarian, and a Senior Librarian at York University in Toronto, Ontario. She is the author of two bibliographies of secondary criticism relating to Canadian literature, published by Scarecrow Press, and is the co-author of *Digital Image Collections and Services* (ARL Spec Kit, 2013). She is the co-editor of the collection *In Solidarity: Academic Librarian Labour Activism and Union Participation in Canada*, published by Library Juice Press in 2014.

Peggy Keeran, Professor, is the Arts & Humanities Librarian at the University of Denver. She is the co-editor of *Successful Campus Outreach for Academic Libraries: Building Community Through Collaboration*, and the co-author of the article "'If You Want the History of a White Man, You Go to the Library': Critiquing Our Legacy, Addressing Our Library Collections Gaps" published in *Collection Management*. Keeran's research interests include library services for graduate students, integrating digital and physical primary source research into the curriculum, and visual literacy for students in non-arts disciplines.

Clayton McCarl is an Associate Professor in the Department of Languages, Literatures and Cultures at the University of North Florida (UNF). He is the founding Director of the UNF Digital Humanities Institute and leads coloniaLab, a workshop for the collaborative edition of colonial Latin American manuscripts and rare print books.

Krista McCracken is a public historian and archivist. They work as an Archives Supervisor at Algoma University's Arthur A. Wishart Library and Shingwauk Residential Schools Centre. McCracken's research focuses on community archives, Residential Schools, access, and outreach.

Miranda Mims is the Special Collections Archivist for Discovery and Access in the Department of Rare Books, Special Collections, and Preservation at the University of Rochester. Mims is also the co-founder of the Nomadic Archivist Project, an initiative devoted to developing relationships and beginning conversations around preserving legacy, memory, connection, and trust in the African diaspora.

Jessica Ruzek is a doctoral candidate and instructor at Concordia University, Montreal, Quebec, where her research focuses on the environmental humanities, arboreal biopolitics, and postcolonial, decolonial, and media studies. In 2017, she conducted research for and helped to create the Kipling Scrapbooks Digital Exhibit at Dalhousie University, Halifax, Nova Scotia.

Angelibel Soto is a Metadata Specialist for Digital Support Services at the University of Florida. Her interests include bilingual metadata, Spanish language authority files, Latin American collections, rare books and manuscripts, and digital humanities.

Jillian Sparks is the Librarian for Special Collections and Archives Instruction at St. Olaf College in Northfield, Minnesota. She holds an MLIS and Certificate in Book Studies from the University of Iowa and an MA in English from the University of Victoria. Her research interests include primary source instruction and literacy, special collections outreach, and libraries and social media.

Jason G. Speck is a Librarian for General and Special Collections Development at the University of Maryland, College Park. He served as Assistant University Archivist at Maryland from 2008-2017 and authored a pictorial history of the university. His previous work has centered on public trust in archives and the archives as a counterbalance to popular myths and legends.

Anne S.K. Turkos is the University Archivist Emerita for the University of Maryland (UMD). She has been a part of the staff of the UMD Libraries' Special Collections and University Archives since 1985. Before retirement in 2017, she worked with campus departments and units, student groups, and alumni to transfer, preserve, and make available permanent university records. She continues to support the Archives through her work on special projects and fundraising.

Margarita Vargas-Betancourt, PhD, is the Latin American and Caribbean Special Collections Librarian at the George A. Smathers Libraries at the University of Florida. In 2016, she was part of the team that received the Society of American Archivists' Diversity Award for the Latin American and Cultural Heritage Archives Section webinar series *Desmantelando Fronteras/Breaking Down Borders.*

504 Archives and Special Collections as Sites of Contestation

Gregory L. Williams has been the Director of Archives & Special Collections, California State University, Dominguez Hills since 2004. He has been an archivist for thirty-eight years. He has written funded grants for NHPRC, NEH, NPS, the Mellon Foundation, the Haynes Foundation, the California State Library, and others; curated several exhibitions (the Watts Rebellion, Japanese American Incarceration During World War II, the Chicano Movement in LA, Movies in San Diego, and others); and published several collection guides, collection and grant-related articles, and served as photo editor for three coffee table books. He is the author of *California State University Dominguez Hills*, a photo history.

Katrina Windon is the Collections Management and Processing Unit Head for the University of Arkansas Special Collections Department. She received her Master of Science in Information Studies from the University of Texas at Austin. Her research interests include issues of rights—including copyright, moral rights, and rights transfers—and the balance between archivists' commitment to access and use and respecting the rights of content creators and donors.

INDEX